Different regions need to explore their own understandings of crime and justice. In doing so, this book draws on an impressive range of contributors to provide an important overview of our understanding of criminalisation, the changing activities of criminal justice agencies and public responses to crime and justice at a key moment in the history of Hong Kong.

Mark Israel, Professor of Law and Criminology, University of Western Australia

Informed by the latest research in the field, the editors and contributing authors help readers navigate some of the profound changes and challenges in the criminal law and processes of criminal justice in Hong Kong over the last decade or so. The book includes some important contributions relating to recent civil protests and the 'Occupy Central' movement, and offers some critical insights into power relations and the changing landscape of criminal justice. The book will serve as a comprehensive resource for students in a wide range of criminal justice, social work and related courses.

Loraine Gelsthorpe, Professor of Criminology and Criminal Justice, Deputy Director, Institute of Criminology, University of Cambridge

I found the second edition of *Understanding Criminal Justice in Hong Kong* well researched and updated to the date of print. A most comprehensive text for anyone interested in Hong Kong's criminal justice system.

Samson Chan, CSDSM, CSMSM, Honorary Lecturer at the Department of Sociology, University of Hong Kong

UNDERSTANDING CRIMINAL JUSTICE IN HONG KONG

In recent years law, crime and justice have become increasingly politicised in Hong Kong. *Understanding Criminal Justice in Hong Kong, Second Edition*, offers a detailed and comprehensive overview of and introduction to the criminal justice system in Hong Kong, building upon recent events and controversies.

This book provides a much-needed overview of the criminal justice system in Hong Kong, including new chapters on criminological research methods, defining crime, fear of crime, the criminal court system, police power and discretion, and plea bargaining. This revised and expanded second edition:

- outlines the basic concepts of criminal law in Hong Kong;
- analyses the process of the criminal justice system, ranging from the reporting of a crime through to the correctional system;
- examines how criminal justice personnel work in practice, and how they deal with the offenders and victims during the criminal justice process; and
- invites readers to consider arguments and debates that surround the controversial issues in the Hong Kong criminal justice system.

This book is a comprehensive resource for students studying this subject as part of a wider course in criminal justice, police studies, law or social work, for practitioners working in Hong Kong in the police, prisons, probation, voluntary agencies, and other criminal justice personnel. Text features include review questions, lists of cases cited and useful websites.

Wing Hong Chui is Professor in the Department of Applied Social Sciences at City University of Hong Kong.

T. Wing Lo is Head of the Department and Professor in the Department of Applied Social Sciences at City University of Hong Kong.

UNDERSTANDING CRIMINAL JUSTICE IN HONG KONG

Second edition

Edited by
Wing Hong Chui and T. Wing Lo

LONDON AND NEW YORK

Second edition published 2017
by Routledge
2 Park Square, Milton Park, Abingdon, Oxon OX14 4RN

and by Routledge
711 Third Avenue, New York, NY 10017

Routledge is an imprint of the Taylor & Francis Group, an informa business

British Library Cataloguing in Publication Data
A catalogue record for this book is available from the British Library

Library of Congress Cataloging in Publication Data
Names: Chui, Wing Hong, editor. | Lo, T. Wing (Tit Wing), 1954- editor.
Title: Understanding criminal justice in Hong Kong / edited by Wing Hong Chui and T. Wing Lo.
Description: Second edition. | Abingdon, Oxon ; New York, NY : Routledge, 2016. | Includes bibliographical references and index.
Identifiers: LCCN 2016009859| ISBN 9781138888746 (hardback) | ISBN 9781138888753 (pbk.) | ISBN 9781315713205 (ebook)
Subjects: LCSH: Criminal justice, Administration of–China–Hong Kong.
Classification: LCC HV9960.H85 U53 2016 | DDC 364.95125–dc23
LC record available at https://lccn.loc.gov/2016009859

ISBN: 978-1-138-88874-6 (hbk)
ISBN: 978-1-138-88875-3 (pbk)
ISBN: 978-1-315-71320-5 (ebk)

Typeset in Sabon
by Taylor & Francis Books

CONTENTS

LIST OF ILLUSTRATIONS

Figures

Tables

CONTRIBUTORS

Michael Adorjan is an Assistant Professor of Sociology at the University of Calgary, Canada. His research and teaching focus on youth crime representations and responses, fear of crime, trust in police, and cyber-risk.

Roderic Broadhurst is Professor of Criminology at the Research School of Social Sciences, Australian National University (ANU). He was Chair of the Hong Kong Criminology Society (2003–06). Recent books include *Policing in Context* (2009, Oxford University Press), *Business and the Risk of Crime in China* (2011, ANU Press), and *Violence and the Civilizing Process in Cambodia* (2015, Cambridge University Press). He has published articles in the *Annals of the Academy of Political and Social Sciences*, *Australian & New Zealand Journal of Criminology*, *British Journal of Criminology*, *Homicide Studies*, *Policing & Society*, *Revue Internationale de Criminologie et de Police Technique et Scientifique*, *Trends in Organized Crime*, and book chapters in *East and South-East Asia: International Relations and Security Perspectives* (2013, Routledge), *Handbook of Asian Criminology* (2013, Springer), *The Oxford Handbook of Organized Crime* (2014, Oxford University Press) and *Transnational Organized Crime* (2014, Sage). His current research includes crime and modernisation, homicide, comparative studies of crime, recidivism, organised crime in China and Asia, and crime in cyberspace.

Ching Yee Chan received a PhD in criminology at The University of Hong Kong. She has published articles in *Asian Journal of Criminology*, *Forensic Science International* and *Homicide Studies*, and in *Global Report on Human Settlements, UN Habitat* (2007). Her current research includes homicide followed by suicide, and domestic violence in Hong Kong.

Wai To Chan worked in the Social Welfare Department (1977–85) with a variety of posts including Group and Community Work, Probation Officer, Aftercare Officer and Training Officer. He has been a Senior Lecturer of the School of Continuing and Professional Education, City University of Hong Kong. He has Master's degrees in social science (socio-legal studies) from the University of Birmingham and in education from The Chinese University of

Hong Kong. He has been appointed by the government to sit on Criminal and Law Enforcement Injuries Compensation Boards (1977–2003) and the Release Under Supervision Board (since 2003).

Wayne W.L. Chan is an Assistant Professor at the School of Arts & Social Sciences, The Open University of Hong Kong, teaching police studies and sociology. He graduated with an MPhil in sociology from the National University of Singapore and a PhD in criminology from the University of Hong Kong. His research interests include community policing, police image and Chinese policing. He is currently conducting a study on the media representations of Hong Kong police and Mainland police.

Kevin Kwok-yin Cheng is an Assistant Professor at the Faculty of Law, The Chinese University of Hong Kong, where he teaches criminal justice and the Hong Kong legal system on the LLB and General Education programmes. His research interests are in the areas of criminology, criminal justice, socio-legal studies, and empirical legal research with particular emphasis on guilty pleas and plea bargaining, procedural justice and public opinion towards crime and criminal justice policies. His works have been published in journals including the *British Journal of Criminology*, *Punishment & Society* and *Social & Legal Studies*. He has received funding, under which this chapter was supported, from the General Research Fund (GRF), Research Grants Council of the Hong Kong Special Administrative Region, China (Project No. CUHK14401214).

Nicole W.T. Cheung is an Associate Professor in the Department of Sociology, The Chinese University of Hong Kong (CUHK). She received her MPhil and PhD from the Department of Sociology, CUHK. She was awarded the Fulbright Hong Kong Senior Scholar in 2008. Her main research interests lie in the fields of sociology of crime and deviance, sociology of youth, and addiction including substance abuse and gambling disorder. Her research publications have appeared in international refereed journals including *Addictive Behaviors*, *Health & Place*, *Journal of Youth & Adolescence*, *Journal of Gambling Studies*, *Social Science & Medicine*, *Sociological Perspectives*, *Substance Use & Misuse* and *Youth & Society*.

Wing Hong Chui is Professor in the Department of Applied Social Sciences, City University of Hong Kong. Prior to this, he was the Associate Dean (Undergraduate Education) of the Faculty of Social Sciences, The University of Hong Kong. His areas of interest include youth studies, social work, criminology and criminal justice. He has published articles in the *Asian Journal of Criminology*, *Australian & New Zealand Journal of Criminology*, *British Journal of Criminology*, *European Journal of Criminology*, *International Journal of Offender Therapy and Comparative Criminology* and *Theoretical Criminology*. He is editor of several books: *Moving Probation Forward* (with Mike Nellis, 2003, Pearson Education), *Social Work and Human*

Services Best Practice (with Jill Wilson, 2006, The Federation Press), and *Research Methods for Law* (with Mike McConville, 2007, Edinburgh University Press). He is also the author of *The Hong Kong Legal System* (with S.H.C. Lo, 2012, McGraw-Hill) and *Responding to Youth Crime in Hong Kong: Penal Elitism, Legitimacy and Citizenship* (with M. Adorjan, 2014, Routledge).

I. Grenville Cross *SBS, SC* is the Vice-Chairman of the Senate of the International Association of Prosecutors, and chairs the Association's Standing Committee on Prosecutors in Difficulty. He served as the Director of Public Prosecutions of Hong Kong from 1997 to 2009. He is a barrister-at-law, and was appointed Queen's Counsel in 1990, becoming Senior Counsel in 1997. He is Honorary Professor of Law, University of Hong Kong, Visiting Professor of Law, Chinese University of Hong Kong, and Adjunct Professor of Law, China University of Political Science and Law. He is the sentencing editor of *Hong Kong Cases* and of *Archbold Hong Kong*, and the co-author of *Sentencing in Hong Kong* (7th edn) (with Patrick W.S. Cheung and Elaine Y.L. Tsui, 2015). In 2010, he received the Silver Bauhinia Star, from the Chief Executive of Hong Kong, for his contribution to the development of prosecution services in Hong Kong, and the Certificate of Merit, from the President of the International Association of Prosecutors, for his services to international prosecutions.

Alistair Fraser is currently Lecturer in Criminology and Sociology at the University of Glasgow, and Honorary Assistant Professor in Criminology in the Department of Sociology, The University of Hong Kong. His interests lie at the intersection of criminology, sociology and youth studies, with a focus on youth gangs in a global and comparative context. He has a particular interest in ethnographic methods, and has carried out fieldwork in Glasgow, Chicago and Hong Kong. His first book, *Urban Legends: Gang Identity in the Post-Industrial City*, was published by Oxford University Press in 2015.

Cora Y.T. Hui is currently a doctoral student in the Department of Applied Social Sciences at City University of Hong Kong. She received her MPhil in Criminology from the University of Cambridge and her MA in Forensic Psychology from John Jay College of Criminal Justice, City University of New York. Her broad research interests include the design, implementation and evaluation of anti-corruption reforms, and the effect of civic awareness on anti-corruption efforts.

Eric C. Ip is an Associate Professor of Law at The University of Hong Kong. He holds a D.Phil. in law from the University of Oxford. His research on regulation, public law, and economic analysis of law has been published in *The American Journal of Comparative Law*, *Oxford Journal of Legal Studies*, *International Journal of Constitutional Law*, and *Supreme Court Economic Review*. He is the author of *Law and Justice in Hong Kong* (Sweet &

Maxwell 2014). He has previously taught at The Chinese University of Hong Kong and University College London.

Paul Vinod Khiatani is a doctoral student at the City University of Hong Kong, where he is working on the intersection of action theory and moral identity theory in the context of student protest. His areas of interest are social and political theory, youth studies, underworld–upperworld relations, casinos and gambling, and critical studies.

Raymond W.K. Lau is a Professor at the School of Arts & Social Sciences, The Open University of Hong Kong. His research interests lie in political-economic theory and mainstream sociology, especially social and sociological theory. In recent years, his interests have also included ancient Chinese thought, both in itself and in comparative perspective vis-à-vis ancient Greece, approached from the perspective of a social and sociological theorist, which is largely (if not entirely) absent in the field.

King Wa Lee is Lecturer at the Department of Sociology, The Chinese University of Hong Kong. He has published articles in *Asian Journal of Criminology, Forensic Science International* and *Security Challenges*, and book chapters in *Community Policing and Peace Keeping* (2009, CRC Press) and *Women and Girls in Hong Kong: Current Situations and Future Challenges* (2012, Hong Kong Institute of Asia-Pacific Studies, The Chinese University of Hong Kong). His current research includes crime and social transformation in Hong Kong, and cross-border drug use.

Maggy Lee is Professor in the Department of Sociology, the University of Hong Kong. She is Principal Investigator on a number of research projects, including the fear of crime in Hong Kong (with M. Adorjan, funded by the Hong Kong Research Grants Council), British lifestyle migration in Asia (with K. O'Reilly and R. Stones, funded by the ESRC/Hong Kong Research Grants Council) and female transnational migrants in Hong Kong (funded by the University Grants Committee). Her books include *Human Trafficking* (2007, Willan) and *Trafficking and Global Crime Control* (2010, Sage).

Stefan H.C. Lo is currently Deputy Principal Government Counsel (Ag.) of the Department of Justice in Hong Kong. He is also a legal practitioner of the Supreme Court of New South Wales, Australia. Prior to joining the Department of Justice, he was an Assistant Professor at the School of Law, City University of Hong Kong, where he taught company law, commercial law and legal theory. He received his LLB, LLM and PhD from the University of Sydney, and is also a Research Affiliate of the Ross Parsons Centre of Commercial, Corporate and Taxation Law, Sydney Law School. He has published numerous articles, including in the *Australian Journal of Corporate Law*, *Common Law World Review*, *Competition and Consumer Law Journal*, *Journal of Business Law* and *Media and Arts Law Review*. He is the author of *Hong Kong Legal*

System (with W.H. Chui, 2012, McGraw-Hill), *In Search of Corporate Accountability: Liabilities of Corporate Participants* (2015, Cambridge Scholars Publishing), *Law of Companies in Hong Kong* (2nd edn) (with C. Qu, 2015, Sweet & Maxwell), and has also contributed chapters in *Chitty on Contracts: Hong Kong Specific Contracts* (4th edn) (2014, Sweet & Maxwell), *Tort Law and Practice in Hong Kong* (3rd edn) (2014, Sweet & Maxwell), *Company Law in Hong Kong: Insolvency* (2015, Sweet & Maxwell), and *Company Law in Hong Kong: Practice and Procedure* (2015, Sweet & Maxwell).

T. Wing Lo is Professor of Criminology and Head of the Department of Applied Social Sciences at City University of Hong Kong. He received his MPhil from the University of Hull in 1984 and PhD from the University of Cambridge in 1991. He had been employed as a youth gang worker for 17 years before he started university teaching in 1990. His research interests are triad societies, anti-corruption, youth gangs, outreach social work, group counselling and corrections. He is a member of the editorial/advisory board of a number of journals, such as the *Asian Journal of Criminology*, *British Journal of Community Justice*, *British Journal of Criminology* and *Youth Justice*.

David K.S. Ng is currently an Adjunct Assistant Professor in the Department of Sociology at The Chinese University of Hong Kong (CUHK). He received his Master's in criminology from the University of Hong Kong, and his PhD in sociology from the CUHK where he is now teaching criminology and policing courses. His research interests include crime and deviance, and subjects relating to policing. He was formerly an Assistant Commissioner of Police in the Hong Kong Police Force, where he served for over 30 years, having spent most of his police career in criminal investigations duties. Apart from his long-term association with the CUHK, he is presently also serving as an Advisory Board member and Honorary Fellow in the Office of Service Learning, Lingnan University.

Rebecca Ong is an Associate Professor with the School of Law, City University of Hong Kong. A barrister at Lincoln's Inn and an advocate and solicitor of the High Court of Malaya, Rebecca practised for 13 years before moving into academia. She teaches on the LLB, JD and PCLL programmes, and has published widely in IT law areas, data protection and privacy. She is also the author of *A Guide to Wills and Probate in Hong Kong*.

Simon N.M. Young is Professor and Associate Dean (Research) in the Faculty of Law, The University of Hong Kong. He is also a practising barrister at Parkside Chambers and appears in court in criminal law and public law cases. He teaches criminal law and evidence in the JD programme and an LLM course on rights and remedies in the criminal process. He is co-director of the Asia-America Institute in Transnational Law and co-editor-in-chief of the *Asia-Pacific Journal on Human Rights and the Law* (Brill). His books include *Hong Kong Evidence Casebook* (2004, Sweet & Maxwell Asia),

National Security and Fundamental Freedoms (with H. Fu and C. Petersen, 2005, Hong Kong University Press), *Interpreting Hong Kong's Basic Law* (with H. Fu and L. Harris, 2007, Palgrave Macmillan), *Civil Forfeiture of Criminal Property* (2009, Edward Elgar), *Electing Hong Kong's Chief Executive* (with R. Cullen, 2010 Hong Kong University Press), *Hong Kong's Court of Final Appeal* (with Y. Ghai, 2014, Cambridge University Press) and *Reforming Law Reform* (with M. Tilbury and L. Ng, 2014, Hong Kong University Press).

Lena Y. Zhong is Associate Professor in the Department of Applied Social Sciences, City University of Hong Kong. She is the author of *Communities, Crime and Social Capital in Contemporary China* (2008). She is a member of the editorial board of the *Asian Journal of Criminology*.

ACKNOWLEDGEMENT

We have received a lot of positive and constructive feedback from students, critical friends, reviewers and professors since the publication of the first edition of the book in 2008. Taking up the task of updating this book has been a daunting and tedious task, particularly for the first editor of the book. Dealing with a considerable number of contributors and reviewers, this almost impossible task would certainly not have been possible without the guidance, strength and wisdom from God. Moreover, the first editor would like to thank Shirley and Adrian Chui for their unfailing support and care. It really is a miracle to see this book materialise after having it spend nearly a decade in our mind palace. He would also like to thank the Institute of Advanced Study, School of Applied Social Sciences and St Mary's College for offering him a COFUND Senior Research Fellowship during his stay at Durham University between May and July 2016. During this fellowship, he was able to find time to review and respond to the editorial materials prepared by the Production Editor.

The principal aim of initiating this book project is to provide students reading criminal justice, criminal procedure, police studies, public administration and social work with an updated account on selected issues surrounding the administration of justice in Hong Kong. Since the publication of the first edition, a number of arguments and debates over controversial issues surrounding the criminal justice system have come to light. Putting these controversial issues into perspective to provide for a critical assessment of the criminal justice system, this book aims not to provide answers or solutions, but to enlighten readers and provoke critical thinking. We are aware of the growth of criminological and criminal justice literature in Hong Kong in the last few years; however, our edited volume draws together a diverse group of talented academics and active researchers – each of whom brings a wealth of knowledge and experience in various practice areas and aspects of criminal justice. We sincerely hope that the outcome of our work is helpful to practitioners and students alike in the fields of criminal justice, social work and law.

Each chapter includes an introduction, structured coursework on a particular topic, concluding remarks by contributors, links to external resource information, review questions and a chapter bibliography. While each contributor had a primary objective for their chapter, we have made every effort to ensure that the contributors applied a common style and provided cross-referencing across chapters. We have striven to ensure consistency and high quality in the material of the book, despite the fact that this was a challenging and time-consuming task. We do hope that readers find the book accessible and coherent.

Last but not least, we are grateful to Paul Vinod Khiatani and Dr Lawrence Ho who have assisted in proofreading earlier drafts of various chapters. We also wish to express our deep gratitude to those contributors who were so diligent and willing to give their time and expertise in contributing to this publication. Without their support, the task of producing this book would have been neither fun nor enjoyable. We owe all contributors a lot and we humbly ask for their forgiveness for bearing with such demanding editors (who appear to be perfectionists ... although do not expect the book to be error-free. Any wrongdoings are the fault of the editors).

Finally, we would like to thank Editorial Assistant Hannah Catterall and Senior Editor Thomas Sutton for their persistence and enduring patience in helping us see through the completion of this book.

Wing Hong Chui
T. Wing Lo
2016

1

THE CHANGING LANDSCAPES OF THE CRIMINAL JUSTICE SYSTEM

Wing Hong Chui and Paul Vinod Khiatani

Introduction

Since the publication of the first edition of this book, a number of events have emerged to increasingly 'politicise' issues relating to law and order, and crime and justice in Hong Kong. Not only the events themselves, but also how the law-makers and law enforcers respond to them are too. There are numerous real-case examples to illustrate the controversies surrounding the administration of justice. For example, protests from civil society, evident in the case of the 'Occupy Central' movement (Erni, 2015; Lee, 2015), and governance over locale-transnational criminal activities, evident in the case of the five missing booksellers (*South China Morning Post* (SCMP) 2016). Reflections on the complexities of these events necessitate a renewed understanding of the criminal justice system. The traditional approach to studying the criminal justice system, that is, the functional approach, needs to be superseded by the accommodation of a more critical, if not radical, lens (Taylor et al., 1973; Ugwudike, 2015). An understanding of the power relations, structural constraints and complexities of how Hong Kong should be administered would prove fruitful to any present-day discussion of the criminal justice system within the larger society.

This chapter will be divided into two parts. The first part of the chapter will draw on secondary data from local newspapers and government statistics to highlight the recent controversial issues relating to criminal justice in Hong Kong. The second part of the chapter will provide readers with an overall structure of the book and brief summaries of the chapters included in this second edition. This edition will feature 19 chapters, covering the basic concepts relating to crime and victimisation, pre-trial (police and corruption), trial (court, prosecution and the legal professionals), and post-trial (probation, prison and crime prevention). It is beyond the scope of this book to offer any concrete solutions to current socio-political problems. Moreover, it is also beyond the scope to cover the full range of issues and controversies surrounding the administration of justice in the past and today. Rather, this book intends to raise some of the issues that are or will be relevant to the study of the criminal justice system in Hong Kong.

Administration of justice today: issues and controversies

Broadly speaking, the changing landscapes of the criminal justice system can be attributed to four emerging trends, including an increasingly blurred line demarcating right from wrong, the changing face of criminal activities, the increasing public demand for accountability and transparency, and the persisting low rates of crime and fear of crime in Hong Kong. Whilst acknowledging that there are a number of significant events that may be out of the scope of the aforementioned trends, it is worth noting that these four trends touch on the core intersection of law, politics, crime and justice since the first edition of this book was published in 2008.

Increasingly blurred line demarcating right from wrong

Recent cases highlight, if anything, a blurred line in the sand when it comes to judging right from wrong in the social realities of Hong Kong. Increased civil unrest and public scepticism about the rulings and processes of the criminal justice system indicate a misaligned understanding of right and wrong between and within the administrative units and citizens in society. Take, for example, the case of 'Long hair' Kwok-hung Leung's challenge to the Correctional Services Department on the hair-length policy as being discriminatory (SCMP, 2015a); the mass protest challenging a prison sentence passed to a female protestor for assaulting a police officer with her 'breast'; Derek Tak-cheung Chan's challenge to the Correctional Services Department that its meal-portion servings are racially discriminatory (SCMP, 2015j); and the pursuit of prison terms by prosecutors from the Department of Justice against four protesters, who were originally given community service orders, for rampaging the doors of the Legislative Council (LegCo) in November 2014 (SCMP, 2015l). The court ruling for the four protestors was changed on 25 August 2015, from 150 hours of community service to a three and a half-month prison term (SCMP, 2015n). One of the aforementioned incidents which received considerable attention from international media was the incident of the 'breast assault' conviction (Time, 2015; BBC News, 2015). On 30 July 2015, in the context of a protest against parallel or cross-border trading, a female protestor was found guilty of assaulting a police officer with her breast during a heated dispute between the two sides of the parallel trading issue by Tuen Mun Magistrates' Court (SCMP, 31 July 2015a), sentencing the protestor to a three and a half-month prison term (SCMP, 2015f). Spiralling from the ruling, on 1 August 2015, a 'Breast Walk' rally of 200 people took place in front of Wanchai Police Station, lambasting the ruling and the police by shouting that the 'breast is not a weapon' (SCMP, 2015g). In the aforementioned cases, it is clear that what were once considered clear-cut, undisputed actions by the criminal justice system are now increasingly being questioned and challenged by the public on grounds of what *should* and *ought to* be right. It is in this cleavage that recent contention between the public and the criminal justice system exists.

The changing face of criminal activities

Another trend that has emerged in recent years is the increasing diversity and sophistication of criminal activities. For example, published as a public announcement on the official website, the Hong Kong Police Force recorded that over the period of January to July 2015, there had been 2,371 reports of telephone deception (the Hong Kong Police Force (HKPF) 2015a) – nearly half the total recorded cases of deception during that period, of 4,875 (HKPF, 2015b). While the upsurge in cases of deception comes as no surprise, especially given that the upward trend has been evident recently (HKPF, 2015b), it is the use of sophisticated technologies, the transnational nature, intended targets and meticulous 'division of labour'-based planning, such as deceiving the victim through group-oriented role-play and storytelling, which gives rise to a relatively new *modus operandi* (HKPF, 2015a; SCMP, 2015k).

In a recent case, a Chinese soprano, Yuanrong Li, was the victim of an elaborate and sophisticated phone fraud, duping her out of HK$20 million. The group of fraudsters impersonated mainland officials, postal officials, prosecutors and the like to convince Li that she had violated mainland law. She was then ordered to pay money via bank transfers into several mainland bank accounts to avoid being prosecuted and sent to prison (SCMP, 2015h).

The aforementioned evolution in telephone-related deception starting in Hong Kong around 2010 (HKPF, 2015a; SCMP, 31 December 2010), poses a pressing challenge to the criminal justice system in Hong Kong. With the accumulation of millions of Hong Kong dollars from duping various targets in Hong Kong, from the elderly to working professionals, since 2010, with striking effectiveness (SCMP, 2010), actors and constituents in the criminal justice system of Hong Kong are forced to adapt and take a firm position in tackling the local problem via international collaborations, especially with Mainland China as most of the fraudsters emerge from Greater China and possess links that extend to South-East Asia (SCMP, 2015i, 2015k).

The increasing public demand for accountability and transparency

There has been an increased dissatisfaction with the performance of constituents of the criminal justice process. This is evident especially in the Hong Kong Police Force, the forefront 'gatekeepers' of the criminal justice process (Traver, 2009). Since the second half of 2013, there has been a striking drop in the rate of public satisfaction in their performance, plummeting from 51.1% in the second half of 2013 to 36.3% and 29.1% in the biannual review of 2014, and further dropping to 28.7% in the second half of 2015 (Public Opinion Programme, 2015a). When compared with the other disciplinary forces, the Hong Kong Police Force has ranked next to last, if not last, in the league tables year after year since the second half of 2012, dropping in satisfaction rates from 67.0 in 2012 to 63.7 in 2013 and 62.4 in 2015 (Public Opinion Programme, 2015b).

Contextualising this dissatisfaction, consider the manner in which the Hong Kong Police Force handled members of the general public – student activists (SCMP, 2014), ethnic minorities (SCMP, 2015c), and people with intellectual disabilities (SCMP, 2015b) – in certain events. This is particularly evident in the incidents that occurred over the 'Occupy Central' period, from September to December 2014, involving allegations of excessive use of force, assault and unnecessary arrests. As a case in point, consider the assault case involving the then Superintendent Franklin King-wai Chu and 'Occupy Central' protestor Osman Chung-hang Cheng. On 26 November 2014, Chu was found hitting demonstrator Osman persistently with a baton at one of the 'Occupy Central' protest sites in Mong Kok (SCMP, 2015d). Having lodged a formal complaint of unlawful assault against Chu through the Independent Police Complaints Council (IPCC), Cheng, as well as the general public, has yet to see the resultant disciplinary action. Arriving at the conclusion that a criminal investigation against Chu was 'substantiated', the IPCC's initial ruling on 10 July 2015 was rejected by the Complaints against Police Officer (CAPO) on 20 July 2015, suggesting that launching a criminal investigation against the then superintendent was 'not fully substantiated' given the evidence (The Standard, 2015). A renewed vote by the IPCC in the same week confirmed its initial stance for 'substantiating' Cheng's complaint against Chu, and the case has since been passed to the Department of Justice. Coinciding with the progress made in pursuing a formal criminal investigation against Chu, Chu retired in the same week (SCMP, 2015d). In this incident, as with the many others that involve public disputes with the police over the 'Occupy Central' movement, the controversial nature and operation of the criminal justice system in handling allegations involving its own criminal justice actors continue to raise eyebrows and agitate sceptics. Feeling the pressure from the rise in controversial cases and mounting public discontent, the Department of Justice has since found it imperative to increase transparency with the public on court rulings and handling of controversial cases, as well as playing down public outcries of 'politically driven' rulings (SCMP, 2015c). This emerging observable trend signals an evolving relationship between the public and constituents of the criminal justice system, especially one grounded in a demand for greater accountability and transparency.

The persisting low rates of crime and fear of crime

Although not a new trend by any account, given Hong Kong's reputation as one of the safest cities in the world with a low violent crime culture, the low crime rate and low fear of crime statistics are a noteworthy trend in this discussion of the changing landscape of the criminal justice system as it relates to a continued 'legitimation of process' the government uses to retain its power and social control (see, for example, Chui et al., 2013; Adorjan and Chui, 2014). Despite its legitimacy being challenged in recent years, the criminal justice system delivers on performance. The crime rate and fear of crime have remained low. Since 2008, the overall crime trend has continued to decrease year on year, by 1.1% from 2008–09, 2.1% from 2009–10, 0.04% from 2010–11, 0.01% from 2011–12, 4.0% from 2012–13, 7.1% from 2013–14 and 1.9% from 2014–15 (HKPF, 2015c). Reflecting the decreasing trend in crime, research conducted on fear of crime in Hong Kong points to a collective perception of a safe city and confidence in the police (Broadhurst et al., 2010; Broadhurst et al., 2007; Adorjan and Chui, 2014). These research studies point to a pre-2010 atmosphere – a time when there was high satisfaction and confidence with the police and the other constituents of the criminal justice system. However, especially after 2013, satisfaction and confidence plummeted (refer to the satisfaction statistics on police performance mentioned in the third trend). In other words, the decreasing crime rate no longer clearly reflects favourable satisfaction and confidence in the criminal justice system.

Contextualising the relationship by considering their role in recent socio-political events, especially during the 2009–15 period characterised by various instances of competing political forces, constituents of the criminal justice system appear to face a challenge to retain their legitimate authority in maintaining law and social order amidst an increasingly disgruntled public. Looking to the recent case of the five missing booksellers, the criminal justice system appears to be under tight scrutiny by the state, civil society and Mainland China, as lawmakers and law enforcers steadily tread the line between provoking the 'One Country, Two Systems' concept, as stipulated by *The Basic Law of the Hong Kong Special Administrative Region of the People's Republic of China* (hereafter referred to as Basic Law) whereby Hong Kong enjoys the autonomy of enforcing laws and having an independent judiciary, and answering to the concerned public (SCMP, 2016).

Taken together, the four aforementioned trends elucidate a change in character and focus of the criminal justice system. Particularly in recent years, actors and constituents of the criminal justice system in Hong Kong have featured prominently in the public light, often over controversies and sensitive cases, spilled over by socio-political upheavals in society, forcing them to be no stranger to the critical eye of the public. Hong Kong has witnessed several social and political protests and acts of civil disobedience concerted by the dissent over the Hong Kong government's handling of internal affairs and its actions, or rather inactions, in furthering Hong Kong's development. These include, but are not limited to, the anti-high speed rail link movement against the proposed Hong Kong Express Rail Link in 2009–10 (Hung, 2014), the movement against the proposal of the Moral and National Education in 2011–13 (Cheng and Ho, 2014; Morris and Vickers, 2015), the protest against parallel trading since 2012 (Laidler and Lee, 2015), and more recently, the 'Occupy Central' movement in 2014 against the Hong Kong electoral system reform package put forward by the Standing Committee of the National People's Congress (Erni, 2015; Lee, 2015). Largely under the administration of the government, yet assumed to uphold justice through impartial administration of the law, the changing dynamics of the various constituents of the criminal justice system, often pursuing different interests and goals in maintaining the collective mission of criminal justice, thus arises as a topic of renewed interest.

About the second edition of *Understanding Criminal Justice in Hong Kong*

Designed as a prescribed text for both undergraduate and postgraduate students undertaking criminal justice and law as they embark on their studies, the aim of the book is twofold. The first aim is to outline basic concepts in criminal law, which is a common approach of defining crime in Hong Kong, and analyse the process by which the criminal justice system operates, ranging from initial reporting of a crime to the correctional system. The second aim of this book is to examine how personnel and actors in the criminal justice system work in practice, and how they deal with the offender and victim during the criminal justice process. In this respect, the updated text does follow along the same lines of covering laws, crimes and victims and various stages of the criminal justice system.

Mirroring the first edition, the ultimate goal of the book is to persuade readers to adopt a more critical approach in understanding the workings of the criminal justice system and to encourage more empirical research on crime and justice. Throughout the text, instead of simply focusing on how different criminal justice agencies operate and function, readers are encouraged to consider the arguments, debates and controversial issues that surround the Hong Kong criminal justice system. For instance, how should we define crime? How do we measure crime? How can the legal system protect the rights of the victims? Should the police be given more power to maintain law and order in society? What is the role of lawyers in safeguarding the rights of the defendant? How do judges make a decision in adjudicating the guilt of the defendant and sentencing? What is the best method of punishing criminals and preventing them from further offending? These issues are not only academic concerns but also 'the daily diet of much of our media' (Muncie and Wilson, 2004: ix). Apart from students interested in criminal justice and law, this updated edition will also appeal to those interested in learning about arrangements for law enforcement, crime control, crime prevention and methods for dealing with convicted offenders in Hong Kong.

Moreover, background information about Hong Kong will be provided for the benefit of non-Hong Kong readers. The book will cover histories of both pre-1997 Hong Kong as a British colony, and post-1997 Hong Kong as a special administrative region of the People's Republic of China (hereafter referred to as HKSAR). Selected themes and topics that subsequent chapters examine will be briefly considered in this opening chapter.

Administration of justice before and after 1 July 1997: an overview

At the outset, it should be emphasised that the following is a brief overview of the government structure in Hong Kong, and readers should consult textbooks on this area such as *The Government and Politics of Hong Kong* (Miners, 1998) and *Political Development in Hong Kong: State, Political Society, and Civil Society* (Ma, 2007) for more details.

Hong Kong, a special administrative region of the People's Republic of China, covers a small area of around 426 square miles. According to the latest estimates, Hong Kong has a population of over 7.299 million (Census and Statistics Department, 2016). Hong Kong was a British colony for more than 150 years, from 1842 to 1997. The colonial status was a result of a series of Anglo-Chinese wars and their 'unequal' treaties, including the Treaty of Nanjing in 1842, the Convention of Beijing in 1860, and the Second Convention of Beijing in 1898 (Lau, 1997; Wesley-Smith, 1998b; Tsang, 2004; Carroll, 2007). Hong Kong was governed by a British-appointed governor, assisted by senior civil servants, including a chief secretary, financial secretary, attorney-general and a group of secretaries responsible for various functions, such as education, health, social welfare and transport (Lo, 2000). Broadly speaking, there were two main branches of the government, namely the Executive and Legislative Councils. During the colonial rule, a large proportion of members of these two councils were primarily official and appointed unofficial members. The Executive Council functioned as the cabinet of the governor whereas the Legislative Council was responsible for making laws, debating issues of public interest, examining and approving public income and expenditure, and monitoring the work of the executive branches and administration of the government (Miners, 1998). Two major constitutional documents handed down by the Queen were the Hong Kong *Letters Patent* and *Royal Instructions*. These outlined the constitutional arrangements, including the powers and responsibilities of the governor and the said councils. In addition to the two branches, the judiciary, led by the chief justice, was independent of the central administration and legislature (Wesley-Smith, 1998a). Jones and Vagg (2007) commented that in many respects law and organisation of criminal justice in Hong Kong has a colonial origin, primarily from Great Britain, but they emphasised that the appointed governor was given some latitude to address local customs and problems:

> In general terms, the key institutions and principles of English law were introduced and applied, but the introduction of the rule of law probably owed as much to the *realpolitik* of the colonial rule as the 'civilising mission' – experience elsewhere had taught the Colonial

> Office that the best means of establishing the *pax Britannica* was by attaching the native population to colonial rule through rule of law and associated institutions.
>
> (Jones and Vagg, 2007: 3)

Despite the lack of democracy, the rule of law has been regarded as a cornerstone of Hong Kong's success as a leading international commercial and financial centre since colonial days. The rights and freedom of citizens were protected, and the rule of law was upheld by the independence of the judiciary. The functioning of the capitalist system and way of life in Hong Kong indicate that the rule of law worked very well before the resumption of the exercise of sovereignty over Hong Kong by the People's Republic of China.

In accordance with the concept of 'One Country, Two Systems', the capitalist system of the HKSAR will remain its existing social and economic systems for 50 years from 1 July 1997. The Basic Law has replaced the *Letters Patent* and *Royal Instructions* as the main constitutional document in Hong Kong. There are several principles enshrined under it. For instance, Article 5 states that 'the socialist system and policies shall not be practised in the [HKSAR], and the previous capitalist system and way of life shall remain unchanged for 50 years'. Article 2 specifies that the governance of the HKSAR will exercise a high degree of autonomy, except in defence and foreign affairs, and enjoy executive, legislative and independent judicial power. In many ways, the Hong Kong legal system has survived, alongside the political, economic and social systems. Article 8 states that the laws previously in force in Hong Kong – that is, the common law, rules of equity, ordinances and customary law – shall be maintained, except for any that contravene the Basic Law and subject to any amendment by the legislature of the HKSAR. Several provisions are concerned with the rights and responsibilities of the Hong Kong residents. Articles 25 and 26 assure that all residents shall be equal before the law and permanent residents of the HKSAR shall have the right to vote and the right to stand for election in accordance with the law. Article 28 specifies that no one shall be subjected to arbitrary or unlawful arrest, detention or imprisonment, and arbitrary or unlawful search of the body of any resident or deprivation or restriction of the freedom of the person shall be prohibited.

There were several significant changes in terms of the government structure in Hong Kong after the transfer of sovereignty. The following are some examples. First, the governor is replaced by the chief executive who is elected by a representative Election Committee in accordance with Annex I of the Basic Law, and the chief executive is appointed by the Central People's Government in Beijing. The chief executive is responsible for implementing the Basic Law, signing bills and budgets, promulgating laws, making decisions on government policies and issuing executive orders. Second, the attorney-general is now called the secretary for justice. Other features of the government have remained basically the same. The secretary for justice, now appointed by the Central People's

Government upon nomination by the chief executive, is the principal legal adviser to the chief executive, to the government, and to the individual government departments and agencies. Third, the Court of Final Appeal was established to replace the United Kingdom's Privy Council as the highest appellate court, which is headed by the chief justice.

Despite these changes, the administration of criminal justice has remained unchanged. In addition to the judiciary, several key government departments are responsible for maintaining law and order, fighting crime, enforcing law and rehabilitating offenders, including the Department of Justice, Hong Kong Police Force, Immigration Department, Independent Commission Against Corruption, Customs and Excise Department, Labour Department, Fire Services Department, Legal Aid Department, Social Welfare Department and Correctional Services Department. It is worth pointing out that while crime control is still very much the state's business and privatisation of criminal justice organisations is not common in Hong Kong, there has been a birth of private policing in places such as banks, shopping malls and private residential areas.

Structure of the book

The book is divided into four main parts: laws, crimes and victims (Part I); pre-trial stage (Part II); trial stage (Part III); and post-trial stage (Part IV). It is hoped that the 18 chapters that follow, divided across the four parts, will provide readers with a comprehensive understanding of the criminal justice system in Hong Kong. It is important to bear in mind that the linear and logical progression of justice from a crime being reported, through investigation or arrest, preparing for court, appearing in court, sentencing and punishment, may not necessarily follow one to another in real life. There are a number of decisions made along these three stages by the principal actors of the criminal justice system. Their decision-making process or use of discretion directly affects how a suspect is processed at various stages of the criminal justice system and whether a defendant will be convicted (Gelsthorpe and Padfield, 2003).

Part I: laws, crimes and victims

Part I consists of six chapters. Chapters 2 to 4 deal with the definition of crime, nature of criminal law and crime trends. Chapters 5 and 6 are concerned with other aspects of crime, including victims and fear of crime. The final chapter of Part I, Chapter 7, introduces how we should measure or research on topics of crime and justice by using social science research methods.

Whilst acknowledging the varied definitions of crime (Bosworth and Holye, 2011; Morrison, 2013), Nicole Cheung and Rebecca Ong define crime from a sociological and legal perspective. Chapter 2 by Nicole Cheung addresses the concept of crime as a function of the harmful consequences rendered, immorality and legal contravention. Crime can also be politically shaped, as reflected in major political challenges to criminal law, including crimes against the state, cross-border crimes and legal bilingualism, which stem from the assumption of sovereignty over Hong Kong by the People's Republic of China in 1997. Although criminal law has been one of the most trusted institutions for people in Hong Kong, it is only one of the geneses of the definition of crime. The socio-cultural beliefs and resulting public perceptions of crime in Hong Kong further indicate that crime is more than an objective attribute and that it involves subjective evaluation.

Chapter 3 by Rebecca Ong provides a general overview of criminal law in Hong Kong by examining the function and purposes of criminal law and elements for criminal liability. Using case law, three basic elements of crime, including *actus reus, mens rea* and defence are discussed. The chapter then goes on to deal with a number of specific offences, including offences against the person, offences against property, offences against public order, offences against public interest, and offences against morals and public policy. It is a well-known fact that the formal legalist definition of crime is commonly adopted in most industrialised countries, and 'no matter how immoral, reprehensible, damaging or dangerous an act is, it is not a crime unless it is made such by the State or international organisations' (Williams, 2012: 24). In this respect, the legal conception of crime determines how we measure the level and volume of crime.

In Chapter 4, Rod Broadhurst, King Wa Lee and Ching Yee Chan use over 50 years of data on crime and victimisation trends to discuss factors related to the changing prevalence and nature of crime, particularly in the context of Hong Kong's political transitions. While overseas studies frequently cite social factors, such as age structure, crime opportunities and social inequalities, in a study on crime trends, this chapter limits itself to examining the impacts of age structure, reporting behaviours, economic change and crime-fighting policies on crime trends in Hong Kong. Various sources of official data, including international surveys on official criminal justice and unofficial victimisation statistics, are used to compare Hong Kong's crime status to that of other countries.

Apart from studying the number of criminals and the volume of crime, Chapter 5 by Wai To Chan considers the ways in which the victim plays an important role in the process of criminal justice. For example, the victim reports an offence to the police, makes a statement, attends identification parades and gives their time by attending court as a witness. Regrettably, amid the criminal justice process, legal professionals are inclined to direct attention to details of an actual offence or the criminal's need by disposing lenient sentences. Consequently, the victims of crime do not get the proper attention they deserve, and that their role in the justice system affords them. Indeed, this chapter also examines whether criminal law processes are sufficiently addressing the needs of the victim. Chan comments that the current provision of victim programmes in Hong Kong seems to be hampered by the absence of a sound philosophical basis for action. The suggested improvement of the *Victims of Crime Charter* (Department of Justice, 2015) and the proposed use of mediation and reparation schemes could be the first step in the course of promoting restorative justice in society. It is hoped that crime victims have the right to be treated with courtesy and respect by criminal justice professionals and are given a prompt and proper response to complaints of crime.

Written by Maggy Lee and Michael Adorjan, Chapter 6 aims at providing some pointers for researchers and students interested in understanding public perceptions of crime as a social issue. Hong Kong has an international reputation as one of the safest cities in the twenty-first century. However, what do Hong Kong citizens actually think and feel about crime and disorder? This chapter sets out a new agenda for the study of public perceptions of crime and disorder in Hong Kong by drawing on the findings of a recent focus group study on people's crime fears and everyday life. Using a 'signal crimes' perspective, Lee and Adorjan argue that people's sense of security is influenced not only by crime events but also by what they perceive as troubling behaviours and disorderly environments that send signals about the distribution of risks and threats in particular locales. Through a discussion of the spatiality of fear in Mong Kok and the sensitised social tensions over parallel trading in border towns, the chapter highlights the significance of foregrounding the social and spatial dimensions and the contributions of a sociologically informed criminology of 'fear of crime'.

Finally in Part I, Chapter 7, by Alistair Fraser, aims to inform the reader of the importance of conducting theoretically grounded, methodologically sound research, which lies at the heart of the criminological enterprise. Whether our audiences are policymakers, the general public or fellow researchers, it is vital to base judgements on valid and reliable empirical evidence. A firm foundation in research methodology is therefore vital, both as a means of evaluating previous research, and to design novel and rigorous interventions. This chapter introduces some of the fundamental issues involved in researching crime and justice, including issues pertaining to settings and contexts, principles and practices, qualitative and quantitative methodologies, politics and ethics. Particular reference is made to the challenges and opportunities involved in conducting criminological research in a Hong Kong context.

Part II: pre-trial stage

Part II consists of four chapters. The pre-trial stage refers to those actions or activities that take place after a crime is reported to the police and before the defendant is summoned to appear in court. In this stage, several major actors, often referred to as 'gatekeepers' of the criminal justice system, are discussed at length – the police (Chapters 8 and 9), the anti-corruption institutional framework (Chapter 10) and the prosecutor (Chapter 11).

In Chapter 8, significant towards developing an understanding of one of the prominent 'gatekeepers', Wayne Chan and Raymond Lau aim to provide an in-depth historical account of the development of the Hong Kong Police Force (HKPF).

Since its establishment in the mid-19th century, following Britain's acquisition of Hong Kong as a crown colony from China in 1842, Chan and Lau trace and contextualise the operational and structural reforms undergone by the HKPF. Apart from discussions on past reform endeavours, Chan and Lau also introduce future prospects for the development of the HKPF in today's Hong Kong.

Furthering the discussion on the HKPF, David Ng writes on present-day challenges that the law enforcers are facing. In a highly politicised society, the challenges to uphold the rule of law, maintain social order, gain public trust and confidence, and remain politically neutral abound. Chapter 9 aims to provide an understanding of these challenges and the existing powers of the HKPF. Ng leads in this chapter with a discussion on the inherent tension and interdependent relationship that exists between society, the law and the police (including, but not limited to, police powers and police duties). Moreover, Ng goes on to discuss the challenges faced by the HKPF since the change of sovereignty in 1997, when Hong Kong transformed overnight from a British colony into an SAR of China.

Writing on the historical developments and reforms undergone by the anti-corruption framework in Hong Kong, Cora Hui and T. Wing Lo in Chapter 10 aim to provide an historical account of local institutional safeguards established to combat corruption. Through an historical perspective, the chapter presents a discussion of five main groups of strategies enacted in Hong Kong to curb corruption since the 1960s and 1970s: effective legislation enacted within the rule of law, the establishment of the Independent Commission Against Corruption, the necessity for strong political will, the emergence of a watchdog culture, and civil service reform. The interdependence and individual functions of the aforementioned strategies are highlighted in the chapter with relevance to the ongoing war for a 'corruption-free' culture in Hong Kong.

In the final chapter in Part II, Chapter 11, I. Grenville Cross aims to provide readers with a comprehensive understanding of the prosecutor as an integral actor in the criminal justice system. A fair trial requires a just prosecutor, and accused persons must always be properly treated, with relevant material which may assist the defence being fully disclosed. While the prosecutor will seek by fair means to secure the conviction of those accused of crime, prosecution must never become persecution, and it is no part of the prosecutor's role to seek a conviction at all costs. Operating at the very heart of the criminal justice system, the prosecutor's ultimate concern is to see that justice is done, and to assist the courts as well as his or her criminal justice partners to achieve a proper outcome to criminal cases. Just as the conviction of the guilty is in the public interest, so also is the acquittal of the innocent.

Part III: trial stage

Part III consists of four chapters. The trial stage covers the process and procedures that take place within the judicial system. Attention has been paid to highlight the distinctions between what happens in lower and higher courts. Chapters 12 and 13 cover issues related to legal representation in the criminal justice system. Chapter 14 provides an in-depth look at criminal courts in Hong Kong. Chapter 15 is concerned with issues related to sentencing.

In Chapter 12, Eric Ip discusses the legal profession as a whole in Hong Kong, often considered to be one of the oldest and most respected in East Asia, and the issue of legal representation in the criminal justice process. An independent legal profession, shielded by legal professional privilege, is regarded by the Hong Kong criminal justice system as integral to the constitutional right of legal representation, arguably the most important procedural right possessed by residents. Several institutions exist to guarantee the quality of legal representation in Hong Kong. The Bar Association, the Law Society and the two major disciplinary tribunals for lawyers maintain high standards of professional ethics and conduct in the solicitors' and barristers' branches of the legal profession, which remain separate. Criminal legal aid, administered by the Legal Aid Department and superintended by the Legal Aid Services Council, is largely free from political interference. The Duty Lawyer Scheme exists *inter alia* to provide eligible defendants with legal representation in the Magistrates' Courts, and legal advice schemes sponsored by the government disseminate legal knowledge across the community.

Kevin Cheng provides an in-depth, critical discussion on plea bargaining in Hong Kong in Chapter 13. Most criminal cases are disposed of by way of guilty pleas, leading some observers to conclude that the criminal justice system is geared towards the mass production of guilty pleas. The purpose of this chapter is to outline the guarantees of voluntariness and plea decisions by the accused stipulated in the law. Hong Kong continues to be restrictive with respect to advanced sentence indications. At the same time, however, this chapter highlights how the criminal justice system encourages defendants to plead guilty, namely through the one-third sentence discount, the intrinsic pressures associated with being caught up in the criminal process, and plea bargaining. The criticisms against the current mechanisms and the justifications of them are discussed.

In Chapter 14, Stefan Lo aims to provide a comprehensive overview of the system of criminal courts in Hong Kong. The chapter discusses in detail the courts in which accused persons can be tried in Hong Kong: the Magistrates' Court, District Court and Court of First Instance of the High Court. The system of appeals is also discussed, including discussion of the appellate roles of the Court of Appeal of the High Court and of the Court of Final Appeal. The chapter outlines some of the main steps in the conduct of a criminal trial in the various courts. Specific aspects of the court system such as the role of the judge and the jury are also covered in this chapter.

Finally in Part III, in Chapter 15, Simon Young presents a detailed discussion of the purposes and principles that animate the law of sentencing in Hong Kong. The chapter identifies and describes a range of options or measures available to the Hong Kong court when sentencing an individual for a criminal offence. Trends on the principles and practice of sentencing, sentencing decisions and options, and aggravating and mitigating factors that inform 'appropriate' sentence decisions are highlighted with respect to judges, the Hong Kong courts, and relevant materials and cases.

Part IV: post-trial stage

Part IV consists of four chapters. The post-trial stage is concerned with the treatment of an offender after being convicted and sentenced. Chapters 16 and 17 are dedicated to an in-depth discussion of non-custodial and custodial sentencing. Chapter 18 reviews and elaborates on issues of crime prevention. Finally, Chapter 19, as the final chapter of the book, attempts to make sense of the challenges the Hong Kong criminal justice system is and will be facing in relation to China's increasing influence in Hong Kong.

A consistent theme emerging from Chapters 16 and 17 is that the ethos of rehabilitation is the dominant sentencing theory and the main intervention method of dealing with offenders. In the post-trial stage, two principal government departments that work with offenders in the community and prison are the Social Welfare Department and Correctional Services Department (CSD). In Chapter 16, Wing Hong Chui introduces the concept of community sentencing. In contrast to the custodial sentencing option, community sentence is a non-punitive approach targeting first-time, non-violent offenders who pose little threat to society. The theoretical underpinning of the probation order and community service order are discussed. Major justifications for community sentences are diversion or deinstitutionalisation, reintegration (or rehabilitation) and reparation. He points out that the Social Welfare Department is primarily staffed by trained social workers who employ various treatment models and interventions to promote pro-social behaviour amongst those being given community sentences. The ingredients of effective intervention with offenders are highlighted, drawing upon empirical evidence. The chapter points to the importance of developing a more systematic and evidence-based criminal justice social work intervention for offenders.

In Chapter 17, T. Wing Lo and Sharon Ingrid Kwok shift the focus to the role and function of the CSD. Custodial sentences are operated by the CSD, formerly the Prisons Department before 1982, which is responsible for the secure, safe and humane custody of offenders. The CSD maintains order and control to minimise the chance of escapes and acts of indiscipline, and its programmes emphasise self-control and discipline. The CSD provides prisoners with a range of psychological and welfare services and opportunities to engage in useful work. To correct their criminal behaviour, it provides education, vocational training, drug addiction treatment, community reintegration programmes, aftercare and support services, and various supervision schemes. Its overall success rate is compatible with that of overseas counterparts.

Overcrowding was common in correctional institutions in the 1990s and 2000s. With a recent decline in the penal population, the overcrowding situation in prisons has been substantially improved. When compared, female institutions have suffered resource issues more than male institutions.

Consistent with what Broadhurst et al. found in Chapter 4, Lena Zhong opines that Hong Kong is among the safest cities around the world, both in terms of official crime statistics and crime victim surveys. Chapter 18 begins with an introduction to the definition of crime prevention, with special emphases placed on the multifaceted nature of crime prevention and the multi-agency approach to crime prevention. Second, the three most commonly used typologies of crime prevention, namely the public health model, the social/situational model, and Tonry and Farrington's Four-level Model, are reviewed. Drawing on the definition and typologies, the chapter reviews various locally initiated crime prevention measures, including some innovative ones. The chapter emphasises that crime prevention measures in Hong Kong should be subject to more vigorous evaluations to assess their effectiveness.

Finally, as a concluding chapter, T. Wing Lo reflects on the future of Hong Kong's criminal justice system against the backdrop of recent events, such as 'Occupy Central', and observable trends, such as the speeding economic and political convergence between Hong Kong and Mainland China. In Chapter 19, Lo provides an overview of the criminal justice system in Mainland China, and the resistance by Hong Kong against the 'mainlandisation' of the local criminal justice system. In talking about the future, moreover, Lo reflects on the felt challenges of the local criminal justice system today, including, but not limited to, the persistence of a legal and political convergence between Mainland China and Hong Kong, a weakened independent commission against corruption, the shifting representation of the police as being a tool for 'political policing', and a growing perception of the courts as an arena of contestation between the dominant and dominated. As Hong Kong continues to undergo political changes, the fate of the local criminal justice system could not be more important, especially if we so desire its independence and the administration of justice through the rule of law.

We want to stress that it is beyond the scope of this introductory text to cover all aspects of criminal justice in Hong Kong. However, its coverage reflects what we believe is essential knowledge that students coming to the field for the first time should acquire. Despite there being 19 chapters and a wide range of topics examined, there are a number of areas that are not included. If space had allowed, we would have liked to discuss the rights of defendants, the role of defence lawyers, and the operation and specific function of various law enforcement organisations that also play an important role in fighting crime. Some examples of these organisations are the Customs and Excise Department, Department of Immigration and Labour Department. Also, a more detailed analysis of the specific criminal procedure for mentally disordered offenders should have been discussed. In this respect, readers are advised to consult other textbooks such as Gaylord and Traver (1994), Wesley-Smith (1998a), Jackson (2003), Jiao (2007),

Jones and Vagg (2007), Gaylord et al. (2009), Lo and Chui (2012), and Whitfort (2012), or the websites listed at the end of this chapter, for further details.

Review Questions

1 What are the major reasons for you to study criminal justice?
2 "A number of events have emerged to increasingly 'politicise' issues relating to law and order, and crime and justice in Hong Kong." How far do you agree with the statement?

References

Adorjan, M. and Chui, W.H. (2014) *Responding to Youth Crime in Hong Kong: Penal Elitism, Legitimacy and Citizenship*, Abingdon: Routledge.

Bosworth, M. and Holye, C. (eds) (2011) *What is Criminology?*, Oxford: Oxford University Press.

Broadhurst, R., Bacon-Shone, J., Bouhours, B., Lee, K.W. and Zhong, L. (2010) *Hong Kong United Nations International Crime Victim Survey: Final Report of the 2006 Hong Kong UNICVS*, Hong Kong and Canberra: The University of Hong Kong and the Australian National University.

Broadhurst, R., Lee, K.W. and Chan, C.Y. (2007) *Crime and Violence in Hong Kong, China*. United Nations. Case study prepared for Enhancing Urban Safety and Security: Global Report on Human Settlements.

Carroll, J.M. (2007) *A Concise History of Hong Kong*, Hong Kong: Hong Kong University Press.

Census and Statistics Department (January, 2016) *Hong Kong Monthly Digest of Statistics*, Hong Kong Government Printer.

Cheng, W.N. and Ho, J. (2014) 'Brainwashing or nurturing positive values: Competing voices in Hong Kong's national education debate', *Journal of Pragmatics*, 74(1): 1–14.

Choi, A. and Lo, T.W. (2004) *Fighting Youth Crime: A Comparative Study of Two Little Dragons in Asia* (2nd edn), Singapore: Eastern Universities Press.

Chui, W.H., Cheng, K.K. and Wong, L.P. (2013) 'Gender, fear of crime, and attitudes toward prisoners among social work majors in a Hong Kong university', *International Journal of Offender Therapy and Comparative Criminology*, 57(4): 479–494.

Department of Justice (2015) *The Victims of Crime Charter*, Hong Kong: Government Printer, www.doj.gov.hk/eng/public/pub200004.html (accessed 15 February 2016).

Erni, J.N. (2015) 'A legal realist view on citizen actions in Hong Kong's umbrella movement', *Chinese Journal of Communication*, 8(4): 412–419.

Gaylord, M.S., Gittings, D. and Traver, H. (eds) (2009) *Introduction to Crime, Law, and Justice in Hong Kong*, Hong Kong: Hong Kong University Press.

Gaylord, M.S. and Traver, H. (eds) (1994) *Introduction to the Hong Kong Criminal Justice System*, Hong Kong: Hong Kong University Press.

Gelsthorpe, L. and Padfield, N. (eds) (2003) *Exercising Discretion: Decision-making in the Criminal Justice System and Beyond*, Cullompton: Willan.

The Hong Kong Police Force (HKPF) (2015a) *Telephone Deception*. www.police.gov.hk/ppp_en/04_crime_matters/ccb/cct_09.html (accessed 15 February 2016).

The Hong Kong Police Force (HKPF) (2015b) *Crime Statistics in Detail.* www.police.gov.hk/ppp_en/09_statistics/csd.html (accessed 15 February 2016).

The Hong Kong Police Force (HKPF) (2015c) *Crime Statistics Comparison.* www.police.gov.hk/ppp_en/09_statistics/csc.html (accessed 15 February 2016).

Hung, S.C.F. (2014) 'Political participation of students in Hong Kong – A historical account of transformation', in J.Y.S. Cheng (ed.) *New Trends of Political Participation in Hong Kong* (pp. 241–275), Hong Kong: City University of Hong Kong Press.

Jackson, M. (2003) *Criminal Law in Hong Kong*, Hong Kong: Hong Kong University Press.

Jiao, A.Y. (2007) *The Police in Hong Kong: A Contemporary View*, Lanham, MD: University Press of America.

Jones, C. and Vagg, J. (2007) *Criminal Justice in Hong Kong*, London: Routledge-Cavendish.

Laidler, K.J. and Lee, M. (2015) 'Border trading and policing of everyday life in Hong Kong', in S. Pickering and J. Ham (eds) *The Routledge Handbook on Crime and International Migration* (pp. 316–328), Abingdon: Routledge.

Lau, C.K. (1997) *Hong Kong's Colonial Legacy: A Hong Kong Chinese's View of the British Heritage*, Hong Kong: The Chinese University Press.

Lee, F.L.F. (2015) 'Social movement as civic education: Communication activities and understanding of civil disobedience in the Umbrella Movement', *Chinese Journal of Communication*, 8(4): 393–411.

Lo, T.W. (2000) 'An overview of the criminal justice system in Hong Kong', in O.N.I. Ebbe (ed.) *Comparative and International Criminal Justice Systems: Policing, Judiciary, and Corrections* (2nd edn) (pp. 113–128), Boston, MA: Butterworth-Heinemann.

Lo, S.H.C. and Chui, W.H. (2012) *The Hong Kong Legal System*, Singapore: McGraw-Hill.

Ma, N. (2007) *Political Development in Hong Kong: State, Political Society, and Civil Society*, Hong Kong: Hong Kong University Press.

Miners, N. (1998) *The Government and Politics of Hong Kong* (5th edn), Hong Kong: Oxford University Press.

Morris, P. and Vickers, E. (2015) 'Schooling, politics and the construction of identity in Hong Kong: The 2012 "Moral and National Education" crisis in historical context', *Comparative Education*, 51(3): 305–326.

Morrison, W. (2013) 'What is crime? Contrasting definitions and perspectives', in C. Hale, K. Hayward, A. Wahidin and E. Wincup (eds) *Criminology* (pp. 3–22), Oxford: Oxford University Press.

Muncie, J. and Wilson, D. (2004) 'Editors' introduction', in J. Muncie and D. Wilson (eds) *Student Handbook of Criminal Justice and Criminology* (pp. ix–xi), London: Cavendish.

Public Opinion Programme (2015a) *People's Satisfaction with the Performance of the Hong Kong Police Force (Half-yearly Average) (7–12/1997 – 7–12/2015)*, Hong Kong: Public Opinion Programme, The University of Hong Kong, hkupop.hku.hk/english/popexpress/hkpolice/halfyr/hkpolice_halfyr_chart.html (accessed 15 February 2016).

Public Opinion Programme (2015b) *People's Satisfaction with the Disciplinary Force*, Hong Kong: Public Opinion Programme, The University of Hong Kong, hkupop.hku.hk/english/popexpress/discipilnaryForces/index.html (accessed 15 February 2016).

Taylor, I., Walton, P. and Young, J. (1973) *The New Criminology: For a Social Theory of Deviance*, London: Routledge.

Traver, H. (2009) 'Hong Kong Police Force', in M.S. Gaylord, D. Gittings and H. Traver (eds) *Introduction to Crime, Law, and Justice in Hong Kong* (pp. 55–75), Hong Kong: Hong Kong University Press.

Tsang, S.Y.-S. (2004) *A Modern History of Hong Kong*, London: I.B. Tauris.

Ugwudike, P. (2015) *An Introduction to Critical Criminology*, Bristol: Policy Press.

Wesley-Smith, P. (1998a) *An Introduction to the Hong Kong Legal System* (3rd edn), Hong Kong: Oxford University Press.

Wesley-Smith, P. (1998b) *Unequal Treaty, 1898–1997: China, Great Britain, and Hong Kong's New Territories* (revised edn), Hong Kong: Oxford University Press.

Whitfort, A. (2012) *Criminal Procedure in Hong Kong: A Guide for Students and Practitioners* (2nd edn), Hong Kong: LexisNexis.

Williams, K.S. (2012) *Textbook on Criminology* (7th edn), Oxford: Oxford University Press.

Newspaper articles cited

BBC News (2015) 'Hong Kong protest over "breast as weapon" conviction', 3 August, www.bbc.com/news/world-asia-china-33754907 (accessed 15 February 2016).

South China Morning Post (SCMP) (2010) 'Police alarmed at success rate of new phone scam', 31 December, www.scmp.com/article/734404/police-alarmed-success-rate-new-phone-scam (accessed 15 February 2016).

South China Morning Post (SCMP) (2014) 'Reform protesters confront Li Fei as Scholarism activists evicted from hotel', 1 September, www.scmp.com/news/hong-kong/article/1582747/students-evicted-hotel-protesters-confront-npcs-li-fei?page=all (accessed 15 February 2016).

South China Morning Post (SCMP) (2015a) 'Hong Kong's "Long Hair" lawmaker goes to court over jailhouse cut', 27 April, www.scmp.com/news/hong-kong/law-crime/article/1777702/hong-kongs-long-hair-lawmaker-goes-court-over-jailhouse-cut?page=all (accessed 15 February 2016).

South China Morning Post (SCMP) (2015b) 'Family blast police over handling of autistic man's arrest, detention', 10 May, www.scmp.com/news/hong-kong/law-crime/article/1791738/family-blast-police-over-handling-autistic-mans-arrest (accessed 15 February 2016).

South China Morning Post (SCMP) (2015c) 'Police say their efforts to include minorities should be model, but activists urge serious action', 21 June, www.scmp.com/news/hong-kong/education-community/article/1824474/police-say-their-efforts-include-minorities (accessed 15 February 2016).

South China Morning Post (SCMP) (2015c) 'Justice Secretary calls for understanding of judicial system after politically sensitive Occupy cases cause controversy', 24 June, www.scmp.com/news/hong-kong/law-crime/article/1825359/justice-secretary-calls-understanding-judicial-system-after (accessed 15 February 2016).

South China Morning Post (SCMP) (2015d) 'Hong Kong police may be told to open criminal probe against senior officer accused of assaulting protester', 23 July, www.scmp.com/news/hong-kong/law-crime/article/1843005/prosecution-top-hong-kong-policeman-hangs-balance-watchdog (accessed 15 February 2016).

South China Morning Post (SCMP) (2015e) 'Woman convicted of "assaulting cop with her breast" maintains she's innocent', 30 July, www.scmp.com/news/hong-kong/law-crime/article/1844878/breast-assault-woman-maintains-her-innocence-over-police (accessed 15 February 2016).

South China Morning Post (SCMP) (2015f) 'Hong Kong magistrate reveals he received threats before sentencing protester accused of assaulting cop with her breast', 31 July, www.scmp.com/news/hong-kong/law-crime/article/1845098/anti-parallel-trade-protester-who-hit-hong-kong-policeman?page=all (accessed 15 February 2016).

South China Morning Post (SCMP) (2015g) '"Breast is not a weapon", Hong Kong protesters shout as they gather at police headquarters', 2 August, www.scmp.com/news/hong-kong/law-crime/article/1845867/hong-kong-protesters-shout-breast-not-weapon-they-gather?page=all (accessed 15 February 2016).

South China Morning Post (SCMP) (2015h) 'Veteran Chinese soprano, 73, cheated out of HK$20m in Hong Kong's largest single phone scam', 10 August, www.scmp.com/news/hong-kong/law-crime/article/1848238/hong-kong-woman-hands-over-hk20-million-largest-single?page=all (accessed 15 February 2016).

South China Morning Post (SCMP) (2015i) 'Hong Kong, mainland Chinese police agree to set up task force to fight phone scammers', 11 August, www.scmp.com/news/hong-kong/law-crime/article/1848442/chinese-soprano-73-cheated-out-hk20m-hong-kongs-biggest (accessed 15 February 2016).

South China Morning Post (SCMP) (2015j) 'Former inmate challenges policy over Chinese and Western meals in Hong Kong prisons', 18 August, www.scmp.com/news/hong-kong/law-crime/article/1850458/former-inmate-challenges-policy-over-chinese-and-western (accessed 15 February 2016).

South China Morning Post (SCMP) (2015k) 'Imprisoned mainland Chinese "forced to make scam calls from Southeast Asia", police liaison officer in Hong Kong alleges', 18 August, www.scmp.com/news/hong-kong/law-crime/article/1850413/mainland-people-being-forced-make-scam-calls-southeast (accessed 15 February 2016).

South China Morning Post (SCMP) (2015l) 'Prosecutors seek jail sentences for four protesters over "near-riot" at LegCo building', 19 August, www.scmp.com/news/hong-kong/law-crime/article/1850658/prosecutors-seek-jail-sentences-four-protesters-over-near (accessed 15 February 2016).

South China Morning Post (SCMP) (2015m) 'Student protesters who pre-empted Occupy Central face justice – 11 months on', 19 August, www.scmp.com/news/hong-kong/law-crime/article/1850653/student-protesters-face-justice-11-months (accessed 15 February 2016).

South China Morning Post (SCMP) (2015n) 'Three Hong Kong protesters jailed using metal barrier LegCo', 26 August, www.scmp.com/news/hong-kong/law-crime/article/1852563/hong-kong-protesters-handed-jail-time-using-metal-barrier (accessed 15 February 2016).

South China Morning Post (SCMP) (2016) 'CY Leung on Hong Kong's missing booksellers: mainland China law enforcement actions "unacceptable"', 5 January, www.scmp.com/news/hong-kong/law-crime/article/1897784/cy-leung-hong-kongs-missing-booksellers-mainland-china-law (accessed 15 February 2016).

The Standard (2015) 'Baton cop ruling likely to stay', 21 July, www.thestandard.com.hk/news_detail.asp?pp_cat=11&art_id=159253&sid=44863692&con_type=1 (accessed 15 February 2016).

Time (2015) 'A Hong Kong woman just got convicted of assaulting a police officer with her breast', 16 July, time.com/3962142/hong-kong-woman-police-breast-assault/ (accessed 15 February 2016).

Legislation cited

Basic Law of the Hong Kong Special Administrative Region of the People's Republic of China

Hong Kong Bill of Rights Ordinance (Cap. 383)
Letters Patent (Hong Kong)
Royal Instructions (Hong Kong)

Useful websites

Basic Law of the Hong Kong Special Administrative Region of the People's Republic of China www.info.gov.hk/basic_law/flash.html
Complaints Against Police Office www.police.gov.hk/ppp_en/11_useful_info/cap.html
Correctional Services Department www.csd.gov.hk
Customs and Excise Department www.customs.gov.hk
Department of Justice www.doj.gov.hk
Fire Services Department www.hkfsd.gov.hk/home/
Hong Kong Police Force www.police.gov.hk
Immigration Department www.immd.gov.hk/index.html
Independent Commission Against Corruption www.icac.org.hk
Independent Police Complaints Council www.ipcc.gov.hk/en/home/index.html
Labour Department www.labour.gov.hk/eng/news/content.htm
Legal Aid Department www.lad.gov.hk
The Legislative Council (LegCo) www.legco.gov.hk/general/english/intro/about_lc.htm
Security Bureau www.sb.gov.hk
Social Welfare Department www.swd.gov.hk/en/index/index.html
South China Morning Post www.scmp.com/frontpage/hk
The Standard www.thestandard.com.hk

Part I

LAWS, CRIMES AND VICTIMS

2

DEFINING CRIME

Nicole W.T. Cheung

Introduction

Crime and criminals attract attention from nearly everyone. Most people know that homicide, robbery, rape, burglary, kidnapping and drug trafficking are crimes, even though they may not be able to define these crimes with legal precision, but what does it actually mean to say this is 'criminal behaviour'? Why should some behaviour be criminalised or decriminalised? Why is it legal to smoke tobacco but not marijuana? Why is property inheritance protected by law but not the expropriation of property to achieve the equitable distribution of wealth? Why is it lawful to bet in a licensed gambling establishment (e.g., The Hong Kong Jockey Club and the casino cruise ships based in Hong Kong), but unlawful in other, unlicensed locations? What about littering, abstracting electricity, loitering, and cheating on income taxes? These acts may amount to crimes or offences in Hong Kong even though they may not be generally considered 'crimes' – at least, not in the same sense as homicide, robbery, rape, burglary, kidnapping and drug trafficking.

Crime as a function of harm and immorality

Most typically, crime is justified in terms of the consequences or the harm rendered. The harmfulness of an act is not confined to physical harm or property damage but extends to potential harm to other interests that are in need of protection so as to sustain a better and more just society. Those interests may be germane to the preservation of public order and safety across a spectrum of activities – for instance, traffic regulation, animal licensing, prohibition of underage gambling and alcohol consumption, safeguarding of intellectual property rights, and the control of obscene and indecent material in various media, including on the Internet. The status of the crime victim is also usually taken into account in the assessment of a crime's harmfulness. Classes of people such as children, the elderly, and people with physical and intellectual disabilities receive extra or special protection under the law.

A second typical criterion for classification as a crime is that the behaviour in question violates the society's moral codes or morality. Moral assessment of behaviour shapes our response, resulting in some actions being treated as crimes while other acts are not. Undoubtedly, this is true of many victimising crimes, particularly those involving violence, which are criminalised not only on the basis of their victimisation and harmful consequences, but also on the basis of the extent to which they are seen as wrong in a moral sense. Nonetheless, victimless crimes, such as drug abuse, prostitution, pornography and gambling, are still often made illegal because they are considered immoral. Victimless acts do not directly threaten the rights of, or inflict harm on, any other individual. They often involve consensual or solitary acts in which no other person is involved. If conducted in private, the most direct and immediate effect of this type of behaviour lies only with the individuals who participate in them.

Female sex work in Hong Kong exemplifies the manner in which a victimless act is demoralised and outlawed. The legal status of sex workers has been determined by Hong Kong's colonial past, in which the laws governing sex work emulate those in the United Kingdom, beginning with the enactment of the *Venereal Disease and Contagious Disease Ordinances* in the 1850s and continuing to the current law introduced in 1978, which adopted the recommendations of the 1957 *Wolfenden Report* (Howell, 2004; Chiu, 2006). Tackling the problem of sex workers in its perceived role of disseminating venereal and contagious diseases, these laws were used to legitimise the biopolitical surveillance of the sex industry on the premise of public health, thereby marking prostitutes as exemplars of deviant and dangerous sexuality (Howell, 2004). The Wolfenden Committee, while assenting that private activities should not be the concern of criminal law and that the law should not penalise the sex workers per se, contended that the function of the law was to 'regulate the sex workers' activities which offended (mainstream) public decency or exposed the average citizen to what was offensive' (Chiu, 2006: 549). By virtue of these precedents, although sex work is not illegal in Hong Kong, nearly all related activities are, such as assuming control over persons for the purpose of prostitution, running a vice establishment, soliciting for an immoral purpose, putting up signs advertising prostitution, living on the earnings of prostitution, or a tenant permitting his or her premises or vessel to be used for prostitution, as specified in the *Crimes Ordinance* (sections 130–145 and 147, Cap. 200).

Sex work has been strongly influenced by local Christian and Chinese conservatism, which emphasises that only sex in marriage is acceptable, which makes sex work and sex workers by definition immoral in Hong Kong (Chiu, 2006). The criminal laws against sex work exacerbate the power differential and structural abuse by law enforcement officers because the status of female sex workers – although legal in itself – alludes to participation in the illegal activities related to prostitution. This keeps female sex workers from seeking legal justice and police assistance when they are the victims of abuse by patrons. They fear that by reporting abuse against them, they may self-identify as sex workers and become liable for criminal prosecution. Such a scenario perpetuates sex work's stigma of immorality and contributes to a cycle of violence in which sex workers can come to be seen as easy prey because violent patrons know that sex workers are unlikely to report an assault to the police (Wong et al., 2011).

It should be noted that the correlation between immorality and criminalisation does not necessarily exist, however. Even if no specific legislation under the criminal justice system (i.e. the formal control mechanism) regulates immorality, society may still condemn such behaviour by means of informal control mechanisms such as family, peers, the education system and religious organisations. The issue of whether morality should be officially defined, enforced and upheld has long been the subject of controversy in jurisprudence. The example of decriminalisation of homosexuality in Hong Kong in 1991 is illustrative of that controversy (Jackson, 2003).

Before decriminalisation, homosexuality was handled under the *Offences Against the Person Ordinance* (Cap. 212), in force since 1865, which prescribed penalties of up to life imprisonment for anal intercourse between men and up to two years' imprisonment for any act of gross indecency by a man with another man, irrespective of whether it is performed with or without consent, in private or in public. From an historical perspective, the query about the appropriateness of the law that governed homosexuality was popularised in Hong Kong in 1980 when a male inspector of the Royal Hong Kong Police Force was found to be a homosexual and committed suicide. This suicide due to homosexual orientation discredited the image of the police force and came as a great shock to the general public because police officers were socially perceived as model citizens (Chan, 2008; Wong, 2010). A motion to debate the decriminalisation of homosexual acts between consenting adults in private places was then initiated by the Law Reform Commission of Hong Kong in 1983 (*Report on Laws Governing Homosexual Conduct*). Although the Law Reform Commission recommended decriminalisation, discussion dragged on for almost a decade before the recommendation came into being in 1991 (Jackson, 2003; Chan, 2008). This delay was partly because the Hong Kong government was keenly sensitive to the local anti-gay culture that considered homosexuality to be a depraved and taboo subject that thus should not be decriminalised. The anti-gay culture also simultaneously emphasised Confucianism (particularly the moral notions of family continuation and filial piety) and Christianity, which were used by the government to stonewall the development of the rights of sexual minorities (Chan, 2008).

In addition, while crimes generate harm and immorality, they may be functional to society from the functionalist perspective (Durkheim, 1938/1964; Liska and Warner, 1991). Crimes delineate the boundaries of acceptable behaviour and solidify society in support of those boundaries. Society will also be informed of the necessity to create new rules or legislation for sustaining social order if new forms of crime arise.

Cybercrime is a good example in this regard. The proliferation of novel criminal opportunities and methods and blurry cyber morality (Thomas, 2005) have been prompted by today's Internet age and information society. The latest trends of cyber or technology crimes that confront Hong Kong include unauthorised access to computer systems, online blackmail, botnets, e-banking fraud, online business fraud, social media deception, online social networking traps, email scams and identity theft (Hong Kong Police Force, 2015). Hong Kong enacted the first piece of legislation directed at computer-related crime, the *Computer Crimes Ordinance*, in 1993 (Lee, 1995). This ordinance prosecutes access to a computer with criminal or dishonest intent and has been subsumed under section 161 of the *Crimes Ordinance* (Cap. 200). At present, computer system and data offences (illegal interception, data interference and system interference), computer-related offences (forgery, fraud and unlawful accessing/altering/damaging of records kept by electronic means), and content-related offences (computer child pornography, using computer systems or networks to spread racism or xenophobia, and online gambling) are also handled by other ordinances (*Control of Obscene and Indecent Articles Ordinance*, Cap. 390; *Gambling Ordinance*, Cap. 148; *Prevention of Child Pornography Ordinance*, Cap. 579; *Theft Ordinance*, Cap. 210; *Telecommunications Ordinance*, Cap. 106) (Jackson, 2005; Wong and Wong, 2005). These laws, however, are neither a comprehensive response to the cybercrime problem nor are they intended to provide Hong Kong with a stand-alone, technology-specific legislative framework. Despite the Security Bureau of the Hong Kong government convening an Inter-departmental Working Group in 2000 (*Inter-departmental Working Group on Computer Related Crime Report*) to review the effects of the changes introduced by the 1993 *Computer Crimes Ordinance* and to consider future developments, Hong Kong's substantive cybercrime legislation remains largely a patchwork of traditional crimes amended to more readily capture their commission in cyberspace (Jackson, 2005; Wong and Wong, 2005). This does not mean that Hong Kong has not kept abreast of technological advances since 1993, but there has been relatively little in the way of further cybercrime legislation.

Legal perspective: crime as a breach of criminal law

Deviance is central to the concept of crime. Most crimes involve a deviation from the expected norms or moral codes of behaviour shared by members of a society. Yet not all deviant behaviour is criminal, unless the behaviour in question invites a legal response. From the legal perspective, crime is defined as a legal wrong (not wrongfulness in a moral sense) that is followed by criminal proceedings stipulated by criminal law rather than by civil law (known as a 'tort').[1] The guilt of a criminal offender must be proven by the prosecuting authority 'beyond a reasonable doubt' on the basis of two coincident liability elements: *actus reus* (guilty act) and *mens rea* (guilty mind). Chapter 3 of this edited book will discuss in great detail the determination of criminal liability under criminal law in Hong Kong.

Hong Kong's criminal law is built upon judge-made law (common law), law developed by the Legislative Council (ordinances), and the *Hong Kong Bill of Rights Ordinance* (Cap. 383) (Jackson, 2003, 2009; Ho, 2011). Common law, which originated from the law of England due to its colonial status before 1997, refers to the prohibition of acts based on the legal principles recorded in past reports of judges' accumulated decisions. It remains the essential body of law in Hong Kong despite the assumption of sovereignty by the People's Republic of China on 1 July 1997. As stated in Article 8 of the *Basic Law*: 'The laws previously in force in Hong Kong, that is, the common law, rules of equity, ordinances, subordinate legislation and customary law shall be maintained, except for any that contravene this Law, and subject to any amendment by the legislature of the Hong Kong Special Administrative Region.' There are many common law offences in Hong Kong.[2] In addition to the principle of common law, judges may retain the power to review the applicability of established offences to new circumstances and to recognise new offences.

Most of Hong Kong's criminal offences are set out in ordinances, which are statutory in nature. Given that the statutory provisions of ordinances are presented in general terms, the consideration and application of common law principles are sometimes necessary. That is, the statutes must be interpreted by judges in particular cases to decide the case. Major ordinances relating to criminal prosecution include, but are not limited to, the *Control of Obscene and Indecent Articles Ordinance* (Cap. 390), *Crimes Ordinance* (Cap. 200), *Dangerous Drugs Ordinance* (Cap. 134), *Drug Trafficking (Recovery of Proceeds) Ordinance* (Cap. 405), *Firearms and Ammunition Ordinance* (Cap. 238), *Gambling Ordinance* (Cap. 148), *Offences Against the Person Ordinance* (Cap. 212), *Organized and Serious Crimes Ordinance* (Cap. 455), *Prevention of Bribery Ordinance* (Cap. 201), *Prevention of Child Pornography Ordinance* (Cap. 579), *Public Order Ordinance* (Cap. 245), *Road Traffic Ordinance* (Cap. 374, stipulating offences in relation to driving), *Societies Ordinance* (Cap. 151, involving criminalisation of activities related to triads), *Summary Offences Ordinance* (Cap. 228), *Theft Ordinance* (Cap. 210), and *United Nations (Anti-Terrorism Measures) Ordinance* (Cap. 575). For further discussion of specific offences under major ordinances, please refer to the Bilingual Laws Information System (BLIS) of the Department of Justice. It is important to note that Hong Kong's criminal law has been increasingly subject to international human rights norms, especially as laid down in the *International Covenant on Civil and Political Rights*, and has been supported by Article 39 of the *Basic Law* (Chan, 1998; Jackson, 2009).

Political perspective: crime is politically shaped

The controversy of Article 23 on national security

Treason and secession are defined as crimes in Mainland China but not in Hong Kong. The event with the strongest potential to influence Hong Kong's criminal law has been the transfer of sovereignty over Hong Kong to the People's Republic of China in 1997. Worries have been expressed about the possible authoritarian use of criminal law to the detriment of Hong Kong's civil liberties in the name of crimes against the state or political crimes. Most significant in this respect was the contentious attempt of the Hong Kong government, in 2003, to implement legislation pursuant to the obligation imposed by Article 23 of the *Basic Law* as the basis of a national security law (Jones and Vagg, 2007; Jackson, 2009). Article 23 states that:

> The Hong Kong Special Administrative Region shall enact laws on its own to prohibit any act of treason, secession, sedition, subversion against the Central People's Government, or theft of state secrets, to prohibit foreign political organizations or bodies from conducting political activities in the Region, and to prohibit political organizations or bodies of the Region from establishing ties with foreign political organizations or bodies.

The government decided to proceed without following the normal legislative process at a time when the public was plagued by the painful process of economic restructuring right after the Severe Acute Respiratory Syndrome (SARS) epidemic from March to May 2003. A demonstration on 1 July 2003 was staged to oppose the anti-subversion law. Some 500,000 people from all walks of life took to the streets to express their grave concern over the enduring 'mainlandisation'[3] of civil liberties and their mistrust of Beijing's expanding influence over Hong Kong's legal system (Lo, 2012), which made this one of the largest popular demonstrations ever held. The march was followed by further demonstrations (on both 9 and 13 July 2003) after the government refused to back down and instead insisted on proceeding with the draft legislation. Mainland political leaders were conscious of the media images of anti-government protests in Hong Kong that could spill over into China (Jones and Vagg, 2007). The pressure from Beijing on the Hong Kong government administration to introduce the laws subsided, and the government formally announced, on 5 September 2003, withdrawal from legislating Article 23 (the so-called *National Security [Legislative Provisions] Bill*).

Although Article 23 remains shelved, social unrest has persisted, roused in part by the government's willingness to seek interpretations of the *Basic Law* from the Standing Committee of the National People's Congress (NPCSC). For example, 'Occupy Central', also known as the Umbrella Movement (Chan, 2015), erupted in September 2014 as a result of restrictions on the proposed electoral reform of Hong Kong's chief executive imposed by the NPCSC. Philosophically, the aforementioned fears about the misuse of criminal law pose a broader query regarding whether or not the criminal law reflects the interests of the members of society at large, or what criminologists call a 'consensus model' (Trevino, 2008). That is, does a consensus of value underlie our criminal law's definition of what behaviour is criminal, or is our criminal law a manifestation of a 'conflict model', whereby the state disproportionately serves the interests of privileged groups at the expense of the less privileged? From the conflict perspective, value dissension characterises the relationship between the powerful and the powerless. Criminalisation of behaviour is a process of power struggle and, hence, only behaviour contrary to the interests of the elite and of state power are criminalised (Chambliss, 1975; Castellano and McGarrell, 1991). Therefore, a thorough understanding of the content of criminal law cannot ignore the presence of political forces.

Cross-border crimes

The surge of cross-border crimes reveals that the assumption of sovereignty by China does not imply cross-application of the criminal law of Hong Kong and that of the mainland. Arrests for cross-border crimes (money laundering, trafficking of female prostitutes, theft rings, loan-sharking syndicates, narcotics trade, unlawful gambling, mobile phone smuggling, circulation of counterfeit Hong Kong banknotes, software piracy and fraudulent companies) in postcolonial Hong Kong have involved more mainland Chinese since the 1990s (Lo, 2009). If they were arrested in Hong Kong, they would be prosecuted under Hong Kong's criminal law rather than that of the mainland.

In addition, a large-scale kidnapping syndicate composed of both Hong Kong residents and mainlanders culminated in a series of cross-border kidnappings in Hong Kong in 2003 (Lo, 2009). The kidnappers smuggled guns and ammunition from the mainland to implement their plans in Hong Kong. This incident further demonstrated the complexity of cross-border crime because the execution took place in Hong Kong and the importation of firearms from the mainland and illegal trading of explosives were preparatory offences to the main and completed offence of kidnapping.

In coping with cross-border crimes, there is no rendition agreement between Hong Kong and China at a formal level, but informal working arrangements have been established. In asking for the rendition of criminals to Hong Kong, the secretary for security would make the request if these conditions are met: 1 the fugitive committed a crime in Hong Kong; 2 the fugitive is a Hong Kong resident; and 3 the fugitive is not currently on trial on the mainland (Wong, 2012).

Nevertheless, such rendition does not apply to mainlanders who commit crimes in Hong Kong but then escape to China. Furthermore, it can be argued that the preparatory offence can be merged with the completed offence to determine the jurisdictional purpose. In this regard, the NPC in China has never intended the preparatory offence to be as serious as the completed offence and has made clear that preparatory offences should be given a lighter or mitigated penalty or should be exempted from punishment (Wong, 2012). Accordingly, preparatory crimes need not be tried in the jurisdiction in which the initial conduct of the preparatory crime transpired, i.e. in China, but in that in which the ultimate consequence of the final crime was felt, i.e. in Hong Kong. The complexity of cross-border crime has tested the limits of the 'One Country, Two Systems' principle. It forces politicians, government officials and the public in both Hong Kong and China to come to terms with the legal issues pertinent to cross-border crime.

Legal bilingualism

A relatively less polemic illustration of the political impact of 1997 on Hong Kong's criminal law pertains to legal bilingualism. The common law that underlies the criminal justice system has been one of the most trusted legal institutions. Post-1997 Hong Kong is one of the very few places in the world in which the common law can be practised in a language (Chinese) other than English (Ng, 2009a). Lawyers and the judiciary are prone to use Cantonese as a factual language in the court proceeding, whereas English continues to be the orthodox language of the law. The present formula of 'Chinese fact, English law' is emblematic of the tension that emanates from the aspiration to move Hong Kong closer to China as an emerging world power and from the reluctance to give up the protection that English common law is able to offer in the still-grim shadow of the rule of man[4] and the fragility of the law in China (Ng, 2009b).

Socio-cultural perspective: public perceptions of crime

Seriousness of the crime

Although the criminal law has been one of the most trusted legal institutions, it is only one of the genus by which crime is defined. Understanding the concept of crime is incomplete without delving into the manner in which crimes are perceived by the public. Popular perceptions of the nature of criminal behaviour constitute a vital area of investigation in the field of criminology and criminal justice. Such an area of investigation departs from the argument by Black (1979) that the seriousness of a crime is more than an objective attribute and is subjectively perceived among the populace. He refuted the contention that the severity of a crime can be derived by reference to the maximum permissible penalty for the offences concerned. As Black argued:

> what is a crime is not merely a matter of fact; it is also an evaluation … the concept of crime does not describe the universe of incidents people experience in their everyday lives, but only the ones they consider worthy of police attention.
>
> (Black, 1979: 20)

Indeed, the manner in which people perceive crime is a leading aspect of normative culture in general and formal social control in particular (Kwan et al., 2002). Specifically, there are two important contributions of research on perceptions regarding the seriousness of crime. First, judgements of seriousness are the chief determinants of public beliefs concerning the intensity of crime in a society. Second, the severity of a crime as perceived by the public influences legal reactions, from the likelihood that it will be reported to the police to the likelihood of the sentence that will be meted out. Any great disparity between the subjectively perceived seriousness of the crime and its legal penalty raises concern about the appropriateness of legal punishment.

A vast international literature on the evaluation of the perceived seriousness of crime has been published since the landmark works of Sellin and Wolfgang (1964), and Rossi and his colleagues (1974). Stylianou (2003) offered a systematic review of studies on perceived crime seriousness conducted from the 1960s to the 2000s. With respect to methodology, the study participants were usually given questionnaires that encompassed a list of behaviours, varying from one to more than 200, and were asked to rate (estimation of magnitude assigning a numerical value of seriousness) or rank (category scaling from 'least serious' to 'most serious') them in terms of seriousness. Moreover, the measurement of popular perception ideally requires the use of probability survey samples from the general population. Although some studies used such samples, much of the extant literature was based on nonprobability samples of general or special populations, including college students, police, prosecutors, judges, correctional officers, inmates and the victimised. Stylianou (2003) also highlighted that the most substantive finding associated with perceived seriousness that was acknowledged by virtually all studies is the act's perceived harmfulness: violent behaviours (causing bodily harm) are perceived as the most serious, followed by property offences (causing property loss or destruction); white-collar violations that result in physical harm are rated as more serious than those that result in economic harm. Victimless crimes, which are generally judged by reference to moral standards, tend to be rated as the least serious.

Thus far there have been few studies of the perceived crime seriousness in Hong Kong, with the exception of two studies by Kwan and his colleagues (2000; Kwan et al., 2002). They selected 15 types of crime: rape, indecent assault, murder, serious assault, robbery, blackmail and intimidation, snatching, burglary, theft, deception, fraud and forgery, drug offences, criminal damage, possession of arms, unlawful society offences, and bribery and corruption. Their study revealed that murder, rape, drug offences, and robbery were considered to be the four most serious crimes, and that theft, snatching, criminal damage, and possession of arms were among those considered the least serious in Hong Kong. Equally noteworthy is the finding that drug offences were perceived as very serious, even more serious than robbery. This finding might be related to the historical colonisation by the British as a result of the Opium Wars. The harm done by illicit drugs such as opium and heroin have been emphasised by the public (Kwan et al., 2000).

Moreover, socio-economic differentials in the perception of the seriousness of a crime were detected in Hong Kong (Kwan et al., 2002). Women rated rape as more serious than men because women tend to be the victims of this crime. In their study, people with tertiary education viewed blackmail as more serious than people with primary education because they were economically better off and had a higher likelihood of being victimised. Older people regarded the possession of arms as more serious than their younger counterparts because older people in Hong Kong lived through social unrest and wars before 1970, which the younger generation has never experienced. Younger people considered bribery to be more serious than older people, possibly because before the founding of the Independent Commission Against Corruption (ICAC) in the 1970s, corruption was so pervasive that it might have been accepted by the populace as a normal practice to get things done. This may explain why there is less sensitivity to bribery among older people. Overall, these differentials imply that the evaluation of crime seriousness is mediated by the social structural context. Different subgroups of a society may have different judgements on the seriousness of crime.

Domestic violence

Culture may also shape the perceived severity of a crime. A specific example concerning the relevance of cultural orientation to public perception in Hong Kong is domestic violence. Domestic violence is a general term used to describe a series of abusive incidents, whether physical or not, that have a cumulative effect on the abused victim. Spouse abuse, elder abuse and child abuse are the three common types of domestic violence. However, there is no specific criminal offence of domestic violence, as such, in Hong Kong. The *Domestic and Cohabitation Relationships Violence Ordinance* (Cap. 189) does not criminalise perpetrators but provides protection from violence for people in familial or cohabitation relationships. If an act of physical or sexual violence arises in a domestic setting, the perpetrator may be prosecuted for an offence under the general criminal law, such as the *Crimes Ordinance* (Cap. 200) and the *Offences Against the Person Ordinance* (Cap. 212), which cover such offences as homicide, wounding, assault, forcible taking or detention of persons, rape, incest, criminal intimidation, unlawful abandonment or exposure of a child under two years of age, and the wilful assault, ill-treatment, neglect or abandonment of a child (Department of Justice, 2009). In determining whether to prosecute a case involving domestic violence, the prosecutor would take the views of the victim into account. Yet the prosecutor is not the legal representative of the victim, and the role of the prosecutor is to represent the state to prosecute and convict the perpetrator in the pursuit of justice for the public.

It has been observed that the perceptions and reporting of abusive behaviour in Hong Kong vary among spouse abuse, child abuse and elder abuse (Chan et al., 2008). Abuse of the elderly and children is more likely to be perceived as abuse and to be reported than that of spouse abuse. This perception appears to be in line with the public understanding that elderly people and children are often helpless and dependent. On the contrary, abuse of a spouse, usually a wife, is least likely to be perceived as abuse. Wives are not thought to be as vulnerable as the elderly and children because there is a Chinese concept of wives as legitimate victims of violence that has been constructed through representations of husband perpetrators as being sick or as being controlled by their impulses, and of women as naggers who trigger men's impulses or potential for violence (Tang et al., 2002). In this vein, women's behaviour is often regarded as the precipitating factor, and men are thus excused from full responsibility for their violent acts. Moreover, there is a traditional Chinese understanding that what happens between a couple is a private family matter (Chan et al., 2008) and should, therefore, be shielded from public scrutiny to avoid the loss of 'face' (*mien-tzu*). Some Chinese people, particularly men, also tend to favour a narrow definition of violence against women that emphasises physical harm and intentionality, rather than adopting a broader definition that includes not only physical acts but also sexual and verbal aggression. There is less emphasis on a broader definition because it defends women's interests, mitigates their submissive status, and may disrupt the patriarchal power distribution between men and women in the Chinese context (Tang et al., 2000). A narrow definition of violence thus renders Chinese people less sensitive to the severity of husband-to-wife abusive behaviour.

Conclusion

The concept of crime is not independent of social and political forces. Whether such forces are a product of consensus that meets the needs of a larger society, or whether they serve the interests of the powerful in conflict with others is a widely debated issue. It is clear, however, that crime can be relative. This is particularly evident in the case of Hong Kong, where the concept of crime as a function of harm, encroachment on morality, and legal wrongfulness is, to a certain extent, a matter of historical development, political process and public evaluation.

Review questions

1. When an act contravenes moral codes, would it be regarded as a crime?
2. How would the functionalist perspective interpret emerging forms of crime and subsequent development of criminal law in Hong Kong?
3. Why do we need to understand the public perceptions of crime?
4. How does Chinese culture shape the public perceptions of crime?
5. In what ways does the politics of Hong Kong affect the definition of crime?
6. How far does the definition of crime embody the interests of most people in society more or less evenly as suggested by the consensus perspective?

Notes

1 Criminal law is concerned with an individual who has transgressed Hong Kong society as a whole and aims to maintain the societal interests, whereas civil law

protects the rights of the individual and recognises duties between individuals, such as contractual relationships or a trust between two parties. The procedural rule, standard of proof that is followed and applied in determining liability and outcome of the proceedings mark the distinction between criminal and civil law in Hong Kong (Jackson, 2003; Ho, 2011). There may be overlap between crime and tort, however. If A attacks and injures B, A is liable for both a criminal conduct (assault) and a civil wrong. Despite the fact that offender A is convicted in criminal proceedings, victim B can still lodge a civil claim for injury and compensation against offender A. The civil liability results from the criminal conduct of the offender (Ho, 2011).

2 Typical common law offences in Hong Kong are murder, manslaughter, kidnapping, conspiracy to defraud, false imprisonment, conspiracy to pervert the course of justice, doing an act tending and intended to pervert the course of justice, and misconduct in a public office (Ho, 2011).

3 Mainlandisation is defined as 'the policy of making Hong Kong politically more dependent on Beijing, economically more reliant on the Mainland's support, socially more patriotic towards the motherland, and legally more reliant on the interpretation of the Basic Law by the PRC National People's Congress' (Lo, 2012: 632).

4 The rule of man in China implies the non-independence of criminal justice from the Chinese Communist Party (CCP). Given that the Constitution of the People's Republic of China adopted a system of the people's democratic dictatorship, all organs are titled 'People's', such as the People's Public Security, the People's Procuratorate, and the People's Court. As the CCP represents the people, all state organs including the judiciary are actually controlled by the CCP. Rule by the people is in fact 'rule by the CCP'. Criminal justice practices must toe the party line correspondingly in China (Lo, 2012).

References

Black, D. (1979) 'Common sense in the sociology of law', *American Sociological Review*, 44(1): 18–27.

Castellano, T.C. and McGarrell, E.F. (1991) 'The politics of law and order: Case study evidence for the conflict model of the criminal law formation process', *Journal of Research in Crime and Delinquency*, 28(3): 304–329.

Chambliss, W.J. (1975) *Criminal Law in Action* (2nd edn), New York: Wiley.

Chan, J.M.M. (1998) 'Hong Kong's Bills of Rights: Its reception of and contribution to international and comparative jurisprudence', *International and Comparative Law Quarterly*, 47(2): 306–366.

Chan, K.M. (2015) 'Occupying Hong Kong: How deliberation, referendum and civil disobedience played out in the Umbrella Movement', *International Journal on Human Rights*, 12(21): 1–7.

Chan, P.C.W. (2008) 'Stonewalling through schizophrenia: An anti-gay rights culture in Hong Kong?' *Sexuality and Culture*, 12(2): 71–87.

Chan, Y.C., Chun, P.K.R. and Chung, K.W. (2008) 'Public perception and reporting of different kinds of family abuse in Hong Kong', *Journal of Family Violence*, 23(4): 253–263.

Chiu, M.C. (2006) '(Han-)Chinese cultural appropriation of sexual legal politics: Post-colonial discourse on law controlling sex work in Hong Kong', *Asian Journal of Social Science*, 34(4): 547–572.

Department of Justice (2009) *The Policy for Prosecuting Cases Involving Domestic Violence*, Hong Kong: Department of Justice.

Durkheim, E. (1938/1964) *The Rules of Sociological Method* (Translated by S.A. Solovay and J.H. Mueller), New York: Free Press.

Heilbronn, G.N. (2002) *Criminal Procedure in Hong Kong*, Hong Kong: Longman.

Ho, W.K.V. (2011) *Criminal Law in Hong Kong*, The Netherlands: Kluwer Law International.

Hong Kong Police Force (2015) *Cyber Security and Technology Crime*, Hong Kong: Hong Kong Police Force, www.police.gov.hk/ppp_en/04_crime_matters/tcd/index.html (accessed 15 February 2016).

Howell, P. (2004) 'Race, space and the regulation of prostitution in colonial Hong Kong', *Urban History*, 31(2): 229–248.

Jackson, M. (2003) *Criminal Law in Hong Kong*, Hong Kong: Hong Kong University Press.

Jackson, M. (2005) 'Law enforcement in cyberspace: The Hong Kong approach', in R. Broadhurst and P. Grabosky (eds) *Cyber-crime: The Challenge in Asia* (pp. 243–267), Hong Kong: Hong Kong University Press.

Jackson, M. (2009) 'Criminal law', in M.S. Gaylord, D. Gittings and H. Traver (eds) *Introduction to Crime, Law and Justice in Hong Kong* (pp. 17–34), Hong Kong: Hong Kong University Press.

Jones, C. and Vagg, J. (2007) *Criminal Justice in Hong Kong*, London: Routledge-Cavendish.

Kwan, Y.K., Chiu, L.L., Ip, W.C. and Kwan, P. (2002) 'Perceived crime seriousness: Consensus and disparity', *Journal of Criminal Justice*, 30(6): 623–632.

Kwan, Y.L., Ip, W.C. and Kwan, P. (2000) 'A crime index with Thurstone's scaling of crime severity', *Journal of Criminal Justice*, 28(3): 237–244.

Law Reform Commission of Hong Kong (1983) *Report on Laws Governing Homosexual Conduct*, Hong Kong: Government Printer.

Lee, M.K.O. (1995) 'Legal control of computer crime in Hong Kong', *Information Management and Computer Security*, 3(2): 13–19.

Liska, A.E. and Warner, B.D. (1991) 'Functions of crime: A paradoxical process', *American Journal of Sociology*, 96(6): 1441–1463.

Lo, S.S.H. (2009) *Politics of Cross-border Crime in Greater China: Case Studies of Mainland China, Hong Kong, and Macao*, Armonk, NY: M.E. Sharpe.

Lo, T.W. (2012) 'Resistance to the mainlandization of criminal justice practices: A barrier to the development of restorative justice in Hong Kong', *International Journal of Offender Therapy and Comparative Criminology*, 56(4): 627–645.

Ng, K.H. (2009a) 'If I lie, I tell you, may heaven and earth destroy me. Language and legal consciousness in Hong Kong bilingual common law', *Law and Society Review*, 43(2): 369–403.

Ng, K.H. (2009b) *The Common Law in Two Voices: Language, Law and the Postcolonial Dilemma in Hong Kong*, Stanford, CA: Stanford University Press.

Rossi, P.H., Waite, E., Bose, C.E. and Berk, R.E. (1974) 'The seriousness of crimes: Normative structure and individual differences', *American Sociological Review*, 39(2): 224–237.

Sellin, T. and Wolfgang, M. (1964) *The Measurement of Delinquency*, New York: Wiley.

Stylianou, S. (2003) 'Measuring crime seriousness perceptions: What have we learned and what else do we want to know', *Journal of Criminal Justice*, 31(1): 37–56.

Tang, C.S.K., Wong, D. and Cheung, F.M.C. (2002) 'Social construction of women as legitimate victims of violence in Chinese societies', *Violence Against Women*, 8(8): 968–996.

Tang, C.S.K., Wong, D., Cheung, F.M.C. and Lee, A. (2000) 'Exploring how Chinese define violence against women: A focus group study in Hong Kong', *Women's Studies International Forum*, 23(2): 197–209.

Thomas, J. (2005) 'The moral ambiguity of social control in cyberspace: A retro-assessment of the golden age of hacking', *New Media and Society*, 7(5): 599–624.

Trevino, A.J. (2008) *The Sociology of Law: Classical and Contemporary Perspectives*, New Brunswick, NJ: Transaction Publishers.

Wong, D. (2010) 'Hybridization and the emergence of gay identities in Hong Kong and in China', *Visual Anthropology*, 24(1–2): 152–170.

Wong, K.C. (2012) *One Country, Two Systems: Cross-border Crime between Hong Kong and China*, New Brunswick, NJ: Transaction Publishers.

Wong, K.C. and Wong, G. (2005) 'Law and order in cyberspace: A case study of cyberspace governance in Hong Kong', *Journal of Computer and Information Law*, 23(2): 249–275.

Wong, W.C.W., Holroyd, E. and Bingham, A. (2011) 'Stigma and sex work from the perspective of female sex workers in Hong Kong', *Sociology of Health and Illness*, 33(1): 50–65.

Legislation cited

Computer Crimes Ordinance
Control of Obscene and Indecent Articles Ordinance (Cap. 390)
Crimes Ordinance (Cap. 200)
Dangerous Drugs Ordinance (Cap. 134)
Domestic and Cohabitation Relationships Violence Ordinance (Cap. 189)
Drug Trafficking (Recovery of Proceeds) Ordinance (Cap. 405)
Firearms and Ammunition Ordinance (Cap. 238)
Gambling Ordinance (Cap. 148)
Hong Kong Bill of Rights Ordinance (Cap. 383)
International Covenant on Civil and Political Rights
National Security [Legislative Provisions] Bill
Offences Against the Person Ordinance (Cap. 212)
Organized and Serious Crimes Ordinance (Cap. 455)
Prevention of Bribery Ordinance (Cap. 201)
Prevention of Child Pornography Ordinance (Cap. 579)
Public Order Ordinance (Cap. 245)
Road Traffic Ordinance (Cap. 374)
Societies Ordinance (Cap. 151)
Summary Offences Ordinance (Cap. 228)
Telecommunications Ordinance (Cap. 106)
Theft Ordinance (Cap. 210)
United Nations (Anti-Terrorism Measures) Ordinance (Cap. 575)
Venereal Disease and Contagious Disease Ordinances

Useful websites

Basic Law Drafting History Online, The University of Hong Kong sunzi1.lib.hku.hk/bldho/home.action

Bilingual Laws Information System (BLIS) (Hong Kong) www.legislation.gov.hk/eng/index.htm

Community Legal Information Centre, Law and Technology Centre, The University of Hong Kong www.clic.org.hk

Hong Kong Legal Information Institute, Faculty of Law and Department of Computer Science, The University of Hong Kong www.hklii.hk

Law Reform Commission, HKSAR www.hkreform.gov.hk

Proposals to Implement Article 23 of the *Basic Law* www.basiclaw23.gov.hk

Security Bureau, HKSAR www.sb.gov.hk

3

CRIMINAL LAW

Rebecca Ong

Introduction

Criminal law is a branch of law that deals with the punishment of an offender for wrongs committed against society. The 'wrong' or crime can be an act (for example stealing) or an omission to act (failure to drive carefully) which the courts consider punishable so as to deter others from committing the offence. In such circumstances, the courts will deal with the offender by sentencing him or her to a term of imprisonment or by imposing other forms of non-custodial sentence such as ordering the offender to pay a fine, serve a community service order or be placed on probation. It can thus be said that the purpose of criminal law is not only to protect societal interests but also to maintain and regulate societal conduct and behaviour.

Who therefore bears this responsibility of protecting the public? It is the government, which is why it is the government that generally initiates criminal proceedings (prosecutes) in the courts. For example, in *HKSAR v Wong*, it is the Hong Kong government against the person charged – Wong, who is also known as the defendant in the case. Before a defendant can be convicted, it is the prosecutor's duty to prove the defendant's guilt 'beyond reasonable doubt' (see *Kwan Ping Bong v R* (1979) HKLR 1). If reasonable doubt is created in respect of any elements of the offence with which the defendant is charged, the prosecution is said not to have made its case and the defendant will be acquitted. The standard of proof coupled with the presumption that a defendant is innocent unless proven guilty (presumption of innocence) imposes an onerous burden on the prosecutor.

Sources of criminal law

It can be said that the main sources of Hong Kong criminal law are law developed through the courts or judge-made law (common law), and law made by the Legislative Council (ordinances). Common law is still very much part of Hong Kong law despite the return of sovereignty to China (see Articles 8 and 18 of the *Basic Law*). Its importance cannot be overlooked, as older crimes such as murder and assault established by common law continue to be recognised. The same holds true for common law defences like insanity and duress. Notwithstanding this, offences established by ordinances are more common. These statutory offences are the most common form. Examples of statutory offences include noisy or disorderly behaviour in a public place, punishable by 12 months' imprisonment and a fine of HK$5,000 – section 17B(2) of the *Public Order Ordinance* (Cap. 245); being a member of a triad society contrary to section 20(2) of the *Societies Ordinance* (Cap. 151), which is punishable on first conviction by three years' imprisonment and a fine of HK$100,000; possessing or using an identity card belonging to another person, punishable on indictment by ten years' imprisonment (summarily for two years) and a fine of HK$100,000 (HK$50,000) – section 7A(1A) of the *Registration of Persons Ordinance* (Cap. 177); and obtaining property by deception, punishable by imprisonment for 20 years – section 17(1) of the *Theft Ordinance* (Cap. 210).

Categorisation of offences

In Hong Kong, criminal offences are divided into categories according to their seriousness. Summary offences are the least serious offences, which are dealt with by the Magistrates' Court summarily. Such offences include littering in public or careless driving (section 38 of the *Road Traffic Ordinance*, Cap. 374). Very serious offences such as murder, manslaughter, rape and drug trafficking are dealt with on indictment. These offences are heard before a judge and a jury of seven (sometimes five or nine) lay people in the Court of First Instance of the High Court. In a trial by jury (trial by your peers), the judge will urge the jury to reach a unanimous verdict on whether the defendant is guilty or not guilty. The jury may, in failing to reach unanimity, arrive at a majority verdict of no fewer than five in a seven-member jury. Between summary and indictable offences is a hybrid offence categorised as offences triable either way. These offences can be dealt with either in the Magistrates' Court, in the District Court or in the Court of First Instance, depending on the seriousness of the offence.

The overall responsibility for the conduct of prosecuting offences in Hong Kong lies with the secretary for justice. However, it is usually the police and the court prosecutors who prosecute. In determining whether or not to prosecute in serious or complicated cases, the secretary for justice considers two issues in making his or her decision. First, whether the evidence is sufficient to justify the institution of proceedings, and second, if it is in the interests of the public for the prosecution to take place.

Criminal liability and elements of crime

Criminal liability is based on the premise that an individual has committed an act prohibited by law. It is thus necessary to determine the prohibited act. This is done by looking at the elements of the offence in common law or under the relevant ordinance. The individual is only criminally liable if the prosecution can prove the prohibited act (*actus reus*) coupled with the guilty state of mind (*mens rea*). Both these elements must co-exist; one without the other will not do (except for offences of strict liability). This can be seen from the principle '*actus non facit reum nisi mens sit rea*': 'an act alone does not make a person criminally liable, the mind must also be legally blameworthy.'

Actus reus

The *actus reus* is the sum of all the elements of the offence other than the *mens rea*. As such, the whole *actus reus* must be proven to establish criminal liability. However, *actus reus* can take a number of forms in that it does not always have to be a positive act. Liability can also be imposed for the failure to act. This can arise where there is a legal duty to act as a result of a parent–child relationship or where the obligation to care for another is undertaken (see *R v Stone and Dobinson* [1977] QB 354). Section 27 of the *Offences Against the Person Ordinance* (Cap. 212), for example, creates an offence of wilful neglect where as a result of a failure to administer proper care, a child is injured. *Actus reus* is also established if the defendant created a dangerous situation and failed to act. For example, in *R v Miller* [1983 2 AC 161], the defendant was convicted of arson for failing to take steps to extinguish a fire that was accidentally started by him.

It is possible for *actus reus* to include the act itself, which does not require proof of result (for example, drink driving), or the circumstances in which the act occurred (for example, having intercourse with a person under 16 years of age). *Actus reus* may also just be the result of the act (for example, criminal damage).

Causation

The defendant is not liable unless the prosecution can prove there exists a causal link between the defendant's act and the prohibited consequences – that is, the defendant can only be liable for the prohibited consequences of his or her act if his or her conduct was both a factual cause (see 'but for' test in *R v White* below) and a legal cause of that act. If the cause that has happened would have occurred anyway irrespective of the defendant's act, then the defendant's act has not brought about that consequence. It must be shown that the defendant's act is the operative, substantial and effective cause of the consequence (legal causation). For the defendant's act to be 'operative and substantial' in law, it must be a reasonably foreseeable course of the defendant's act. As such, there is no *actus reus* if the defendant's course of conduct fails to bring about the prohibited consequences – for example, there is no assault if the individual at whom the defendant is directing his fist, ducks; there may, however be a charge of attempted assault. In *R v White*, as the mother died of natural causes rather than as a result of the defendant's poisoning, the 'but for' test was not satisfied. The mother would have died anyway irrespective of the defendant's act of poisoning (see *R v White* [1910] 1 KB 124). However, if a causal link exists, then it matters not that the defendant's act is one of a number of causes of the prohibited consequence. It is important to establish causation before questions of intent are answered, as in *HKSAR v Chan Man Lok & Others* [2003] HKCA 159 (the Hello Kitty case).

Novus actus interveniens

As mentioned earlier, the defendant does not commit an offence if a causal link between his or her prohibited act and the prohibited consequences is not established. In other words, there must be a casual relationship between conduct and results. Accordingly, it is possible for an (independent) intervening act or *novus actus interveniens*. The causal link, however, is not broken if the third party's intervening act was foreseeable by the defendant or if the medical treatment received by the victim was inadequate or negligent (see *R v Smith* [1959] 2 All ER 193).

Mens rea

As *mens rea* is the mental element of an offence, the commission of a prohibited act will not render the person guilty of an offence unless it is accompanied with a guilty mind – '*actus non facit reum nisi mens sit rea*'. As such, once the defendant is found responsible for committing the physical elements (*actus reus*) of the offence, he or she must also be shown to have the necessary mental state for its commission. The mental state (*mens rea*) of an offence can include intention, recklessness and negligence. Thus it must be proven that the defendant intended the consequences of the prohibited act or that he or she was reckless as to its consequences or that he or she did not care what the consequences were.

In *Chan Wing Sui v R* [1985] A.C. 168 (PC) it was said:

> The test of mens rea is subjective. It is what the individual accused contemplated that matters. As in other cases where the state of an accused's mind has to be ascertained, this may be inferred from his conduct and any other evidence throwing light on what he foresaw at the material time including [any explanation he gives in evidence or to the police].

Mens rea varies with each offence. For example, for the offence of theft, the prosecution needs to prove the defendant intended to dishonestly deprive the rightful owner permanently of his goods, whilst in manslaughter, it is acting recklessly thereby causing death, as in *Kong Cheuk-kwan v R* [1986] HKLR 648. In *R v Adomako* [1995] 1 AC 171, the *mens rea* was a grossly negligent act (omission) resulting in death. In this case, an anaesthetist was held to have breached his duty when he failed to notice and reconnect a tube that had become disconnected during an operation.

Intention

In its narrow sense, intent can be said simply to mean that the defendant intended the consequences of his or her prohibited act, or a result was intended if it was the purpose of the doer. However, through a combination of various common law decisions, intention has taken on a much wider meaning. In order to determine intention, foresight of consequences and the extent to which the consequences might have been foreseen is important. Questions such as whether death was a natural and probable consequence of the prohibited act and the degree of probability will be relevant in *R v Moloney* [1985] AC 905, and *R v Hancock & Shankland* [1986] 2 WLR 357. The defendant cannot be said to have the culpable mental state if he or she had merely foreseen the consequences of the prohibited act although foresight of the consequences is admissible as evidence of the defendant's intention. In such cases, it is necessary to prove that the defendant is virtually certain of the probability of that consequence occurring as a result of his act (see *R v Nedrick* [1986] 1 WLR 1025).

In Hong Kong, it has been accepted that if juries are to be directed on the defendant's foresight, the 'virtual certainty' direction would be a correct direction to be given. This was so in *R v Wong Tak Shing* [1989] 2 HKC 94, where the court held that juries should be directed that they may infer that a result is intended, though not desired, when the result is a virtually certain consequence of the act and the doer knows that it is a virtually certain consequence. It should be noted, however, that whether or not a defendant intends or foresees a consequence is determined by the court or the jury by reference to all the evidence, drawing such inferences from the evidence as appear proper in the circumstances (see section 65A of the *Criminal Procedure Ordinance*, Cap. 221).

Recklessness

As far as recklessness as a mental state is concerned, a person is reckless if he or she consciously and wilfully takes on an unjustifiable risk. This is subjective recklessness – where the defendant knew there was a risk or has foreseen the risk and proceeded to take it (see *R v Cunningham* [1957] 2 QB 396). This narrower test as opposed to *Caldwell recklessness* was adopted by the House of Lords in *R v R and G* [2003] UKHL 50. In *R. v Caldwell* ([1982]AC 341), a person can be liable if he takes on an obvious risk that no reasonable person would take (objective recklessness) and he did so either without giving any thought to the risk or he had consciously and wilfully ignored the consequences of the risk.

In Hong Kong, the opportunity to consider the application of the decision in *R v R and G* arose in *Sin Kam Wah & Anor v HKSAR* [2005] 8 HKCFAR 192.

In *Sin*, the Court of First Instance agreed that Caldwell recklessness 'exposed the defendant who caused a risk of injury to another of a serious crime although he did not genuinely perceive the risk'. This could lead to an unjust conviction of the defendant on the strength of not what the defendant had himself apprehended but on what another person would have apprehended. The court continued by holding that juries in Hong Kong should be directed in terms of *R v R and G* subjective interpretation of recklessness such that 'it had to be shown that the defendant's state of mind was culpable in that he acted recklessly in respect of a circumstance if he was aware of a risk that it would occur, and it was circumstances known to him, unreasonable to take the risk'. *Sin* was an important decision in that in addition to clarifying Hong Kong's position with respect to recklessness, the court went further to hold that the defendant must genuinely appreciate or foresee the risks involved in his or her actions before he or she can be held liable. Failure to appreciate or foresee the risks of his or her actions can be due to age or personal characteristics. In *Sin* the court overruled *R v Chau Ming Cheong* [1983] 1 HKC 68 and *R v Dung Shue Wah* [1083] HKC 30. The former cases were decisions based on Caldwell recklessness.

Negligence

Negligence is the failure of the accused to foresee a consequence that a reasonable man or woman would have foreseen and avoided. Although the Privy Council in *Kong Cheuk-kwan v R* [1986] HKLR 648 equated gross negligence and recklessness, negligence clearly still has a part to play in certain offences under the *Road Traffic Ordinance*, e.g. careless driving. Section 38(1) of the *Road Traffic Ordinance* provides 'A person who drives a motor vehicle on a road carelessly commits an offence and is liable to a fine at level 2 and to imprisonment for 6 months'. Section 38(2): '(1) A person who drives a motor vehicle on a road carelessly commits an offence and is liable to a fine at level 2 and to imprisonment for 6 months. (Amended 33 of 2000 s. 3) (2) A person drives carelessly within the meaning of this section if on a road he drives a vehicle without due care and attention or without reasonable consideration for other persons using the road'.

Knowledge

The defendant can also be required to prove he or she had knowledge of the circumstances. This can arise if the establishment of the offence refers to the existence of specified circumstances. For example, section 118(3) of the *Crimes Ordinance* provides: 'a man commits rape if (a) he has unlawful sexual intercourse with a woman who at the time of the intercourse does not consent to it; and (b) at that time he *knows* that she does not consent to the intercourse or he is reckless as to whether she consents to it.'

In the offence of rape, knowledge can be actual knowledge that the woman does not consent to intercourse or that the defendant is reckless or indifferent as to whether she consents or not. In determining recklessness, the courts will adopt the subjective test laid down in *Sin Kam Wah & Anor*.

Strict liability

Although generally, the prosecution must prove *mens rea* in respect of any one of the elements of *actus reus*, there are offences that do not require such proof. Such offences are called strict liability offences. Strict liability offences do exist in common law but the majority of the offences are created by statute. It is thus the duty of the court to ascertain the legislative intention of the provision to determine if *mens rea* is a requirement. In so doing, the court first presumes that *mens rea* is required before a person can be convicted of any offence unless it is rebutted by necessary implication in the statute. This is particularly the case where the offence is truly criminal in nature.

The only situation in which the presumption can be rebutted is where the statute is concerned with issues of social concern such as public safety. Even in such circumstances, the presumption of *mens rea* still applies unless the imposition of strict liability is required to effectively achieve the purpose of the statute, for example to prevent the prohibited act by promoting and ensuring greater vigilance. It is important to note that in *Gammon (Hong Kong) v Attorney General of Hong Kong* [1985] 2 HKC 661, the case is of social concern as it was dealing with construction site safety and maintenance. Other social concerns would include food safety and hygiene, public health and environment, or, as in the case of *A-G v Demand Enterprise Ltd* [1987] HKLR 195, employment of underage children.

Factors affecting liability

A person can only be held liable if he or she voluntarily carries out the elements of the offence with the necessary *mens rea*. There are a number of factors, however, that can reduce or negate the person's criminal responsibility for the offence.

Age

The criminal responsibility of a person may be affected by his or her age. Section 3 of the *Juvenile Offenders Ordinance* (Cap. 226) provides that it shall be conclusively presumed that no child under the age of ten years can be guilty of an offence. This means the child is '*doli incapax*' – incapable of committing any offence although he or she might have carried out the elements of the offence. There is, however, a rebuttable presumption if the child is over ten years old but under 14. In such circumstances, it is necessary for the prosecution to prove beyond reasonable doubt that when committing the criminal act, the child knew that the act was 'seriously wrong' – that he or she had a 'mischievous discretion'. In *A v DPP* [1992] Crim LR 34, it was held that the child must know that what he or she did was not just wrong but seriously wrong. Children (under the age of 14) and young persons (between the age of 14 and 16) are dealt with in the Juvenile Court, and if found guilty of an offence will only be committed to prison if there are no other suitable methods of dealing with them.

Insanity

A factor that the court has to consider with respect to criminal responsibility is a person's mental capacity. A defendant is not capable of forming the requisite *mens rea* for an offence if he or she is found to be insane. In determining if the defendant is insane, the courts in Hong Kong apply the M'Naghten test, which states:

> to establish a defence on the ground of insanity, it must be clearly proved that at the time of committing the act, the party accused was labouring under such a defect of reason, from the disease of mind as not to know the nature of the act he was doing or if he did know it, that he did not know what he was doing was wrong.
>
> (*M'Naghten Case* [1843] 10 CL & F 200)

As such, it must be proven that the defendant was suffering from such disease of mind as to impair his or her reasoning, memory and powers of understanding. In considering disease of mind, it is immaterial if the condition is curable, incurable, transitory or permanent (see *R v Kemp* [1957] 1 QB 399). Disease of the mind has been held to include sleepwalking (*R v Burgess* [1991] 2 QB 92), epilepsy (*Bratty v Attorney General for Northern Ireland* [1963] AC 386), hyperglycaemia (*R v Hennessy* [1989] 1 WLR 287), and arteriosclerosis resulting in blackouts (*R v Kemp* [1957] 1 QB 399). The defence of insanity can only be established if the defect of reason has resulted in the defendant not knowing the physical nature of the act, or if he or she did know, he or she did not know that it was wrong. The defence cannot be said to be established if the defendant knew what he or she was doing and knew the act he or she was committing was wrong, but cannot stop him- or herself from so acting – for example, uncontrollable behaviour due to battered baby syndrome, as in *Pang Bing Yee v R* [1984] HKLR 298.

The existence of insanity may have the effect of rendering the defendant unfit to stand trial. For a trial against the defendant to proceed, it is vital to prove not only that the defendant understands the charges against him or her, but is able to raise a defence to those charges, as in *R v Podola* [1960] 1 QB 325. Such is the importance of the issue of insanity that it must be determined by the jury as soon as it arises according to section 75(3) of the *Criminal Procedure Ordinance*.

The defence of insanity is normally raised by the defendant, although it may be raised by the judge or the prosecution. As the court proceeds on the basis that 'everyone is presumed sane' (presumption of sanity), the burden will be on the defendant to prove insanity on the balance of probabilities. If the M'Naghten test is satisfied, the jury must return a verdict of not guilty by reason of insanity (see section 74 of the *Criminal Procedure Ordinance*). In such circumstances, the court must make an order committing the defendant to a mental hospital or the Correctional Services Department Psychiatric Centre (see sections 76(1) & (2) of the *Criminal Procedure Ordinance*).

Automatism

Akin to insanity is involuntary conduct or automatism. Automatism has been described as:

> an act which is done by the muscles without any control of the mind, such as spasm, a reflex action or a convulsion; or an act done by a person who is not conscious of what he is doing such as an act done whilst suffering from concussion or whilst sleepwalking ...
>
> (*Bratty v A-G for Northern Ireland* [1963] AC 386)

Thus for automatism to succeed, the defence must prove that the commission of the act by the defendant was the result of an unconscious and a total lack of control over his or her actions; that he or she was acting in a 'trance-like' state, unaware and unable to control his or her actions. A mere declaration that he or she cannot remember what happened (amnesia) or that his or her mind just went blank or that his or her actions were the result of an 'irresistible impulse' is not sufficient. The Court of First Instance in *R v Chan Tak Kwong* [1997] HKLY 225, took the view that what was required to raise a defence of automatism was a 'total destruction of voluntary control of the defendant'. Reduced or partial control is insufficient to find for the defence (as in *A-G Reference* (No. 2 of 1992) (1994) QB). The issue of post-traumatic automatism, hysterical disassociation and malingering was raised and discussed in *HKSAR v Luk Chiu-Ki* [2005] HKEC 390 CFI.

Automatism may be caused by internal or external factors. If the automatism is caused by a disease of mind within the M'Naghten rules (internal factor), it is called insane automatism and will be treated in the same way as insanity. Consequently, the considerations are the same as for insanity, as in both *R v Kemp* [1957] 1 QB 399, and *R v Burgess* [1991] 2 QB 92. Further, as in the defence of insanity, the defendant who raises insane automatism bears the burden of laying the proper evidential foundation for the defence. It is only when this has been done that the court will leave the defence to be considered by the jury (as in *R v Mohammed Hussain* [1993] 1 HKCLR).

Non-insane automatism, on the other hand, includes unconscious acts due to external causes such as a blow to the head resulting in concussion, or low blood sugar, as in *R v Budd* [1962] Crim LR 49, and *R v Quick & Paddison* [1973] QB 910. Automatism may also be caused by the defendant having taken drugs or alcohol. However, such automatism is regarded as 'self-induced' and is a restricted defence in that it does not negate liability for a basic intent offence, as in *R v Bailey* [1983] 1 WLR 760.

Intoxication

There are circumstances when the consumption of alcohol or drugs has impaired the mental faculties of the defendant so as to negate criminal liability (see *R v Yeung Ka Wah* [1992] HKLY 299, where the court held that the defendant bears a persuasive burden to show that he was so affected by the drug that he did not form the intent to rob). Intoxication can be self-induced (voluntary) where the defendant knowingly consumes alcohol, drugs or other intoxicating substances. Voluntary intoxication is only admissible where the offence is a specific intent offence (*DPP v Majewski* [1977] AC 443, reaffirming *R v Beard* [1920] AC 479), and where the offence requires proof of intention (*MPC v Caldwell* [1982] AC 341). Accordingly, it is not a defence for an offence requiring basic intent or in circumstances where recklessness as *mens rea* of the offence suffices.

The admissibility of intoxication as a defence thus requires a determination of whether the offence is a specific intent or a basic intent offence.

Specific intent offences

A specific intent offence requires the prosecution to prove that 'the purpose for the commission of the offence extends to the intent expressed or implied in the definition of the crime' (see Lord Simon in *DDP v Majewski* at p. 479). By comparison, 'the mens rea in crimes of basic intent does not go beyond the act and its consequence ... as defined in the actus reus' (see Lord Simon in *DPP v Morgan* [1976] AC 182).

Basic intent offences

In *HKSAR v Chan Ping Kwan* [2005] 2 HKLRD 5, the defendant was charged with making a call of menacing character – an offence contrary to section 20(a) of the *Summary Offence Ordinance* (Cap. 228). The court held that the offence was completed once it was proven that it was the defendant who had sent the message of menacing character. The *mens rea* here was that the defendant was aware of the message's menacing character – the intent required for the offence was a basic intent.

Other examples of crimes of basic intent are common assault, assault occasioning actual bodily harm, indecent assault, manslaughter, assault on a police officer in the execution of his or her duty, taking a conveyance without the owner's authority, arson or criminal damage, and rape. As for specific intent crimes, these include theft, burglary, wounding with intent to cause grievous bodily harm, handling stolen goods, and murder.

Intoxication may be involuntary in that it arose as a result of consuming a prescription drug, or where the defendant was unaware that the drink or food he or she had consumed was laced with an intoxicating substance. Involuntary intoxication might only be used if it negates the *mens rea*. If it merely disinhibits the defendant, it is not a defence, as in *R v Kingston* [1995] 2 AC 355. As such, despite the defendant asserting and proving that he or she was involuntarily intoxicated, the prosecution must still prove beyond reasonable doubt that the defendant had the necessary *mens rea* for the offence despite the involuntary intoxication.

Duress and necessity

A person who commits an offence under an imminent threat of death or serious violence against him-/herself or another is not criminally liable. The threat or violence must be of death, personal injury or of other dangers of similar nature (see *R v Valderrama-Vega* [1985] Crim LR 220). A connection must exist between the threat and the defendant's decision to act in the manner he or she did. In *DPP v Rogers* [1998] Crim LR 202, the defendant drove a car with excess alcohol in his bloodstream because he believed his life was in danger but there had been no threat of violence to him. It was held on appeal from the Magistrates' Courts that the defence of duress was not available where there had been no threat to the defendant.

In circumstances where there is in fact no threat or violence, duress is available if the defendant has good cause to fear and honestly believes that the threat or violence would be carried out if the defendant did not commit the offence, as in *R v Howe* [1987] AC 417, approving *R v Graham* [1982] 1 WLR 294. Accordingly, the defence is not available if steps can be taken to remove the threat or if the threat is as a result of the defendant knowing and voluntarily associating with organisations likely to use violence such as triad societies and terrorist organisations. The defence is also not available for offences such as murder, attempted murder and treason.

Necessity and duress of circumstances

Necessity is a defence where the defendant is asserting that he or she was left with little choice but to do as he or she did in view of the threatened harm. The defence can only arise if pressure is exerted on the defendant's will from wrongful threats or violence threatening the defendant, his or her family, or other persons. To assert the defence, the defendant must also be said to be acting reasonably and proportionately in order to avoid a threat of death or serious injury. Once the defence is raised, it is to be left to the jury to decide: 1 whether the defendant was impelled to act as he or she did because of what he or she reasonably believed to be the situation and had good cause to fear that otherwise death or serious physical injury would result; and 2 if so, if a sober person of reasonable firmness would have responded to that situation by acting as the defendant did. If the answer to both questions is 'yes', the defendant will be acquitted (see Simon Brown J in *R v Martin* [1989] 1 All ER 652).

In *A-G v Chan Yuen Long* [1989] 1 HKC 470, the court held that necessity can be relied upon only if: 1 the conduct was to avoid consequences that, if they had followed, would have inflicted upon the defendant or upon others whom he or she was bound to protect, inevitable or irreparable evil; 2 no more was done than was reasonably necessary for the purposes; and 3 the evil inflicted was not disproportionate to the evil avoided. Simon Brown J's summary of the factors in *R v Martin* constituting duress of circumstances was applied successfully more recently in *HKSAR v Ip Chung San* [2005] HKEC 1338, where the defendants were charged with dangerous driving, failing to stop after a motor collision, and criminal damage.

Offences against the person

Homicide is the killing of another life in being and can include murder, manslaughter, infanticide and child destruction. A person commits murder if he or she unlawfully kills another with the intent to kill or to cause grievous bodily harm. However, not all acts of killing are unlawful. For example, it is not murder if the unlawful act is aimed at an unborn child or a dead person. The act of killing may also be justified in certain circumstances such as where it was carried out in accordance with the law – for instance, the execution of a prisoner – or in self-defence. Further, the defendant may not be guilty of murder if the act was the result of provocation or if the defendant was suffering from diminished responsibility.

Murder is a very serious offence, punishable by life imprisonment, according to section 2 of the *Offences Against the Person Ordinance*. With the severity of the punishment imposed, it is crucial for the prosecution to prove that the act of killing was accompanied by either the intention to kill or to cause grievous bodily harm (see *R v Moloney* [1985] AC 905, *R v Nedrick* [1986] 1 WLR 1025, and *Lau Cheong and Anor v HKSAR* [2002] 2 HKLRD 612). Proof of forethought or premeditation is not required; rather, what is necessary is that the relevant intention exists at the time of killing and it was the defendant's unlawful act or omission that was the cause of the victim's death, as in *R v Lo Yung-kan* [1985] 1 HKC 302, and *R v Yeung Lung-fai* [1991] 2 HKC 102. In this regard, one should note section 65A of the *Criminal Procedure Ordinance*, which provides:

> A court or jury, in determining whether a person has committed an offence:
>
> a shall not be bound in law to infer that he intended or foresaw a result of his acts or omissions by reason only of its being a natural and probable consequence of those acts or omissions but

b shall decide whether he did intend or foresee that result by reference to all the evidence drawing such inferences from the evidence as appear in the circumstances.

Voluntary manslaughter

Voluntary manslaughter is where the defendant commits murder but circumstances exist where the conviction for murder is reduced to manslaughter on grounds of provocation or diminished responsibility. This means that the defendant is not subject to a mandatory sentence of life imprisonment.

Provocation

Provocation is a statutory defence available only where a defendant is accused of murder. In *R v Duffy* [1949] 1 QB 63, Devlin J. said:

> Provocation is some act or series of acts, done by the dead man to the accused, which would cause in any reasonable person, and actually causes in the accused, a sudden and temporary loss of self-control, rendering the accused so subject to passion as to make him or her for the moment not master of his mind.

Section 4 of the *Homicide Ordinance* (Cap. 339) provides:

> Where on a charge of murder there is evidence on which the jury can find that the person charged was provoked (whether by things done or by things said or by both together) to lose his self control, the question whether the provocation was enough to make a reasonable man do as he did will be left to be determined by the jury; and in determining that question the jury shall take into account everything both done and said according to the effect which in their opinion, it would have on the reasonable man.

The question to be considered by the jury thus is: 1 whether the defendant was provoked to lose his or her self-control (a subjective test); and 2 whether the provocation was so serious as to make a reasonable man or woman act as he or she did (an objective test). Accordingly, there must be a direct causal connection between the provoking conduct of the victim and the defendant losing his or her self-control. The time lapse between the two must not be too long, as in *R v Vu Van Thang* [1991] 2 HKC 90. The court (jury), in considering whether a reasonable man or woman would have been provoked to act as the defendant did, must take into account a person having the power of self-control expected of an ordinary person of the sex, age and characteristics of the defendant that they think would affect the gravity of the provocation to him or her (see *R v Camplin* [1978] AC 705 (HL)). Characteristics like 'race', 'sexual inclination' and 'mental capacity', whether normal or abnormal, could be taken into account by the jury when they were trying to determine whether the provocation was enough to make a reasonable man or woman do as the defendant had done. In fact, in *Luc Thiet Thuan v R* [1996] 2 All ER 1003 (PC), the Privy Council opined that it is necessary for the provocation to have been directed at the relevant characteristics of the defendant, where he was the subject of taunts by the deceased (see also *HKSAR v Mok Tsan Ping v Ors* [2001] 2 HKLRD 325).

The Court of Appeal in Hong Kong confirmed the authority of *Luc* in *Mok Tsan Ping*. Therefore when considering provocation in Hong Kong, the courts are guided to *Luc* for characteristics. It should be noted that personality defects and/or mental infirmity that reduce a person's self-control below that expected of a reasonable person are irrelevant. However, individual peculiarities that bear on the gravity of the provocation should be taken into account, as in *HKSAR v Pang Kam-Chuen* [2003] HKCA, and *HKSAR v Chung Kei Tung* [2004] HKCA 297. Once the defence is raised, the prosecution bears the burden of proving that the defendant did not lose his or her self-control (see *R v Tran Dihn Thannh & Anor* [1994] 2 HKC 260).

Diminished responsibility

A defendant who kills another person whilst suffering from such an abnormality of mind so as to substantially impair his or her mental responsibility for his or her acts commits manslaughter according to section 3(1) of the *Homicide Ordinance* (Cap. 339). Like provocation (above), diminished responsibility is a special defence to a charge of murder. The abnormality of mind must be the result of retarded development of the mind, inherent causes, or be induced by disease or injury. Consequently, neither self-induced intoxication through drink or drugs, nor extreme emotion such as anger or jealousy can amount to abnormality of the mind, as in *HKSAR v Leung Wai Chung* [1999] 2 HKC 471. Thus the defendant must prove more likely than not that his or her mental responsibility at the time of the killing was substantially impaired – the impairment being more than merely trivial (see *HKSAR v Tsui Chu Tin, John* [2005] 1 HKC 518). Whether the impairment was sufficiently substantial is a question for the jury. It should be noted that although it is accepted that the cause of the disease of the mind may be self-inflicted (the effects, for example, of long-term drinking or drug taking), a purely transient state brought on by recent consumption of drugs or alcohol is to be disregarded for the purpose of the defence of diminished responsibility, as in *HKSAR v Liu Chun Yip* [2006] HKEC 1616.

Involuntary manslaughter

Involuntary manslaughter is unlawful killing without the intention to kill or to cause grievous bodily harm. It can be committed either by an unlawful and dangerous act or by gross negligence.

In the case of the former, what is required is the intention to carry out the act coupled with any fault required to make the act unlawful. It is irrelevant that the defendant was not aware of the unlawful nature of the act or that it was dangerous or that he or she had failed to foresee its consequences, as in *R v Lamb* [1967] 2 QB 981. The act, however, must be a crime, thus making it unlawful. The test to be applied must be that which was previously stated in *R v Church* [1966] 1 QB 59, that '[t]he unlawful act must be such as all sober and reasonable people would recognize must subject the other person to some risk of harm albeit not serious harm' (see also *DPP v Newbury* [1977] AC 500).

Manslaughter by gross negligence, on the other hand, requires the consideration of the ordinary principles of negligence in the sense whether: 1 there is a duty of care; 2 the defendant has breached his or her duty of care; and 3 such breach resulted in the death of the victim. In such circumstances, the jury must consider whether the defendant's breach was so grossly negligent that it amounted to a criminal act or omission. The jury must (in the words of Lord Mackay LC) be satisfied there is a 'reckless disregard of danger to the health and welfare of the infirm person. Mere indifference is not enough. The defendant must be proved to have been indifferent to an obvious injury to health or actually to have foreseen the risk but to have determined nevertheless to run it' (see *R v Adomako* [1995] AC 171).

Thus, what is required is: 1 the creation of an obvious and serious risk of causing injury to others by a wrongful act of the defendant; and 2 the defendant proceeded with his or her wrongful act either a) without giving consideration to the risk of injury, or (b) having recognised the risk, and taken it, as in *R v Kong Cheuk-kwan* [1986] HKLR 648, and *R v Chang Wai Kwan* [1994] 1 HKC 301. The approach adopted justifiably reflects the sentiments of society in that conduct exposing others to an obvious and serious degree of risk to injury should be penalised severely.

Assault

It is common for the word 'assault' to cover both the threat of violence (assault) and the actual unlawful use of force (battery). An important element of assault is that there must be a threat of violence calculated to cause immediate apprehension or fear in the victim. Therefore, any act by which a person intentionally, or recklessly, causes another to apprehend *immediate* and unlawful personal violence is an assault (see *R v Burstow* [1998] AC 147 HL, and *R v Venna* [1976] QB 421 at 429). As such, a threat to use violence at some time in the future is not an assault. Thus, throwing a chair at a person or a shout of 'Get out the knives' would be an assault, as in *R v Wilson* [1955] 1 All

ER 744. Any person who is convicted of a common assault shall be guilty of an offence triable either summarily or upon indictment, and shall be liable to imprisonment for one year according to section 40 of the *Offences Against the Person Ordinance*.

Assault includes assault occasioning actual bodily harm where the injury caused by the assault must be calculated to interfere with the health or comfort of the victim and wounding or inflicting grievous bodily harm (see sections 39, 17 and 19 of the *Offences Against the Person Ordinance*). In *HKSAR v Law Kwok Fai* [Unrep. Criminal Appeal No. 204 of 2003], the court held that 'grievous bodily harm' should be given its natural and ordinary meaning of really serious bodily harm. In *Law Kwok Fai*, the victims suffered lacerations of the scalp, which required suturing, as well as bruising, swellings and abrasions.

Although it is not necessary for such harm to be permanent or dangerous, grievous bodily harm does extend to serious psychological or biological harm. Thus, infecting a person with HIV will amount to inflicting grievous bodily harm, as in *R v Mohammed Dica* [2004] EWCA Crim 1103, and *R v Konzani* [2005] EWCA Crim 706. Defences in respect of assault include consent (this does not include consent to the satisfaction of sado-masochistic desires or the infliction of bodily harm), lawful correction, self defence, defence of property, and necessity.

Offences against property

The most important offences relating to property are covered by the *Theft Ordinance*. These offences include theft (sections 3–7 and 9), burglary (section 11) and handling stolen goods (section 24). Theft is defined as the dishonest appropriation of property belonging to another with the intention of permanently depriving the other of it. All the elements of theft are defined and provided for in the ordinance, as with the offences of burglary and handling stolen goods. In addition to offences created by the *Theft Ordinance*, one should note section 60(1) of the *Crimes Ordinance* (Cap. 200), which provides for the offence of criminal damage to property.

Conclusion

Criminal law is an essential part of every society. It can be said that the basis of criminal law is to promote and maintain a sense of security, well-being and harmony within society. It does this by regulating a great part of our daily life, activities and relationships with others and their interests/property, from something as trivial as how we should behave in a public area to instilling respect and care for the property of others to regulating and prohibiting matters of a more serious nature such as killing, grievously wounding another, drug trafficking or becoming a member of a terrorist organisation. It matters not that criminal offences are established either by common law or by statute. What is of paramount importance is that before criminal liability can be imposed, all the elements of the offence and its requisite mental state must be proven. Even when this is sufficiently proven, the defendant might still not be convicted of the offence if a defence is successfully raised.

Review questions

1 Is criminal law important? What is the purpose of criminal law?
2 Distinguish between the categories of offences in Hong Kong. Why is the distinction important?
3 Can a child aged 11 years old commit an offence? What does the prosecution need to prove?
4 Is there a difference between duress and necessity?
5 In what circumstances can a conviction of murder be reduced to manslaughter? What must be proved?
6 Name some offences relating to property and some of the offences that affect the moral values of society.

References

Findlay, M., Howarth, C. and Dobinson, I. (1996) *Criminal Law in Hong Kong: Cases and Commentary* (2nd edn), Hong Kong: Butterworths Asia.

Jackson, M. (2003) *Criminal Law in Hong Kong*, Hong Kong: Hong Kong University Press.

Legislation cited

Crimes Ordinance (Cap. 200)
Criminal Procedure Ordinance (Cap. 221)
Homicide Ordinance (Cap. 339)
Juvenile Offenders Ordinance (Cap. 226)
Offences Against the Person Ordinance (Cap. 212)
Public Order Ordinance (Cap. 245)
Registration of Persons Ordinance (Cap. 177)
Road Traffic Ordinance (Cap. 374)
Societies Ordinance (Cap. 151)
Summary Offence Ordinance (Cap. 228)
Theft Ordinance (Cap. 210)

Cases cited

Hong Kong cases

A-G v Chan Yuen Long [1989] 1 HKC 470
A-G v Demand Enterprise Ltd [1987] HKLR 195
Gammon (Hong Kong) v Attorney General of Hong Kong [1985] 2 HKC 661

HKSAR v Chan Ping Kwan [2005] 2 HKLRD 5
HKSAR v Chung Kei Tung [2004] HKCA 297
HKSAR v Ip Chung San [2005] HKEC 1338
HKSAR v Law Kwok Fai (Unrep. Criminal Appeal No. 204 of 2003)
HKSAR v Liu Chun Yip [2006] HKEC 1616
HKSAR v Leung Wai Chung [1999] 2 HKC 471
HKSAR v Luk Chiu-Ki [2005] HKEC 390 CFI
HKSAR v Mok Tsan Ping v Ors [2001] 2 HKLRD 325
HKSAR v Pang Kam-Chuen [2003] HKCA
HKSAR v Tsui Chu Tin, John [2005] 1 HKC 518
Lau Cheong and Anor v HKSAR [2002] 2 HKLRD 612
Kong Cheuk-kwan v R [1986] HKLR 648
Kwan Ping Bong v R (1979) HKLR 1
Pang Bing Yee v R [1984] HKLR 298
R v Chan Tak Kwong [1997] HKLY 225
R v Chang Wai Kwan [1994] 1 HKC 301
R v Chau Ming Cheong [1983] 1 HKC 68
R v Dung Shue Wah [1983] HKC 30
R v Lo Yung-kan [1985] 1 HKC 302
R v Mohammed Hussain [1993] 1 HKCLR
R v Tran Dihn Thannh & Anor [1994] 2 HKC 260
R v Vu Van Thang [1991] 2 HKC 90
R v Wong Tak Shing [1989] 2 HKC 94
R v Yeung Ka Wah [1992] HKLY 299
R v Yeung Lung-fai [1991] 2 HKC 102
Sin Kam Wah & Anor v HKSAR [2005] 8 HKCFAR 192

English cases

A-G Reference (No. 2 of 1992) (1994) QB
Bratty v Attorney General for Northern Ireland [1963] AC 386
DPP v Majewski [1977] AC 443
DPP v Morgan [1976] AC 182
DPP v Newbury [1977] AC 500
DPP v Rogers [1998] Crim LR 202
Luc Thiet Thuan v R [1996] 2 All ER 1003 PC
M'Naghten Case [1843] 10 CL & F 200
MPC v Caldwell [1982] AC 341
R v Adomako [1995] 1 AC 171
R v Bailey [1983] 1 WLR 760
R v Beard [1920] AC 479
R v Budd [1962] Crim LR 49
R v Burgess [1991] 2 QB 92
R v Burstow [1998] AC 147 HL
R v Caldwell [1982] AC 341
R v Camplin [1978] AC 705
R v Church [1966] 1 QB 59
R v Cunningham [1957] 2 QB 396

R v Duffy [1949] 1 QB 63
R v Graham [1982] 1 WLR 294
R v Hancock & Shankland [1986] 2 WLR 357
R v Hennessy [1989] 1 WLR 287
R v Howe [1987] AC 417
R v Kemp [1957] 1 QB 399
R v Kingston [1995] 2 AC 355
R v Konzani [2005] EWCA Crim 706
R v Lamb [1967] 2 QB 981
R v Martin [1989] 1 All ER 652
R v Miller [1983] 2 AC 161
R v Mohammed Dica [2004] EWCA Crim 1103
R v Moloney [1985] AC 905
R v Nedrick [1986] 1 WLR 1025
R v Podola [1960] 1 QB 325
R v Quick & Paddison [1973] QB 910
R v R and G [2003] UKHL 50
R v Smith [1959] 2 All ER 193
R v Stone and Dobinson [1977] QB 354
R v Valderrama-Vega [1985] Crim LR 220
R v Venna [1976] QB 421 at 429
R v White [1910] 1 KB 124
R v Wilson [1955] 1 All ER 744

Useful websites

Basic Law of the Hong Kong Special Administrative Region of the People's Republic of China www.info.gov.hk/basic_law/flash.html
Bilingual Laws Information System (BLIS) (Hong Kong) www.legislation.gov.hk/eng/index.htm

4

CRIME TRENDS

Roderic Broadhurst, King Wa Lee and Ching Yee Chan

Introduction

This chapter examines crime trends in Hong Kong (HK) over the past 50 years and discusses factors that might have impacted on the prevalence and nature of crime. Hong Kong was formerly a British colony and became the Hong Kong Special Administrative Region (HKSAR) of the People's Public of China on 1 July 1997 (Lo and Chui, 2012). Our discussion of crime trends covers both the period before and after the transfer of sovereignty, therefore provides an opportunity to examine crime trends during a period of political transition. In Western literature, frequently cited factors that affect crime trends include the age structure, economic inequalities, firearm prohibition, gangs and organised crime, illegal drug markets, public and media attitudes to crime, anti-crime measures and opportunities for crime (Siegel and Worrall, 2016). Due to space, our discussion of crime trends is limited to a few of these factors: the impacts of the age structure, reporting behaviour of victims, economic change, and crime and justice policies in HK.

Levels of crime in HK are usually measured by official statistics and crime victim surveys (CVS) but have occasionally involved self-report youth delinquency surveys (Wong, 1992; Vagg et al., 1995; Chui and Chan, 2012). Official crime statistics frequently underestimate crime due to under-reporting and recording practices. This 'dark figure' of unreported crime is addressed by surveys that estimate the 'true' victimisation rate, but are also subject to sampling and non-sampling errors. We can compare HK's crime rates to other countries, like Singapore, with the help of United Nations (UN) international surveys that report both official criminal justice and self-reported victimisation statistics (Bouhours and Broadhurst, 2015). Despite being significantly important, some ten years have passed since the last CVS was conducted in 2006 (Broadhurst et al., 2010). To begin with, we look at some international comparisons of official crime statistics.

An overview of the crime situation: where Hong Kong stands

As one of the safest cities in the 21st century, HK ranked low in overall recorded crime per capita among industrialised countries surveyed in the *Tenth United Nations Survey of Crime Trends and the Operations of Criminal Justice Systems* (10th UN CTS) (see UN Office on Drugs and Crime (UNODC), 2008 for more information). According to the 10th UN CTS, HK's *official total of recorded crimes in city* rate per 100,000 population was 1,222.5 (or 1.22%) in 2006, which was lower than cities in Malaysia (1,787.0), Japan (1,932.3), the USA (2,517.1), Canada (5,483.2), Argentina (7,016.7), Italy (8,181.9), England and Wales (12,367.5), and Sweden (17,544.8), but was higher than Singapore (900.6), Thailand (596.9), and the Philippines (134.4) in the same year. A shortcoming of these comparisons is that figures were based on official criminal justice statistics. The grand total of recorded crimes, however, is often subject to changing reporting and recording practices.

A comparison of international homicide statistics, which are considered less susceptible to under-reporting, would illustrate a picture different from the official total crimes statistics. The *total recorded committed intentional homicides in city* rate per 100,000 for HK in 2006 was 0.55, which was lower than Italy (0.96), Sweden (1.27), Canada (1.82), the Philippines (2.07), England and Wales (2.25), Argentina (3.83), Malaysia (4.43), Thailand (5.78), and the USA (7.30), but higher than Japan (0.43) and Singapore (0.39) (UNODC, 2008). Perceptions of corruption were much higher in some countries with lower total crime rates but higher homicide rates than HK, like the Philippines and Thailand (Transparency International, 2006). This suggests that official crime rates of some countries were likely distorted by malpractice. Notably, HK ranked 15th among 163 countries participating in the 2006 CPI. Along with Singapore (fifth), HK was perceived as one of the least corrupt in Asia, suggesting official crime statistics in both places were relatively reliable. This continues to be the case despite a recent drop in the latest 2015 CPI rank for both places (HK now ranks 18th and Singapore 8th).

The *United Nations International Crime Victim Survey* (UN ICVS) provides an alternative measure for comparing the crime situation across countries. The UN ICVS surveyed a total of 38 countries and 30 cities, including that of HK (van Dijk et al., 2007). The HK sample surveyed 2,083 households about their crime victimisation experience, for example sexual victimisation, assault/threat, and personal property theft, during 2001–05 (Broadhurst et al. 2010). For instance, 7.9% of HK citizens experienced at least one crime in 2005. The HK ICVS also suggests theft from households in HK was generally low. While only 0.5% of respondents experienced theft from a car and 0.1% motorcycle theft, and there was no report of car theft in 2005.

Crimes outside the household setting were more common in HK. Some 1.7% reported experiencing bicycle theft and 3.6% personal theft. Predatory crime like robbery was relatively rare (0.4%), but sexual victimisation (0.7%) and assault or threats (1.2%) were higher. Compared to other industrialised countries surveyed in 2003–04, crime victimisation in HK was lower than most Western countries but similar to other Asian countries such as Japan (van Dijk et al., 2007). Compared to Japan, HK had lower household crime such as vehicle theft, burglary and especially bicycle theft, but higher personal victimisation like assault and threat, robbery and in particular sexual assault against women and personal property theft (see Table 4.1). With a relatively low crime status, respondents felt rather secure about HK as the majority (92.7%) reported feeling 'fairly safe' or 'very safe' walking alone in their own neighbourhood after dark (Broadhurst et al. 2010). International victim surveys in general reflected a similar low crime status as HK, but the prevalence was overall much higher (HK ICVS victimisation rate: 7.9%; official rate: 1.2%).

In fact, the current low crime status of Hong Kong conforms to a global decline of crime incidents since the mid-1990s onwards (van Dijk et al., 2007). A recent report of the UN secretary-general on the *State of Crime and Criminal Justice Worldwide* stated that stable trends or a steady decline in the level of violent crimes (intentional homicide, robbery and rape) have been observed in most developed economies (United Nations, 2015). Being one of the advanced economies, Hong Kong was no exception – its homicide rates were among the lowest in the world (UNODC, 2013). However, HK's crime trends have fluctuated over the past 50 years, as illustrated by both police statistics and periodic crime victim surveys. We now take a closer look at HK's crime trends before examining the factors that may influence them.

Official crime trends

HK was not always a safe place, and in the early days of the colony it was considered a place full of 'vagabonds', 'thugs' and 'villains' (Fortune, 1847, cited in Faure, 1997: 19). Even by the 1950s and 1960s the safe image of HK had not been established. Although the recorded crime rates of that time were low in comparison with later years, they were not lower than other major jurisdictions. For instance, the HK homicide rate in 1950 was 1.31 per 100,000 persons, compared with 0.78 in the UK and 1.1 in Australia. In 1980 the HK robbery rate was 184 per 100,000 compared with the world average of about 40 (Shaw, 2003). However, a less lethal picture emerges for HK homicide rates in 2000 and 2005, which were 0.6 and 0.5 per 100,000 respectively, compared with 1.6 for the UK and 2.0 per 100,000 for Australia in 2001. Similarly, in 2000 the robbery rate for HK dropped to 51 compared with the world average of 60 per 100,000 (Shaw et al., 2003).

HK has experienced several 'crime waves' after three major civil disturbances (the 1956, 1966 and 1967 riots) in the last half century. After the riots in 1967, HK recorded a continual increase in crime, which triggered the colonial government to embark on a new era of politically driven crime prevention models that had various unintended consequences (Scott, 1989). The official overall

Table 4.1 Hong Kong UN ICVS 2006 compared with selected countries participating in the fifth UN ICVS (2005) and 2005 EU ICS: one-year prevalence rates (%)

	Surveyed year	Car theft	Theft from car	Motor-cycle theft	Bicycle theft	Burglary	Attempted burglary	Robbery	Personal property theft	Sexual victimisation**	Assaults and threats
Australia	2003	1.1	4.5	0.1	1.2	2.5	2.4	0.9	3.6	n/a	3.8
Canada	2003	0.8	4.8	0.2	2.7	2	1.7	0.8	4	0.8	3.0
England and Wales	2004	1.8	6	0.8	2.6	3.5	2.7	1.4	6.3	0.9	5.8
France	2004	0.6	3.2	0.3	0.9	1.6	1.2	0.8	3.3	0.3	2.1
Japan	2003	0.1	1.1	0.7	5.1	0.9	0.7	0.2	0.3	0.8	0.6
Sweden	2004	0.5	4.2	0.6	5	0.7	0.1	1.1	2.4	1.3	3.5
USA	2003	1.1	5.2	0.3	2.9	2.5	2.6	0.6	4.8	1.4	4.3
Average*	2003/2004	0.8	3.6	0.3	2.9	1.8	1.7	1.0	3.8	0.6	3.1
Hong Kong	2005	0	0.5	0.1	1.7	0.6	0.4	0.4	3.6	1.2	1.2

Source: (van Dijk et al., 2007)

Notes: * Countries in 2005 UN ICVS include: Australia, Bulgaria, Canada, Estonia, Iceland, Japan, Mexico, New Zealand, Northern Ireland, Norway, Poland, Scotland, Switzerland, USA. Countries in 2005 EU ICS include: Austria, Belgium, Denmark, England and Wales, Finland, France, Germany, Greece, Hungary, Italy, Luxembourg, Netherlands, Portugal, Spain, Sweden. ** Sexual assault against women.

police recorded crime in HK featured a rapid rise during the early 1970s, but soon stabilised between 1974 (1,294 per 100,000) and 1995 (1,493 per 100,000). The overall crime rate rose from 407 per 100,000 in 1963 to a peak of 1,610 in 1983. The violent crime rate rose tenfold from 48 in 1963 to peak at 477 per 100,000 in 1976. Thereafter violent crime declined, but increased again from 1986 (259) to 1991 (340). The year of the handover, 1997, saw a comparatively low overall (1,038 per 100,000) and violent (212 per 100,000) crime rate.

The rise in the overall crime and violent crime rates seems to match with the changing proportion of ages 15–24 in the population – an age group some consider to have a higher risk of offending (see Figure 4.1). However, the fact that a drop in violent crime in 1976 preceded the emergence of an ageing population in 1980 and yet overall recorded crime maintained a high level, suggests that mechanisms other than 'age' were in place.

One reason for the fluctuation in recorded offences included a change in police definitions of crimes and/or how statistics were compiled over time. For example, in 1987, the number of violent crimes was reduced from 21,215 to 14,303 (–32%) due to re-categorisation of several types of minor and public order offences; in 1990 'throwing objects from a height' was reclassified from 'serious assault' to 'other crimes', producing a 6.4% decline in serious assault and 2% decline in total violent crime; and in 2003, the minimum age of criminal responsibility was increased to ten from seven years old (Chui, 2006; Adorjan and Chui, 2014). Thus, trends in crime may be significantly influenced by recording practices.

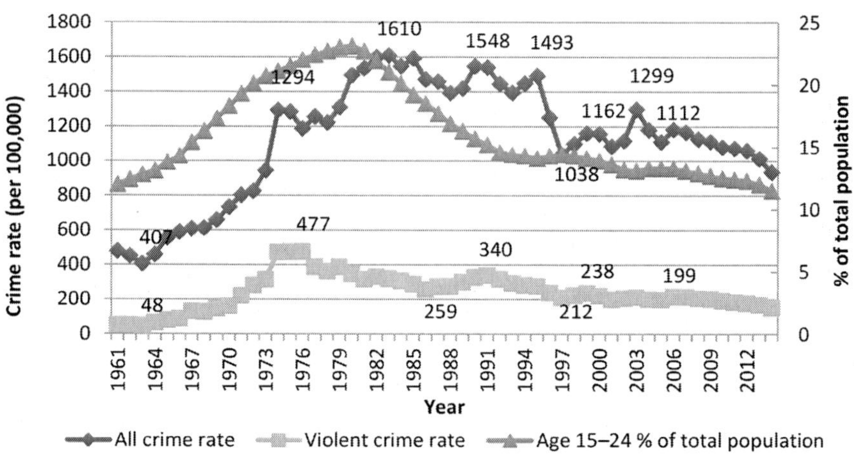

Figure 4.1 All crime and violent crime rates in Hong Kong, 1961–2014
Source: Hong Kong Police, 1961–68, 1998–2014; Royal Hong Kong Police, 1969–97; Crime Wing, Statistics Office, 1978–2001, 2002–2005; Hong Kong Census and Statistics Department, 1961–2014.

Serious offences such as homicide, rape and robbery (with firearms) exhibited periodic 'waves' between 1961 and 2005 (see Figure 4.2). Homicide is regarded as a robust temporal measure of violent crime because it is much less subject to the vagaries of reporting, recording and definitional changes. Homicide rates increased 3.5 times from 0.79 (n=17) in 1961 to 2.79 (n=115) in 1972. The spike in 1967 was a direct consequence of the civil disturbances that occurred in that year. The homicide rate then dropped quickly between 1972 and 1977 before turning upwards again to 2.03 in 1981, reaching a second peak of 2.4 in 1990 (n=137) before gradually decreasing to 0.49 (n=34) in 2005. Rates for firearm robbery experienced a similar trend and reached a peak of 1.5 per 100,000 in 1975 (n=66), thereafter declining, but spiking to 1.16 in 1990 (n=66) before declining tenfold to 0.11 per 100,000 in 2005 (n=8). Previous studies have suggested incidents of firearm robberies in Hong Kong, especially those committed by cross-border gangs, were extremely lethal and highly associated with an increase in homicide rates in a particular year, like 1975 and 1980 (Lee, 2009).

The trend for rape illustrates the systematic under-reporting of early police statistics. Changes in recorded rape often reflect the shifting patterns of victim reporting behaviour and/or improving police administrative procedures, rather than the 'real' fluctuations in this sexual offence. In 1961 there was only one police-recorded rape incident (0.03 per 100,000) in a population of 3,168,100. Over the next few years (1962–65) incidents numbered around five cases per annum. From 1968 onwards the reported rape rate rose quickly, reaching a peak rate in 1974 of 2.34 (n=101), thereafter fluctuating between 1 and 2 per 100,000 with a second peak in 1989 at 2.08 (n=120). Sociologists argued that

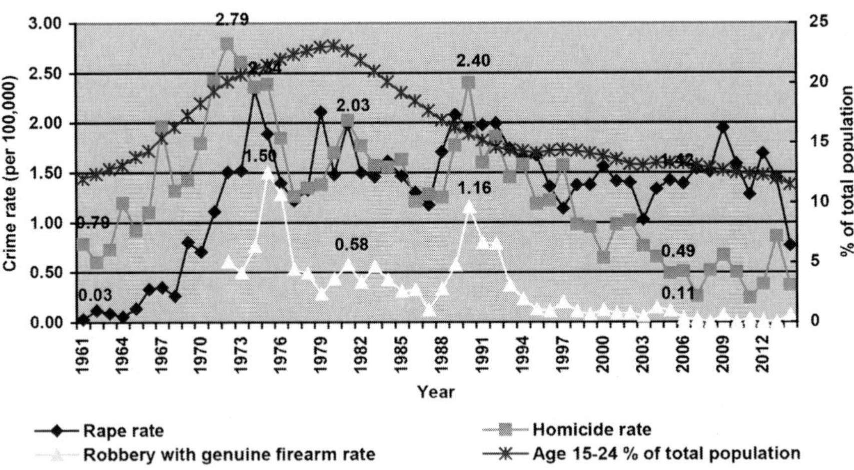

Figure 4.2 Rate of homicide, rape and robbery with a firearm in Hong Kong, 1961–2014
Source: Hong Kong Police, 1961–68, 1998–2014; Royal Hong Kong Police, 1969–97; Crime Wing, Statistics Office, 1978–2001, 2002–2005.

there was a 'crime-reporting' wave generated by feminist movements in HK (Lethbridge, 1980). The phenomenon of 'under-reporting' prompts us to describe alternative, perhaps more accurate, measures concerning experiences of crime in HK.

Victim surveys in Hong Kong: an alternative measure of crime

Addressing the systematic under-reporting problem, the Census and Statistics Department has conducted seven sweeps of the HK Crime Victim Surveys (HKCVS; note – different from HK ICVS) to estimate the actual risk of criminal victimisation in 1978, 1981, 1986, 1989, 1994, 1998 and 2005. The last survey, conducted by the government between January and May in 2006, interviewed 20,100 households out of a population of 6,904,300. The response rate was 83%. The survey scope is confined to crimes against the person or household crimes, and excludes some serious crimes (such as corruption and commercial crime such as corruption and commercial crime. These crimes are later covered by Broadhurst et al. (2011, 2013) for Chinese cities including Hong Kong in the UN International Crime Against Business survey, which reported that 19.5% of Hong Kong businesses in 2005 had experienced a commercial crime (fraud, bribery, extortion) similar to Shanghai but lower than the 27.9% percent of business in Shenzhen and the 25.3% of business in Xi'An). The HKCVS, like other victim surveys, is subject to non-sampling errors because it depends on the respondent's memory, honesty and willingness to cooperate, but face-to-face interviews can help to reduce ambiguous and inconsistent responses about victimisation over the past year. Large samples tend to produce more reliable estimates. The HKCVS sample is large, but even so, for some rare crimes the sample may be too small for reliable estimation. Repeated surveys thus provide valuable guidance on trends and the impact of crime policies (Broadhurst, 2005).

Overall 358,800 criminal incidents were estimated for 2005. Some 205,200 persons aged 12 and above experienced 214,100 criminal events, at a rate of 3.53% for personal crime. Some 120,700 households experienced 144,700 criminal events, at a rate of 6.57% for household crimes, which is lower than the previous year. The general trends of personal crime victimisation show a slight increase in risk in 2005 compared to previous sweeps. There is, however, a significant drop in the percentage of crime incidents reported to police in 2005 in all categories (see Table 4.2).

Overall, 9.1% of the crimes reported to the HKCVS involved crimes of violence like assault and robbery, 34.2% theft from persons, and 40.3% crimes affecting households such as burglary and theft of cars. According to the survey, about 0.1% (4,500 persons) of the population experienced three or more criminal events in 2005, indicating that some segments of the population are at higher risk of repeated victimisation. In terms of age, young women 12–19 and 20–29 are at highest risk of all personal crimes (51.8 and 49.0 per 1,000),

Table 4.2 Trends in HKCVS estimates of crime, 1978–2005

	1978	*1981*	*1986*	*1989*	*1994*	*1998*	*2005*
All personal							
% population	2.19	3.92	4.02	2.43	3.32	3.40	3.53
% report to police	18.0	37.7	39.1	42.2	38.9	36.3	20.9
Crimes of violence							
% population	0.98	0.98	0.95	0.67	1.05	0.92	1.07
% report to police	28.4	41.2	38.4	44.6	34.5	31.3	17.6
Personal crimes of theft							
% population	1.20	2.94	3.01	1.75	2.27	2.47	2.46
% report to police	9.5	36.6	39.4	41.3	40.9	38.2	22.4
All household crimes							
% population	4.65	8.64	7.37	6.12	9.34	7.98	6.57
% report to police	18.7	15.0	19.6	24.2	22.2	20.7	16.5

Source: Fight Crime Committee and Census and Statistics Department, 1979, 1982, 1987, 1990, 1995, 1999, 2007.

including the highest rates for crimes of violence (15.9 and 17.5 per 1,000), due mainly to indecent assault (11.8 and 10.2 per 1,000). Young men aged 12–19 and 20–29, on the other hand, are at much higher risk of wounding and assault (5.8 and 9.4 per 1,000) than women of the same age group (n.a. and 2.1 per 1,000).

Table 4.3 shows that police statistics and crime victim surveys could be contradictory in their results. For instance, police statistics showed a decline in crimes of violence in recent years but HKCVS indicated the trend has stabilised. In terms of sexual assaults, HKCVS showed an increase in the overall rate of indecent assault and rape in recent years, whereas police statistics indicated a

Table 4.3 HKCVS and Hong Kong police trends for selected offences (per 100,000)

	1978	*1981*	*1986*	*1989*	*1994*	*1998*	*2005*
Crimes of violence							
HKCVS rate	980	980	950	670	1,050	920	1,070
Police rate	364	318	259	301	284	224	199
Indecent assault and rape							
HKCVS rate*	30	20	70	80	100	220	230
Police rate	34	33	33	41	39	39	18

Source: Fight Crime Committee and Census and Statistics Department, 1979, 1982, 1987, 1990, 1995, 1999, 2007.

Note: Rates per 100,000 total population are rounded to the nearest whole number. * Category: rape only included in HKCVS in 1998 sweep and before.

slow decline. A possible explanation for the contradictory trends is that a dramatic decline in reporting rates in recent years has distorted the official figures (see Table 4.2 for a comparison of 1989 and 2005 reporting rates). Regardless of an increase or decrease in crime incidents, the HKCVS illustrated victimisation rates are much higher than reported to the police in HK.

What influences official crime trends?

A visual inspection of official crime trends from 1961 to 2014 (see Figures 4.1 and 4.2) indicates four crime waves in HK. The first occurred in 1963 and escalated in 1971. The second wave continued after the first, reaching a peak in 1982. The third rose from 1988 but ended abruptly in 1995. The fourth crime wave appears to be a temporary rebound after the 1997 changeover. Together the last three 'waves' form a crime 'plateau' that has lasted for 30 years in HK. These fluctuations in crime have often been attributed to the impact of various demographic and socio-economic factors, as well as reporting behaviour and law enforcement policies and practices. We now turn to discuss these issues to account for the changes in crime in HK.

Reporting behaviour

Traver (1991) argued that the first crime wave was the result of the combined effect of an increased willingness to report crime and the dissolution of widespread corruption within the police and other agencies. He argued that the first crime wave accelerated when the anti-corruption campaigns within the police were followed by the establishment of the Independent Commission Against Corruption (ICAC) in 1974. This dealt with every aspect of corruption in HK society. Active promotion of anti-corruption measures along with consensus-style policing led to the dissolution of the symbiotic relationship between police and triads (organised criminals) observed during the 1940s to 1960s. The breakdown of 'informal policing' by the triads resulted in a rapid surge in street crime. Simultaneously the decolonisation and re-legitimisation of the HK police force was achieved by implementing the community-policing model and the establishment of the Fight Crime Committee, both of which led to positive increases in the public's willingness to report crime (Lethbridge, 1985; Traver, 1991; Lo, 1993; Gaylord and Traver, 1995; Leung, 1996).

Nevertheless, the proportion of respondents who claim to have reported offences to the HK police appears to have peaked in the 1989 HKCVS sweep, thereafter declining, especially for crimes of violence (see Table 4.2). The extent to which decreases in crime after 1990 are accounted for by decreased willingness to report crime has yet to be ascertained.

The reporting rates for personal crimes of theft remain fairly stable at around two in five cases since the mandatory requirement to carry a universal identification card for all those over 15 was introduced in 1980. Household crime is not often reported, despite the incentive of insurance, but this crime includes a large number of criminal damage offences, attempted burglary, and other minor thefts where the victim suffered little or no loss. In 2005, about 22.3% of all crimes reported to HKCVS suffered no loss. Of those suffering loss, 41.1% suffered losses of HK$450 or less. For crimes of violence 65.7% of victims sustained no injuries. Yet, the reporting rate is higher if victims suffered greater loss or were injured. HKCVS for 2005 indicated that 29% of victims losing HK $950 reported this to the police, compared to those with no loss (15.5%). Up to 35.5% of injured victims of crimes of violence in HKCVS reported this to the police, compared to 7.4% who suffered no injury.

According to the government HKCVS for 2005, people failed to report victimisation for many reasons: most (37.9%) did not report it because they had not lost much or had suffered no loss; more than one-fifth (23.9%) believed there was a lack of evidence, and 8.9% considered that the police could not or would not do anything; a further 10.8% attributed not reporting to 'cumbersome reporting procedures', the 'police station too far' away, or being 'too busy'; and a further 3.1% were afraid of reprisal. Of those who reported their crime to the police in the government HKCVS for 2005, the majority (51.5%) hoped that the offender would be caught, and did so as a prerequisite to get documents replaced or to claim insurance (13.4%), they felt it was the duty of a citizen to report crime (13.1%) and hoped to alert the police to improve anti-crime measures (12.2%). Of all personal crimes, older victims (aged 50–64) (28.5%) and males (24.3%) were also more likely than younger ones (aged 12–19) (17.3%) and females (18.2%) to report their victimisation (Fight Crime Committee and Census and Statistics Department, 2007).

Comparing Hong Kong's crime reporting rates from UN International Crime Victim Surveys to Japan data, those in HK were less likely to report sexual victimisation, personal property theft, attempted burglary, bicycle theft, motorcycle theft and theft from a car, but were more likely to report assaults/threats, robbery and burglary (see Table 4.4). Victim reporting rates for HK differ across different types of offence, as is typical in all jurisdictions.

Analysis of international victim surveys shows that the better-educated and higher-income groups are more likely to report crimes to the police. There is also considerable variation in the levels of reporting depending on the gravity of the offence and the relationship of the victim to the offender. Respondents also may tend to over-report that they or a friend have contacted the police or assume the victimisation was only a private matter (van Dijk and van Kesteren, 1996).

Socio-economic causes

Poverty and income inequality are often thought to influence crime trends because theft is usually about material gain. Gaylord and Lang (1997) examined the correlation between real wages and the robbery rate from 1970 to 1980, and they argued that in the case of robbery:

Table 4.4 Reporting rate (%) by crime, UN ICVS

	Surveyed year	Car theft	Theft from car	Motorcycle theft	Bicycle theft	Burglary	Attempted burglary	Robbery	Personal property theft	Sexual victimisation	Assaults and threats
Australia	2000–04	94	55	84	57	86	39	55	39	n/a	38
Canada	2000–04	94	63	87	39	74	39	46	33	31	37
England and Wales	2000–04	88	69	93	70	88	47	60	60	73	36
France	2000–04	77	64	89	48	77	45	44	47	18	40
Japan	2000–04	100	66	74	49	63	18	25	87	13	46
Sweden	2000–04	93	79	91	57	77	39	49	52	61	35
USA	2000–04	87	64	65	38	77	38	61	48	35	43
Average	2000–04	83	62	78	49	74	38	46	46	25	33
Hong Kong	2001–05	76	28	59	6	74	29	40	29	11	33

Source: van Dijk et al., 2007.

Notes: Estimates based on the last incident reported in the past five years: HK 2001–05, for other countries 2000–04.

> the absence of a social safety net and when most of the population live close to the margin of survival relative to local standards of consumption, an economic downturn that substantially reduces average real wages will be reflected quickly in an increase in crimes involving little prior knowledge of criminal methods, planning and personal risk.
>
> (Gaylord and Lang, 1997: 17)

On the other hand, the post-war ethos of utilitarian familism (Lau, 1982) suggested there was a lack of informal social control in the 1960s and 1970s, and crime prevention incentives were extremely low given the lack of concern towards one's surrounding neighbourhood. This lack of organisation of the community and the rising aspiration towards material success might be reasons for the early 'crime wave'. Meanwhile, an improved economy and rising wages could reduce the motivation to commit robbery, and this may account for the continual decline of certain violent crimes since 1976 (Figure 4.1).

Traver (1991) asserted that observed increases in crime during the second crime wave (1978–82) are largely a result of increased illegal or even legal opportunities combined with a lessening of social constraints in a modernising and urbanising society. Rejecting the view that HK had a crime and disorder problem due to the invasion of capitalist investment, he argued crime trends would eventually decline or level off as the effects of rapid social and economic change begin to lessen, and prosperity and opportunities are more evenly distributed in society. The data support such a contention as the overall crime rate was in decline from 1982, albeit slowly, but more significantly in the mid-1990s onwards (Figure 4.1). This was a period when the social security system was also expanding fast, but the Gini coefficient (which signifies the gap between the poor and the rich) also worsened in the 2000s, suggesting social control mechanisms other than the optimistic trickledown effect are probably in place.

Expanding business opportunities during the 1980s provoked keen competition, particularly in some sectors, and enabled triad gangs to expand protection markets via franchising their different brands of violence (Chu, 2000; Lee et al., 2006; Broadhurst and Lee, 2009). After the dissolution of the police–triad symbiosis in the 1970s they soon found new footholds in various legitimate or semi-legitimate businesses such as the management of entertainment premises or acting as 'arbitrators' in debt disputes. Triad gang-related blackmail or wounding was rare during the latest 2000s crime wave. The open market economy in China during the 1980s and 1990s also amplified the effect of income inequality. Cross-border crimes, such as firearm robbery, illegal immigration and smuggling, increased rapidly throughout this period (Vagg, 1991; Lo, 2009).

The reasons for the abrupt decline in the overall crime rate between 1995 and 1997 and thereafter a significant reduction in rates are less clear. Although the economic development of HK was stable, we note that the decline observed is far less evident in the data from crime victim surveys. The enactment of the

Organized and Serious Crimes Ordinance (Cap. 455) in 1994 also impacted on triad activities but had a minor influence on the overall crime rate.

HK has gone through several crises since the People's Republic of China (PRC) resumed sovereignty in July 1997. Shortly after the transfer of sovereignty, HK's economy suffered as a result of the collapse of the Thai stock market and the subsequent Asian financial crisis, which triggered the 1998 recession in the HK property market. An epidemic of Severe Acute Respiratory Syndrome (SARS) in 2003 further depressed the already weakened HK economy. These events intensified social instability and may have been reflected in the small increase in the overall crime rate in 1999 and 2003 (Figure 4.1), but the effect was temporary because the overall crime rate soon returned to the previous lower level in subsequent years. Formal and informal responses to these problems (such as tax relief and social security) appear to have had a dampening effect on prolonged social instability.

In 2006 the Heritage Foundation/*The Wall Street Journal* ranked HK first out of 157 countries in their 'Index of Economic Freedom' – for the 11th consecutive occasion. In fact, Hong Kong is still ranked number one in the world by the Heritage Foundation in the *Index of Economic Freedom 2016* (The Heritage Foundation, 2016). The gross domestic product at purchasing power parity per capita (GDP [PPP] per capita) of HK reached HK$346,710 in 2006. HK also ranked eighth in GDP (PPP) per capita among 181 members of the International Monetary Fund in 2005, which was the highest among all the Asian members. Hong Kong continues to do well as the median monthly domestic household income doubled between 1991 and 2014 (Table 4.5). The percentage of the population in higher education increased from 42.9% in 1991 to 59.4% in 2011 (Table 4.5, adding upper secondary and matriculation, and tertiary). Nonetheless, HK's economic success is not shared by all sectors, and the Gini coefficient, as noted, increased from 0.476 to 0.537 between 1991 and 2011 (Table 4.5), reflecting greater income inequality. Yet, the official crime trends for two key instrumental offences – burglary and robbery – as well as all violent crime declined during the same period (Table 4.5). This does not devalue Gaylord and Lang's (1997) hypothesis, as an ageing HK population possibly offsets the negative impact of growing income inequality. Certainly, social control exercised by the criminal justice system is also playing a key role in the suppression of crime.

Criminal justice policy

Considering crime control and 'punitiveness', the 10th UN CTS survey showed HK ranked as one of the largest police forces per capita with 431.9 *total police personnel* per 100,000 persons in 2006. The closest 'policed' countries would be Portugal (420.2) and Italy (551.8). Most other Asian jurisdictions had proportionally smaller forces (e.g. Philippines 133.2, Japan 199.0, Singapore 394.8, and Thailand 336.5). HK's large police force exceeds that of most industrialised

Table 4.5 Key social index and crime rates in Hong Kong

	1991	*1996*	*2001*	*2006*	*2011*	*2014*
Median monthly domestic household income (HK$)	9,964	17,500	18,705	17,100	20,200	23,500
Gini coefficient*	0.476	0.518	0.525	0.533	0.537	–
Population aged 15 and over by educational attainment (highest level attended)						
Upper secondary and matriculation (% by population =>15)	1,383,848 (31.7%)	1,712,019 (33.8%)	2,001,771 (35.8%)	1,931,193 (32.6%)	2,005,373 (32.1%)	–
Tertiary (% by population =>15)	490,891 (11.2%)	768,520 (15.2%)	918,500 (16.4%)	1,361,473 (23.0%)	1,703,031 (27.3%)	–
All crime (rate per 100,000 population)	1,541	1,253	1,086	1,183	1,074	936
All violent crime (rate per 100,000 population)	340	241	202	217	185	153
All burglary (rate per 100,000 population)	794	617	570	616	555	348
All robbery (rate per 100,000 population)	158	62	47	22	10	4

Source: Crime Wing, Statistics Office, 1978–2001, 2002–2005; Hong Kong Police 2006-2014; Hong Kong Census and Statistics Department, 2001, 2006, 2011.

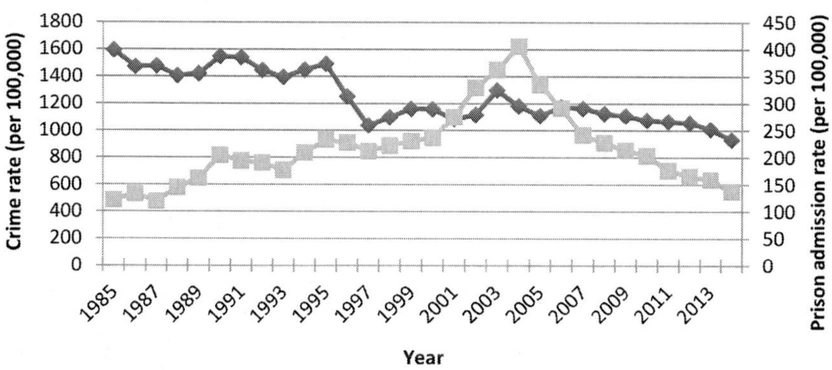

Figure 4.3 Prison admission rate for convicted sentenced to imprisonment and total reported crime rate (1985–2014)
Source: Crime Wing, Statistics Office, 1985–2001, 2002–2005; Hong Kong Police 2006–2014; Hong Kong Correctional Services Department, 1985–97a, 1997b–2014.

countries such as Sweden (191.2), Canada (191.7), the USA (225.7), and England and Wales (264.1; 2005 data). According to the 10th UN CTS survey, HK also has a moderately high *total persons incarcerated* rate per 100,000 of 168.4 in 2006, which was higher than Japan (63.5), Sweden (79.8), Italy (104.2), Canada (108.8), Portugal (119.5), England and Wales (142.6; 2005 data), but was notably lower than Thailand (238.9) and Singapore (291.2) (UNODC, 2008).

Since the 1980s, HK has given extensively used custodial sentences, and substantial 'net widening' in the 1970s and 1980s in the juvenile justice system was noted by Gray (1991) and continued into the 1990s. From 1985 to 2004, there was a threefold increase in prison admission rates (excluding remands, recalls and those sentenced to drug treatment centres) from 121 to 406 per 100,000 population, despite a general decline in overall crime rates during the same period (see Figure 4.3). This punitive sentiment might partially contribute to the decrease in the crime rate by incapacitating at-risk persons – a factor widely recognised in Western literature about penal policy (Levitt, 2004; Tseloni, 2010). However, local scholars suggest that the surge in the prison admission rate in the early 2000s was also caused by the mandatory imprisonment of convicted illegal migrant workers following the opening of the border between HK and Mainland China (Lee, 2007). Nonetheless, prison admission rates fell significantly from 2004 onwards and the rate has returned to a low level comparable to 1985 – a condition that matches the falling crime rates.

Until recently HK's relative freedom from large-scale public disorder partly reflects the success of a proactive strategy of crime prevention and control. Partnerships between the private sector, government and the community are strongly encouraged. Since the 1970s, the police have actively engaged in youth work and sponsoring youth clubs – notably *Junior Police Call* with over 130,000 children regularly involved. Following the British model of crime control that focuses on offender rehabilitation, HK has developed its own integrated welfare-control correctional model. For instance, in 2014 more than one-fifth of the HK government budget was spent on security (8.4%, HK$35,784 million) and social welfare (14.1%, HK$60,066 million). The security budget includes the administration of justice, anti-corruption, immigration control, internal security, legal administration and legal aid. Social welfare policies have also received increasing attention reflected by the rising proportion of the government's budget devoted to this area from 2002 (12.1%) to 2014 (14.1%) (see Table 4.6).

The successful transition from a once suppressive colonial quasi-military police force into the current service-based, client-oriented community policing practice of the modern period contributed to effective crime prevention (Gaylord and Traver, 1995; Lo and Cheuk, 2004). Whether the low crime rate in HK reflects the effectiveness of law enforcement as indicated by the relatively high incarceration rate, large police force and the significant public resources allocated, remains a matter for further research given the role of other structural factors we discuss below. In reality, state action accounts for only part of the reason for the stability and low crime levels experienced, as other less visible social factors are equally relevant to the decline of crime.

Ageing society vs. youth moral panic

Lastly, we argue that age can be a crucial factor in shaping HK's crime trends (see Table 4.7). Between 1990 and 2014 the absolute number of arrested persons declined for all age groups. Yet, the proportions in the younger 16–30 age group arrested dropped from 51% to 29%, whereas the older (31+) group increased

Table 4.6 Total public expenditure by policy area group, 2002/03 to 2014/15, selected years

Policy area groups	*2002/03*	*2004/05*	*2006/07*	*2008/09*	*2010/11*	*2012/13*	*2014/15*
Total public expenditure (HK$ million)	263,520	257,137	264,889	330,968	320,570	400,179	426,004
Social welfare (%)	12.1	12.9	13.7	11.9	12.6	11.5	14.1
Security (%)	10.3	9.9	10.2	8.5	10.2	8.2	8.8

Source: Hong Kong Special Administrative Region, 2001–14.

from 34% of those arrested to 67%. Meanwhile, the proportion of the HK population in the age group 15–29 decreased from 26% to 18%, while the 30 or above age group increased from 52% to 70%. The proportion of violent crime as a percentage of all reported crime also declined from 21% to 17% in the same period. These figures suggest the proportion of higher-risk juveniles and youths in HK may be an influential factor in previous 'crime waves'. The initial contribution of juveniles to crime and the subsequent youth moral panic has merited additional government attention in the form of various interventions, sanctions and social policies that unintentionally also widened the justice net for youths since the 1970s. While youths have gradually retreated from the 'crime scene', perhaps the ageing offender population warrants further discussion as proportionally more and more elders go through the criminal justice system in the future.

Conclusion

In the past four decades, many jurisdictions, including HK, experienced rising crime until the mid- and late 1990s. Nevertheless, how HK has emerged as a 'safe' city is complex and can only be partially addressed in this chapter. On average the HK government spends one-tenth of its public expenditure on security. The HK police have long been equipped with extensive powers of 'stop and search' and are one of the largest police forces deployed. Having striven to improve their image and relations with the public, the HK police have in general obtained the support of the HK people, and successfully transformed from the 'rough and corrupt bullies' of the colonial past into a professional and modern police service. This high level of legitimacy despite sporadic criticism about police misbehaviour and corruption reflects these efforts. According to the 2006 UN ICVS, 94% of respondents reported that the police in their area had done a 'fairly good job' or a 'very good job' in controlling crime.

HK's service-oriented policing, however, constantly faces new challenges. Some recent challenges are not only about the threat of transnational crime and traditional crime and its evolution in cyberspace, but the demand for proactive action on domestic violence such as the increasing incidence of homicide-suicide (Chan et al., 2003), where the would-be guardians may be the perpetrators themselves (specifically see Broadhurst, 2013). This requires balancing the role of state intervention in family disputes with heightened respect for civil rights while at the same time ensuring that social services and the police collaborate in crime prevention. However, one of the consequences of the large-scale civil disobedience that occurred during the Umbrella Movement in 2014 has been that the police–community relationship has deteriorated, especially among the young (for more information on people's satisfaction with the performance of the Hong Kong Police Force, please see Public Opinion Programme, 2016). The impact of this troubling period on the legitimacy of the police and on the character of crime trends has yet to be played out.

Table 4.7 Age and arrest rate

	1990	*1995*	*2000*	*2005*	*2010*	*2014*
Overall crime (no.)	88,300	91,886	77,245	77,437	75,965	67,740
Overall crime rate (per 100,000)	1547.9	1492.6	1159.0	1111.7	1074.8	932.2
Violent crime (no.)	18,820	17,087	14,812	13,890	13,456	11,073
Violent crime (rate per 100,000)	329.9	277.6	222.2	199.4	191.7	152.4
Violent crime (% of all crime)	21	19	19	18	18	17
Total arrest (no.)	43,713	53,098	40,930	40,804	37,956	33,679
Total arrest (rate per 100,000)	766.3	862.5	614.1	585.8	537.0	463.5
Arrested aged 16–30 (no.)	22,312	23,950	17,442	14,737	12,060	9,713
Arrested aged 16–30 (% of all arrests)	51	45	43	36	32	29
Population aged 15–29 (no.)	1,503,400	1,410,600	1,458,300	1,396,700	1,412,200	1,334,200
Population aged 15–29 (% of all)	26	23	22	20	20	18
Arrested aged 31 or above (no.)	14,818	22,425	17,259	21,536	22,320	22,454
Arrested aged 31 or above (% of all arrests)	34	42	42	53	59	67
Population aged 30 or above (no.)	2,974,800	3,550,400	4,138,400	4,587,500	4,807,800	5,121,300
Population aged 30 or above (% of all)	52	58	62	66	68	70

Source: Crime Wing, Statistics Office, 1978–2001, 2002–14.

Note: Juveniles those aged 7–15 prior to July 2003, thereafter those aged 10–15 due to the change in the minimum age of criminal liability.

Hong Kong's low level of crime contests assumptions that dense urban environments are criminogenic. What are the likely explanations? The protective value of cultural and ethnic homogeneity combined with the preservation of traditional Confucian values and extended kinship structures are crucial. As noted, 'utilitarian familism' resulted in minimal social organisation rather than strong integration (Lau, 1982). In a cultural sense, though, familism might amplify the shaming effect of crime because such shame is shared by the entire family. Considering the role of the state, widespread penal elitism and lack of democratic institutions and traditions result in a government with little interest in taking into consideration the populists (Adorjan and Chui, 2013, 2014) and becoming extremely hostile to crime. This reinforces conservative criminal justice policies in Hong Kong which are pre-emptive in a good sense but possibly also 'construct' more crime – like the previously proposed compulsory drug test that possibly widened the justice net further. Strict gun laws have effectively reduced firearm robbery to almost zero and not a single incident of domestic violence was perpetuated with a firearm in the past ten years. The successful suppression of cross-border crime by way of mandatory identity cards and coordinated efforts with the Public Security Bureau of the PRC has had significant impact on an enclosed jurisdiction like HK (Broadhurst, 2005). Punishment is also generally severe on either side of the border, as reflected by the high incarceration rate in HK and the death penalty in the PRC.

The densely populated nature of urban high-rise living also provides higher levels of natural or informal surveillance by facilitating the presence of capable guardians and reduces opportunity for crime. The availability of attractive wealthy targets within the city has a limited stimulus on crime opportunity due to the large numbers of private security officers employed; approximately 130,000 people are registered security providers, and most are employed to provide a guarding service. In addition, advanced crime prevention technologies including closed-circuit television are installed in public housing, public recreational areas and crime hot spots, and these serve to reduce potential offenders' willingness to commit crime. Private security operates in areas such as shopping malls and middle-class fortress estates, and this has impacted on social control in Hong Kong (see Shearing and Stenning, 1983).

Various measures that attempted to bring the public and state together in fighting crime have been successfully implemented since the late 1960s. The continual localisation and professionalisation of the HK Police Force also overcame the challenge caused by the rising proportion of at-risk youths during the 1970s and the cross-border crime waves in the late 1980s and early 1990s. The Fight Crime Committee and the HK police work closely with the public to develop programmes that aim at reducing youth offending and recidivism. District Fight Crime Committees proactively coordinate the local community's efforts to fight against crime and retain their potency as a means for mobilising public responses to crime (see also Chapter 18 of this edited volume, on crime prevention).

There are limitations to this chapter. We focus mainly on street crimes but omit crimes of the powerful, such as corruption and other white-collar crimes. We only touch on some crimes and we did not discuss the impact of drug use, media or technology on crime trends. Nonetheless, age, economic factors, policy and changes in the willingness to report crime have impacted on crime trends at different times. Compared to other nations, the low crime rate observed in HK is the outcome of a complex mixture of cultural traditions, proactive crime prevention and the emergence of a legitimate 'consensus' style of law enforcement. Thus family-oriented Confucian values, a large professionalised and localised police service, strict gun laws, effective suppression of cross-border crime, high levels of formal or informal surveillance, ethnic homogeneity, proactive efforts against organised crime and corruption, and severe punishment of the convicted all serve to reduce opportunity for crime. However, with the society ageing, more attention will be needed to curb the growing victimisation of the elderly but also to cater for the need of an ageing offender population.

Review questions

1 To what extent have changes in the youth population contributed to declines in HK's crime rates?
2 Discuss why strict gun laws may have made robbery less commonplace in HK.
3 Crime victim surveys show that reporting behaviour can be a crucial determinant in changes in crime rates, but why do they vary so much for different offences?
4 Is the criminal justice system in Hong Kong becoming more punitive? Does the use of custodial sentences reflect community attitudes to social control?
5 What will the crime trends in Hong Kong be like in the next five to ten years?

References

Adorjan, M. and Chui, W.H. (2013) 'Colonial responses to youth crime in Hong Kong: Penal elitism, legitimacy and citizenship', *Theoretical Criminology*, 17(2): 159–177.

Adorjan, M. and Chui, W.H. (2014) *Responding to Youth Crime in Hong Kong: Penal Elitism, Legitimacy and Citizenship*, Abingdon: Routledge.

Bouhours, B. and Broadhurst, R.G. (2015) 'Violence against women in Hong Kong: Results of the International Violence Against Women Survey', *Violence Against Women*, 21(11): 1311–1329.

Broadhurst, R.G. (2005) 'Crime trends in Hong Kong', in R. Estes (ed.) *Social Development in Hong Kong: The Unfinished Agenda* (pp. 185–192), New York: Oxford University Press.

Broadhurst, R. (2013) 'Uncertainty and the case of police constable "Tiger" Tsui Ka Po', *Policing and Society*, 23(3): 390–407.

Broadhurst, R., Bacon-Shone, J., Bouhours, B., Lee, K.W. and Zhong, L. (2010) *Hong Kong United Nations International Crime Victim Survey: Final Report of the 2006 Hong Kong UNICVS*, Hong Kong and Canberra: The University of Hong Kong and the Australian National University.

Broadhurst, R., Bacon-Shone, J., Bouhours, B. and Bouhours, T., with Lee, K.W. (2011) *Business and the Risk of Crime in China: the International Crimes Against Business Survey 2005–2006*, Canberra: ANU Press.

Broadhurst, R., Bouhours, B. and Bouhours, T. (2013) 'Business and the risk of crime in China', *British Journal of Criminology*, 53(2): 276-296.

Broadhurst, R.G. and Lee, K.W. (2009) 'The transformation of triad "dark" societies in Hong Kong: The impact of law enforcement, and socio-economic and political change', *Security Challenges*, 5(4): 1–38.

Chan, C.Y., Beh, S.L. and Broadhurst, R.G. (2003) 'Homicide-suicide in Hong Kong, 1989–1998', *Forensic Science International*, 137(2/3): 165–171.

Chu, Y.K. (2000) *The Triads as Business*, London: Routledge.

Chui, W.H. (2006) 'Avoiding early intrusion in the lives of children: The need for juvenile justice reform in Hong Kong', *Journal of Youth Studies*, 9(1): 119–128

Chui, W.H. and Chan, H.C. (2012) 'An empirical investigation of social bonds and juvenile delinquency in Hong Kong', *Child and Youth Care Forum*, 41(4): 371–386.

Crime Wing, Statistics Office (1978–2001, various issues) *Crime and Enforcement Report*, Hong Kong: Government Printer.

Crime Wing, Statistics Office (2002–05, various issues) *Crime in Hong Kong*, Hong Kong: Government Printer.

Faure, D. (ed.) (1997) *Society*, Hong Kong: Hong Kong University Press.

Fight Crime Committee and Census and Statistics Department (1979) *Crime and its Victims in Hong Kong in 1977*, Hong Kong: Government Printer.

Fight Crime Committee and Census and Statistics Department (1982) *Crime and its Victims in Hong Kong in 1981*, Hong Kong: Government Printer.

Fight Crime Committee and Census and Statistics Department (1987) *Crime and its Victims in Hong Kong in 1986*, Hong Kong: Government Printer.

Fight Crime Committee and Census and Statistics Department (1990) *Crime and its Victims in Hong Kong in 1989*, Hong Kong: Government Printer.

Fight Crime Committee and Census and Statistics Department (1995) *Crime and its Victims in Hong Kong in 1994*, Hong Kong: Government Printer.

Fight Crime Committee and Census and Statistics Department (1999) *Crime and its Victims in Hong Kong in 1998*, Hong Kong: Government Printer.

Fight Crime Committee and Census and Statistics Department (2007) *Crime and its Victims in Hong Kong in 2005*, Hong Kong: Government Printer.

Gaylord, M.S. and Lang, G. (1997) 'Robbery, recession and real wages in Hong Kong', *Crime, Law & Social Change*, 27(1): 49–71.

Gaylord, M.S. and Traver, H. (eds) (1994) *Introduction to the Hong Kong Criminal Justice System*, Hong Kong: Hong Kong University Press.

Gaylord, M.S. and Traver, H. (1995) 'Colonial policing and the demise of British rule in Hong Kong', *International Journal of the Sociology of Law*, 23(1): 23–43.

Gray, P. (1991) 'Juvenile crime and disciplinary welfare', in H. Traver and J. Vagg (eds) *Crime and Justice in Hong Kong* (pp. 25–41), Hong Kong: Oxford University Press.

The Heritage Foundation (2016) *2016 Index of Economic Freedom: Hong Kong*, www.heritage.org/index/country/hongkong (accessed 15 February 2016).

Hong Kong Census and Statistics Department (2001) *Population Census 2001: Summary Results*, Hong Kong: Government Printer.

Hong Kong Census and Statistics Department (2006) *Population By-Census 2006: Summary Results*, Hong Kong: Government Printer.

Hong Kong Census and Statistics Department (2011) *Population Census 2011: Summary Results*, Hong Kong: Government Printer.

Hong Kong Census and Statistics Department (2016) *Population by Age Group and Sex (1961–2014)*. Retrieved online: http://www.censtatd.gov.hk/hkstat/sub/sp150.jsp?tableID=002&ID=0&productType=8.

Hong Kong Correctional Services Department (1982–97a, various issues) *Annual Review*, Hong Kong: Government Printer.

Hong Kong Correctional Services Department (1997b–2014, various issues) *Annual Report*, Hong Kong: Government Printer.

Hong Kong Police (1961–68, 1998–2014, various issues) *Annual Report*, Hong Kong: Government Printer.

Hong Kong Special Administrative Region (2001–14, various issues) *The Budget, Hong Kong Special Administrative Region Government*, Hong Kong: Government Printer.

Lau, R.W.K. (2004) 'Community policing in Hong Kong: Transplanting a questionable model', *Criminal Justice: The International Journal of Policy and Practice*, 4(1): 61–80.

Lau, S.K. (1982) *Society and Politics in Hong Kong*, Hong Kong: Chinese University Press.

Lee, K.W. (2009) 'Applying time-series cross correlation analysis to examine the nexus between firearms and homicide in Hong Kong', *Asian Journal of Criminology*, 4(1): 31–46.

Lee, K.W., Broadhurst, R.G. and Beh, S.L. (2006) 'Triad-related homicides in Hong Kong', *Forensic Science International*, 62(1/3): 183–190.

Lee, M. (2007) 'Women's imprisonment as a mechanism of migration control in Hong Kong', *British Journal of Criminology*, 47(6): 847–860.

Lethbridge, H.J. (1980) 'Rape, reform and feminism', *Hong Kong Law Journal*, 10(3): 260–291.

Lethbridge, H.J. (1985) *Hard Graft in Hong Kong: Scandal, Corruption and the ICAC*, Hong Kong: Oxford University Press.

Leung, B.K.P. (1996) *Perspectives of Hong Kong Society*, Hong Kong: Oxford University Press.

Levitt, S.D. (2004) 'Understanding why crime fell in the 1990s: Four factors that explain the decline and six that do not', *Journal of Economic Perspectives*, 18(1): 163–190.

Lo, S.H.C. and Chui, W.H. (2012) *The Hong Kong Legal System*, Singapore: McGraw-Hill.

Lo, S.S.H.. (2009) *The Politics of Cross-Border Crime in Greater China: Case Studies of Mainland China*, Hong Kong and Macao, New York, and London: M.E. Sharpe.

Lo, T.W. (1993) *Corruption and Politics in Hong Kong and China*, Buckingham: Open University Press.

Lo, W.H.C. and Cheuk, C.Y.A. (2004) 'Community policing in Hong Kong: Development, performance and constraints', *Policing: An International Journal of Police Strategies & Management*, 27(1): 97–127.

Public Opinion Programme (2016) *People's Satisfaction with the Performance of the Hong Kong Police Force*, www.hkupop.hku.hk/english/popexpress/hkpolice/ (accessed 15 February 2016).

Royal Hong Kong Police (1969–97, various issues) *Annual Report*, Hong Kong: Government Printer.

Scott, I. (1989) *Political Change and the Crisis of Legitimacy in Hong Kong*, Hong Kong: Oxford University Press.

Shaw, M., Dijk, J.V. and Rhomberg, W. (2003) 'Determining trends in global crime and justice: An overview of results from the United Nations Surveys of Crime Trends and Operations of Criminal Justice Systems', *Forum on Crime and Society*, 3(1/2): 35–63.

Shearing, C.D. and Stenning, P. (1983) 'Private security: Implications for social control', *Social Problems*, 30(5): 493–506.

Siegel, L.J. and Worrall, J.L. (2016) *Introduction to Criminal Justice* (15th edn), Boston, MA: Cengage Learning.

Tonry, M. and Frase, R.S. (eds) (2001) *Sentencing and Sanctions in Western Countries*, New York: Oxford University Press.

Transparency International (2006) *Corruption Perceptions Index 2006*, www.transparency.org/research/cpi/cpi_2006#background (accessed 15 February 2016).

Traver, H. (1991) 'Crime trends', in H. Traver and J. Vagg (eds) *Crime and Justice in Hong Kong* (pp. 10–24), Hong Kong: Oxford University Press.

Tseloni, A., Mailley, J., Farrell, G. and Tilley, N. (2010) 'Exploring the international decline in crime rates', *European Journal of Criminology*, 7(5): 375–394.

United Nations (2015) *State of Crime and Criminal Justice Worldwide* (Report of the Secretary-General at Thirteenth United Nations Congress on Crime Prevention and Criminal Justice, United Nations, A/CONF.222/4), New York: United Nations.

United Nations Office on Drugs and Crime (UNODC) (2008) *Responses by Country to: Questionnaire for the Tenth United Nations Survey of Crime Trends and Operations of the Criminal Justice Systems, covering the period 2005–2006*, www.unodc.org/documents/data-and-analysis/All_countries.pdf (accessed 15 February 2016).

United Nations Office on Drugs and Crime (UNODC) (2013) *Global Study on Homicide*, Vienna: UNODC.

Vagg, J. (1991) 'Illegal immigration and cross-border crime', in H. Traver and J. Vagg (eds.) *Crime and Justice in Hong Kong* (pp. 83–97), Hong Kong: Oxford University Press.

Vagg, J., Bacon-Shone, J., Gray, P. and Lam, D.O.B. (1995) *Research on the Social Causes of Juvenile Crime*, Hong Kong: Government Printer.

van Dijk, J.M. and van Kesteren, J.N. (1996) 'The prevalence and perceived risk seriousness of victimisation by crime; some results of the international crime victim survey', *European Journal of Crime, Criminal Law and Criminal Justice*, 4(1): 48–71.

van Dijk, J., van Kesteren, J. and Smit, P. (2007) *Criminal Victimisation in International Perspective: Key Findings from the 2004–2005 ICVS and EU ICS*, Tilburg: University of Tilburg and UNODCP.

van Kesteren, J.N., Mayhew, P. and Nieuwbeerta, P. (2000) *Criminal Victimisation in Seventeen Industrialized Countries: Key-findings from the 2000 International Crime Victims Survey*, The Hague: Ministry of Justice.

Wong, S.W. (1992) *Youth Problems in North District: An Integrated Study on Unruly and Delinquent Behaviours*, Hong Kong: Working Group on Youth Problem, North District Board (in Chinese).

Legislation cited

Organized and Serious Crimes Ordinance (Cap. 455)

Useful websites

Census and Statistics Department www.censtatd.gov.hk
Centre for Criminology, University of Hong Kong www.crime.hku.hk
Hong Kong Police Force www.police.gov.hk
Hong Kong Yearbook www.yearbook.gov.hk

Security Bureau www.sb.gov.hk
Transparency International (Germany) www.transparency.org
United Nations un.org
United Nations Surveys on Crime Trends and the Operations of Criminal Justice Systems www.unodc.org/unodc/en/crime_cicp_surveys.html

5

VICTIMS OF CRIME

Wai To Chan

Introduction

Victims of crime play various roles in the criminal justice process. For instance, they report offences to law enforcement agencies, provide evidence, make statements, attend identification parades in police stations and attend court as witnesses. However, in contemporary society, considerable attention has been paid to the defendant, and those persons at the receiving end of the crime (notably the crime victims) have not been given corresponding equal attention. Quite often, both the rights and interests of crime victims are neglected. In the criminal sciences literature, crime victims are rightly called 'forgotten persons' (United Nations, 1999a: 1; see also United Nations, 1999b).

In view of the above, it seems that the victims of crime are left to fend for themselves from statutory resources or assistance from family and/or community groups or non-governmental organisations. This chapter attempts to review the present provision of various victim programmes and to discuss the drawbacks as well as the absence of a sound philosophical basis for action.

Who are 'crime victims'?

The definition of 'crime victims' is controversial. Generally, the term refers to those persons at the receiving end of a crime. According to a legal definition, crime victims are those persons who, individually or collectively, have suffered harm, loss or damage through acts or omission that are in violation of criminal laws (Sutherland, 1949: 31; see also Walklate, 2011; Daigle, 2013). A human rights definition implies that crime victims are those persons who have been deprived of basic human rights (Schwendinger and Schwendinger, 1970: 148). A social process definition widens the category of crime victims by considering all those who have suffered pain as a consequence of social interaction (Cohen, 1973: 624). In other words, they are the ones being victimised by the process of social perception and reaction as applied and interpreted by agents of the state authorities.

The above definitions throw light on the meaning of the crime victims from different angles. Yet, upon closer scrutiny, it is very difficult for all academics, professionals, practitioners or clients to reach unanimous agreement on the exact category of both 'direct' and 'indirect' or 'primary' and 'secondary' victims of crime. For instance, victimisation surveys in Hong Kong (Census and Statistics Department, 1979, 1982, 1987, 1990, 1995, 1999) distinguish between household crimes and personal crimes. On typical household crimes, statements such as 'burglary does not cause serious problems of interpretation' are common. However, with personal crimes like theft of a vehicle, the circle of victims may be defined differently by various groups of respondents. Some parents may see themselves as victims when their child's vehicle is stolen, yet others may not. Equally, no conclusion can be arrived at on the question of whether family members of victims of crimes of violence must be considered as crime victims.

Even international bodies such as the United Nations (UN) and the European Committee on Crime Problems have different emphases on the conception of crime victims. The UN, on the occasion of its Seventh Congress on the Prevention of Crime and the Treatment of Offenders, defined crime victims as 'persons who, individually or collectively, have suffered harm ... through acts or omissions which are in violation of criminal laws operative within Member States, including those laws which proscribe criminal abuse of power' (Colvin, 1988: 57). The European countries, at their 16th Criminological Research Conference, defined crime victims as 'persons who stand a reasonable chance of winning a civil law suit against the perpetrator of an act which is defined by positive law as a crime' (European Committee on Crime Problem, 1984: 11). Seen in the above definitions, the UN, in a much more restrictive sense, considers crime victims to be those within the legal framework or criminal justice system, while in Western Europe the term refers to the broader civil law concept of the damaged person. This covers all persons who have suffered any form of damage such as pain arising from the consequence of the offence under consideration in legal terms.

In short, there is no unanimous agreement on the concept of 'crime victims' as the notion can be principally examined from legal, human rights and social process perspectives. The situation is further complicated by the fact that the exact category of 'crime victims' can be quite arguable (as in the case of personal crimes according to the legal definition). The lack of unified formal definition of 'crime victims', indeed, poses considerable problems within the criminal jurisprudence in general and in the field of victimology in particular.

In reality, the number of victims always being a 'dark figure' could be explained by the following:

- those involved may know that an offence has been committed, but are willing parties to it (e.g. illegal abortion, under-age sexual relations or drinking under age);
- the offender may know that he or she has committed a crime, but the victim may not be aware of it (e.g. shoplifting or sexual assaults on children);

- the non-reporting of offences is due to: 1 victims' fear, 2 feelings of helplessness and the perceived powerlessness of police, and 3 the threat of further retaliation by offender(s) and further victimisation from authorities (Kidd and Chayet, 1984);
- the police, with its discretionary power, may fail to record crimes simply because of lack of resources and power, and at times might have the view of not wanting to antagonise the general public by pursuing every single incident.

The costs of victimisation may include such things as damaged property, pain and suffering, time lost from work, and so forth. The explanation of victimisation depends on how the problem is being conceptualised (Siegel, 2007: 75): 1 victimisation precipitation theory asserts that victims provoke criminals either through active or passive precipitation; 2 lifestyle theory suggests that victims put themselves in danger by going out late at night or associating with peers of dubious character; 3 deviant place theory argues that victimisation is related to neighbourhood crime rate; and 4 routine activities theory maintains that a pool of motivated offenders exists and that these offenders will take advantage of unguarded or suitable targets.

Indeed, the treatment of victims depends on different victimological schools of thought. Some programmes help victims by providing court services, economic compensation, crisis intervention, public education and so forth. Some countries have even created a victim's bill of rights or victim's charter. Nevertheless, rather than relying on the justice system, victims are often left to fend for themselves in the community or through support from community groups for self-protection or rehabilitation. The relationship between community care and crime victim is not distant at all, to say the least.

The relationship between community care and crime victim

At first sight, both the terms 'community care' and 'crime victim' appear to be totally unrelated. While the former refers to health and social services being provided for those who require more care and support from others because they are elderly, mentally ill, mentally challenged or physically disabled (notably not crime victims), the latter refers to those persons who are at the receiving end of a crime as defined in the contemporary criminal justice system.

The concept of 'community care' (in the sector of health and welfare) generally aims to provide sufficient support to allow the individual to lead as normal a life as possible and to develop his or her ability to the maximum, resulting, it is hoped, in complete independence for the individual. However, the 'crime victim' (in the sector of criminal justice) is not placed at the centre since the system of justice is primarily concerned with the maintenance of rules of law, and not much with victims' interests or needs.

However, allowing the differences in aims, the two terms are not totally unrelated, particularly before the emergence of the modern criminal justice system (Harding, 1982). Victims in the past used to have greater involvement and to exert considerable influence throughout the conflict resolution in their own communities. Nowadays, community care is important, particularly to crime victims, not only because they are marginal members of the criminal justice system, but also because they are often the forgotten people in the field of social services or welfare provision. More crucially, in view of the government's current philosophy of welfare provision which aims to minimise its obligation, crime victims cannot expect much from the government's intervention on the basis of a collective well-being. Rather, individual crime victims have to solicit assistance from statutory programmes in the community and from non-government services rendered by those community groups or organisations entirely outside the criminal justice system.

In this respect, both the terms 'community care' and 'crime victim' become closely connected, particularly with the core problem of crime victims being their loss of social trust and their feeling of alienation from their community (Smale, 1984). This urgently calls for a redevelopment of 'community' which can be achieved through the mobilisation and integration of a diverse range of organised social resources, including both voluntary and state-financed (Clarke, 1982: 465–469). Indeed, the statutory victim programmes in the community and those voluntary efforts sustained by community groups or local volunteers have significant and complementary roles to play to help the crime victim.

Provision of victim programmes in Hong Kong

The major provision of victim programmes can be categorised: statutory provisions of both a Compensation Order, and Criminal and Law Enforcement Injuries Compensation, and voluntary efforts sustained by non-governmental organisations such as Harmony House for Battered Wives and Services for Sexually Assaulted Victims (see, for example, Tsun and Lui-Tsang, 2005; Chui and Fu, 2007).

Compensation Order

Since 1972, the use of court-ordered compensation has been the most direct way for offenders to recompense their victims. The courts can require the offenders to pay compensation to the victim for any injury, or loss of damage resulting from the offence of which he or she has been convicted and any other offence taken into consideration. The court has the power to ensure that the offender pays what he or she can afford, even if it is not what the victim is fully entitled to.

Both the *Criminal Procedure Ordinance* (Cap. 221) and *Magistrates Ordinance* (Cap. 227) provide the court with full power to compensate the victims of crime through the offenders. Section 73 of the *Criminal Procedure Ordinance* provides:

> Where a person is convicted of an offence, the court may, in addition to passing such sentence as may otherwise by law be passed or making an order under section 107(1), order the person so convicted to pay any aggrieved person such compensation for personal injury; loss of or damage to property; or both such injury and loss or damage; as it thinks reasonable.
>
> The amount ordered as compensation under subsection (1) shall be deemed a judgment debt due to the person entitled to receive the same from the person so convicted, and the order for payment of compensation may be enforced in such and the same manner as in the case of any costs or expenses ordered by the court to be paid under section 72.

Section 98 of the *Magistrates Ordinance* provides:

> Where a magistrate makes an order under section 36(1) or convicts a person of an offence and passes such sentence (if any) as may otherwise by law be passed, he may in addition to the order or sentence, order the offender to pay to any aggrieved person such compensation for personal injury; loss of or damage to property; or both such injury and loss or damage; not exceeding HK$100,000 as he thinks reasonable.

Unfortunately, figures related to the use of the orders are not systematically kept and are quite often difficult to obtain from the judiciary for in-depth analysis. The inherent constraints of this programme are obvious in at least three areas. First, a compensation order can only be imposed after the defendant has been convicted. Second, the offender's means to pay must be considered by the court. It is often difficult to make impoverished offenders comply with regulations, especially if payment extends over a long period of time. Finally, compensation orders are not awarded equitably. Crime victims of violent crimes are more frequently awarded compensation orders than victims of personal crimes of theft or crimes against households (e.g. burglary, theft from a vehicle, criminal damage to property). Perhaps the core problem is that crime victims do not regularly file for compensation claims because they are not aware of their legal right to do so.

Criminal and Law Enforcement Injuries Compensation scheme

The scheme was first introduced in May 1973. The scheme is operated by the Criminal and Law Enforcement Injuries Compensation Boards (the Boards) appointed by the then governor for decision making, and administratively serviced by the Social Welfare Department. The scheme aims to assume government responsibility for compensating victims sustaining personal injuries in crimes of violence and law enforcement exercises. The objective is to provide ex-gratia compensation to all qualifying victims or their dependants without an age limit, residential qualification, test of means, and on a non-contributory basis.

Specifically, the scheme administered by respective Boards provides monetary compensation to victims suffering personal injury arising out of the following: a crime of violence (including arson and poisoning); an arrest or attempted arrest of an offender or suspected offender; the prevention or attempted prevention of an offence; and the giving of help to any police officer or other person who is engaged in arresting or attempting to arrest an offender or suspected offender, or preventing or attempting to prevent an offence.

During the initial phase of implementation, only 282 applications (within the first ten months) were received in 1973. In the following three decades, the number of cases reached its peak (consistently around 1,000) throughout the 1980s. In the 1990s, it reduced slightly to between 650 and 950, and the total number of new cases paid each year was between 500 and 700. Notably, in the last 15 years, the number of applications has gradually decreased from 637 (2003/04) to 563 (2004/05) to 436 (2005/06) to 332 (2010/11) and finally to 237 (2013/14), which is the lowest since the launch of the scheme.

If victim compensation is an adequate gauge, the scheme appears to be a success. Yet, a number of shortcomings are apparent. First, compensation is paid only to claims of personal injury caused by crime. Property loss caused by property crimes, which constitute a significant proportion of reported crime, is not compensated. Second, the victim must not have contributed to their own injury, or have helped to cause the crime of which he or she is the victim. Thus, members of the Boards may be inclined to be more biased against those victims with criminal records or dubious character. Third, effective from December 1982, the scheme has been extended to victims of family violence, provided they follow strict prosecuting procedures before receiving compensation. Thus, the chance of family reunion would be discouraged. Fourth, victims are only eligible for compensation if they satisfy the Boards' requirement to report crimes to the police without reasonable delay. This practice is thought to be a government safeguard against fraudulent claims because it is assumed that the longer a victim waits to report a crime, the more complicated and, perhaps, dishonest the claims may be. Although members of the Boards cannot check the validity of claims or the circumstances surrounding the alleged offence, failure to report to and cooperate with the police could deter compensation or may even result in the amount being eventually reduced. Finally, the scheme has been criticised because only those crime victims with 'serious' injuries, as defined by medical examiners, have a real incentive to apply. 'Serious' injuries justifies a minimum of three days' sick leave from work. Although this rule does not apply to cases where the victim is killed or has sustained permanent disability, or where the victim sustained injury while trying to prevent crime, the effect is that the scheme does not encourage victims suffering 'less grievous' harm from applying for the compensation they deserve. This scheme's major shortfall could be related to the methodology employed by members of the Boards to award compensation. Rather than focusing on victims' needs, the Boards tend to support the notion that only those 'deserving' or 'innocent' victims warrant the government's sympathy. The end result is that the scheme is more of a symbolic gesture of pity for selected crime victims, rather than a panel that awards remuneration to all those who may be deserving. From the official statistics, the number of victims awarded compensation, in general, has been very limited as compared to those who are eligible to apply (see Tables 5.1 and 5.2).

House for battered spouses

The voluntary welfare sector has been more responsive to the growing incidence of broken homes and those problems experienced by victims of family violence, who are mostly the battered wives and/or their children. In early 1985, Harmony House, with its capacity of 40, was established to provide a retreat for women, with or without children, who are in immediate danger of violence. Its primary task is to provide for the safety of victims of violence and give them necessary financial and practical support, while the ultimate goal is to help battered spouses find the strength, self-confidence and resources to lead a life free from the threat of violence.

In late 1986, the government also began to assume its responsibility by running a similar place of refuge for victims, known as the Wai On Home for Women under the administration of the Social Welfare Department. The admission criteria, apart from battered spouses, are extended to girls aged 13 and over who are ill-treated or sexually molested, or in emotional crisis resulting from serious conflict with their parents or unexpected hospitalisation of parents or guardians. The designed capacity is 40, broadly categorised into the family section for spouses and children, and single-person section for girls at risk. In 1996, a similar establishment known as Serene Court (run by another non-governmental organisation, the Christian Family Service Centre) began its service for battered wives and abused children. The accommodation capacity is also 40.

All of the above houses operate around the clock. While the accommodation is offered free of charge, residents may be required to pay for their own meals and daily necessities. Battered women coming to stay with or without children and/or girls at risk or abused are given individual counselling and supportive group services. Essentially, this kind of victim programme is a crisis service, and the victims are anticipated to be reintegrated into their own families rather than creating a dependency role for the clients. The period of stay varies across victims. However, as an emergency service, the maximum period of residence is three months.

This victim programme fails to reach the vast majority of the victims. The number of admissions to Harmony House in the first three years was quite steady: 166 in 1987/88, 105 in 1988/89 and 141 in 1989/90; while the cases known to the Social Welfare Department were 685 in 1987/88, 433 in 1988/89

Table 5.1 Application for Criminal and Law Enforcement Injuries Compensation and total number of new paid cases

Year	*Applications for criminal injury (a)*	*Applications for law enforcement injury (b)*	*Total Applications (a)+(b)=(c)*	*Total no. of new cases paid*
1973/74	280	2	282	193
1974/75	719	3	722	362
1975/76	853	3	856	514
1976/77	623	–	623	475
1977/78	582	–	582	412
1978/79	546	–	546	325
1979/80	710	1	711	317
1980/81	900	1	901	410
1981/82	996	1	997	450
1982/83	1,300	–	1,300	545
1983/84	1,325	3	1,328	585
1984/85	1,192	3	1,195	656
1985/86	1,329	–	1,329	690
1986/87	1,117	–	1,117	931
1987/88	1,206	–	1,206	824
1988/89	1,138	1	1,139	887
1989/90	1,025	3	1,028	680
1990/91	1,094	3	1,097	801
1991/92	930	2	932	696
1992/93	766	3	769	686
1993/94	867	2	869	601
1994/95	979	–	979	707
1995/96	760	1	761	555
1996/97	800	–	800	568
1997/98	663	–	663	604
1998/99	760	–	760	557
1999/2000	756	–	756	447
2000/01	679	–	679	351
2001/02	589	–	589	388
2002/03	759	–	759	370
2003/04	637	–	637	325
2004/05	563	–	563	314
2005/06	436	–	436	305
2006/07	442	0	442	197

Year	*Applications for criminal injury (a)*	*Applications for law enforcement injury (b)*	*Total Applications (a)+(b)=(c)*	*Total no. of new cases paid*
2007/08	391	1	392	211
2008/09	409	0	409	163
2009/10	393	0	393	237
2010/11	332	0	332	176
2011/12	332	0	332	162
2012/13	285	0	285	146
2013/14	237	0	237	166

Source: Compiled from the *Annual Reports* of Criminal and Law Enforcement Injuries Compensation Boards, various issues.

and 252 in 1989/90 (Shin, 1990). However, starting from the early 1990s, rapid social changes began to have a great impact on families and marriages. Domestic violence became more serious than ever. From 1993 to 1997, the annual number of battered spouse cases soared from 198 to 491, representing a fivefold increase over five years on police records (Harmony House, 2005: 3). The number of battered-spouse cases, as reported by the Social Welfare Department, further rose from 1,171 in 1998 to 1,292 in 1999 (the first ten months) with 5% of cases involving wives attacking their husbands. The figures are alarming and believed to be just the tip of the iceberg, particularly starting from the turn of the century.

One sample survey recently conducted by the University of Hong Kong in 2006 (as part of the UN International Violence Against Women Survey) revealed that about 20% of Hong Kong women suffer at least one violent incident in their lifetime; 14% experience physical attacks, while 16% experience sexual violence (Faculty of Social Sciences, 2006). The survey further revealed that the city's annual physical and sexual violence victimisation rates (being 1.7% and 2.1%, respectively) were much higher than in the police and official crime reports. In response to the serious problem, the Jockey Club Harmony Link Domestic Violence Prevention Centre opened in 2006, funded by the Hong Kong Jockey Club Charities Trust and providing one-stop, integrated services for families affected by domestic violence.

Indeed, it is very difficult to know the full extent of violence against spouses, since it is probable that many incidents go unrecorded. This may occur because women and men feel ashamed or guilty about confessing that their marriage has gone wrong. Alternatively, they may fear that disclosure would probably lead to further attacks or that nothing can be done to help them. In short, the official statistics provide no more than an indication of the extent of the problem. The vast majority of victims could hardly be contacted or even helped. Such programmes could only be regarded as a humanitarian response to people in

Table 5.2 Breakdown of applications for criminal injuries compensation

Year	*91/92*	*92/93*	*93/94*	*94/95*	*95/96*	*96/97*	*97/98*	*98/99*	*99/00*	*00/01*	*01/02*	*02/03*	*03/04*	*04/05*	*05/06*	*06/07*	*07/08*	*08/09*	*09/10*	*10/11*	*11/12*	*12/13*	*13/14*
Application No.	930	766	867	979	760	800	663	760	756	679	589	759	637	563	436	442	391	409	393	332	332	285	237
Types of Violence																							
Homicide, Murder and Manslaughter	45 (91)	59 (125)	45 (95)	33 (90)	32 (81)	46 (95)	33 (92)	38 (57)	37 (76)	31 (52)	20 (69)	42 (78)	23 (61)	16 (41)	14 (39)	18 (35)	9 (35)	14 (37)	13 (51)	9 (32)	9 (22)	8 (38)	6 (59)
Robbery, Theft and Burglary	198 (1760)	157 (1628)	132 (1449)	130 (1520)	89 (1403)	92 (1039)	81 (782)	91 (866)	156 (946)	107 (791)	93 (802)	121 (939)	100 (673)	78 (495)	46 (382)	58 (375)	33 (325)	37 (305)	34 (254)	12 (210)	11 (190)	14 (156)	8 (101)
Assault and Wounding	670 (7032)	537 (6765)	656 (6854)	799 (7316)	622 (7879)	624 (7500)	517 (7507)	558 (7574)	535 (7832)	503 (7016)	457 (6906)	581 (7211)	492 (6 761)	458 (7 441)	370 (7 798)	355 (8715)	337 (8378)	348 (8242)	305 (7783)	309 (7137)	310 (6986)	253 (6852)	223 (6163)
Rape and Sexual Assault	3 (100)	4 (88)	3 (95)	3 (119)	4 (113)	6 (27)	5 (25)	6 (22)	7 (28)	9 (14)	8 (16)	8 (60)	4 (53)	4 (61)	2 (68)	3 (68)	4 (67)	1 (75)	3 (62)	1 (46)	1 (40)	5 (53)	0 (29)
Arson	4	1	17	5	8	23	12	55	7	26	5	1	9	0	2	1	0	1	2	0	0	0	0
Falling Object	10	8	14	7	5	5	10	10	12	3	5	4	7	5	2	1	7	8	36	1	1	1	0
Others	0 (92)	0 (96)	0 (126)	2 (68)	0 (95)	4 (137)	5 (109)	2 (128)	2 (139)	0 (119)	1 (113)	2 (120)	2 (87)	2 (113)	0 (95)	6 (142)	1 (134)	0 (134)	0 (158)	0 (133)	0 (109)	4 (89)	0 (60)
Remark of Family Violence	9	3	13	15	10	3	16	19	31	11	8	6	9	15	10	10	6	6	15	10	13	6	11

Source: Compiled from the *Annual Reports* of Criminal and Law Enforcement Injuries Compensation Boards, various issues.

Notes: Figures shown in brackets () represent the number of cases reported to the police. In police records, 'arson' and 'falling object' are grouped under 'others'.

trouble, the fulfilment of the psycho-social need of the victims, and an indispensable crisis service provided by groups of welfare personnel. This programme falls along the conservative lines of enquiry, focusing more on the psycho-social dimension, rather then seeing the more diffuse and subtle relationships of power and oppression between both sexes in society. From the official statistics, many victims rarely ask for assistance or compensation and, in fact, the number of cases involving family violence in the Criminal and Law Enforcement Compensation scheme has been surprisingly low for many years (see Table 5.2).

Services for sexual assault victims

Services to victims of rape were initiated by the Family Planning Association in 1977. The service was started for adolescents and young adults with problems concerning general sexual development as well as a victim programme specifically related to rape or sexual assault. Clients include victims of rape, indecent assault, incest, child abuse and so forth, who are referred by police, school, parents, social workers, friends or the client themselves. The association recorded 1,114 clients, with the average figure of about 80 per year from 1977 to 1989 (Kwan, 1990). From the early 1990s, the association was able to maintain more or less 100 cases every year until the turn of the century (see Table 5.3). The association eventually ceased this special service in July 2003 with the opening of a 24-hour one-stop Rape Crisis Centre by another service provider, Rainlily. However, the association, since 1979, has been greatly appreciated in catering for the sexual and reproductive health needs of the mentally or physically challenged, or persons with impaired hearing, who could be potential victims of abuse. From the service statistics, around a few hundred clients have been served annually in the last 25 years (see Table 5.4).

Other non-governmental organisations such as Against Child Abuse (formed in 1980), the Association Concerning Sexual Violence Against Women (formed in 1997) and the End Child Sexual Abuse Foundation (formed in 1998) are actively rendering a variety of services to those in need in society.

The service statistics or programmes indicate the extent of the seriousness of the problem of abuse in the community, and yet the services may fail to reach the vast majority of victims who feel too guilty or embarrassed to report the incidents to external bodies. Moreover, victims of sexual abuse or domestic violence can hardly be detected by others since a large number of indoor cases may occur in the victims' own homes and victims may be familiar with their abusers. Also, victims may feel stigmatised while they receive practical help or counselling. It is particularly true that in the present ethical and cultural context, rape or serious sexual assault, or indecent assault would bring disgrace, misfortune or guilt on the family and/or community.

In brief, this victim programme is generally considered to be a humanitarian response to people who are in trouble. It separates the problem from the psycho-social dimension of the individual rather than a re-examination of the

Table 5.3 Sexually assaulted victim service

	91/92	92/93	93/94	94/95	95/96	96/97	97/98	98/99	99/00	00/01	01/02	02/03	03/04 (Apr–Jul)
Case reporting													
Reported cases (known to police)	68	56	67	62	57	34	40	43	28	43	27	23	4
Unreported cases (not known to police)	37	56	48	29	47	45	54	65	71	77	59	44	16
	(105)	(112)	(115)	(91)	(104)	(79)	(94)	(108)	(99)	(120)	(86)	(67)	(20)
Types of sexual assault													
Acquaintance rape	36	42	31	44	45	18	34	46	37	54	41	39	10
Victim under drug/alcohol influence	-	-	-	-	12	23	27	16	13	32	16	13	4
Blitz rape	18	22	27	20	19	20	6	14	18	11	9	4	0
Suspected rape	14	12	16	7	9	6	13	11	5	10	6	3	2
Gang rape	9	8	5	3	4	3	4	7	4	2	1	1	0
Indecent assault	4	5	5	2	6	1	5	5	18	5	6	6	2
Drug rape	5	6	11	4	7	6	3	5	2	3	6	0	2
Incest	2	7	4	4	2	1	1	4	2	3	1	1	0
Buggery	9	2	1	4	–	1	1	–	–	–	–	–	–
Unspecified	8	8	15	3	–	–	–	–	–	–	–	–	–
Current age of victims													
Under 16	35	39	39	26	38	30	25	21	18	57	24	22	4
16–20	31	43	40	25	25	25	45	44	34	11	27	24	11
Over 20	39	30	36	40	41	24	24	43	37	47	34	17	5
	(105)	(112)	(115)	(91)	(104)	(79)	(94)	(108)	(89)	(115)	(85)	(63)	(20)

Source: Compiled from the *Annual Reports* of the Family Planning Association of Hong Kong, various issues.

Notes: As some victims reported more than one incident of assault, the number of victims does not equal the number of cases.

Table 5.4 Special sexual and reproductive health service for the disabled

Year	*96/97*	*97/98*	*98/99*	*99/00*	*00/01*	*01/02*	*02/03*	*03/04*	*04/05*	*05/06*	*06/07*	*07/08*	*08/09*	*09/10*	*10/11*	*11/12*	*12/13*	*13/14*	*14/15*
No. of clients	374	476	500	501	291	303	505	378	367	348	276	216	187	179	167	155	128	116	116

Source: Compiled from the *Annual Reports* of the Family Planning Association of Hong Kong, various issues.

Notes: Services specially catering for the sexual/reproductive health needs of people who are mentally or physically challenged, or have impaired hearing. Contraceptive advice, counselling and health services are rendered by counsellors, sign language interpreters and medical staff.

inadequacy of the justice system and structural or societal forces that constitute the social problem of sexual assault or abuse.

Examination of current ideologies of crime victim programmes

As a matter of fact, our crime victim programmes vary significantly in their objectives, structure, forms of help, target of victims and so forth. Generally speaking, the underlying ideological currents can be discerned, namely, a 'care' or 'welfare' ideology, a 'retributive' ideology and a 'rights-based' model.

'Care' or 'welfare' ideology

The first conceptual approach, known as the 'care' or 'welfare' model, is mainly based on the principle that the community should, as far as possible, absorb the burden of severe hardship suffered by individual citizens as a consequence of misfortunes such as illness, accident or unemployment. Emphasis is placed on providing for victims rather than on the criminal nature of the offence. The problems of crime victims are perceived to be a manifestation of stress, psychological trauma or economic need. No specific reference is made to the moral aspect of crime or to the punishment of the offender, providing that the victims' injuries or trauma are treated professionally and hardship is alleviated. The Criminal and Law Enforcement Injuries Compensation scheme, refuges for battered spouses, services for the victims of sexual assault, and other related social welfare services are typical examples.

The conceptual framework of the 'care' and 'welfare' model can be challenged on a number of grounds:

- Should the needs of crime victims be viewed as problems of a more general psychological or economic nature?
- Would these services avoid the unintended side-effect of generating expectations among victims which cannot be satisfied?
- Would these services be free from the stigmatising features of the established welfare institutions as victims might often be unduly labelled as persons in need of treatment?
- Indeed, victim programmes characterised by the 'care' ideology bear moralistic overtones and represent a form of charity act or a humanitarian response to people in trouble, and in no way will this model promote social justice for victims at all.

'Retributive' ideology

The second model is based on the principle that the offender should be punished in proportion to the seriousness of the offence. This approach advocates a punitive penal measure according to the damage inflicted on both victim and society, and considers compensation of the victim as one of the primary aims of sentencing. The use of compensation orders in court is a typical example.

While this kind of ideology seems to gain support from the public, it does not necessarily imply that victims share the same view of imposing punishment on the offenders. This model of practice does not answer the most pressing questions related to victims' desire for greater participatory rights within the criminal justice process.

'Rights-based' model

The 'rights-based' model has taken hold in Hong Kong for the past decade. The *Victims of Crime Charter* (Department of Justice, 1996) was first publicised through concerted efforts from various government departments such as the Hong Kong Police Force, Social Welfare Department, Judiciary, Department of Justice, Legal Aid Department, Independent Commission Against Corruption, Hospital Authority and Security Branch.

As defined by the charter, a victim is a person 'who suffers physical or emotional harm, or loss or damage to property, as a direct result of a criminal offence'. The definition covers 'anyone who has suffered directly from the commission of the offence [which] may include, for example, the parent of a child who has been sexually abused or the immediate family of a murder victim'. The charter sets out both the duties and rights of victims. Victims have a duty to help maintain law and order such as abiding by the law, taking proper precautions, reporting crime, giving assistance to the police and attending court as witnesses. On the other hand, victims have their rights: 1 to be treated with courtesy and respect; 2 to receive a proper response to complaints of crime; 3 to information including reporting the crime, investigation and prosecution; 4 to access proper court facilities; 5 to be heard in court; 6 to seek protection; 7 to privacy and confidentiality; 8 to property; 9 to access support and aftercare; and 10 to seek compensation. In this model, the ideal would be that victims have the opportunity to influence the key decision in dealing with the victimisation experience, not simply as witnesses in law courts against the offender.

Regrettably, the definition of victim is largely confined to the legal framework or criminal justice system. The charter (despite revisions by the Department of Justice in early 2000, 2003 and 2007) seems to be simply a workplace moral guideline for personnel within the criminal justice process. No legal jurisdiction has been made to safeguard those who are not fully exercising their power. The charter has no legal status at all, and courts in this jurisdiction cannot be compelled to accept any impact statement from the victim.

Could the criminal justice personnel involved be more humanised so as to address victims' needs and rights? Public education and wide publicity of the charter are indispensable. The latest crime victimisation survey (Census and Statistics Department, 1999: 20) revealed that only 8% of persons aged 12 or above had heard of the charter, and the major channel was through the mass media, such as television (66%), newspapers (20%) and radio (17%). Notably, the channels had rarely been made known to victims from the professionals within the system or related community organisations at the time of the survey.

By contrast, much less attention is paid to victims despite them making a major contribution such as reporting crime to the police, detecting unlawful acts, providing evidence and so forth. Quite often, they need a great deal of support from family and friends after their traumatic experiences, with particular regard to crimes of violence. The costs of victimisation are not simply time lost from work, property loss or damage, physical injury and the like. Some victims may begin to suffer depression and low self-esteem. It is probable that they may shy away and lose confidence in the justice system.

In short, victims' needs and feelings are ignored by professionals at various criminal justice stages. The victim, in general, has no accepted role to play other than being functionally and legally 'just another witness in court' (Shapland, 1982: 21–23), despite the fact that the place of victims within the system has been addressed through the introduction of the *Victim's Charter* in England and Wales (Home Office, 1986, 1988, 1990, 2001).

It is noticeable that the provision of victim programmes in Hong Kong is characterised by their diversity in theoretical assumptions, objectives, selection criteria of victims, forms of help, sources of referral, year of establishment and organisational bases, financial sources and so forth. For instance, the Criminal and Law Enforcement Injuries Compensation scheme aims to compensate victims for personal injuries resulting from violent crimes; the Compensation Order aims to compensate victims for injury, loss or damage by the offender through the monetary payment from offenders; the refuges for battered spouses endeavour to provide voluntary short-term practical assistance and psychosocial help to victims; the services to victims of rape aim to reduce clients' anxieties and fears. However, the current major provision of victim programmes seems to be hampered by the absence of a sound philosophical basis for action.

None of the current practice models can be considered satisfactory: namely, the 'care' or 'welfare' model, being typified by refuges for battered spouses, services to victims of rape, and criminal and law enforcement injuries compensation schemes; the 'retributive' model, being demonstrated by the Compensation Order; and the 'rights-based' model, seen in the *Victims of Crime Charter*. The first model symbolises an act of charity or a humanitarian response to people in trouble, and in no way can this promote social justice. The second model focuses on punishing the offender without genuine consideration of victims' needs and participatory rights within the criminal justice process. The third model has no legal status or jurisdiction at all throughout the entire criminal justice process.

Perhaps what is needed is a comprehensive review of victim programmes and a debate or discussion on the underlying philosophical framework prior to action. A combination of a humanised criminal justice system and a network of outreach victim support with a strong input from the local community could be just the starting point (van Dijk, 1988), and research findings tend to support that 'a guiding principle for working with victims of crime is inter-agency partnership, and this at least will provide some grounds for optimism in the search for more effective public policy for crime victims in the next decade' (Davis, 2003: 119).

Finally, attention should be paid to the fact that crime victims have their rights to both remedial and restorative services aimed at addressing the difficulties and inconveniences caused by crime. It would be worthwhile considering some kinds of mediation or reparation practices as well as innovative services for both the victim and offender, with the ultimate goal of achieving restoration in society (Braithwaite, 1998; Fattah and Peters, 1998).

The way ahead

The 'rights-based' model that has taken hold in Hong Kong, as evidenced by the *Victims of Crime Charter*, is the starting point of victim protection. It is hoped that the charter will be given legal status in due course. On the other hand, the courts and the general public may wish to consider that instead of simply imposing punishment on wrong-doers, there is a growing concern about restorative justice which emphasises restitution as a means of restoring both parties, and reconciliation of both parties is considered an important goal (Umbreit, 1995, 1999, 2001; Wright, 1999; Morris and Maxwell, 2001; Weitekamp and Kerner, 2003).

Victims of crime, despite their unforgettable victimisation experiences, are human beings in need of love, respect and care throughout the justice process. They would no longer be the forgotten people in society if we were all to aim for the well-being of victims through cooperation among professionals and volunteers heading for the goal of restoration. I believe that this is highly desirable in the course of reconstructing a caring, harmonious and civilised community.

From the victim's perspective, there is a great need for a paradigm shift from the current retributive justice to restorative justice. The basic differences between these two models, as Zehr (1995) and Zehr and Harry (1998) have respectively pointed out, are summarised in Table 5.5.

The proposed shift of paradigm (from retributive justice to restorative justice) puts a great emphasis on the process whereby all parties with a stake in a particular offence come together to resolve collectively how to deal with the aftermath of the offence and its implications for the future (Marshall, 1998: 32).

Put simply, restorative justice programmes encourage the voluntary efforts brought forward by the victims, offender, their families and community representatives. They arrange to meet one another so as to bring about reconciliation between the two sides of the offence or victimisation. In some countries like Australia, both the police and the court, as a form of youth justice model, can even refer cases to a community or youth justice conference, for young people

Table 5.5 Retributive and restorative justice

Retributive justice	*Restorative justice*
Wrong as a violation of rules	Wrong as violation of people, relationships
Wrongs create guilt	Wrongs create liabilities and obligations
Crime seen as categorically different from other harms	Crime recognised as related to other harms and conflicts
Focus on past	Focus on future
Debt paid by taking punishment	Restitution as a means of restoring both parties
Imposition of pain to punish and deter	Harm by offender balanced by making right
Harm by offender balanced by harm to offender	Harm by offender balanced by making right
Offender denounced	Harmful act denounced
Justice serves to divide	Justice aims at bringing together
Victim's needs and rights ignored	Victim's needs and rights central
Ignores social, economic and moral contest of behaviour	Total context relevant
Process alienates	Process aims at reconciliation
State monopoly on response to wrongdoing	Victim, offender and community roles acknowledged
Community on side-line, represented abstractly by state	Community as facilitator in restorative process

(aged ten to 16 inclusive) when they break the law (Chui et al., 2005). The outcome of conferencing based on extensive literature review has been quite encouraging (Hayes and Daly, 2003), and the general impression is that getting both parties of an offence involved in the reconciliation process enables them to face the consequences of victimisation or assume active responsibility for their offending behaviour (Hayes and Daly, 2003).

The above-suggested use of offender–victim mediation and reparation schemes is the initial step in the course of advocating restorative justice and might be considered at different stages of the justice process. The suggestion could be justified on two grounds: victims have a greater involvement in the process, and offenders have the chance to appreciate the impact of their crime and to provide reparation in a much wider sense, such as restoring stolen property to the victim, repairing damage inflicted on the victim's property, performing services for a victim, a group of crime victims generally or the community at large, and making an apology (oral and/or written) to the victim of the offence. Theoretically speaking, the model could be beneficial to both parties from the rehabilitative perspective.

From the victim's perspective, he or she may gain material compensation for the loss incurred, other than the monetary payment. In addition, the victim may benefit in psychological terms from meeting the offender. Fear or feelings of insecurity may fade away upon visualising that the 'offender' was recognisably human after all, with sympathetic problems and emotions. It would also give the victim a chance to feel a certain reintegration into the community after understanding the circumstances leading to the offence, the psycho-social make-up of the criminal, and the way of helping the criminal to reform.

From the offender's viewpoint, reparation may encourage the criminal to accept responsibility for the misdeed or harm inflicted on the victim, to face the reality of the crime that has been committed without resorting to such self-defence as neutralisation techniques (Siegel, 2007), to understand the impact on victimisation and have a positive attitude or behaviour change accordingly.

Furthermore, the use of victim-offender encounter groups could be considered as mediation initiatives in the post-sentence stage. Distinctive from normal 'own offender' and 'own victim' methods of mediation or reparation, this kind of encounter-group model involves the meeting of offenders (particularly of burglary) with unrelated victims through the creative use of therapeutic group processes and dynamics. The main purpose is to provide adequate opportunities for two parties to challenge each other's prejudices, stereotypes and rationalisation related to the offence. This model has two merits: in terms of group composition, it involves 'voluntary' offenders and a variety of victims of solved, unsolved and unreported crimes; and in terms of optimal timing of group encounter, both parties are able to decide when they feel ready to meet each other, because there are great individual differences in recovery from victimisation, and thus an honest exchange is seen.

The above proposals are simply some suggested innovative programmes for consideration. In full recognition of various thought-provoking practice models of restorative justice (particularly in youth justice, see Adorjan and Chui, 2014 for more information) as documented and submitted to the Security Bureau (Lo et al., 2003, 2005), it is the right time to place 'victims of crime' at the centre of further thought. It is an important step believed to be in the right direction of victim protection or a restoration movement in Hong Kong.

The development of victim programmes in Hong Kong seems to be much affected by the absence of a sound philosophical basis for action. Frustrated by the criminal justice policy in contemporary society (which is essentially retributive), an alternative model, which protects the community and makes sure that the offender is held responsible in a constructive way, is therefore suggested. This model, broadly known as 'restorative justice', could be the guiding philosophical framework in the future. I hope that this chapter will lead to further discussion on the use of restorative justice while working with victims of crime, who are equally important participants in the justice process. Whether or not it is a myth or reality depends much on our perception, attitude and our devotion to making it possible.

Review questions

1 Why is the definition of 'crime victim' so controversial in the field of criminology or victimology?
2 What is the relationship between community care and a crime victim?
3 Compare and contrast the strengths and weaknesses of various victim programmes in Hong Kong.
4 Should the *Victims of Crime Charter* be improved along the line of restorative justice?

References

Adorjan, M. and Chui, W.H. (2014) *Responding to Youth Crime in Hong Kong: Penal Elitism, Legitimacy and Citizenship*, Abingdon: Routledge.

Braithwaite, J. (1998) *Restorative Justice: Assessing an Immodest Theory and a Pessimistic Theory*, Canberra, ACT: Australian National University.

Census and Statistics Department (1979, 1982, 1987, 1990, 1995, 1999) *Crime and its Victim in Hong Kong*, Hong Kong: Government Printer.

Chui, W.H. and Fu, X. (2007) 'Victim's rights and protection in the Hong Kong criminal justice system', in H. Zhang (ed.) *Studies on Victim Protections* (pp. 267–297), Beijing: Court Press (in Chinese).

Chui, W.H., Kidd, J. and Preston, C. (2005) 'Treatment of child and juvenile offenders in Queensland, Australia', in T.W. Lo, D.S.W. Wong and G. Maxwell (eds) *Alternatives to Prosecution: Rehabilitative and Restorative Models of Youth Justice* (pp. 171–205), Singapore: Marshall Cavendish Academic.

Clarke, M. (1982) 'Where is the community which cares?', *British Journal of Social Work*, 20(2): 459–469

Cohen, S. (1973) 'The failures of criminology', *The Listener*, November 8: 622–625.

Colvin, G. (1988) 'Report on the 7th United Nation Congress on the Prevention of Crime and the Treatment of Offenders', *Crime and Social Justice*, 25: 55–61.

Daigle, L.E. (2013) *Victimology: The Essentials*, Thousand Oaks, CA: Sage.

Davis, P. (2003) 'Crime victims and public policy', in P. Davis, P. Francis and V. Jupp (eds) *Victimization: Theory, Research and Policy* (pp. 101–120), London: Palgrave Macmillan.

Department of Justice (1996, 2000, 2003, 2007) *The Victims of Crime Charter*, Hong Kong: Government Printer.

European Committee on Crime Problems (1984) *Research on Victimization* (Collected Studies in Criminological Research), Strasbourg: Council of Europe.

Faculty of Social Sciences (2006) *Press Release – United Nations International Violence Against Women Survey: The Hong Kong Part*, Hong Kong: Faculty of Social Sciences, The University of Hong Kong.

Family Planning Association of Hong Kong (various issues) *Annual Reports*, Hong Kong: Family Planning Association of Hong Kong.

Fattah, E. and Peters, T. (1998) *Support for Victims of Crime in a Comparative Perspective*, Leuver: Leuver University Press.

Harding, J. (1982) *Victims and Offenders: Needs and Responsibilities* (NCVO Occasional Paper No. 2), London: Bedford Square.

Harmony House (2005) *Annual Report of 2004/2005*, Hong Kong: Harmony House.

Hayes, H. and Daly, K. (2003) 'Youth justice conference and re-offending', *Justice Quarterly*, 20(4): 725–764.

Home Office (1986) *Criminal Justice: A Working Paper*, London: Home Office.

Home Office (1988) *Victims of Crime* (Home Office Circular 20), London: Home Office.

Home Office (1990) *Victim's Charter: A Statement of the Rights of Victim*, London: Home Office.

Home Office (2001) *A Review of the Victim's Charter*, London: Home Office.

Kidd, R.F. and Chayet, E.F. (1984) 'Why do victims fail to report? The psychology of criminal victimisation', *Journal of Social Issues*, 40(1): 39–50.

Kwan, M. (1990) 'Service rendered by the Family Planning Association of Hong Kong to sexually assaulted victims', in F. Cheung, R. Andry and R. Tam (eds) *Research on Rape and Sexual Crime in Hong Kong* (pp. 47–51), Hong Kong: Institute of Asia-Pacific Studies, The Chinese University of Hong Kong.

Lo, T.W., Wong, D.S.W. and Maxwell, G. (2003) *Measures Alterative to Prosecution for Handling Unruly Children and Youth Persons: Overseas Experiences and Options for Hong Kong* (Report submitted to the Security Bureau of Hong Kong SAR Government), Hong Kong: Youth Studies Net, City University of Hong Kong.

Lo, T.W., Wong, D.S.W. and Maxwell, G. (eds) (2005) *Alternatives to Prosecution: Rehabilitative and Restorative Models of Youth Justice*, Singapore: Marshall Cavendish Academic.

Marshall, T. (1998) *Restorative Justice: An Overview*, St Paul, MN: Centre for Restorative Justice and Mediation, University of Minnesota.

Morris, A. and Maxwell, G. (eds) (2001) *Restorative Justice for Juveniles: Conferencing, Mediation and Circles*, Oxford: Hart Publishing.

Schwendinger, H. and Schwendinger, J. (1970) 'Defenders of order or guardian of human right?', *Issues in Criminologist*, 5(2): 148–152.

Shapland, J. (1982) 'The victim in the criminal justice system', *Home Office Research Bulletin*, 14: 21–23.

Shin, K. (1990) 'Battered spouse: A community responsibility?', Address at Annual General Meeting of Harmony House on 28 September 1990, Hong Kong.

Siegel, L.J. (2007) *Criminology: Theories, Patterns, and Typologies* (9th edn), Belmont, CA: Wadsworth/Thomson Learning.

Smale, G.J.A. (1984) 'Psychological effects behavioural changes in the cases of victims of serious crime', in R. Block (eds.) *Victimization and Fear of Crime: World Perspectives* (pp. 87–92), Washington, DC: US Department of Justice.

Sutherland, E. (1949) *White Collar Crime*, New York: Dryden Press.

Tsun, A.O.-K. and Lui-Tsang, P.S.-K. (2005) 'Violence against wives and children in Hong Kong', *Journal of Family and Economic Issues*, 26(4): 465–486.

Umbreit, M. (1995) 'The development and impact of victim offender mediation in the United States', *Mediation Quarterly*, 12(3): 263–276.

Umbreit, M. (1999) *The Handbook on Justice for Victims*, New York: United Nations.

Umbreit, M. (2001) *The Handbook of Victim/Offender Mediation: An Essential Guide to Practice and Research*, San Francisco, CA: Josey Boss.

United Nations (1999a) *Guide for Policy Makers on the Implementation of the United Nations Declaration of Basic Principles of Justice for Victims of Crime and Abuse of Power*, New York: United Nations.

United Nations (1999b) *Handbook on Justice for Victims: On the Use and Application of the Declaration of Basic Principles of Justice for Victims of Crime and Abuse of Power*, New York: United Nations.

van Dijk, J. (1988) 'Ideological trends within the victims movement: An international perspective', in M. Maguire and J. Pointing (eds) *Victims of Crime: A New Deal* (pp. 115–126), Milton Keynes: Open University Press.

Walklate, S. (eds) (2011) *Handbook of Victims and Victimology*, Abingdon: Routledge.

Weitekamp, E.G.M. and Kerner, H.-J. (eds) (2003) *Restorative Justice in Context: International Practice and Directions*, Cullompton: Willan.

Wright, M. (1999) *Restoring Respect for Justice: A Symposium*, Winchester: Waterside Press.

Zehr, H. (1995) *Changing Lenses*, Scottdale, PA: Herald Press.

Zehr, H. and Harry, M. (1998) 'Fundamental concepts of restorative justice', *Contemporary Justice Review*, 1(1): 47–55.

Legislation cited

Criminal Procedure Ordinance (Cap. 221)
Magistrates Ordinance (Cap. 227)

Useful websites

Community Justice & Reconciliation www.restorativejustice.org
International Victimology Institute of Tilburg www.victimology.nl
National Association of Community and Restorative Justice nacrj.org
National Centre for Victims of Crime victimsofcrime.org
The Victims of Crime Charter (Hong Kong) www.doj.gov.hk/eng/public/pub200004.htm
World Society of Victimology www.worldsocietyofvictimology.org/#

6

PUBLIC PERCEPTIONS OF CRIME AND SAFETY

Maggy Lee and Michael Adorjan

Introduction

The study of public perceptions and reactions towards crime has become prominent in the criminology of 'fear of crime' since the 1980s. As Smith suggested in one of the early formulations of the concept, fear of crime broadly refers to 'an emotional response to a threat: an admission to self and others that crime is intimidating; and an expression of one's sense of danger and anxiety at the prospect of being harmed' (Smith, 1987: 2).

There is now a rich tradition in criminology that typically revolves around the study of the prevalence, distribution and multifaceted meanings and experiences of crime fears as being related to 'people' (e.g., the socio-demographics, social relations and identities of people with crime concerns), 'places' (e.g., spatial or structural contextual conditions that shape crime concerns), or 'problems' (e.g., social exclusion, unemployment, poverty, environmental planning) (Innes, 2014: 5–6; see also Pain, 2000). In societies where high levels of crime have become a routine social fact (Skogan, 1990; Garland, 2001; Farrall et al., 2009), public concerns about crime may spur moral panics signalling wider anxieties about social order, underscoring boundaries of 'us' (respectable, law-abiding society) versus 'them' (the criminals, social deviants) (Cohen, 2002 [1972]; Goode and Ben-Yehuda, 2009). In many Anglo-Western societies such as the USA and the UK, fears tend to focus on stereotypical 'others' on the margins of society whose presence threatens mainstream life and values. As Garland (1996: 461) has pointed out in relation to 'criminologies of the other', the association of danger with the 'threatening outcast, the fearsome stranger, the excluded and the embittered', is also invoked by politicians to 'govern through' the fear of crime (Simon, 2007; see also Roberts et al., 2003). To what extent can these criminological insights help us make sense of social reactions to crime and public sentiments about safety in low-crime societies beyond Anglo-Western contexts?

This chapter examines public perceptions of crime and disorder in Hong Kong. Hong Kong has consistently been described as one of the safest cities in the world and was ranked 11th out of 50 global cities in terms of overall safety in the 2015 *The Economist* Safe Cities Index (Economist Intelligence Unit, 2015). According to official figures, Hong Kong's crime rate per 100,000 population in 2012 was 1,061. 'Though higher than that of Singapore (584), the figure was lower than those of Paris (10,455), London (9,500), New York (2,361) and Tokyo (1,387). This indicate[s] that the overall law and order situation in Hong Kong [is] rather good when compared with other major cities' (Hong Kong Police press release, 28 January 2014, 'Overall law and order situation further improved in 2013'). On the surface, Hong Kong does not exhibit the conventional signs of disorder which may point to crime and social decline central to the oft-cited 'broken window thesis' in other high-crime societies (cf. Wilson and Kelling, 1982). There are 'very few outward signs of grave physical disorder such as public drinking and vandalism. In Hong Kong, people do not write on the walls or drink in public' (La Grange, 2011: 1190). Against this background, the subject of fear of crime has been 'virtually unexplored' in Hong Kong (Chui et al., 2012: 479). So what do people in Hong Kong actually think and feel about crime and disorder? Do they feel safe, and if not, why not?

This chapter aims at providing some pointers to researchers and students interested in understanding public perceptions about crime as a social issue. Our starting point is that public sentiments and perceptions about safety are not a simple correlate of overall crime levels and aggregate crime rates. Instead, people's sense of security is influenced by crime as well as what they perceive as troubling behaviours and disorderly environments that send 'signals' (Innes, 2004, 2014) to them about the distribution of risks and threats in particular locales. Furthermore, people's fear of crime is multifaceted, changeable, and embedded in the local details of individuals' circumstances and everyday experiences in their neighbourhood and beyond. As Pain (2000: 368) suggests, 'we all move in and out of shades of fear over our life courses, influenced by our own experiences and by spatial, social and temporal situation'. In the rest of this chapter, we provide a brief review of the existing (largely quantitative) studies of crime victimisation and public perceptions of safety in Hong Kong. We then draw on the findings of our focus group study on fear of crime in Hong Kong in order to understand what citizens think and feel about dangerous 'others' and anti-social behaviour through their 'crime talk' (Sasson, 1995). We conclude by highlighting the potential of the 'signal crimes perspective' (Innes, 2014) in providing new directions for understanding the situated and local nature of people's crime fears and perceptions of safety in Hong Kong.

Hong Kong as a safe city?

With just over 7 million residents living within its 426 square miles, Hong Kong boasts one of the lowest rates of violent crime and victimisation in the world (63.4 homicides per year on average from 1991 to 2011) (Broadhurst et al., 2007: 11; Jones and Vagg, 2007).[1] The overall crime rate, highest during the 1980s, has continued to decline into the 1990s and post-colonial period (UN HABITAT, 2007; see also Broadhurst et al., Chapter 4 of this volume). In 2014, the overall crime rate dropped to a record low of 936 per 100,000 population (South China Morning Post, 2015). By and large, official data confirm Hong Kong's international reputation as 'one of the safest cities in the twenty-first century' (see Chapter 4, this volume, for a detailed explication).

Other quantitative data provide a similar picture about the low level of crime victimisation (Broadhurst et al., 2007: 10–11). These surveys focus on levels of victimisation but not public concerns about crime per se. A more useful study was the 2006 United Nations International Crime Victim Survey (UNICVS) which included Hong Kong. The survey indicated that overall Hong Kong citizens rated slightly below the international average regarding their perceived likelihood of being robbed, and significantly lower regarding fear of street crime (Broadhurst et al., 2010). Specifically, the 2006 UNICVS findings indicate 93% of Hong Kong residents felt 'very' or 'fairly safe' walking alone in their own neighbourhood at night (Broadhurst et al., 2007: 16). This is in striking contrast to international research which often relates higher levels of fear of crime to the unknown that 'lurks' behind the veil of darkness at night (Warr, 1990; Enders et al., 2008).

However, Hong Kong's overall low levels of crime victimisation and crime fears must be qualified in terms of differences across gender, age and class. Findings from the 2006 UNICVS reveal that 'females are significantly more likely to become victims of theft in Hong Kong ... than males', and that 'women are more likely than men to be assaulted in a domestic context' (Broadhurst et al., 2010: xx). Official victimisation surveys dating back to the colonial period also repeatedly suggest that women are more likely to be victims of personal crimes than men (see Leung, 2001: 44). Broadhurst and colleagues (2007: 11) report that 'overall, women are more at risk of personal theft and violence, but males have higher risks of violent offences in the 12–19 years age group and women in the 40–49 age group. Violent and personal crime victimization peaks for either sex in the younger 12–19 age groups'.

The 2006 UNICVS was the first major crime survey in Hong Kong to examine public fear of crime. Similar to other international surveys, its gauge of crime fear was based on two questions – one related to concern about being burgled in one's home, and the other related to concern about walking on the streets near one's home at night. Respondents were asked, 'What would you say are the chances that over the next twelve months someone will try to break into your home? Do you think this is very likely, likely or not likely?' (Broadhurst et al., 2010: 33). The findings further underscore public perceptions of Hong Kong as a comparatively safe city. The survey reports that 'nearly three-quarters (71.8%) felt it was unlikely that their home would be burgled in the coming year' (ibid.). Slightly more females (30.5%) than males (25.6%) indicated they feel being burgled is 'likely' or 'very likely' over the next year, and slightly more of those aged 55 and over (23%) indicated the same level of concern as opposed to those aged 25 to 34 (34.3%) (ibid.: 34).

Fear of crime was also assessed in the 2006 UNICVS by asking respondents, 'How safe do you feel walking alone in your area after dark? Do you feel very safe, fairly safe, a bit unsafe, or very unsafe?' (Broadhurst et al., 2010: 35). As summarised above, 'only 5.6% of respondents indicat[ed] that they felt "a bit" or "very unsafe" in the street after dark' (ibid.). This is significantly lower than the international average of 32% among main cities surveyed (ibid.). While age had no significant effect on fear of street crime, females expressed greater concern than males (7.1% vs. 3.8%, respectively) (ibid.: 34). As for socio-economic status, the 2006 UNICVS found that respondents 'from the lowest household income group (less than HK$10,000) felt significantly more "unsafe" in the street than respondents from other income groups. Yet the poorest respondents were those least likely to have been victims of street crimes' (ibid.: 35).

Although victimisation surveys are an important source of information about the hidden figure of crime (i.e. when compared to official crime statistics), they have inherent limitations. Scholars have pointed to a number of epistemological and operational issues in quantitative approaches to the study of crime and the fear of crime in particular. As Rachel Pain (2000: 368) has argued:

> Most fundamental is that 'quick tick' surveys are used inappropriately to quantify human behaviour, given the psychosocial complexities of experiencing and fearing crime. This not only arguably promotes errors in reporting but also exacerbates the tendency for survey analysis to relate what is measured – present-day fear of crime – solely to individuals' immediate social or environmental circumstances.

Victimisation surveys also tend to be under-theorised and reveal little about the complexities of people's feelings about crime and disorder and how individual reactions to personal troubles may in fact be inextricably linked to public issues of social changes, relations and divisions. For example, Leung's (2001) quantitative study of fear and risk perception among 124 subjects found that in general, women held statistically significant higher levels of fear than men over robbery/mugging, pickpocketing and rape. Not surprisingly, the largest gap in gender differences in fear of personal crimes was over rape (ibid.: 26). Leung also found that a higher proportion of women (79.1%) than men (52.6%) claimed to avoid unsafe places during daytime; the majority of women (95.5%) also indicated their avoidance of unsafe areas at night, with only 71.9% of men making the same claim (ibid.: 28). Leung concluded that women's higher level of fear is 'rational … due to the high victimization rate' (ibid.: 48). The gendered nature of crime fears was also found in a recent survey of university social work students, which concluded that female students 'showed significantly greater fear of all crimes except for fear of "being cheated, conned, or swindled out of your money"' (Chui et al., 2012: 486). Fear of rape and sexual assault was identified as a 'prime concern' for the female students sampled and a 'significant predictor of fear of other crimes' (ibid.: 488–9). While these findings are broadly consistent with international research (Warr, 1985; but see Gilchrist et al., 1998; Scott, 2003; Rader and Haynes, 2011), they leave many important questions unanswered – for example, how gendered meanings of fear and fearlessness about particular types of crime are culturally produced and locally situated.

In order to explore the context and culturally specific 'thick descriptions' (Geertz, 1973; see also Fraser, Chapter 7, this volume) of crime and safety, we examined public understandings of crime through a series of focus group discussions conducted in different neighbourhoods of Hong Kong.[2] As many researchers have suggested, focus groups are useful in unpacking the 'situated character' of experience within the 'practical and mundane contexts' of people's everyday lives (Sparks et al., 2001: 888; see also Madriz, 1997; Morgan, 1997; Stewart et al., 2007).

Between 2011 and 2013, we conducted 30 focus groups with a total of 156 discussants. The groups were conducted in a range of geographical locations including Hong Kong Island, Kowloon, the New Territories and some outlying islands. We covered a wide spectrum of demographic and socio-economic groups, for example, age, gender, employment, those living in private and public housing, middle-class communities, satellite towns and areas near the Hong Kong–Mainland China border. The groups ranged from three to eight members. Half of our discussants were aged 16–29 and 42% of our discussants were aged 30–59, with a few in the retired age group. Half the sample had a junior-secondary education while 21% of them held a Bachelor's university degree qualification. In terms of occupation, the highest percentage of discussants (37%) were in full-time paid work, with the second highest (27%) being students, followed by housewives (16%). Only 3% of the sample were unemployed. We asked them about their impressions of Hong Kong in terms of safety and security, crime, and policing.[3] Overall, we are interested in identifying a sociologically informed approach to understand what local citizens think and feel about crime and safety, and the social meaning of their crime fears amidst broader changes and social tensions played out in different locales.

Signal crimes and signal disorders

Our research indicates, overall, that participants felt Hong Kong is a 'safe city' and did not feel frightened of crime. This was the case even when respondents have had personal experiences of victimisation, including pickpocketing (22 cases), theft (16 cases) and fraud (11 cases). However, feelings of unsafety do not emerge solely from direct experiences of victimisation, nor only from events formally defined as crime (Enders et al., 2008: 199; Farrall et al., 2009: 74). Here, the 'signal crimes' perspective developed by Martin Innes (2014) is particularly instructive:

> The signal crimes perspective provides an optic for viewing social reactions to crime, disorder, and control, and how public perceptions and reactions gravitate around particular incidents. Stated simply, it maintains that some events matter more than others in terms of their impact upon individual and collective security because of how they symbolize wider social problems.
>
> (Innes, 2014: 22)

According to Innes (2014), 'signal disorders' that can be anticipated to indicate the presence of particular risks, opportunities and threats are often stronger and more coherent triggers for public concerns than the types of crime that the criminal justice system tends to focus upon. More specifically, he identified two types of signal disorders – 'social signal disorders', which are types of behaviour that breach situated conventions of social order (for example, groups of rowdy youths), and 'physical signal disorders', which are instances of physical damage and deliberate environmental degradation (for example, vandalised public utilities, graffiti or large amounts of litter in public spaces) (ibid.: 12–14). Seen in this light, signal disorders exemplify not only broader socio-economic conditions and cultural changes in the society but also the resulting sensitised tensions that are played out differently in particular neighbourhoods.

Even where the problem is ostensibly criminal, such as drug related, people's concerns are often directed at criminal incidents as well as the health and safety risks caused by drug users. For example, some female focus groups expressed concern over 'head bashing' robberies involving drug users ('You don't know what they are holding. Suddenly they may rob us because they don't have money, like crazy men, I am afraid of that'). Other focus group participants living in public housing estates and subdivided units in industrial buildings were more concerned about quality of life environmental issues associated with drug use, such as blocked fire exits, discarded syringes, strangers loitering and poor lighting.

Physical and social signal disorders in a neighbourhood function as a visible index of safety, as they convey a sense of the distribution of risks across social space. Significantly, signals are not interpreted in isolation from each other (Innes, 2014: 13–14). As citizens encounter a number of individually 'weak' signal disorders within the local neighbourhood, the accumulation of these signals amplifies the overall impact upon how they view the area:

> I have a lot of people living above me in the building. They would throw all kinds of things out of the window, like cigarette stubs. I live on low-level floors and on the balcony, I can find all kinds of things. Sometimes things thrown down will set a fire. Those living upstairs would even throw a knife out of the window. I wonder if they are crazy!
>
> (Male focus group, aged 30s and 40s)

The volume and types of physical detritus and incivilities in public spaces frame the impressions that local residents have of the neighbourhood situation. Individually, the instances of physical disorder may not be consequential, but their cumulative presence serves as a cue about the state of the local social order:

> I see these 40 or 50 year-old men gambling instead of going to work. Doesn't matter how many local police officers there are, it is still insufficient. The police can't stand guard here everyday ... This problem is, how shall I put it, the society is not healthy, the social values are not good. It makes each household not able to live in harmony, kids can't study well, it drags down the neighbourhood.
>
> (Female focus group, aged 40s and 50s)

In appraising crime and safety in Hong Kong, people constantly react to and make sense of a range of crime incidents as well as disorder problems which are troubling but not necessarily illegal. Taken together, these signals carry 'deeper messages about the distribution of risk and threat, identity and belonging' in a local social order (Innes, 2014: 45). In the next sections, we illustrate the significance of social and spatial dimensions in the criminology of 'fear of crime' by using two local examples: social tensions over parallel trading in border towns, and the spatiality of crime in Mong Kok.

Sensitised social tensions

In Hong Kong, especially in border towns in the New Territories, there have been heightened tensions over the liberalisation of internal border controls with Mainland China and cross-border parallel trading of everyday items such as infant milk formula, food and nappies. In focus groups, residents of these border areas expressed feelings of anxiety and anger directed at a range of anti-social activities by mainland Chinese parallel traders or suspected traders in public spaces. As Laidler and Lee (2014) have explained:

> Local Chinese-language newspapers ran a number of stories of how parallel traders were hated by local residents for disrupting their lives and social stability, for example, by creating shortages of daily necessities, obstructing the roads and local shopping centres, creating noise and rubbish with their unpacking and repacking activities, and endangering the safety of local residents, especially children and the elderly, by recklessly pushing their heavy trolleys in the streets.
>
> (Laidler and Lee, 2014: 321)

The following exchanges of a group of teenagers residing in Fan Ling near the border with Mainland China illustrate how personal experience of certain kinds of troubles and interpretation of the experiences of others serve to signal a neighbourhood 'under siege':

> The frequent gatherings of parallel traders in the last few years have created a big issue. When you go out, you will find the place is crowded, even in shopping malls, you notice there are plenty of those people who deliberately make purchases to ship them to Mainland China … because many of them have flooded into Hong Kong, there's bound to be more conflicts, more arguments, and therefore more physical fighting.
>
> I think these people pose a danger. They carry and move the goods in suitcases and trolleys. I'm always afraid these suitcases and trolleys would hurt small kids … these people just jaywalk and dash across the streets. I've seen a number of accidents happening because of that …
>
> What I see is Fan Ling has become just like Mainland China. One has to be wary about everything, wary about things being stolen … you would not feel comfortable putting things in your bag, you don't dare taking things out, you worry that there are thieves and pickpockets everywhere.
>
> (Male focus group, teenagers)

Although local citizens (including students and housewives) were reportedly involved in the illicit market activities, public hostilities were largely focused on the influx of mainland Chinese couriers and routine border crossers who were portrayed as presenting a putative threat to Hong Kong's way of life. These public sentiments illustrate that people do not always make clear distinctions between those issues definable as crimes and other forms of disruptive behaviour attributable to particular unwanted groups. More importantly, when there are heightened social tensions, people are sensitive to and interpret an array of social and physical incidents as signals of disorder.

The spatiality of fear: unpacking perceptions of Mong Kok

In general, Hong Kong citizens' cognitive maps of crime and disorder are structured by an understanding that there are particular places and times where troubles concentrate. In other words, 'crime talk' (Sasson, 1995) is often about particular spaces perceived to be dangerous as much as abstract notions of particular forms of crime (Sparks et al., 2001). In Hong Kong several locales were typically mentioned when participants were asked to identify places associated with crime and feelings of unsafety, with Mong Kok being singled out as the most frequently cited area that signalled disorder and crime.

Our focus group respondents often made reference to securing their personal belongings while walking through Mong Kok. Female participants referred to guarding their handbags and wallets more closely. One female participant recalls:

> Places that have many people are not safe ... I have experienced it personally. My wallet was stolen in Ladies Market [a popular street market attracting locals and tourists alike] in Mong Kok.

Others referred to being cheated and extorted in the Ladies Market. Men also referred to being 'more careful' with belongings such as their wallets in 'black zones' like Mong Kok. Yet, people's appraisals of safety in Mong Kok are shaped not only by experiences of direct victimisation but also by their interpretations of social spaces and social relations in the urban setting.

Described by the chief executive as 'not exactly the most genteel part of Hong Kong' (ATV Newsline interview, 19 October 2014) during the Umbrella Movement in 2014, the increase in Mong Kok's local and international profile was manifold when images of thousands of protesters taking to the streets and occupying its major intersections were beamed around the world. Mong Kok is a working-class urban area and one of the most densely populated places in the world (Forrest et al., 2002: 229). It has been subject to a number of urban renewal projects and drastic re-commodification of traditional industries such as its bird and flower markets into consumable heritage spaces in recent decades (Ho, 2012; Tang, 2005). Its position as a 24 hour major transportation interchange node point that integrates extensive local and cross-border transportation networks, means its roads are choked with cars, buses and mini-buses amidst a constant flow of people around the clock. The hybridised character of Mong Kok as a 'hyper-densed consumption space', 'marginal urban labyrinth' and a 'youth underground space' (Tang, 2005: 75) is best characterised by the glitzy neon lights and beckoning signs for top-end electronics chain stores as well as traditional mahjong and massage parlours; the official open-air night market alongside the unofficial on-street hawking zone selling cheap commodities and mobile services; the state-of-the art skyscrapers for shopping and entertainment as well as small shopping malls and cramped stores concealed in commercial buildings, selling everything from CDs, DVDs, books and Japanese comics to copies of pirated software and illegal pornographic movies. The complex and unpredictable flows of licit and illicit workers, residents, tourists and pedestrians in the bustling residential-cum-commercial spaces; the urban labyrinth structures criss-crossing its run-down residential and commercial buildings, red-light district, street food stalls and dimly lit alleyways, all exemplify what urban sociologists have variously described as unruly or 'wild zones' (Stanley, 1997), 'parafunctional spaces' or 'in-between wastelands' where 'social life is not simply abandoned or wasted ... [but] continues in ambiguous and unconventional ways' (Papastergiadis, 2002: 45).

Participants across the focus groups made references to these hybridised, anonymous and unpredictable qualities of Mong Kok as unruly and criminogenic. They referred to literally colliding into random people in the area. One female in her 30s commented, 'it is easy to have fights or disputes, so it makes [Mong Kok and its surrounding area] not so safe'. Another male participant explained:

> I don't find Mong Kok very safe. You see a lot of old walk-up tenements in the area. The place could be very dark at night and people of different backgrounds could be found there. There could be some drug abusers. It is likely you could find a bunch of syringes lying on the floor of some back alleys ... In the trash cans, you could find some ... ummm ... needles and all sorts of rubbish. Anyhow, those places are comparatively unruly at night ... Prostitutes and women of the sort hang around there too.
>
> (Male focus group, aged 20s)

The huge flows of people from varied backgrounds and their unpredictable behaviour, rather than criminal activity per se, were identified as signals of trouble, making Mong Kok anarchic and potentially dangerous. Seen in this light, people were nervous and fearful about travelling to Mong Kok not only because of the crime risks but also because of the ambiguous spatial practices that function as signals of disorder in urban environments.

In sharp contrast to non-residents, participants who live in Mong Kok often interpreted the physical and social disorders as less threatening. Even when they referred to the presence of disorder, they mediated their interpretation of disorderly incidents through established social ties and situated knowledge about the locale. For instance, one group of men who reside in Mong Kok and the nearby area commented on the reputation of Mong Kok as the heartland of triads. One male said he was 'not that frightened' of Mong Kok:

> [I got] accustomed to it. The triads don't target ordinary citizens like us. The things they are interested in have nothing to do with us; they need to maintain a peaceful environment in order to let their gangs continue with their business. If they disturb normal citizens, they will receive complaints. It then creates problems for them and affects their 'big plans'.

These statements reveal that different people interpret 'hot spots' for crime and disorder differently. As Innes (2014: 47–48) has argued, having established social relations and 'local contextual knowledge' provides 'the possibility of mitigating perceptions of any risks or threats posed' and 'defining the deviancy down' in some cases. These sentiments are echoed by our focus group participants who live in (or previously resided in) Mong Kok and its nearby area in Kowloon.

Conclusion

In Hale's (1996) extensive review of fear of crime research, he suggested that:

> Too much reliance has been placed upon the use of surveys as a method and too great an emphasis given to research based upon responses to questions about feeling safe out at night. Any new

> research should look for at [sic] triangulation of methods. Ethnographic studies, life histories and individual and group interviews all have much to contribute and are currently relatively ignored as methods by researchers into fear.
>
> (Hale, 1996: 132)

We argue here that qualitative approaches to the fear of crime are especially vital when examining how and why men and women, the young and the old, say they are worried about particular people, places and problems in their neighbourhood. 'Crime talk' (Sasson, 1995) often reveals as much about personal perceptions and experiences of trouble as wider social forces related to broader anxieties and public issues. What these anxieties point to is empirically specific to the particular culture examined, but can also be linked to wider currents of globalisation and the long reach of the 'risk society' paradigm (Beck, 1992). While criminologists have understandably gravitated to examining fear of crime in nations with relatively high levels of violent crime, such as the USA and UK (Garland, 2001), much may be gleaned from detailed examinations of societies with relatively low levels of violent crime. Hong Kong, as we have shown, is a safe city by international standards; nevertheless, our qualitative research reveals that it is neighbourhood incivilities, more than crime per se, which are foremost on the minds of many Hong Kong citizens. Seen in this light, the signal crimes perspective provides a useful theoretical framework to help us understand the links between people's concerns, identities and their everyday experiences of order and disorder. Incivilities may be perceived through signs of social disorder such as encounters with 'troublesome' youths or the presence of parallel goods traders from Mainland China, or through physical signals of disorder such as discarded syringes and insufficient illumination. Significantly, our focus group discussions also revealed multiple standpoints regarding problem places. While many people were quick to identify an array of signal disorders in criminogenic 'hot spots' in Hong Kong (e.g. Mong Kok), residents draw from more direct, experiential sources of knowledge regarding daily life and routines. This direct knowledge and familiarity helps deflect negative perceptions and fear and facilitates a process of 'defining deviancy down' (Innes, 2014: 47–48).

Research on fear of crime indicates that although direct victimisation experience does impact fear of crime and risk perception, it is not necessarily foremost when compared with how individuals may feel 'uncomfortable, threatened or helpless' in the face of wider sociological shifts related to 'globalization, emancipation, international migration and secularization' (Cops, 2010: 387). A distinct line of research has emerged that examines how expressions of fear of crime are 'more or less directly rooted in abstract anxieties about modernization', as well as its accompanying social and economic changes (Roberts et al., 2003: 61; Hirtenlehner and Farrall, 2013: 6). Hirtenlehner and Farrall (2013: 7, 19) observe 'fear of crime surfaces as an expression of an unspecific insecurity nurtured by diffuse existential fears and elusive future-oriented anxieties', and that greater attention needs to be paid to 'sociocultural and political-institutional context' in comparative research (Nelken, 2010). Against this background, some researchers have found that the greater the anxiety about long-term social change, the greater their levels of fear (Jackson, 2004; Gray et al., 2011). In the Hong Kong context, public fears and anxieties about parallel trading in border towns reflect not only concerns about criminality and urban disorder but also identity and belonging amidst growing 'mainlandization of the Hong Kong polity' (Lo, 2007: 179; Laidler and Lee, 2014). Clearly, more work is required to explore how citizens' crime fears may be linked to a broader sense of social breakdown and 'societal unraveling' (Sasson, 1995: 84). A sociologically informed criminology of the fear of crime has the potential to provide a more nuanced and grounded approach to understanding how people construct their local orders of reality, and how they think and feel about safety in their neighbourhood amidst broader social changes.

Review questions

1 What do existing victimisation surveys in Hong Kong reveal about the level of crime victimisation in Hong Kong? What are the strengths and weaknesses of these surveys as a source of knowledge about the crime problem in Hong Kong?
2 How does the signal crimes perspective advance our knowledge and understanding about crime and social order?
3 Identify the different types of social and physical signal disorders revealed through focus group discussions with Hong Kong citizens. What do these signal disorders tell us about the links between private troubles and public ills in Hong Kong?

Notes

1 Figures retrieved from the Hong Kong Police Force's *Police in Figures* and *Fight Crime Committee* reports. See www.police.gov.hk/ppp_en/09_statistics/ and www.sb.gov.hk/eng/pub/index.htm. The average homicide rate was 96.4 from 1990 to 1997, the year of the handover, dropping to 44.6 from 1998 to 2011.
2 The project 'Fear of crime and trust in crime control in Hong Kong' was funded by the Research Grants Council of Hong Kong (HKU 740211H) between January 2012 and December 2014. We are grateful to the RGC and to Ms Garlum Lau for her assistance with the fieldwork, and the research participants for sharing their stories with us.
3 The research findings regarding perceptions of the Hong Kong Police Force are beyond the scope of this chapter and not explicated here.

References

Beck, U. (1992) *Risk Society: Towards a New Modernity* (M. Ritter, trans.), London: Sage.

Broadhurst, R., Bacon-Shone, J., Bouhours, B., Lee, K.W. and Zhong, L. (2010) *Hong Kong United Nations International Crime Victim Survey: Final Report of the 2006 Hong Kong UNICVS*, Hong Kong and Canberra: The University of Hong Kong and the Australian National University.

Broadhurst, R., Lee, K.W. and Chan, C.Y. (2007) *Crime and Violence in Hong Kong, China*. United Nations. Case study prepared for Enhancing Urban Safety and Security: Global Report on Human Settlements.

Census and Statistics Department (1990) *Crime and its Victims in Hong Kong in 1989: A Report on the Crime Victimisation Survey*, Hong Kong: Census and Statistics Department.

Census and Statistics Department (1999) *Crime and its Victims in Hong Kong in 1998: A Report on the Crime Victimisation Survey*, Hong Kong: Census and Statistics Department.

Census and Statistics Department (2011) *Population Census: Summary Results*, Hong Kong: Census and Statistics Department.

Chui, W.H., Cheng, K.K.-Y. and Wong, L.P. (2012) 'Gender, fear of crime, and attitudes toward prisoners among social work majors in a Hong Kong University', *International Journal of Offender Therapy and Comparative Criminology*, 57(4): 479–494.

Cohen, S. (2002) [1972] *Folk Devils and Moral Panics* (3rd edn), London: Routledge.

Cops, D. (2010) 'Socializing into fear: The impact of socializing institutions on adolescents' fear of crime', *Young*, 18(4): 385–402.

Economist Intelligence Unit (2015) *The Safe Cities Index 2015: Assessing Urban Security in the Digital Age*, www.economistinsights.com/infrastructure-cities/analysis/safe-cities-index-2015 (accessed 15 February 2016).

Enders, M., Jennett, C. and Tulloch, M. (2008) 'Revisiting fear of crime in Bondi and Marrickville: Sense of community and perceptions of safety', in M. Lee and S. Farrall (eds) *Fear of Crime: Critical Voices in an Age of Anxiety* (pp. 188–210), Abingdon: Routledge-Cavendish.

Farrall, S., Jackson, J. and Gray, E. (2009) *Social Order and the Fear of Crime in Contemporary Times*, Oxford: Oxford University Press.

Forrest, R., La Grange, A. and Yip, N.-M. (2002) 'Neighbourhood in a high rise, high density city: Some observations on contemporary Hong Kong', *Sociological Review*, 50(2): 215–240.

Garland, D. (1996) 'The limits of the sovereign state', *British Journal of Criminology*, 36(4): 445–471.

Garland, D. (2001) *The Culture of Control: Crime and Social Order in Contemporary Society*, Chicago, IL: The University of Chicago Press.

Geertz, C. (1973) *The Interpretation of Cultures*, New York: Basic Books.

Gilchrist, E., Bannister, J., Ditton, J. and Farrall, S. (1998) 'Women and the "fear of crime": Challenging the accepted stereotype', *British Journal of Criminology*, 38(2): 283–298.

Girling, E., Loader, I. and Sparks, R. (2000) *Crime and Social Change in Middle England: Questions of Order in an English Town*, London: Routledge.

Goode, E. and Ben-Yehuda, N. (2009) *Moral Panics: The Social Construction of Deviance* (2nd edn), Malden, MA: Wiley-Blackwell.

Gray, E., Jackson, J. and Farrall, S. (2011) 'Feelings and functions in the fear of crime: Applying a new approach to victimisation insecurity', *British Journal of Criminology*, 51(1): 75–94.

Hale, C. (1996) 'Fear of crime: A review of the literature', *International Review of Victimology*, 4(2): 79–150.

Hirtenlehner, H. and Farrall, S. (2013) 'Anxieties about modernization, concerns about community, and fear of crime: Testing two related models', *International Criminal Justice Review*, 23(1): 5–24.

Ho, K.-Y. (2012) *Embedded Coloniality in Hong Kong: From Flower Cultivation to Culture-led Urban Renewal in Mong Kok Flower Market*, unpublished Master of Philosophy dissertation, Hong Kong: The University of Hong Kong.

Innes, M. (2004) 'Signal crimes and signal disorders: Notes on deviance as communicative action', *British Journal of Criminology*, 55(3): 335–355.

Innes, M. (2014) *Signal Crimes*, Oxford: Oxford University Press.

Jackson, J. (2004) 'Experience and expression: Social and cultural significance in the fear of crime', *British Journal of Criminology*, 44(6): 946–966.

Jones, C. and Vagg, J. (2007) *Criminal Justice in Hong Kong*, London: Routledge-Cavendish.

La Grange, A. (2011) 'Neighbourhood and class: A study of three neighbourhoods in Hong Kong', *Urban Studies*, 48(6): 1181–1200.

Laidler, K.J. and Lee, M. (2014) 'Border trading and policing of everyday life in Hong Kong', in S. Pickering and J. Ham (eds) *The Routledge Handbook on Crime and International Migration* (pp. 316–328), London: Routledge.

Leung, K.-M. (2001) *Gender Differences in Risk Perception in Hong Kong*, unpublished Master of Social Sciences thesis, Hong Kong: The University of Hong Kong.

Lo, S. (2007). 'The Mainlandization and recolonization of Hong Kong: A triumph of convergence over divergence with Mainland China', in J.Y.S. Cheng (ed.) *The Hong Kong Special Administrative Region in its First Decade* (pp. 179–223), Hong Kong: City University of Hong Kong Press.

Madriz, E. (1997) *Nothing Bad Happens to Good Girls: Fear of Crime in Women's Lives*, Berkeley, CA: University of California Press.

Morgan, D. (1997) *Focus Groups as Qualitative Research* (2nd edn), Thousand Oaks, CA: Sage.

Nelken, D. (2010) *Comparative Criminal Justice: Making Sense of Difference*, London: Sage.

Pain, R. (2000) 'Place, social relations and the fear of crime: a review', *Progress in Human Geography*, 24(3): 365-387.

Papastergiadis, P. (2002) *Traces Left in Cities in Leon Van Schaik Poetics in Architecture*, London: Architectural Design, Wiley Academy.

Rader, N. and Haynes, S. (2011) 'Gendered fear of crime socialization: An extension of Akers's social learning theory', *Feminist Criminology*, 6(4): 291–307.

Roberts, J., Stalans, L., Indermaur, D. and Hough, M. (2003) *Penal Populism and Public Opinion: Lessons from Five Countries*, Oxford: Oxford University Press.

Sasson, T. (1995) *Crime Talk: How Citizens Construct a Social Problem*, New York: Walter de Gruyter, Inc.

Scott, H. (2003) 'Stranger danger: Explaining women's fear of crime', *Western Criminology Review*, 4(3): 203–214.

Simon, J. (2007) *Governing through Crime: How the War on Crime Transformed American Democracy and Created a Culture of Fear*, Oxford: Oxford University Press.

Skogan, W. (1990) *Disorder and Decline: Crime and the Spiral of Decline in American Neighborhoods*, Beverly Hills, CA: Sage.

Smith, S.J. (1987) 'Fear of crime: Beyond a geography of deviance', *Progress in Human Geography*, 11(1): 1–23.

Sparks, R., Girling, E. and Loader, I. (2001) 'Fear and everyday urban lives', *Urban Studies*, 38(5–6): 885–898.

Stanley, C. (1997) 'Not drowning but waving: Urban narratives of dissent in wild zones', in S. Redhead, D. Wynne, and J. O'Connor (eds) *The Clubcultures Reader: Readings in Popular Cultural Studies* (pp. 36–54), Oxford: Blackwell.

Stewart, D., Shamdasani, P. and Rook, D. (2007) *Focus Groups, Theory and Practice* (2nd edn), London: Sage.

Tang, S.-H.W. (2005) *Beyond Hybridization: The Spatial Histories of Mong Kok, Hong Kong*, unpublished Master of Philosophy dissertation, Hong Kong: The University of Hong Kong.

Warr, M. (1985) 'Fear of rape among urban women', *Social Problems*, 32(3): 238–250.

Warr, M. (1990) 'Dangerous situations: Social context and fear of victimization', *Social Forces*, 68(3): 891–907.

Wilson, J. and Kelling, G. (1982) 'Broken Windows', *The Atlantic Online*, www.theatlantic.com/magazine/archive/1982/03/broken-windows/304465/ (accessed 15 February 2016).

Newspaper articles cited

South China Morning Post (2015) 'Hong Kong crime rate fell to a 41-year low in 2014, says police chief', 27 January, www.scmp.com/news/hong-kong/article/1693327/hong-kong-crime-rate-fell-41-year-low-2014-says-police-chief (accessed 15 February 2016).

Useful websites

Hong Kong Police Force (Crime Statistics) www.police.gov.hk/ppp_en/09_statistics/

Hong Kong Public Opinion Programme www.hkupop.hku.hk

Hong Kong United Nations International Crime Victim Survey papers.ssrn.com/sol3/papers.cfm?abstract_id=2077438

The Economist: The Safe Cities Index 2015 www.economistinsights.com/infrastructure-cities/analysis/safe-cities-index-2015

United Nations Office on Drugs and Crime www.unodc.org/unodc/en/data-and-analysis/Crime-Victims-Survey.html

United Nations Settlements Programme (UN-HABITAT). (Oct 1, 2007) Hong Kong: The World's Safest City? Nairobi. www.unhabitat.org

7

RESEARCHING CRIME AND JUSTICE

Alistair Fraser

Introduction

Why does Hong Kong have a low crime rate? How have triad societies persisted over time? What are 'young night drifters' and why are they seen as a problem? In what ways has the period of British colonialism impacted on Hong Kong's justice system? Why does Hong Kong have such a high rate of female imprisonment? These questions are not only of interest to the public, as issues of political or topical importance, but also as the foundations of criminological research. If you are interested in investigating these issues as criminological research questions, we must delve deeply into one of the key foundations of criminological knowledge: research methods. Criminology is a diverse field of knowledge, held together by a commitment to rigorous and scholarly efforts to understand crime, criminalisation and harm. Criminologists may vary in their disciplinary backgrounds, philosophical traditions and focus of attention, but all seek to deepen and enrich our knowledge of this thing we call 'crime'.

In this chapter, the focus will be on the fundamentals of research methods – namely, the 'tools of the trade' needed to answer the kinds of questions posed above. To do this, we must first travel backwards, to the early origins of criminology; travel sideways, to the development of research methods in the USA and Europe; then, finally, we will stay put and look at some of the ways that researchers have studied crime and justice in Hong Kong. Along the way, we will cover some core issues that must be dealt with for any student wishing to design a research project in Hong Kong.[1]

The ability to conduct theoretically grounded, methodologically sound research lies at the heart of the criminological enterprise. Whether our audiences are policymakers, the general public or fellow researchers, it is vital to base judgements on valid and reliable empirical evidence (Bauman and May, 2001). A firm foundation in research methodology is therefore vital, both as a means of evaluating previous research, and to design novel and rigorous interventions. This is particularly important in the context of Hong Kong. While criminological research has a relatively long history in Hong Kong in comparison to other parts of Asia (Lee and Laidler, 2013), there are a large number of areas of criminological interest that remain unexplored, or underexplored. While some topics have attracted a reasonable level of attention – youth crime and justice, drug use, organised crime, and policing – many others, such as the study of prisons, transnational crime, subcultures and racism, have lain dormant. As a result, the criminological knowledge base in Hong Kong remains far from solid.

One consequence of these gaps in knowledge has been an over-reliance on concepts, ideas and theories developed within the context of the USA and Europe. Rather than growing new knowledge organically from a local context, theories have been transplanted from Anglo-American criminology with little heed for their relevance or applicability to the local context. While research should not proceed from a starting point of assumed difference – given the parallels brought about by processes of globalisation and migration – criminological knowledge production in Hong Kong contains echoes of the development of criminal justice in the colonial era, in which institutions, laws and ordinances were transferred directly from England (Adorjan and Chui, 2013, 2014). One objective of this chapter, therefore, is to encourage the development of a robust understanding of the principles and practice of research methods, in order to develop a criminology that is tuned in to the subtleties, nuances and realities of the landscape of crime and justice in Hong Kong. The chapter therefore aims to introduce some of the fundamental issues pertaining to settings and contexts, principles and practices, qualitative and quantitative methodologies, politics and ethics. Relevant case studies and examples from the developing criminological literature of Hong Kong will be drawn on as appropriate. Due to the constraints of space, this overview will be necessarily brief and introductory, sketching the principal contours of research problems for those relatively new to research. Issues such as data analysis, writing and the practical meanings of various research methods will therefore not be covered. Readers are directed to more broad-based texts on criminological research methods (see, for example, King and Wincup, 2008; Davies et al., 2011) for further analysis of these issues.

Settings, contexts and funding

Every country has a unique culture of social research, and Hong Kong is no exception. This often relates to the status of criminology within a given national context, including the independence of its universities, the relationship between criminologists and the national government, and the level of transparency within systems of criminal justice. These factors in turn shape the nature of research within that national context, dictating both the projects that will get funded and the level of access that will be granted to carry out independent research. Before starting to plan a research study in Hong Kong, therefore, it is important to have some awareness of the various settings and contexts in which that research would take place, and the likely sources of funding.

Settings

Criminology is an eclectic, 'rendezvous' discipline that draws from sociology, anthropology, psychology, geography, law, social work, economics and politics, among others. It covers the study of the nature of crime itself, the character of those who break the law, the impact on the victims of crime, and the functioning of the criminal justice system. It also, however, covers the social and cultural causes of criminalisation, the harms caused by poverty and inequality, discrimination and corruption, and crimes of the state. It is therefore a very 'broad church', involving intense debates between individuals steeped in different traditions and approaches. Not only are there different types of research, but there are also different types of researcher. Understanding the social, political and cultural settings within which research into crime and criminal justice takes place is therefore crucial for informing the formulation of research problems and questions and the design of appropriate research methods. Criminal justice agencies and institutions can be difficult research environments, usually requiring careful access negotiations and complex ethical considerations. Undertaking research on crime, criminals and victims brings a different set of issues surrounding access, ethics and context (King and Wincup, 2008).

Criminological research tends to focus on a range of different settings depending on which group, phenomenon or problem is under investigation (King and Wincup, 2008). A study of youth gangs, for example, would be most likely to take place in a street or community-based context (Lo, 2012), while a study of policing might take place in a police headquarters, station, patrol car or in a courtroom. The setting in which a study takes place is dependent not only on the nature of the phenomenon under investigation, however. Another crucial factor determining setting is *access* – the extent to which a researcher is allowed to spend time in that setting. This is often determined by what is known as a *gatekeeper*, meaning the individual or institution that decides whether or not a researcher may access a particular social milieu. This can be a formal procedure in the case of criminal justice institutions such as prisons, or an informal procedure in the case of negotiating access to street-based contexts. A famous example of the latter can be found in William Foot Whyte's (1943) study *Street Corner Society*. Whyte hoped to study community life in a disadvantaged neighbourhood in Boston, which he called 'Cornerville'. In a methodological appendix to the study, Whyte describes his good fortune in meeting Doc, the leader of a group of 'corner boys', early in the study, who instantly grasped the nature of the project and went to considerable lengths to facilitate research access. (For further discussion on the role of gatekeepers, see Noaks and Wincup, 2004: 56–60.)

Finally, in planning a new criminological research study, it is important to think about where the research will be situated *globally* – be it Hong Kong, China, Taiwan or elsewhere – as well as where the research will be sited *locally*, be it in a classroom, a boardroom or a protest camp. This allows the researcher to think, too, about *how* access to the field site will be negotiated, and potential problems and biases that may arise from one's choice of gatekeeper. Since access via the criminal justice system is relatively limited, the majority of criminological research in Hong Kong has been carried out through social work agencies and non-governmental organisations. Social work in Hong Kong is not centrally administered; rather, it is at arm's length from the government administration by a wide range of third-sector organisations. This allows greater autonomy for arranging research access, and many of the largest-scale studies of crime and deviance in Hong Kong have been carried out with their assistance.

Contexts

Criminology as a discipline developed critical mass in the context of the USA, UK and mainland Europe in the early part of the 20th century. Its foundations therefore lie in the development of modern techniques of government during this period, particularly the use of administrative statistics – government efforts to quantify features of populations in order to manage them – and subsequent efforts to reduce social problems. As Garland (2002) summarises, the modern enterprise of criminology emerged from the coming together of the 'Lombrosian' project, which sought to distinguish correlations between offending behaviour and individual pathologies, and the 'governmental' project of enhancing the administration of systems of criminal justice. This took place within a broader context – in the UK at least – of colonial expansion, and a correspondingly strong economy. As the British government sought to increase their transnational reach, so forms of criminology and criminal justice were also exported (Brown, 2005).

The context in which criminological research is carried out in Hong Kong, therefore, must be located within a broader context of power, post-colonialism and international relations. For better or worse, the apparatus of government assembled by the British colonial administration included a significant statistical component, and data pertaining to the operation of crime and justice have been more accessible than in much of the Asian region (Adorjan and Chui, 2013, 2014). In addition, the relative strength, competitiveness and independence of Hong Kong's university sector, along with the predominance of English-language instruction and publication, have created an institutional space in which criminology has developed critical mass. As a result, there is a growing cache of conceptual tools drawn from empirical study that capture the unique hybridities, contradictions and cultural distinctions of crime and justice in Hong Kong.

In formulating new criminological studies of Hong Kong and the wider region, therefore, it is important to ground understandings within the context of local knowledge. Hong Kong-based scholars in particular have started to build a foundation for a new 'criminology of the periphery' (Lee and Laidler, 2013; see also Chen, 2010), which privileges the voices of scholars in non-Western contexts, and seeks to build a new empirical base with which to construct meaningful dialogue with concepts and theories from the North. This project seeks to build the foundations of a democratic, cosmopolitan criminology that is rooted in lived experiences in the Asian region in a bid to create discursive forms of knowledge between centre and periphery.

Funding

A primary concern when designing a criminological research project, aside from setting and context, is the issue of research funding. Carrying out research can be expensive. Research assistance, travel, data collection, transcription and translation, possible remuneration for participants, buy-outs from teaching – these can add up to significant sums. An application for criminological research to the main funding body in Hong Kong, the University Grants Committee (UGC), might request over HK$500,000 to be spent over three years.

The funding landscape in Hong Kong is, however, considerably more straightforward than in the USA or Europe. The UK has a wide range of different funding bodies – from charitable organisations to private trusts, research councils to public funds. (For an overview of the UK funding landscape, see Noaks and Wincup, 2004: 24–27.) Hong Kong's funding systems are more streamlined. The UGC fund most large-scale social research projects in Hong Kong through their General Research Fund, Early Career Scheme and Public Policy Scheme. This is a tremendously competitive source of funding, with less than a third of applicants gaining funding. The other principal source of funding is at the university level. Most, if not all universities in Hong Kong have research funds available for competitive application from full-time staff, principally designed to cover small projects and 'start-up' costs towards larger applications. For students carrying out independent research, little or no funding is required; for those intending to pursue a research career, however, 'grant capture' is increasingly important.

Now that the wider context for knowledge production in Hong Kong has been established, we can turn our attention to the practical and philosophical aspects of starting your own research project.

Starting your research: from ideas to questions

If a journey of 100 miles starts with a single step, a research journey starts with a single idea. Ideas for criminological research projects are all around us – in the conversations we have, the news we read, the movies we watch, the jobs we do. We are surrounded by questions of crime and justice, both old and new, and are tapped into unique social, cultural and professional networks that can help us develop them. The first step is to find a topic that is interesting, relevant and timely – be it parallel trading, the Umbrella Movement or the treatment of young offenders. Find something that you are interested in, passionate about or otherwise engaged with. This is the seed of an idea, and finding the right one is a crucial first step. However, initial ideas tend to be quite broad and unfocused. As Pamela Davies notes:

> While 'The Fear of Crime', 'Women and the Police', 'Mass Media and Violence', 'Juvenile Crime' etc might be general areas within which you choose to study, they are far too broad as dissertation topics. If unrefined, such broad topics are likely to lead to the 'kitchen-sink' approach to conducting research.
>
> (Davies, 2011: 43)

In order to allow the idea to grow, therefore, it is critical to understand the current state of knowledge as it relates to your chosen topic. This is what is termed a *literature review*, and at its best it should constitute a comprehensive, critical review of all available sources of information on your chosen topic. This can include a range of sources, including statistics, media representations or professional experience, but must be rooted fundamentally in relevant academic literature. If your topic is an established criminological area, such as youth offending, there will be a wealth of literature at your fingertips. learn to use your academic library, online journal databases, and academic handbooks such as the *Oxford Handbook of Criminology*. Between these sources, you will find a starting point to help your idea develop and mature. If your topic is a new or emergent one, such as the Umbrella Movement, there may not be much in the way of primary academic research. In this situation, you must focus on finding the correct criminological 'frame' for your study, for instance by looking at the academic literature on youth politicisation, social movements or street politics. Whatever your topic, the aim of a literature review is to blend current academic knowledge with other sources to identify two things: a 'gap' in the literature, and an 'angle' with which to pursue a research project.

Once you have completed a literature review, you are in a position to determine two other core components of a research project: research design and research questions. First, the *research design* is a framework for the collection and analysis of data, representing a blueprint for every aspect of the study. Second, the *research questions* clearly elucidate the research problem and translate the initial 'big' ideas into smaller, more feasible questions. Questions should be researchable, connected to literature, linked to one another, and neither too broad nor too narrow. As Gilbert (2008: 512, quoted in Davies, 2011: 37) points out, research requires an 'overarching question that defines the scope, scale and conduct of a research project … [and which] focuses research design and methods towards the provision of evidenced answers'.

To take an example, a few years ago I became interested in the criminological significance of Hong Kong's Kowloon Walled City.[2] After reading a wide range of literature on the topic, I found that while there had been a number of published and unpublished studies of the Walled City – in the fields of law, social work and history – as well as autobiographical, photographic and popular accounts, there had been little space afforded to the voices and experiences of individuals who grew up and lived in the area, and the relationship between crime and everyday life. At the same time I began thinking about the importance of 'history from below'. The historian E.P. Thompson distinguishes between 'history from above' – based on government documents and archives, told by people in positions of power and authority – and 'history from below'. 'History from below', far rarer, is history as told from the margins, often in the form of social documents, letters and testimonies. While the Walled City has been represented in a range of historical and media narratives, there remain very few dedicated efforts to reconstruct how life was lived inside the enclave. Having developed a topic (Kowloon Walled City), a 'gap' in the literature (crime and everyday life), and an 'angle' ('history from below'), I was then in a position to devise a set of *research questions*:

1 In what ways do English- and Chinese-language sources differ in their representations of crime within the Walled City?
2 What are the principal ways in which crime and everyday life in the Walled City are narrated by those who lived and worked there?
3 How do these narratives relate to broader patterns of social, cultural and historical change in Hong Kong?

This brief sketch highlights some important aspects of the early stages of the research process. First, while good research often starts with a good idea, this idea must be developed and matured in dialogue with the relevant research literature. As important as a topic may appear, without an adequate grounding and positioning within the literature it cannot make a valuable contribution to knowledge. Second, putting in the work early on is repaid later. A clear research design, predicated on a robust understanding of the significance of the project, facilitates progress towards the collection of valuable data. A messy or unclear research design can, conversely, lead to problems at later stages of the research process. Having solid research questions and research design provide a guiding blueprint through these later stages. Finally, however, these should not be thought of as a straitjacket but as a guide. It is important to be both clear and open minded in the unfolding of a research project.

Choosing the right approach: quantitative and qualitative research

Once you have established a good idea, located it within the context of relevant literature and started to sketch your research design, questions of methodology and methods become very important. The *methodology* of a research project involves not only research methods, but also the theoretical and philosophical underpinning of your approach to research. Your choice of methods reflects your view of the nature and production of knowledge – theory, method and data are closely related. The *research methods* involved in the project represent the tools you use to collect data in line with that broader philosophical intention, and may take the form of structured interviews, focus groups, observations, or content analysis of newspapers.

In the Walled City example, I was interested in exploring the intersections of space, youth and order, as well as their broader political, sociological and historical significance. Had the Walled City not been demolished in the 1990s, I may have opted for an ethnographic approach in which I lived in the community, or a survey-based approach in which I recorded data from residents. As it was, I decided that oral history interviews with professionals who worked with young people in the area, and a number of residents, would be the best means of excavating this 'history from below'. In making these decisions in your own research, it is important to understand the distinctions between the epistemologies of *positivism* and *interpretivism* as well as the practical aspects of conducting research within the *quantitative* and *qualitative* paradigms.

Quantitative approaches

The roots of quantitative approaches in criminology can be found in the pioneering work of Adolphe Quetelet and Emile Durkheim in the 19th century. In the context of enormous growth in statistical knowledge of the population – the so-called 'avalanche of printed numbers' (Hacking 1990) in which government statistics increased by a staggering degree – Quetelet was among the first to recognise patterns in the data relating to crime and other social factors, for example gender, age, occupation and religion. Quetelet's 'insight' was bold and striking:

> one passes from one year to the other with the sad perspective of seeing the same crimes reproduced in the same order and bringing with them the same penalties in the same proportions. Sad condition of the human species! The share of prisons, chains, and the scaffold appears fixed with as much probability as the revenues of the state. We are able to enumerate in advance how many individuals will stain their hands with the blood of their fellow creatures, how many will be forgers, how many poisoners, pretty nearly as one can enumerate the births and deaths which must take place.
>
> (Quetelet, 1831, quoted in Hayward et al., 2010: 15)

The contingent nature of social life, and the ability to discover these patterns through empirical research, formed the basis for the work of Emile Durkheim (1895). Durkheim sought to establish sociology as an independent discipline, and as such drew on the natural sciences, which were rising in prominence, in this project. For Durkheim, categories such as 'class', 'occupation' and 'religion' were not simply descriptors, but could be conceptualised as having an objective 'existence' which could have a discernible impact on one another. Through study of these variables – which he termed 'social facts' – Durkheim believed it possible to identify 'natural laws' within society that were akin to the laws of physics or the natural sciences. The first generation of social scientists therefore sought out patterns in statistics, from which to test theories of the new discipline of sociology.

This approach formed the basis for the epistemological approach known as *positivism*, which holds that the social world adheres to certain patterns and social laws, which can be discerned through numeric quantification and analysis; that there are knowable rules governing the operation of social life that are akin to the 'natural laws' of biology and physics (Carrabine et al., 2004). While much has changed since Durkheim's pioneering work – ever-more sophisticated modelling, complex computer programming, ever-expanding webs of 'big data' – the basic principles of quantitative methods have remained based on these core concerns. In essence, researchers seek causal links between key variables – be it between experiences of violence and violent behaviour, social class and risk of victimisation, or income and job satisfaction. In seeking correlations of this kind, one variable is treated as the *independent variable*, meaning that it exerts an influence, while the other is the *dependent* variable, meaning that it is influenced. To take one of the above examples, we might be interested in the job satisfaction of prison officers. We might hypothesise that greater income will lead to greater job satisfaction – in this case, income might be treated as an independent variable and job satisfaction the dependent variable, while controlling for other variables. The emphasis is therefore on *quantification* in the process of data collection, and a *deductive* approach to the relationship between theory and research.

The means of data collection for quantitative studies are multiple and various, but many rely on the use of *survey instruments*. These involve a sequence of questions or statements that can be answered in clear-cut ways, which in turn create data from which to draw correlations between variables. Questions might ask, for example, about household income, savings, property and education level to evaluate social class, or on self-reported offending to assess crime and victimisation. There are several critical aspects in such survey designs. The first of these is *sampling*. The intention in a survey is for a small sub-set of respondents to 'represent' a larger population – for example, for a sample of 1,000 voters to 'represent' the likely result of an election. The extent to which randomised sampling is robust – that is, truly random and not affected by the 'selection bias' of convenience or lack of representativeness – will affect the *generalisability* of the research, namely how large a population it might apply to. Another key aspect in survey design is *validity*, meaning measures to assess the internal integrity of the research findings. For example, *measurement validity* refers to the degree to which a measure reflects a concept (see Bryman, 2004: 61–82; Bachman and Schutt, 2011).

Examples of this approach in Hong Kong can be found in the United Nations (UN) Violence Against Women Survey (Broadhurst et al., 2010), and in Chui et al. (2015), who conducted a telephone survey relating to sex-offending policies in Hong Kong. Broadhurst and colleagues' study is part of a broader international study of 'women's experiences of physical and sexual violence by men, including intimate partners' (Broadhurst et al., 2010: 1), involving 12 countries. The Hong Kong study is based on a telephone survey, with a sample size of 1,297. As the study used standardised measures, it was possible to make comparisons reliably across these diverse contexts, demonstrating the powerful value of quantitative methodologies in understanding crime and victimisation in a comparative context. In Chui and colleagues' (2015) study, a randomised sample of 202 respondents – with roughly similar characteristics to the general population of Hong Kong – gave their views on sex offending. The value of this approach, in both cases, is the ability of respondents to answer questions in an anonymous and confidential manner, thereby generating powerful insights into sensitive topics, as well as their generalisability to a larger population.

Quantitative studies that deal directly with crime and deviance – rather than victimisation or perception – are often criticised from the perspective of *interpretivism*. This was summarised by David Matza (1964) in his book, *Delinquency and Drift*. For Matza, quantitative methods often seek out the *differences* between offenders and non-offenders, representing the 'criminal' as 'a specific type of person' who 'differs from others' and is 'driven' into crime 'through factors outside his or her control' (Carrabine et al., 2004: 62–63). For Matza, in reality the causes of crime are rooted in social and cultural processes that are messy and unpredictable, and as such cannot be captured by survey instruments. From this perspective, the attempt to apply natural laws to social life ignores the subjectivity inherent in human behaviour, implying that the world is static, not fluid, and fails to capture variation in identity and action. As Jock Young (2004: 25–26) argues, while certain phenomena are capable of definition, 'there are many others that are blurred ... because it is their nature to be blurred'. These critiques tap into a different research tradition in criminology: qualitative methods.

Qualitative approaches

The qualitative study of crime and deviance finds its roots in the Chicago School of Sociology, in the early 20th century (Faris, 1967). The Chicago School sought to distinguish patterns of interaction, association and order amidst the rapid population and urbanisation of the city. One of the most prominent methods of discovering these patterns was through direct observation of the phenomenon being studied. As Park, a former journalist, famously exhorted his students: 'Go and sit in the lounges of the luxury hotels and on the doorsteps of the flophouses; sit on the Gold Coast settees and on the slum shakedowns; sit in the Orchestra Hall and in the Star & Garter Burlesk. In short, gentlemen, go get the seat of your pants dirty in *real* research' (Robert E. Park, speaking circa 1920, quoted in Lofland, 1971: 2). Part of the enduring reputation of the Chicago School was in discerning regularised structures amid seemingly chaotic or disorganised terrain (Downes and Rock, 2003: 64–69). Combining analysis of urban ecology with the lived experiences of those in so-called 'zones of transition', students of the Chicago School were able to locate deviance in its particular social and cultural context, as a 'kind of surrogate social order ... explained as a functional response to deprivation, to the social and moral structures imported by immigrants and to the experience of growing up in the inner-city' (Downes and Rock, 2003: 71). Qualitative research traditions such as these draw from the epistemology of *interpretivism*. This theory of knowledge is premised on the view that social reality does not have an *objective* reality 'out there', waiting to be discovered, but conversely that the social universe is made up of a complex web of *subjective* relations – that is, that the world as we know it is socially constructed, or interpreted, out of the tissue of cultural understanding.

This approach became established in criminology during the 1960s as part of a more generalised backlash against the perceived abstraction of the positivist method. Foremost among these 'new deviancy theorists' was Howard Becker, who turned the search for 'causal mechanisms' for crime on its head. Rather than starting with incarcerated prisoners and working backwards, Becker's starting point was in the meanings of social and cultural behaviour, the processes by which certain behaviours became problematised and criminalised, and the impact of these labels on the individuals. This approach was premised on a view that crime, or deviance, is a wholly contingent categorisation. Deviance is not inherent in individuals, but a label imposed by systems of authority: '[t]he central fact about deviance: it is created by society' (Becker, 1963: 8). The Centre for Contemporary Cultural Studies or Birmingham School brought Chicago School methods of participant observation to the study of youth culture in 1970s Britain, emphasising the collective routes through which cultural identities are formed (see, for example, Hall et al., 1978). For Becker (1963), this line of thinking opens the door to questioning the very foundations of law and justice:

> All social groups make rules and attempt, at some time and under some circumstances, to enforce them. Social rules define situations and the kinds of behavior appropriate to them, specifying some actions as 'right' and forbidding others as 'wrong'. When a rule is enforced, the person who is supposed to have broken it may be seen as a special kind of person, one who cannot be trusted to live by the rules agreed on by the group. He is regarded as an outsider.
>
> (Becker, 1963: 1)

Qualitative research, by and large, therefore takes the view that social reality – what we see, hear and experience – does not have an 'objective' aspect that acts independently on individuals, but rather is *socially constructed* out of 'subjective' understandings. This approach therefore places emphasis not on numbers and quantification, but on words and their cultural meanings. Rather than starting from a 'top-down', deductive hypothesis, qualitative researchers approach data in an inductive way, building theory from the 'bottom up'. The intention is often to view reality through the eyes of participants, and make sense of their actions from that perspective, rather than seeking causal explanations in abstract variables such as 'social class' or 'victimisation'. When researching 'hard-to-reach' groups, or sensitive topics, quantitative methods may not be appropriate.

As with quantitative data collection, there are different research methods that can be brought to bear in qualitative work. These range from participant observation and ethnography, in which the researcher embeds him- or herself within a particular social environment for an extended period, to semi-structured interviews, in which the researcher asks an open-ended, thematic series of questions to a specific respondent. Other examples include focus groups, in which the researcher facilitates a 'guided discussion' among a group of individuals on a certain topic, and visual methods, which may include photography, film or other creative methods. What unites these methods is an effort to 'see through the eyes' of research participants – to tap into their daily lives and the meanings they attribute to the world around them.[3]

Two examples of qualitative research in Hong Kong can be found in the work of Groves and colleagues (2012) in their study of young night drifters, and Laidler (2005) in her study of club drug use. Groves and colleagues set out to understand the unique phenomenon of young people who 'colonise' the night in Hong Kong in gaming centres, snooker halls, 24-hour McDonald's and public parks – using time rather than physical space as a means of carving out space for individual identity. As 'the goal of this research was not simply to quantify the amount of time youth spend on various pursuits or even to understand their subjective conceptualization of time', the researchers used ethnographic methods, accompanying social work outreach workers on their 'nightly patrols' (Groves et al., 2011: 6–7). This enabled the researchers to gain deep and grounded insights into the everyday routines and rhythms of the so-called 'young night drifters'. In this way, qualitative researchers seek to gain an 'appreciative' (Matza, 1964) view of participants' lives – be they gang members, police officers or victims of crime – in a way that privileges their voices and experiences. For ethnographers in particular, the focus is often on giving voice to individuals who are marginalised, stereotyped and stigmatised in society (Ferrell and Hamm, 1998). Critics of qualitative methods, however, argue that the data gathered are too subjective, creating overly impressionistic and unsystematic findings. Replicability may be difficult, and the findings not necessarily generalisable.

One way of shoring up the challenges and shortcomings of both approaches is by utilising a mixed-method research design. Laidler's (2005) work on club drug use in Hong Kong, for example, was part of a larger worldwide assessment for the UN, and drew on mixed methods to explore both a comparative and local context. The wider UN study sought to 'examine the local supply, demand, and marketing mechanisms for drugs over the 5-year period from 1995–2000' (Laidler, 2005: 1259) – as such, Laidler's team drew on a standardised questionnaire, with expert interviewees, relating to issues such as drug availability, pricing and seizures. The study, however, was also concerned with tracking the market in dance-drug use in Hong Kong, and therefore involved an additional component of observations in nightclubs and parks, and interviews with drug users. This allowed the research team to generalise their findings, and compare with experiences overseas, whilst complementing these data with more experiential observations.

In designing your own study, however, a note of caution should be sounded. Too often students suggest a mixed-method design as it appears to be the 'safe option'. Mixed methods have a particular value, but risk minimising the real advantages of each method. For some ethnographers, passing out a survey would be unthinkable. Before making your choice, therefore, think deeply about which methodological approach you feel is most appropriate to answer your research questions, and start from there.

Ethics and politics

The final issue that bears mentioning is the ethics and politics of criminological research. Social research is seldom carried out in a vacuum, but given that issues of crime, victimisation and justice are often politically sensitive, criminological research is often particularly fraught with ethical and political dilemmas. If a research participant discloses that they have been the victim of a crime, what do you do? If a funder tries to suppress key findings because your research discloses a negative view of their organisation, what principles should be followed? How can we avoid our sensitive data falling into the wrong hands, and what are the legal issues at play? These questions fall largely within the ambit of ethics and politics of criminological research.

In Hong Kong, as in the UK and USA, academic research is governed by a set of ethical principles that are internally regulated at university level by ethics committees, and externally by professional societies such as the British Society of Criminology. At the university level, each research project – including student work that includes human participants – must be vetted according to certain key principles of informed consent, confidentiality and harm. Before embarking on your own research, therefore, you must ensure that you have gained appropriate ethical clearance. This is designed to protect both your potential participants and you as a researcher. As Liebling and Stanko (2001) note:

> Ethical research is typically defined as that which safeguards the rights and feelings of those who are being researched. Assuring confidentiality, minimizing the impact of recalling and reporting stressful events, and avoiding deception are three components of any ethical expectation for social science researchers.
>
> (Liebling and Stanko, 2001: 424)

Research participants should be given full information regarding the nature, form and consequences of their participation – usually taking the form of an informed consent form – and know how the data will be stored, used and published. Their participation must be entirely voluntary, and should not expose them to any greater risk than they might experience in everyday life – including risks to privacy. As such, all data should be confidential, and participants anonymised (Bryman, 2004).

In practice, however, these principles are frequently put to the test. Ethics *on paper* is a very different prospect to ethics *in the field*. While it is essential to evaluate potential ethical risks and dilemmas in advance, and minimise them where possible, it is also vital to remain ethically aware and morally sensitised whilst in the field. Burman et al. (2001), for example, reflect on the ways in which very careful planning for research on young women's experiences of violence did not fully prepare them for the reality of discussions. In one example, a role-play exercise was dropped from the research methodology as the research team felt that it was creating a potentially violent situation. While the role-play exercise received ethical approval from a university-based research ethics board/internal review board, the researchers made changes to the methodology of their project during the course of their engagement with participants. This is an example of how research objectives and ethical concerns must be balanced in the field (see Wahidin, 2011; King and Wincup, 2008).

Conclusion

This chapter has focused on fundamental philosophical and practical issues relating to the design, implementation and evaluation of criminological research in Hong Kong. Issues relating to the settings, contexts and funding of crime and justice research in Hong Kong have been introduced, along with some of the fundamentals of research design and the development of a research project. The chapter has sketched the contours of the two main epistemological approaches to researching crime and justice – interpretivism and positivism – and connected these traditions with specific research methodologies, such as surveys or participant observation. Where possible, examples drawn from the criminological canon in Hong Kong have been offered by way of illustration. Finally, issues relating to politics and ethics have been introduced.

As mentioned in the introduction, while research on issues of crime and justice in Hong Kong has recently been developing a critical mass, there is a pressing need for a broadening and deepening of knowledge. This chapter has sought to lay a methodological grounding for this project. If Hong Kong criminology is to grow and prosper, however, there is also a need to look beyond Hong Kong field sites in the construction of new ideas. Issues relating to global and comparative criminology have come increasingly to the fore of the discipline, as well as the building of a 'theory from the South' rooted in critical, post-colonial perspectives. A blending of these theoretical insights, coupled with a global and comparative sensibility, would make for an exceptionally fruitful future direction for criminology in Hong Kong, and one that would inform criminology elsewhere. Drawing together knowledge and experiences from China, Asia and the criminological heartlands of Europe and North America, the future of Hong Kong criminology looks bright.

Review questions

1 What are some of the challenges associated with the settings, contexts and funding of criminological research?
2 What are the main differences between positivism and interpretivism, and what are their historical roots?
3 Drawing on empirical examples, critically assess the importance of both qualitative *and* quantitative methods for a rounded understanding of crime.
4 Choose *three* of the following concepts and evaluate their importance to criminological research methods: politics; epistemology; validity; ethics; research design; sampling; research questions.
5 In what ways do issues of ethics and politics relate to the planning of criminological research?

Notes

1 The author would like to thank students on the Master's degree-level 'Research Methods in Criminology' class at the University of Hong Kong, and the anonymous reviewer, for their feedback and assistance in developing the ideas that underpin this chapter. Any errors – or 'selection bias' towards qualitative methods – lie with the author.
2 The Kowloon Walled City was an enclave in Hong Kong during British colonialism that had a legally ambiguous status, with both the UK and China claiming sovereignty. As a result of this ambiguity, the area attracted a thriving 'grey' economy of illegal dentists, gambling dens, drug dealing and prostitution. For an overview, see Lambot and Girard (2014).
3 For an overview of the use of qualitative research, see Mason (1996); for qualitative methods in criminology, see Wincup (2004). On ethnographic methods in criminology, see Hobbs (2001).

References

Adorjan, M. and Chui, W.H. (2013) 'Colonial responses to youth crime in Hong Kong: Penal elitism, legitimacy and citizenship', *Theoretical Criminology*, 17(2): 159–177.

Adorjan, M. and Chui, W.H. (2014) *Responding to Youth Crime: Penal Elitism, Legitimacy and Citizenship*, Abingdon: Routledge.

Bachman, R. and Schutt, R.K. (2011) *The Practice of Research in Criminology and Criminal Justice*, Thousand Oaks, CA: Sage.

Bauman, Z. and May, T. (2001) *Thinking Sociologically*, Oxford: Blackwell.

Becker, H.S. (1963) *Outsiders: Studies in the Sociology of Deviance*, New York: Free Press of Glencoe.

Broadhurst, R., Bacon-Shone, J., Bouhours, B., Lee, K.W. and Zhong, L. (2010) *Hong Kong United Nations International Crime Victim Survey: Final Report of the 2006 Hong Kong UNICVS*, Hong Kong and Canberra: The University of Hong Kong and the Australian National University.

Brown, S. (2005) *Understanding Youth and Crime: Listening to Youth?* Maidenhead: Open University Press.

Bryman, A. (2004) *Social Research Methods* (2nd edn), Oxford: Oxford University Press.

Burman, M., Brown, J. and Batchelor, S. (2001) 'Researching girls and violence: Facing the dilemmas of fieldwork', *British Journal of Criminology*, 41(3): 443–459.

Carrabine, E., Iganski, P., Lee, M., Plummer, K. and South, N. (2004) *Criminology: A Sociological Introduction*, London: Routledge.

Chen, K-h. (2010) *Asia as Method: Toward Deimperialization*, London: Duke University Press.

Chui, W.H., Cheng, K.C. and Ong, R. (2015) 'Attitudes of the Hong Kong Chinese public towards sex offending policies: The role of stereotypical views of sex offenders', *Punishment and Society*, 17(1): 94–113.

Davies, P. (2011) 'Formulating criminological research questions', in P. Davies, P. Francis and V. Jupp (eds) *Doing Criminological Research* (pp. 36–53), London: Sage.

Davies, P., Francis, P. and Jupp, V. (eds) (2011) *Doing Criminological Research*, London: Sage.

Downes, D. and Rock, P. (2003) *Understanding Deviance: A Guide to the Sociology of Crime and Rule-Breaking*, Oxford: Oxford University Press.

Durkheim, E. (1895/1966) *The Rules of Sociological Method*, New York: Free Press.

Faris, R.E.L. (1967) *Chicago Sociology, 1920–1932*, San Francisco, CA: Chandler Pub. Co.

Ferrell, J. and Hamm, M. (1998) *Ethnography at the Edge: Crime, Deviance and Field Research*, Boston, MA: Northeastern University Press.

Garland, D. (2002) 'Of crimes and criminals: The development of criminology in Britain', in M. Maguire, R. Morgan and R. Reiner (eds) *The Oxford Handbook of Criminology* (3rd edn) (pp. 7–50), Oxford: Oxford University Press.

Groves, J., Ho, W.Y. and Siu, K. (2012) 'Youth studies and timescapes: Insights from an ethnographic study of "young night drifters" in Hong Kong's public housing estates', *Youth & Society*, 44(4): 548–566.

Hacking, I. (1990) *The Taming of Chance*, Cambridge: Cambridge University Press.

Hall, S.M., Critcher, C., Jefferson, T., Clarke, J. and Roberts, B. (1978) *Policing the Crisis: Mugging, the State and Law and Order*, London: Macmillan.

Hayward, K., Maruna, S. and Mooney, J. (eds) (2010) *Fifty Key Thinkers in Criminology*, Abingdon: Routledge.

Hobbs, D. (2001). 'Ethnography and the study of deviance', in P. Atkinson, A. Coffey, S. Delamont, J. Loftland and L. Loftland, (eds) *Handbook of Ethnography* (pp. 204–219), London: Sage.

King, R. and Wincup, E. (eds) (2008) *Doing Research on Crime and Justice*, Oxford: Oxford University Press.

Laidler, K.J. (2005) 'The rise of club drugs in a heroin society: The case of Hong Kong', *Substance Use & Misuse*, 40(9/10): 1257–1278.

Lambot, I. and Girard, G. (2014) *City of Darkness Revisited*, London: Watermark.

Lee, M. and Laidler, K.J. (2013) 'Doing criminology from the periphery: Crime and punishment in Asia', *Theoretical Criminology*, 17(2): 141–157.

Liebling, A. and Stanko, B. (2001) 'Allegiance and ambivalence: Some dilemmas in researching disorder and violence', *British Journal of Criminology*, 41(3): 421–430.

Lo, T.W. (2012) 'Triadization of youth gangs in Hong Kong', *British Journal of Criminology*, 52(3): 556–576.

Lofland, J. (1971) *Analysing Social Settings: A Guide to Qualitative Observation and Analysis*, Belmont, CA: Wadsworth.

Mason, J. (1996) *Qualitative Researching* (2nd edn), London: Sage.

Matza, D. (1964) *Delinquency and Drift*, New York: Wiley and Sons.

Noaks, L. and Wincup, E. (2004) *Criminological Research: Understanding Qualitative Methods*, London: Sage.

Wahidin, A. (2011) 'Ethics and criminological research', in P. Davies, P. Francis and V. Jupp (eds) *Doing Criminological Research* (2nd edn) (pp. 287–306), London: Sage.

Whyte, W.F. (1943/1993) *Street Corner Society: The Social Structure of an Italian Slum*, Chicago, IL: University of Chicago Press.

Wincup, E. (2004) *Criminological Research: Understanding Qualitative Methods*, London: Sage.

Young, J. (2004) 'Voodoo criminology and the numbers game', in J. Ferrell, K. Hayward, W. Morrison and M. Presdee (eds) *Cultural Criminology Unleashed* (pp. 13–28), London: Routledge/Glasshouse.

Useful websites

Census and Statistics Department, HKSAR www.censtatd.gov.hk

Correctional Services Department, HKSAR – Annual Review www.csd.gov.hk/english/pub/pub_ar/pub_ar.html

Hong Kong Fight Crime Committee Reports www.sb.gov.hk/eng/pub/index.htm

Hong Kong Police Force (Crime Statistics) www.police.gov.hk/ppp_en/09_statistics/

Independent Commission Against Corruption – Annual Survey www.icac.org.hk/en/useful_information/sd/sd/index.html

Social Welfare Department, HKSAR – Publications www.swd.gov.hk/en/index/site_pubpress/page_publicatio/

University Grants Committee (for Research Funding) www.ugc.edu.hk/eng/rgc/fs/fs.htm

Part II

PRE-TRIAL STAGE

8

THE POLICE FORCE

Wayne W.L. Chan and Raymond W.K. Lau

Introduction

In many ways, the Hong Kong Police Force (HKPF) can be regarded as one of the world's finest police organisations. Surveys show that the public generally regard the HKPF as free of serious corruption, as professional, efficient and effective in maintaining law and order in Hong Kong (OffBeat, 2012). However, this has not always been the case. The HKPF was once a target of public hatred (Grant, 1992: 70). The HKPF has not become complacent over its present achievements, but strives to move forwards in order to keep abreast of the changing demands of Hong Kong society. How has the HKPF developed into what it is today, and what are the prospects of it moving further ahead? This chapter attempts to address these questions.

We begin by explaining how the HKPF, formed soon after Hong Kong became a British colony in 1841, was established along the lines of the classic colonial paramilitary model. Just as the character of the colonial regime remained essentially unchanged up to the early 1970s, the HKPF retained its colonial paramilitary nature throughout the entire period. In the early 1970s, Britain changed the style of colonial governance, as a result of which policing reform was implemented in the mid-1970s. The law enforcement or anti-crime policing function, previously neglected, began to acquire increasing prominence. However, the establishment of the Independent Commission Against Corruption (ICAC) in 1974, as part and parcel of the overall reforming of the HKPF, undermined the HKPF organisationally, as well as damaging police morale. In 1977, a police 'mutiny' against the ICAC erupted, in the aftermath of which corruption offences prior to 1977, with rare exceptions, were generally pardoned. Despite the pardon, corruption as a way of life in the HKPF was gone forever. The pardon allowed the HKPF to recuperate and continue to reorient itself to becoming, by the mid-1980s, a professional force employing coercive tactics in maintaining law and order.

Political developments in the late 1980s and since, however, have impelled the HKPF to abandon its previous strong-arm public order maintenance tactics. In the mid-1990s, under the impact of the radical reforms of the last colonial governor, Chris Patten, the HKPF launched its strategy of transforming itself into a 'service of quality'. This strategy has been maintained up until the present, despite Patten's departure, in the context of political and socio-political developments since Hong Kong's return to Chinese sovereignty in 1997.

Throughout the period of almost continuous reorientation of the HKPF from the mid-1970s until today, the HKPF has emphasised the importance of maintaining its paramilitary capabilities and hard anti-crime tactics. We argue that the maintenance of these capabilities and tactics, generally supported by all and sundry in Hong Kong, is conducive to the retention of a traditional police culture, which does not serve to facilitate the HKPF's attempt to reorient itself into a 'service of quality'. On the other hand, however, in the context of the above-mentioned political and socio-political developments, in terms of daily street patrolling and the policing of public order events, the HKPF's approach has indeed become service oriented. Furthermore, as a result of what we call the 'governability' crisis in Hong Kong since 1997, police authority at street level has been significantly eroded. Thus, the HKPF today and its future developmental trajectory are pulled by contradictory forces. It is still highly effective in maintaining law and order. However, whereas the top brass is committed to the service strategy, there is evidence that a significant number of experienced frontline police still steeped in traditional values are demoralised due to the erosion of street-level police authority, while under these circumstances, the development of a strong sense of organisational and professional commitment among new recruits appears to be encountering some difficulties. Finally, the first edition of this book was published in 2008; for this second edition, we add an addendum at the end of this chapter to take into account developments between 2008 and mid-2015.

The HKPF up to the early 1970s: a classic colonial paramilitary force

Hong Kong became a British colony in 1841. With regard to the policing of colonies, Jeffries (1952) opined that colonial police forces go through three phases: improvised arrangements to secure basic law and order in the initial period of colonisation; establishment of a paramilitary force; and development into a civilian force as colonial rule relaxes and developments towards democratisation and/or decolonisation occur. As a descriptive thesis, Jeffries's view is useful for gaining an overview of the HKPF's development from 1841 to the present day.

The paramilitary model is based upon the recognition of a hostile (usually indigenous) population ruled (usually by an alien colonial power) primarily by coercion with the threat of armed force. The main purpose of the armed police is to suppress disorder without having to resort to the military. The principle of policing strangers (the indigenous population) by strangers (the police staffed and/or controlled by aliens) is practised. Police lived mainly in barracks, and police stations were heavily fortified. The three general functions of the police have been: 1 maintaining public order (e.g. dealing with riots, policing demonstrations, etc.); 2 law enforcement (i.e. dealing with crime); and 3 the provision of miscellaneous services (e.g. regulating traffic). Maintaining public order can further be divided into two sub-categories. One is of a political nature (e.g. policing riots and protests), and the other is of a non-political nature (e.g. dealing with drunkards causing disturbance in a public place, settling disputes between neighbours). In order to distinguish between these two sub-categories, in this chapter we confine maintaining public order to the first sub-category, i.e. in relation to incidents of a political nature, while the latter sub-category will be referred to as peacekeeping. We will also on occasion refer to peacekeeping and service provision collectively as civilian police work. Among the three general functions of the police, public order maintenance was given primacy, law enforcement being secondary, while civilian police work was regarded as a nuisance. Special units were established to gather political intelligence and engage in political policing against political activists considered unfriendly to the government (Tobias, 1972; Andrade, 1985; Anderson and Killingray, 1992). All these features could be found in the HKPF right up to the mid-1970s.

Policing arrangements in Hong Kong began haphazardly upon colonisation with the recruitment of British and (in a well established practice of British colonialism at that time) Indian rejects from the local garrison. In 1944, the HKPF was formally established and subsequently developed on the lines of the classic colonial paramilitary model (Crisswell and Watson, 1982). As shown in Table 8.1, the ethnic composition was as follows (the years 1941–42 and 1946–47 are selected for illustrative purposes).

It can be observed that all gazetted officers were recruited from the British Isles, with only a very small number of inspectors recruited locally. Though locals were recruited to rank and file positions, mostly for linguistic reasons, the classic tactic of policing strangers (locals) by strangers (aliens) was adopted in the rank and file by the use of South Asians and Shandong natives. The departure of the South Asians in 1946–47 was due to the independence of India and Pakistan in 1947. The HKPF wished to replace them by recruiting Portuguese, but the exercise was unsuccessful and thenceforth it was forced to man the rank and file mostly by locals. For decades, only European officers carried firearms. Unmarried European officers as well as the alien rank and file were housed in fortified barracks. Police stations were built like fortresses with high walls and barbed wire.

In 1925–26 an anti-imperialist general strike erupted in Hong Kong led by communist agitators. In its aftermath, the HKPF formed the Emergency Unit (EU) and the Anti-Communist Squad. The latter was a political police unit which subsequently became the Special Branch (SB, *zhengzhibu*) in 1938. The EU's function was to deal with civil disturbances, and to take control at the scene of major incidents. In addition to the EU, the Police Training Contingent (PTC) was later created to provide anti-riot training. All new recruits underwent PTC training early in their career, and refresher training was provided

Table 8.1 Ethnic composition of the HKPF in the 1940s

	1941–42		*1946–47*	
*Officers**	*% of total*	*Number*	*% of total*	*Number*
Gazetted officers (overseas)**	0.8	16	1.0	25
Gazetted officers (local)	0.0	0	0.0	0
Inspectorate (overseas)	12.9	265	10.2	244
Inspectorate (local)	2.5	52	3.7	88
Rank and file*				
Cantonese (i.e. local)	39.0	797	72.9	1,749
Northern Chinese (from Shandong)	8.0	164	8.0	193
Indians/Pakistanis	36.8	752	0.1	3
Portuguese	0.0	0	4.1	99

Source: Adapted from Gaylord and Traver, 1995: 34.

Notes: * 'Officers' refers to inspectors and above; rank and file to their subordinates (constables, sergeants and station sergeants). The latter are now known as junior police officers (JPOs).
** 'Gazetted officers' refers to officers at superintendent rank and above; 'overseas officers' refers to those recruited from the British Isles.

periodically. PTC graduates returned to serve at the local level, but in what is called an Internal Security (IS) situation, i.e. in case of serious civil disorder, local police formations could instantly mobilise PTC graduates of the formation into an anti-riot squad. Police stations underwent regular 'station attack' dry runs.

In 1966, serious anti-colonial protests occurred; the following year, riots led by local communist activists erupted; the HKPF mobilised into IS structure. After these incidents, the Police Tactical Unit (PTU) replaced the PTC. The titles of PTUs (company, platoon, etc.) were all military in origin. Instead of immediately returning to local formations after training, PTU graduates were deployed to a PTU company for a period of time. Thus, PTU became a permanent anti-riot formation, with the EU as a further backup. 'Station attack' dry runs continued. Local police formations continued to have the ability to mobilise instantly into IS structure. Training at both the Police Training School (PTS, for new recruits) and at the PTC/PTU was militarised. Trainees were bare chested and subject to physical punishment. Discipline, loyalty and group solidarity were emphasised.

Up until the early 1970s, crime was only a secondary concern (Munn, 1995). This is strikingly evidenced in the tolerance of the police–triad symbiosis by the HKPF's top brass (Sinclair, 1983; Gaylord and Traver, 1995), in which police kept crime 'under control' by protecting triad-operated vice trade and establishments in return for bribes paid in an organised manner and shared by locals and Europeans alike, a practice that began from the very first days of the HKPF's founding, and reached its peak in the 1950s and 1960s.

Over the decades, some changes to the above did occur, such as the replacement of barracks after the departure of the South Asian rank and file, and the gradual increase in the local ratio of the officers' ranks (mostly at the inspectorate level). However, all the other paramilitary features remained, such as in structure and organisation (EU, PTC/PTU, SB), processes (e.g. militarised training), and practices (e.g. 'station attack' dry runs).

Mid-1970s: first step towards policing reform

Up until the early 1970s, the local administration was a typical colonial regime in the worst sense of the term. Although the 1967 riots were closely related to the Cultural Revolution raging on the mainland during that period, the 1966 disturbances were a spontaneous indigenous anti-colonial incident, while the 1967 disturbances also began as an indigenous labour dispute (Cheung, 2000).

The 1966–67 events were a watershed, both for Hong Kong as a whole and for the HKPF. The colonial regime had always been doubtful of the loyalty of local police. Perhaps to its surprise, local police by and large were prepared to defend the colonial regime against both indigenous anti-colonial and local pro-Beijing activists and protesters. For instance, in our discussions with police informants from that period, we have been informed of only one high-profile resignation by a local inspectorate officer in protest against the HKPF during the course of the 1967 events. In the later stages, the 1967 riots developed into indiscriminate bombing, which alienated most of the local population, and hence local police's willingness to suppress at this stage was easier to understand. The HKPF were prepared to go into suppression mode right from the beginning, in 1966 and again in the initial stages of the disturbances in 1967.

Up to the early 1970s, in the same way as the colonial regime was seriously degenerate, the HKPF was thoroughly corrupt and abusive. At that time, there were several common local sayings that aptly summed up how the public viewed the police: 'the good boy does not join the police'; police were dubbed 'rascals with a licence'. Official inquiries into the 1966–67 events revealed that many protesters in 1966 were anti-police as much as anti-colonial (Scott, 1989). In short, the police, including local police, were beneficiaries and accomplices of the degenerate colonial regime. This probably played a significant part in local police's spontaneous preparedness to defend the regime under challenge. From a social psychological perspective, once the initial preparedness was there, as officers engaged in ongoing conflict with protesters, the conflict itself served to strengthen the *esprit de corps*, as a result of which local police's antipathy towards the protesters became battle hardened.

Local police's readiness to defend the colonial regime surprised and greatly gratified Britain. As a reward, the HKPF was conferred the title of 'Royal' and became the Royal Hong Kong Police Force, a name retained until 1997. In practical terms, with the previous distrust of local recruits considerably reduced, the local ratio of the officers' ranks increased (Gaylord and Traver, 1995).

The 1966–67 events, nonetheless, showed Britain that modifications to the style of colonial governance in Hong Kong were necessary in order to shore up the colonial regime's legitimacy. In 1971, Murray MacLehose was appointed governor. His appointment denoted a sharp break from past practices, as it demonstrated that, unlike previous governors, he did not come from the Colonial Service, and he was known to have socialist sympathies (being pro-Labour in Britain). Clearly, Britain wanted to begin a new era of colonial rule in Hong Kong in which social reforms would be implemented to bridge the gap between the rulers and the ruled – which MacLehose did indeed do soon after his assumption of governorship by introducing massive social reforms such as the ten-year public housing programme (Lo, 1993).

Official inquiry into the 1966–67 events also revealed that official corruption (with the HKPF being most publicly visible) was a social time bomb. Hence, a change in governance style would require tackling official, especially police, corruption head on. Up until then, corruption was investigated by the Anti-Corruption Branch (ACB) of the HKPF, which was a unit within the Criminal Investigation Detective (CID). Such an arrangement was obviously problematic, not only because it meant police investigating police corruption, but also because of the low ranking of the ACB. In 1971, the colonial government raised the issue of setting up an independent anti-corruption body, to which the HKPF objected. Nonetheless, under pressure, the HKPF agreed to take corruption investigation away from the CID, and upgraded the ACB by establishing the Anti-Corruption Office (ACO), headed by an assistant commissioner of police. The ACO's performance was to be reviewed after three years, as a result of which it showed much greater investigative determination than its predecessor. In 1973, the ACO launched an investigation into Chief Superintendent Peter Godber, then deputy district commander of Kowloon. However, Godber managed to flee Hong Kong, sparking massive public outcry and street protests (Lo, 1993).

Meanwhile, in 1972, the management consultants McKinsey & Co., commissioned to look into civil service reform, reported that a sizeable portion of the community hated the police (Grant, 1992: 70). Reform of the HKPF was clearly overdue. MacLehose proceeded on two fronts: first, as a result of the Godber scandal, he set up the ICAC in 1974 despite the HKPF's objection (Lo, 1993); second, several major reform schemes (borrowed from London) were implemented by the HKPF in 1974.

The objective of the HKPF's 1974 reforms was to improve its relations with the public. We have examined these reforms in detail elsewhere (Lau, 2004a); here we shall simply mention one for illustration. The Police Community Relations Officer (PCRO) at the Division (now called District) level was established in 1974 to liaise with the community and improve police–public relations by taking into consideration 'public opinion', and to 'advise, assist and guide' the community. Under the PCRO, there were officers responsible for liaising with schools, local organisations and so on. This set-up has continued to the present day.

At the same time, the function of law enforcement also began to acquire increasing importance. Initially, this was triggered by the beginning of the end of organised police corruption. With the ACO taking a more determined effort to investigate police corruption in the early 1970s, the police–triad symbiosis began to break up, a process further accelerated by the creation of the ICAC in 1974. For this reason, among others, the violent crime rate soared (Traver, 1991). In 1973, the government set up the Fight Violent Crime Committee, which became the Fight Crime Committee (FCC) in 1975. In 1976, District Fight Crime Committees (DFCCs) were formed. Both the FCC and DFCCs remain functioning today with representation from the HKPF.

The police 'mutiny' in 1977 and the HKPF's reorientation towards professionalism

The creation of the ICAC had a serious impact on the HKPF. This is because organised corruption syndicates existed in all police formations, with each syndicate having a 'treasurer'. An arrested treasurer who cooperated with the ICAC often led to the arrest of dozens of officers from the same formation. This not only disrupted police work, but also seriously undermined police morale. In October 1977, police hostility towards the ICAC boiled over. Hundreds of off-duty police gathered at a mass rally held at Police Headquarters. Many subsequently marched to the ICAC headquarters, with some physically breaking into its offices. MacLehose defused the 'mutiny' by announcing a general pardon of all corruption offences committed before 1 January 1977, except for the most heinous cases (Miners, 1998: 97).

In retrospect, the pardon turned out to be instrumental in reorienting the HKPF towards professionalism. While individual corrupt acts did continue after the pardon, it was also clear that corruption as a way of life in the police was gone forever. Those unprepared to accept this would over time leave, either through retirement or resignation; new recruits and those opting to remain would from now on have to focus on doing proper police work. Large-scale arrests of previously existing corruption syndicates ceased completely, allowing the HKPF to recuperate and reorient itself under the changed circumstances.

As a matter of fact, reorientation had begun even before the general pardon. As said, the break-up of the police–triad symbiosis and the government's emphasis placed on fighting crime in the mid-1970s raised the importance of the function of law enforcement. In July 1977, the beat radio was introduced, which greatly enhanced police efficiency at the street level. The breathing space given to the HKPF by the general pardon, and the demise of corruption as a way of life among police, enabled the HKPF to press ahead with its reorientation. In the early 1980s, the organisational structure was overhauled. The previous territorial structure comprising District (of which there were four), Division and Sub-division was changed to the new structure (which has lasted until the present day) comprising Region (of which there are now six), District (equivalent to the previous Division), and Division (equivalent to the previous Sub-division). This overhaul effectively upgraded the rank of the local command. For instance, previously the divisional commander was of senior superintendent rank; now the equivalent post (district commander) is of chief superintendent rank. With this upgrading of the local command, considerable decision-making authority has been decentralised to the local command, with the objective of enhancing efficiency. At the same time, great efforts were put into upgrading the HKPF's equipment and crime-fighting capacity (personal communication to the author from senior police commanders).

As a result, by the mid-1980s, the HKPF had more or less completed a first round of reorientation – namely, the change from a thoroughly corrupt and abusive colonial paramilitary force that focused on public order maintenance into a force which, though still steeped in paramilitary traditions and equipped with paramilitary capabilities, was much professionalised and generally free of organised corruption, with law enforcement now being accorded equal priority with public order maintenance. For convenience, we can call this a reorientation towards professionalism, meaning that proper police work (in contrast to the previous corruption as a way of life) now occupied centre stage, with the HKPF's capabilities in carrying out proper police work being much upgraded.

However, it should be noted that the HKPF remained very much a coercive force, always ready to use the strong arm of the law against the public. A good illustration of this is its strict enforcement of the then very stringent *Public Order Ordinance* (Cap. 245) (POO), as a result of which protesters were often barred from using loudhailers or from marching in groups exceeding 20 in number.

The HKPF's reorientation towards service from the mid-1990s onwards

No sooner had the HKPF more or less completed its reorientation towards professionalism, but it was compelled to engage in a second round of reorientation, this time towards service (Lau, 2004a). In policing parlance, a service is contrasted to a force, for which civilian police work is accorded equal priority. Under the impact of neo-liberal ideology since the early 1990s (see below), service also denotes a customer-service culture in the performance of all policing functions, and not only civilian work. For example, in maintaining public order, a force would emphasise strict enforcement of the relevant laws, if necessary by coercion, whereas a service would aim at facilitating demonstrations as far as that is consistent with minimising disruption to the public. In law enforcement, a force would emphasise the coercive power of control, whereas a service would pay more respect to the rights of individuals. This round of reorientation (hereinafter referred to as service reorientation) occurred due to two intervening events.

The first was the mass rallies and marches after the Tiananmen Square incident on 4 June 1989. Because of the sheer size of these events, the POO was unenforceable. Even after the mass events had died down, local political activists continued to defy the POO, usually with impunity – the political atmosphere after 1989 made return to the previous strict enforcement socially unacceptable. In short, the coercive approach that the HKPF retained prior to 1989 was, in its aftermath, starting to crumble with regard to public order maintenance.

Second, in October 1992, Chris Patten was appointed as the last colonial governor. For reasons best known to himself and Britain, he introduced a number of drastic reforms, of which we shall discuss only one – namely, turning public service into 'customer service'. The background to the 'customer service' idea was that in the late 1970s the neo-liberal right wing ascended to power in Britain and America. It drastically reduced the role of government and introduced market principles into the public service. In 1991, British Prime Minister John Major put forth the Citizens' Charter, which demanded that civil servants serve the public like serving customers. Upon his arrival, Patten, a close political ally of John Major, pushed the same agenda in Hong Kong.

Shortly before Patten's arrival, the HKPF hired a British management consultancy to review its command structure. As usual, these British consultants simply recommended that Hong Kong follow the latest developments in Britain, and hence, inspired by John Major's Citizens' Charter, recommended that the HKPF adopt a more customer-oriented approach. Whether or not this recommendation would have been implemented had it not been for Patten's arrival and demand to adopt this approach for the entire civil service is a moot point. In any case, it was after Patten's programmatic declaration that in May 1994, the HKPF established the Service Quality Wing (SQW), with the mission to develop a customer-service culture among police and transform the HKPF into a 'service of quality'.

In March 1995, the SQW launched the Force Strategy on Quality of Service (Hui, 1995). In December 1996, two documents, *Force Vision* and *Statement of Common Purpose and Values* (Royal Hong Kong Police Force, 1996), collectively known in the Force as 'the Values', were promulgated. Several rounds of 'Living-the-Values' workshops were held on a force-wide basis (Hui, 2001). In early 2001, the slogan-cum-motto of 'We Serve with Pride and Care' was adopted, implying that what the HKPF is providing is a service, which is delivered with care to (in contrast to coercive imposition upon) the public. To instil 'the Values' in new recruits, new subjects on 'the Values' and the 'Bill of Human Rights' (a new ordinance enacted in the early 1990s) were added to the recruit training syllabus. In December 2001, a new uniform was designed; after consultation and trial, it was adopted in December 2004. It should be noted that this new uniform is very similar to the uniform of most private security guards. Apparently, this similarity was intentional, with the purpose of 'civilianising' the police in appearance – the old uniform was too paramilitary-like, hence projecting an image of being separate from, and above, the public, whereas the new uniform would supposedly eliminate this gap.

If the main impetus for the HKPF's service reorientation was initially externally driven by Patten's edict, there can be little doubt that the HKPF's top management was intent on pressing on with the reorientation even after Patten's departure. To understand why and how this came about, it is necessary to examine a third intervening event – namely, the reign of Chee-wah Tung.

Tung became the chief executive (CE) of the Hong Kong Special Administrative Region (HKSAR) under Chinese sovereignty on 1 July 1997. For several months, he enjoyed widespread endorsement among the public, probably because Hong Kong's economy was then riding on the crest of a boom. At the end of 1997, however, the Asian financial crisis struck, and Hong Kong began a long period of economic decline which was to last for some six years or so, with unemployment reaching prolonged record levels. At the same time, a series of unfortunate incidents and Tung's political ineptitude landed his regime in a legitimacy crisis. In 1998, the bird flu epidemic struck Hong Kong; in the same year, the new airport's computer system collapsed on the very first day of operation; and the Severe Acute Respiratory Syndrome (SARS) epidemic killed several hundred people in 2003. While the government's handling of the bird flu crisis and the SARS epidemic won praise internationally, and the removal of the entire airport operation from Kai Tak to Chep Lap Kok literally overnight was no mean feat at all, the media and public opinion focused solely on the negative effects of these incidents. Before becoming the CE, Tung announced the '85,000 policy', trying to provide more affordable housing to the needy. It was a well-intentioned policy enjoying widespread support. However, the property market collapsed with the onset of the Asian financial crisis. Lacking political wisdom, Tung quietly abandoned the policy. In mid-2000, property developers demanded the policy's abandonment in a high-profile manner. Tung decided to make it public that the policy no longer existed, but fearing that such an announcement might be taken as giving in to the developers' demand, he also announced that the policy had in fact been secretly abandoned prior to the developers raising their demand. For a politician to say that he had secretly abandoned a policy was, of course, political stupidity of the first degree. These are just some of the coincidences and examples of Tung's political ineptitude for illustration.

This was not helped by the fact that the local media, from being generally pro-establishment prior to 1997, had post-1997 become one of the world's most fierce critics of, even hostile to, government. This applied not only to media organisations such as *Apple Daily* (a local Chinese newspaper generally regarded as being 'anti-China'), but also to media that are generally regarded as taking a friendly stand towards the Chinese and the HKSAR governments. For instance, *Oriental Daily* (another local Chinese newspaper) might be comparatively friendly towards Beijing or the CE, but when it came to fault finding with the civil service and civil servants, it was no less critical.

The legitimacy crisis of Tung's regime affected not only Tung and his principal officials, but the entire civil service (and other public bodies). Prior to 1997, Hong Kong's civil service was highly praised for its efficiency. Soon after

1997, the same civil service, functioning on the same systems and processes, staffed by mostly the same people, suddenly came to be seen as grossly inept and inefficient. What changed was not the system or the people, but the public's and the media's attitudes towards government and civil servants, and the high demands placed upon them in a radically changed social and socio-political environment, to be discussed as we proceed.

With regard to the police, previously most members of the public tended to submit to police authority (Lau, 2004b), but now, under the radically changed socio-political environment, police authority at the street level is often challenged. Defiance of police authority, resistance to and even assault against officers occur regularly. 'Assault' in such cases usually means physical resistance resulting in police being injured, as opposed to deliberate attack intended to wound. To cite just a few cases from 1997 up to the late 2000s, on 28 September 1999, police responding to a complaint against noise nuisance caused by mahjong playing were injured when the individuals concerned defied the police and resisted (Singpao Daily, 1999); on 23 October 2005, two officers trying to issue a fixed-penalty ticket on a car were confronted by three people and suffered injury during the resistance (MingPao, 2005a); on 26 February 2006, freelance musicians performing in Tuen Mun Park and their fans angrily confronted and hurled verbal abuse at police and Leisure and Cultural Services Department officers who tried to stop the performance on receiving a complaint of noise disturbance (Apple Daily, 2006). A most dramatic case occurred on the night of 11 February 2003 (Oriental Daily, 2003). A squad of officers stopped a group of suspected triad members for identity checks in Yau Ma Tei which is one of the busiest districts in Kowloon after midnight. The group told the officers that after midnight the area was under their, and not police, control. The officers called for reinforcement, as a result of which the media (which were able to tap into police communications) also arrived. The suspected triads' defiance of the police continued right in front of the reporters.

The challenge against street-level police authority is not hard to understand. Because of the legitimate crisis of the Tung regime, principal officials found themselves in a very weak position. As a result, when they appeared on radio talk-shows, they were often 'grilled' and humiliated at will. In the sociology of the media, it is well known that the very nature and format of talk-shows favour simplistic criticism and attack, and make rational all-round explanation difficult. Besides the weak legitimacy position of top officials of Tung's regime, this is another reason why they were often humiliated at will by hosts. If even the CE and his top officials were indiscriminately humiliated in public on a regular basis, why should members of the public pay any respect to minor civil servants such as a beat police officer?

An indication of how bad the situation had become can be gained from the following incident. In May 2001, a protester was arrested in a demonstration and brought back to a police station. Legislator-cum-solicitor Ka Fu Cheng gained access to the arrested protester as his legal representative (MingPao,

2001). While they were conferring alone, Cheng let his mobile phone be used by the arrestee to carry out a live radio interview. This would appear to constitute a breach of a lawyer's professional code of conduct, and incensed police staff associations wanted to lodge a complaint with the Law Society of Hong Kong against Cheng. However, after the intervention of the police commissioner, the staff associations dropped their protestation.

This erosion of authority not only affects the police, but the entire civil service, such that we can properly speak of a governability crisis consequent upon the Tung regime's legitimacy crisis. Even with the departure of Tung, this governability crisis has continued, as it has already acquired its own momentum.

In addition to the governability crisis, the 'customer service' campaign has also produced significant effects. By transforming citizens into consumers, the double emphasis of rights and responsibilities in the concept of citizenship has given way to the one-sided emphasis of rights in the concept of consumerism (Lau, 2006). Citizens-as-consumers are entitled to lodge whatever complaint they see fit. Add the governability crisis and the 'customer service' campaign together, and we have as a result a public that does not respect police authority and feels it to be their right to complain against the police at will.

In letters to newspaper readers' columns and through other channels, frontline police have voiced their concerns about the situation. In our own informal exchanges with various frontline police, it is clear that the feeling of eroded authority at the street level is significant and prevalent, and as a result of this, as well as the desire to avoid being made the subject of complaint, many frontline officers are not prepared to carry out their duties with a firm attitude – in some cases, even avoiding carrying out their duties altogether.

There is, however, one area in which current policing practice largely retains the former coercive style – namely, in some anti-crime tactics such as the regular use of 'carpet searches' of nightspots, which in some cases involve hundreds of police.

In these operations, police enter nightspots for inspection during which the venue's normal activities are suspended for a considerable time. As a result, dozens or even hundreds of ordinary patrons are, at the very least, inconvenienced; at worst, treated as though they were suspects – for example, police sometimes command males to stand on one side, females on the other, and then proceed to check everybody's identity. It is interesting to note that in public order events, any hint of police strong-arm tactics would incur the wrath of human rights activists; by contrast, these strong-arm law enforcement tactics rarely raise an eyebrow, even among the same activists. One possible explanation for this is that Hong Kong has one of the lowest crime rates in the world, and the police receive credit for it from the public (though research worldwide generally provides no support for any correlation between police strength or tactics and crime). Thus, long-established anti-crime tactics have become taken for granted by the public as serving society well, and because of this, even if some human rights activists are aware of the implications of these tactics (which we doubt), it would be politically unwise to question them.

Despite what is being said, however, even in anti-crime operations, police are sometimes challenged due to the erosion of police street-level authority. For instance, on 21 October 2003, a group of seven Special Duty Squad officers carrying out an operation against illegal gambling in a public place, found themselves surrounded by 200 onlookers and had to call for reinforcements. On 12 November 2005, in an anti-crime operation in Mongkok, a team of 12 officers carrying out a liquor licence check were physically confronted by alleged triads who refused to cooperate (MingPao, 2003, 2005b).

To sum up, as a result of social and socio-political changes since 1989, the HKPF's public order maintenance has now become very much a service – facilitating demonstrations – though it must be emphasised that this change notwithstanding, the HKPF's paramilitary capabilities remain intact, as demonstrated in the policing of the protests at the ministerial-level World Trade Organization conference in mid-December 2005. In similar conferences in various parts of the world in previous years, violent confrontations between police and anti-globalisation activists from around the world invariably occurred. On this occasion, several thousand anti-globalisation activists from around the world came to Hong Kong, including the famously (or infamously, depending on one's political standpoint) militant Korean farmer activists. To cope with the challenge, the HKPF mobilised some 9,000 officers, almost a third of the disciplined manpower of the force, to police the protests (WenWeiPo, 2005). Negotiations were held with the protest organisers well ahead of time. Several barricaded protest zones in the vicinity of the conference venue as well as various routes for protest marches were designated. This demonstrated the service role played by the HKPF in the maintenance of public order.

On the first several days of the week-long conference, the protests proceeded in a generally orderly manner. Violent clashes between some protesters (mostly Korean farmer activists) and police did occur at the barricades, in which pepper spray was used by the police. Nevertheless the incidents were relatively minor, almost ritualistic in character, and the police were able to cope with them with little problem.

On the evening of 17 December 2005, the night before the final day of the conference, the Korean farmer activists were determined to make a serious attempt to break through police cordons to reach the conference venue. Marching along the pre-agreed route, some protesters suddenly broke away from the main protest contingent. Perhaps lulled by the orderly manner in which the previous marches had proceeded, the first line of police defence that guarded the march was breached, as a result of which hundreds of protesters were able to reach within 100 metres or so of the conference venue. The second line of police defence was, however, able to hold the line, and violent street battles between police and marauding protesters occurred. Teargas was fired and eventually the police rounded up around 1,000 protesters in Gloucester Road, the main thoroughfare 200 metres away from the conference venue. The protesters were detained (contained) there until the next morning when they were taken to the police station. Despite breaching the first line of defence, the police generally rose to the challenge, thereby illustrating their paramilitary capabilities when called upon to make use of them.

With regard to ordinary street-level policing, the HKPF's previous coercive presence (in the above-mentioned sense that the majority of the population dispositionally deferred to the police) has largely disappeared. It is in this context – of the changes in the HKPF's environment in terms of public order maintenance and street-level policing – that the HKPF's continuation to press on with the service reorientation, even after Patten's departure, should be appreciated.

Despite this change on the part of the police, in a social climate in which the public remains ever dissatisfied (see Lau, 2006), complaints against police have remained high. Thus, reducing complaints is a top HKPF priority. The HKPF top brass believe that the means to do this is to push ahead with the service reorientation. In 2005–06, the HKPF took two significant steps in this direction. In January 2006, the PTS was upgraded to become the Hong Kong Police College (HKPC), for which the HKPF contracted a local university to teach two modules to new police recruits – namely, social studies in policing (aiming to prepare new recruits to face Hong Kong's changed social and socio-political environments for policing), and psychology in policing (aiming to enhance the police's ability to handle cases such as domestic violence so as to avoid complaint). In 2005, a comprehensive plan for providing 'psychological competency' training to serving officers was drawn up and began to be implemented (in phases) with the help of local academia, one major objective of which was the same as the teaching of psychology in policing at the HKPC.

It is clear that the HKPF has changed radically from the pre-1989 era. The HKPF top brass are aware of this change and are committed to follow through with the service reorientation to suit Hong Kong's changed social and socio-political environments. The remaining questions are: What is the deeper reality of the HKPF's change since 1989, and what are the future prospects of its service reorientation?

Future prospects of the HKPF's service reorientation

As explained, transformation into a service involves two aspects: giving equal priority to civilian police work, and adopting a customer-service culture and ethos in all police work. To what extent have these aspects been realised?

Concerning the first aspect, it will be recalled that a paramilitary force gives first priority to public order maintenance; a professional police gives equal priority to public order maintenance and law enforcement (hereinafter, these two types of police work will be referred to as frontline operational work) through reliance on coercive tactics. Ideally, a police service values civilian police work as highly as frontline operational work. In this respect, the HKPF is apparently still under the influence of its historical roots and retains an emphasis on frontline operational work.

First, all of the HKPF's paramilitary structures (e.g. EU, PTU), processes (e.g. ready mobilisation into IS structure) and so on have been retained. This is partly due to the general emphasis placed by the government and the public on the need to maintain Hong Kong's political stability, but it is also partly determined by the HKPF's historical roots. Second, priority is apparently still given to frontline operational work, informally regarded as 'core' duties in the HKPF. 'Core' duties are informally given greater weight in comparison to non-'core' duties (e.g. training, community work) in terms of career advancement. Thus, of the two deputy commissioners of police (DCPs), namely, DCP (Operations) and DCP (Management), when the commissioner retires, it is usually DCP (Operations) who succeeds to the post. It should, however, be underlined that the retention of the HKPF's historically entrenched values, such as those mentioned above, is not the conscious intention of the HKPF's top management. The impression that we have gained from our own contact with some members of the top management and other senior commanders is that the wish to follow through with the service reorientation is genuine. Our argument is that such retention occurs on a subconscious level.

As to the second aspect, the impression gained from our informal exchanges with various veteran frontline police can nicely be summed up in this comment: 'we are now polite towards ordinary citizens, that's mainly to avoid complaint. But that's on the surface. Deep down, there's no concept of service at all. That's very hard to acquire.' There is general scepticism among experienced frontline officers towards the concept of consumerism (public service as customer service) in policing. Thus, the generally known nickname given to SQW is 'idiotic wing' (in Cantonese 'Shaw Q wing'). This is not peculiar to Hong Kong. Research elsewhere also finds that ingrained police attitudes inimical to the service ethos are hard to change (Guyot, 1991; Dixon and Stanko, 1993; Bennett, 1994; Lurigio and Rosenbaum, 1994). Whereas we believe that the above is the case with many experienced frontline officers, whether or not with the establishment of the HKPC a stronger service culture can be cultivated among the new breed of recruits is an issue that awaits future research.

The HKPF and its future developmental trajectory are in some ways pulled by contradictory forces. On the one hand, the top management sincerely wishes to follow through with the service reorientation. On the other hand, the maintenance of its paramilitary capabilities and hard law enforcement tactics provides fertile soil for the persistence of a professional but hard law enforcer culture among police. In contradiction to this, the erosion of police authority in ordinary street-level policing has been significant. Among experienced officers still largely steeped in traditionalist values, this has considerably affected morale. In the pre-1989 era, when such a contradictory situation did not exist, new recruits quickly became 'police-ified', i.e. they were initiated into the prevalent police culture and developed a strong sense of organisational-professional belonging. In the past several years, the top management have come to notice that this sense of organisational-professional belonging among new recruits is weak. Why is this so?

While in-depth research is required to answer this fully, we believe it has a lot to do with the diminished morale of many experienced frontline police, through whom new recruits' initiation into the organisation and its culture occurs, and the erosion of street-level police authority (new recruits begin their career on beat patrol). As various frontline officers have remarked to me, many (both the experienced and the new) now regard the job simply as a job; the previous sense of organisational-professional *esprit de corps* has been comparatively weakened.

Despite this, the HKPF is still able to function effectively – a testimony to its well-established capabilities and professionalism. However, it is clear from the above that the only viable position to take in public under Hong Kong's current social and socio-political climate (which is unlikely to change in the foreseeable future), namely, to press on with the service reorientation, is creating tension with the determination (ironically, also supported by the public) to maintain its paramilitary capabilities and hard law enforcement tactics, which serve to reproduce traditionalist police culture. With street-level police authority eroded, this tension has so far been 'resolved' in the engendering of low morale among many experienced officers and a relatively low sense of organisational-professional belonging and commitment among new recruits.

To conclude, despite the subconscious retention of the priority given to frontline operational work, civilian police work is now given much greater weight than previously. The HKPF's history in terms of certain anti-crime tactics and ingrained police values is still exerting an influence, at least among some members of the force, but in terms of ordinary street-level policing and the policing of public order events, the approach now taken by the HKPF is service oriented. This juxtaposition reflects the above-explained underlying tension facing the HKPF. It will be interesting to see how the resolution of this tension will unfold in the coming years.

Addendum (as of April 2015)

There have been a few notable background developments and one large public order incident since the first edition of this book was published in 2008.

During the SARS epidemic in 2003, the central government greatly relaxed restrictions on mainland Chinese visitors to Hong Kong in order to help revive the latter's economy. This created several unintended consequences, including the bidding up of local property prices and increase in mutual animosity between many locals and the mainland tourists (*South China Morning Post* (SCMP) 2014b). As a result, a pro-independent mentality has developed among a not insignificant number of locals (SCMP, 2014a). In July 2012, Chief Executive Chun-ying Leung took office. The opposition has begun a continuous sabotage campaign against his administration, including the repeated use of filibustering (SCMP, 2013). The crisis of governance mentioned above has thus worsened.

According to Article 45 of the *Basic Law* and the political reform blueprint adopted in 2007, universal suffrage for electing the CE would be introduced in 2017, with the power of nominating candidates given to an Election Committee. In 2014, details of the arrangements for 2017 were being worked out. The opposition demanded to bypass the Election Committee and called for civil nomination. Several oppositional figures such as the 'Occupy Central' founder, Benny Tai, announced that if this demand was not met, they would call for an 'Occupy Central' struggle ('Central' refers to the local core business district) (SCMP, 2014c). The central government took the 2017 arrangements to be a sovereignty issue and refused to budge (SCMP, 2014f).

In the autumn of 2014, 'Occupy Central' materialised and a 79-day protest occurred, sometimes dubbed the 'umbrella revolution' by the media (SCMP, 2014d). Revolution or not, it indeed very much constituted an insurrection, with violent clashes occurring on many occasions, while the pro-independent mentality surfaced prominently among a significant number of protesters (SCMP, 2014e). The government and the police initially used teargas in attempts to prevent the occupation of the area around government headquarters, but this failed, whereupon occupiers paralysed several major traffic arteries. The government then changed tactics and allowed the occupation to continue, letting it cause as much damage as possible to the daily life of the travelling public. This tactic worked and eventually sentiments among probably the majority of the public turned against the occupiers, and the police were finally able to restore normality. Under the current and foreseeable socio-political environment, it is worth putting further thought into how the police force maintains its paramilitary capabilities for public order events despite the commitment to a service culture.

Review questions

1 In what ways was the HKPF a classic colonial paramilitary force up to the early 1970s?
2 In this chapter, an implicit theme is that the main impetuses to the HKPF's almost continuous reorientation since the mid-1970s have been externally derived. Explain this with reference to the reforms of the mid-1970s, the service strategy begun in the mid-1990s, and the continued commitment to the service reorientation after Patten's departure until today.
3 How would you describe the character of the HKPF today?

References

Anderson, D.M. and Killingray, D. (1992) *Policing and Decolonization: Politics, Nationalism and the Police 1917–65*, Manchester: Manchester University Press.

Andrade, J. (1985) *World Police and Paramilitary Forces*, Basingstoke: Macmillan.

Bennett, T. (1994) 'Community policing on the ground: Developments in Britain', in D.P. Rosenbaum (ed.) *The Challenge of Community Policing: Testing the Promises* (pp. 224–246), Thousand Oaks, CA: Sage.

Cheung, K.W. (2000) *Inside Story of 1967 Riot in Hong Kong*, Hong Kong: The Pacific Century Press Ltd (in Chinese).

Crisswell, C. and Watson, M. (1982) *The Royal Hong Kong Police (1841–1945)*, Hong Kong: Macmillan.

Dixon, B. and Stanko, E. (1993) *Serving the People: Sector Policing and Public Accountability*, Uxbridge: Brunel University.

Gaylord, M. and Traver, H. (1995) 'Colonial policing and the demise of British rule in Hong Kong', *International Journal of the Sociology of Law*, 23(1): 23–43.

Grant, I. (1992) *1997: The Implications for Community Policing in Hong Kong*, unpublished MA thesis, Exeter: University of Exeter.

Guyot, D. (1991) *Policing as Though People Matter*, Philadelphia, PA: Temple University Press.

Hui, K-O. (1995) *A Service of Quality: Speech to the Australian Chamber of Commerce in Hong Kong*, Hong Kong: Government Printer.

Hui, K.-O.. (2001) 'Management reforms in the Police Force', in A.B.L. Leung and J.C.Y. Lee (eds) *Public Sector Reform in Hong Kong: Into the 21st Century* (pp. 167–199), Hong Kong: The Chinese University Press.

Jeffries, C. (1952) *The Colonial Police*, London: Max Parrish.

Lau, R.W.K. (2004a) 'Community policing in Hong Kong: Transplanting a questionable model', *Criminal Justice*, 4(1): 61–80.

Lau, R.W.K. (2004b) 'History as obstacle to change: A neo-institutionalist analysis of police reform in Hong Kong', *International Journal of the Sociology of Law*, 32(1): 1–15.

Lau, R.W.K. (2006) 'Fetishistic forms of rationality and the culture of blame', conference paper presented at the 16th World Congress of Sociology, Durban, South Africa, July 2006, organised by the International Sociological Association.

Lo, T.W. (1993) *Corruption and Politics in Hong Kong and China*, Buckingham: Open University Press.

Lurigio, A.J. and Rosenbaum, D.P. (1994) 'The impact of community policing on police personnel: A review of the literature', in D.P. Rosenbaum (ed.) *The Challenge of Community Policing: Testing the Promises* (pp. 147–163), Thousand Oaks, CA: Sage.

Miners, N.J. (1998) *The Government and Politics of Hong Kong* (5th edn), Hong Kong: Oxford University Press.

Munn, C. (1995) '"Scratching with a rattan": William Caine and the Hong Kong magistracy', *Hong Kong Law Journal*, 25(2): 213–238.

Royal Hong Kong Police Force (1996) *Force Vision* and *Statement of Common Purpose and Values*, Hong Kong: Royal Hong Kong Police Force.

Scott, I. (1989) *Political Change and the Crisis of Legitimacy in Hong Kong*, Hong Kong: Oxford University Press.

Sinclair, K. (1983) *Asia's Finest: An Illustrated Account of the Royal Hong Kong Police*, Hong Kong: Unicorn.

Tobias, J.J. (1972) 'Police and the public in the UK', *Journal of Contemporary History*, 7, 201–220.

Traver, H. (1991) 'Crime trends', in H. Traver and J. Vagg (eds) *Crime and Justice in Hong Kong* (pp. 10–24), Hong Kong: Oxford University Press.

Newspaper articles cited

Apple Daily (2006) 「康文署出動保安員 人鏈護送離開　公園表演受阻百人圍兩警」, 27 February.

MingPao (2001) 「警搶手機阻拘留者電臺控訴」, 10 May.

MingPao (2003) 「警廟街掃賭遭200人包圍」, 22 October.

MingPao (2005a) 「兩漢小故襲警 胡椒噴霧降服」, 24 October.

MingPao (2005b) 「酒吧查牌6煞推撞12 警員報稱受傷」, 13 November.

OffBeat (2012) 'Force scores high ratings in surveys', *OffBeat: The Newspaper of the Hong Kong Police Force*, 4–17 July, www.police.gov.hk/offbeat/970/eng/n05.htm (accessed 15 February 2016).

Oriental Daily (2003) 「不滿查證六漢圍警挑釁」, 12 February.

Singpao Daily (1999) 「惡男女竹戰擾人清夢　狂毆投訴鄰居　反抗傷兩警員」, 29 September.

South China Morning Post (SCMP) (2013) 'Filibusters disrupt 11 planned events', 2 May, www.scmp.com/news/hong-kong/article/1227772/filibusters-disrupt-11-planned-events (accessed 15 February 2016).

South China Morning Post (SCMP) (2014a) '"Independence" groups want a stronger local voice in how city is run', 4 January, www.scmp.com/news/hong-kong/article/1396879/independence-groups-want-stronger-local-voice-how-city-run (accessed 15 February 2016).

South China Morning Post (SCMP) (2014b) 'Hong Kong may amend its race hate law to protect mainland visitors', 20 February, www.scmp.com/news/hong-kong/article/1432229/hong-kong-may-amend-its-race-hate-law-protect-mainland-visitors (accessed 15 February 2016).

South China Morning Post (SCMP) (2014c) 'Upbeat Occupy Central founder Benny Tai hints at long-term fight', 9 September, www.scmp.com/news/hong-kong/article/1588015/occupy-central-founder-benny-tai-hints-long-term-fight (accessed 15 February 2016).

South China Morning Post (SCMP) (2014d) 'TIMELINE: How Occupy Central's democracy push turned into an Umbrella Revolution', 9 October, www.scmp.com/news/hong-kong/article/1612900/timeline-how-occupy-centrals-democracy-push-turned-umbrella (accessed 15 February 2016).

South China Morning Post (SCMP) (2014e) 'Occupy Central organisers want independent Hong Kong, People's Daily claims', 20 October, www.scmp.com/news/hong-kong/article/1620149/occupy-central-organisers-want-independent-hong-kong-peoples-daily?page=all (accessed 15 February 2016).

South China Morning Post (SCMP) (2014f) 'China leaders stress Hong Kong should stick to strict reform framework', 26 December, www.scmp.com/news/hong-kong/article/1668655/premier-li-keqiang-praises-cy-leung-administration-pledges (accessed 15 February 2016).

WenWeiPo (2005) 「強調警方有能力平亂 無需求助駐軍 一哥⊠街頭圍困900示威者」, 18 December.

Legislation cited

Public Order Ordinance (Cap. 245)

Useful websites

Hong Kong Police Force (HKPF) www.police.gov.hk/index.html
The Independent Police Complaints Council www.ipcc.gov.hk/tc/home/index.html
The Metropolitan Police Service (London) – HKPF's early model of police service www.met.police.uk

9

POLICE POWERS

David K.S. Ng

Introduction

In Western societies, the relationship between society, the law and police is regarded as 'the triangle of tension' (Edwards, 2011: 6). This tension appears to be universal as the police and the policed may at times be seen by some to be standing in opposing positions. However, the Hong Kong Police's role is rather unique as they witnessed and experienced rapid changes in the society in the past few decades that were of a scale unmatched by most other societies. After the two civil disturbances in the 1950s and the 1960s, the economy of Hong Kong took off in the 1970s, when Hong Kong became an industrial and manufacturing port. Then, it transformed to become a financial and service regional centre in the 1980s, before the transfer of sovereignty in 1997.

Once regarded as a utilitarian society where people were apathetic about politics, the citizens of Hong Kong were happy with a stable political, social and economic environment ensured by the British colonial government that allowed them to simply make their living. Lau (1984: 13) described people of Hong Kong as 'utilitarian familism'. He explained that many people were, in some sense, refugees fled from Mainland China before 1949 in order to escape communism, they counted on family members or relatives to support their welfare and did not expect much from their government. The colonial government and its paternal style of governing were taken for granted and relatively few challenges against its authority were staged. People simply enjoyed a stable environment in which they were left alone to continue to work hard to improve their standard of living. During this period, the primary task of the Hong Kong Police was simply to maintain law and order under a rather homogeneous society. Police power was rarely an issue.

While the economy of Hong Kong continued to thrive in the 1980s and the 1990s, higher educational opportunities and social upward mobility were also enhanced. The society became more diversified, the public demand and expectation of the government also increased. People began to expect a more accountable and transparent government. In tandem with this development trend, the colonial government adopted a more open approach and was more responsive to public demands. In the same period, the Hong Kong Police first introduced community policing, and then later the service-oriented approach. Community policing in the Hong Kong Police was introduced in 1974 when the Police Community Relations Office in each police division (now district) was set up. The service-oriented approach was launched in the mid-1990s.

Facing the return of sovereignty to Mainland China in 1997, many people of Hong Kong began to raise their political concerns about the future, and society became very divided. Many people pledged loyalty to the Beijing government, and became very supportive of the new Hong Kong Special Administrative Region (HKSAR) government, whilst some people were concerned that the capitalistic free society of Hong Kong might sooner or later be eroded by communism, or at least by the notionally communist government of Mainland China. To ensure freedom and democracy under the 'One Country, Two Systems' arrangement, such people became keen on challenging governance by the government of the HKSAR, querying whether autonomy was being maintained, and if the People's Republic of China was controlling the former from behind the scenes. Under such a conflicting political environment, some people in Hong Kong are becoming more and more prepared to adopt a more confrontational attitude to advocate for human rights issues. We can see similar situations around the world where people are launching large-scale protests against their governments. These include the Jasmine Revolution that took place in Tunisia in 2010, the Occupy Wall Street movement in the USA in 2010, and the Sunflower Movement in Taiwan in early 2014.

These movements are believed by some to have far-reaching impacts in the globalised world, and in recent years there has been increasing demand in Hong Kong society for greater public participation in government. For a number of years now, after the handover of sovereignty, protests made by people against the Hong Kong government have not ceased. Some protests have been getting more openly confrontational, and this culminated in the Occupy Central movement that started in September 2014. Although the protesters started to express their dissatisfaction with the proposed political reform package at first, the police were caught in the middle, and subsequently became a subject of protests themselves with the consequence that police legitimacy became severely challenged. The political reform package was about the Hong Kong chief executive election arrangement for 2017. The controversy related to how to achieve universal suffrage.

Hong Kong is now facing a series of post-1997 governance crises. Many studies have been conducted to assess the causes of these from different perspectives (Lui and Wong, 2000; Cheung, 2005; Chiu and Lui, 2009). No matter what the reasons may be, the Hong Kong Police, being the forefront executive arm of the government of the HKSAR, charged with the responsibility to uphold law and order, can be perceived as a suppressive power against the people of Hong Kong. When people protest against the government, lawfully or unlawfully, the police are always there to maintain law and order. Just to regulate any public order events and to ensure public safety, the police may find themselves caught up in confrontations with the demonstrators, when they might be compelled to enforce the law in a manner that could be construed as using their powers against the people. The demonstrators may in turn find the police acting in excess of their powers. Under the current political environment, the Hong Kong Police are often standing in between the Hong Kong government and the people challenging the governance of Hong Kong. The amount of pressure the Hong Kong Police face may be viewed as some kind of thermometer that partly reflects the intensity of political conflicts in society and the amount of people's support to the government of the HKSAR.

Police power is becoming a contentious issue in Hong Kong. The dilemma is, at least to some people: ought police powers be significantly curbed or do we still want the police to do their job well and can we still expect the police to effectively discharge their duties to maintain law and order, prevent and detect crime, protect lives and property? This short chapter attempts to offer a few insights for a better appreciation of police power in the context of socio-political changes in Hong Kong.

Society, the law and police power

The very first question we have to ask is, where does the power of the police come from? No matter how much privacy, democracy and human rights we desire, we have to recognise that for public safety and stability, civil society needs not only an effective body of law but also the means to enforce the law diligently.

In modern societies, there is an ideological assumption that the police are a functional prerequisite of social order so that without a police force chaos would ensue (Reiner, 2010). Sociologically speaking, the power vested in the police is to enforce the laws enacted to uphold valued social norms, and to guard against deviant behaviour that has been commonly defined, defied and criminalised by society. Inevitably, some people may find these laws, determined by the powerful group, imposing or restrictive of their rights and freedom.

A developed and orderly society should have its police enforcing the law for the overall benefits of all its citizens. Yet a problem is that law pervades the lives of every single citizen in their interactions with others. For example, in Hong Kong, freedom does not entitle us to harm others physically; we are not entitled to drive a car on a road without a driver's licence; a driver is not entitled to drive whilst under the influence of alcohol; and people are not entitled to carry an offensive weapon such as a knife in a public place. The police are not only empowered but also expected to enforce the law to protect the innocent.

A perspective exists that there are always two camps holding different and conflicting views on where the thin line should be drawn. The 'law and order' camp always supports the extension of police power and argues against the rights of suspects that would erode the police power, tipping the scale of justice too far in the interests of the offenders, helping them to hide their guilt

(Koffman, 1985: 12). The opposing camp maintains that the extension of police power would be a pernicious step on a path towards paramilitarisation, as 'a draconian increase in police powers, in precisely those areas of activity which feature heavily in military policing' (Lea and Young, 1993: 254).

It is emphasised here that in a modern society, and also in the case of Hong Kong, it is the society that gives the police a wide range of powers to act on its behalf to enforce the laws the society has enacted. In doing so, society has created an organisation with the powers and resources to police itself, potentially against the wishes of its members (Edwards, 2011: 15). Understanding this from a more societal perspective, police officers are only enforcing the law, may be arresting an offender, on behalf of society, to uphold the overall benefits of all. From this perspective, offenders or those who fight against the police should understand that the police are exercising powers against them as entrusted and expected by their own society, and it is society that decides how much power should be given.

The officers of the Hong Kong Police are working within a very complex political environment, influenced by a range of citizens and interest groups, and by the media to professional groups. As in many other places, these different interests can often make law enforcement a difficult and politicised profession (Worrall and Schmalleger, 2015). In recent years, the number of public order events in Hong Kong kept rising. Public order events refer to public processions and public meetings in a public place where the police have a duty to regulate to ensure public order and safety. It climbed from 1,190 in 1997 to 6,818 in 2014, representing an almost sixfold increase. Table 9.1 shows the trend of these public order events since 1997, and these activities are largely protests against the government. The police whose duty has been to exercise their powers to regulate these events, have from time to time been criticised for acting in abuse of their authority.

Police power and police duty

In the UK, the political debate about policing often evolves around whether the police have sufficient legal powers to deal with the ever-changing problems of crime and disorder apparently threatening society (Rowe, 2014: 65). In Hong Kong, we may debate the same question today, and it has been opined that the Hong Kong colonial police force was set up in the past to improvise arrangements to secure basic law and order. The policing model under the earlier, more paramilitary colonial policing ethos was that the use of coercion by means of a police force instead of by military forces was needed to regulate a hostile population being ruled by an alien power (Jeffries, 1952). Be that as it may, with such an inheritance and mission, the Hong Kong Police have since been developed as the agency of first response and last resort. When we put the power of the police in context, there is nothing substantial, at least not referenced by studies, to indicate that the Hong Kong Police have any greater power than the police in other societies.

Table 9.1 Number of public order events in Hong Kong, 1997–2014

Year	*Number of public order events*
1997	1,190
1998	2,247
1999	2,326
2000	2,046
2001	2,347
2002	2,303
2003	2,705
2004	1,974
2005	1,900
2006	2,228
2007	3,824
2008	4,287
2009	4,222
2010	5,656
2011	6,878
2012	7,529
2013	6,166
2014	6,818

Source: Support Wing, Hong Kong Police.

The duties of the Hong Kong Police are laid down in section 10 of the *Police Force Ordinance* (Cap. 232) (PFO) (see Table 9.2). As can be seen, today the police duties are still wide in range variety, including preserving the peace; preventing and detecting crimes; and preventing injury to life and property. They have to deal with dangerous criminals, as well as stray animals. For the police to effectively fulfil the obligations of carrying out these diverse duties, they need adequate legal powers.

The PFO provides a wide range of police power, ranging from the power to administer found property disposal, to the power of taking an intimate body sample from a suspect. However, the most frequently used police powers are under sections 50 and 54. Section 50 provides for the 'Power of arrest, detention and bail of suspected person and seizure of suspected property'; Section 54 provides for the 'Power to stop, detain and search' any person who acts in a suspicious manner in any street or other public place. Discussing these two sections, Wong (2010: 8) believed that the 'Hong Kong Police has legally unlimited and operationally non-reviewable powers to stop and if need be search people in the street, at will'. Are police powers really unlimited and non-reviewable? This, in fact, is arguable from a legal point of view. In a number of

Table 9.2 Duties of the Hong Kong Police

	The duties of the police force shall be to take lawful measures for: -
a.	preserving the public peace;
b.	preventing and detecting crimes and offences;
c.	preventing injury to life and property;
d.	apprehending all persons whom it is lawful to apprehend and for whose apprehension sufficient grounds exist;
e.	regulating processions and assemblies in public places or places of public resort;
f.	controlling traffic upon public thoroughfares and removing obstructions therefrom;
g.	preserving order in public places and places of public resort, at public meetings and in assemblies for public amusements, for which purpose any police officer on duty shall have free admission to all such places and meetings and assemblies while open to any of the public;
h.	assisting in carrying out any revenue, excise, sanitary, conservancy, quarantine, immigration and alien registration laws;
i.	assisting in preserving order in waters of Hong Kong and in enforcing port and maritime regulation therein;
j.	executing summonses, subpoenas, warrants, commitments and other process issued by the courts;
k.	exhibiting information and conducting prosecutions;
l.	protecting unclaimed and lost property and finding the owners thereof;
m.	taking charge of and impounding stray animals;
n.	assisting in the protection of life and property at fires;
o.	protecting property from loss damage;
p.	attending the criminal courts and, if specially ordered, the civil courts, and keeping order therein;
q.	escorting and guarding prisoners;
r.	executing such other duties as may by law be imposed on a police officer.

Source: Section 10 of the *Police Force Ordinance*.

judicial reviews lodged by people of Hong Kong in recent years, the Court of Final Appeal ruled that exercise of police powers should be subject to the tests of 'proportionality', 'necessity' and 'reasonableness'. The relevant judicial review cases are *Leung Kwok-hung & others v HKSAR* (CFA FACC Nos. 1 & 2 of 2005, 2), and *Yeung May-wan & others v HKSAR* (CFAFACC No. 19 of 2004).

Besides the PFO, more police powers are supplemented by derivative and delegated powers in other legislations, for example, in *Dangerous Drugs Ordinance* (Cap. 134), *Public Order Ordinance* (Cap. 245), *Road Traffic Ordinance* (Cap. 374), and *Summary Offences Ordinance* (Cap. 228).

The Hong Kong Police are also a restrictive regulatory authority. The commissioner of police is vested with different legislative powers to issue various licences and permits, and to sanction public activities. These onerous duties include controlling firearm licences, pawnbroker licences, security personnel permits and registration under the *Societies Ordinance* (Cap. 151), etc. In sanctioning public activities under the *Public Order Ordinance*, the police can issue objections to the notifications of public meetings and public processions.

Exercise of police power

Hong Kong society has given a wide range of duties to the police, and enacted the law to create the necessary powers for them to fulfil these duties. Very often, the police are called by the public to arbitrate disputes and are expected to do so with authority, yet without being authoritarian. The police are expected to behave in a manner that is both authoritative and acceptable to the public that is more diverse and socially aware than ever before (Edwards, 2011: 95). It is therefore necessary for the police to faithfully discharge their duties and exercise their powers in a way that the society expects.

Serving a population of over 7 million people, the approximately 28,000 officers of the Hong Kong Police must be well equipped to exercise their powers in a professional manner. The nature of police work allows no room for error. Very often police officers are walking the beat alone, and they have to make a decision alone within a split second of whether or not to stop and search a suspect, and whether or not to make an arrest at the scene. The officers must therefore be very conversant with their powers, and well trained on how to use them. Officers may have an unlimited number of opportunities in a shift to come across a citizen against whom they have to exercise their police powers, but to this citizen, it may be the once-in-a-lifetime encounter with the police. Making a wrong decision would not only impart a very negative experience to this citizen, but would also likely result in a miscarriage of justice.

Although the enforcement and investigatory powers rest with the police, the Department of Justice (DOJ) separately holds the power to prosecute. This is a good balance of power intended within the Hong Kong criminal justice system. In determining legal or evidential questions, the police may consult the Prosecution Division of the DOJ. The police can also seek advice on the ways to collect sufficient evidence before preparing and making a criminal charge. Overall, the Hong Kong Police and the DOJ work very closely together, and they 'invariably co-operate harmoniously in pursuit of shared objectives' (Cross, 2008: 116). Details on the subject of the prosecution principles and mechanism are in Chapter 11 of this book.

Police officers may find their average day's work mundane and uneventful, but there will be many times that they face challenges, potentially having to exercise their police powers. Every scenario they face in a day can be different; it is impossible to codify precisely when and how exactly they should act. They have to exercise their discretion under the particular circumstances they find as to whether they should stop and search a suspicious person, arrest, or whether they should release a minor offender with a caution, or issue a summons. Police discretion is always a hot topic that politicians and criminologists are interested in exploring.

A stable society needs a police organisation that provides a reliable and trustworthy service. The members of the public have to be confident that when they call upon the police for help, they can expect, with minimal uncertainty, basically what they will get. Even though the police are allowed to exercise their powers with some discretion, the way they act in dealing with cases and reports must be within reasonable expectations, so that the members of the public can predict the consequences of law breaking. For example if anyone steals, the police will arrest the thief, and if anyone is criminally victimised, the police will help him or her and submit the perpetrators to justice. The fact that the police can be expected to respond diligently to the public's demand and enforce their powers professionally is reassuring for public safety and can reduce a general fear of crime. At the same time, there is a deterrent effect on crimes: criminologists Cohen and Felson in their Routine Activity Theory (1979) posited that crimes take place when there is an absence of a capable guardian, while a motivator offender exists and the opportunity arises.

In order to establish their role of being a capable guardian, the police, in exercising their powers, must act under some important principles:

1 Lawfulness: rule of law is the cornerstone of the stability of Hong Kong (Chui and Lo, 2008; Lo and Chui, 2012). Legality is the first and most basic level of legitimacy (Beetham, 2013). The police must act within the parameters of the law and cannot act exceeding the powers they have been given. To exercise their powers lawfully, the police must exercise their powers in good faith. If the police find a problem they cannot tackle without more powers, they should seek the additional powers they need through the legislative process.
2 Consistency: public confidence in law and order is reinforced when the ways the police operate and the ways they exercise their powers are consistent. However, consistency can be influenced by difference in personal attitude between police officers (Stith, 1990). Consistency in context here means the police discharging their duties to a similar standard and exercising their powers within similar principles over time. To lay down these principles and guidelines and to minimise ambiguity, the Hong Kong Police have a fairly detailed *Force Procedure Manual*, and publish instructions written in Headquarters Orders and Standing Orders from time to time. These materials are reviewed and updated regularly to cope with the changes in society.
3 Uniformity: the need to, and benefits of, policing with uniformity have been widely recognised (Stockdale and Gresham, 1995). In dealing with about 70,000 crimes and many miscellaneous reports a year in Hong Kong, it is not at all easy to handle these cases in an absolutely uniform manner. Failure to do so will cause confusion for the public. It is understandable

that absolute uniformity across the board is impossible because each locality has its own uniqueness, some being more densely populated, some having more crime problems, some with more high-risk premises, some being very urban and some being rural in nature. We cannot expect the police officers in different districts to focus on the same things. Difference in attention aside, the police officers should exercise their powers in a uniform fashion. That is, they should by and large apply the same policing principles and considerations.

4 Fairness: it is very important for police officers to exercise their powers fairly, showing no favouritism to any one. Because the police are the most visible face of power of the government to most citizens, they are expected to be impartial and fair (Skogan and Frydl, 2004). Fairness is also a subjective perception. When two parties are involved in a dispute, the police are often called to arbitrate; they will find themselves standing in a very difficult and awkward position, as both sides could perceive that the police are not helping them but favouring the other side. Acting with a sense of fairness should therefore not only to be done, but also to be seen to be done. In a diverse society like Hong Kong, the police have to be fair to people from all backgrounds.

5 Empathy: today the public not only expects the police to discharge their duties lawfully, but also empathetically. An empathetic relationship can help a police officer to communicate better with victims and offenders and to understand them more easily (Blagden, 2012). For instance, society expects special care and consideration for young people and elders, who might have breached the law owing to ignorance, senile dementia or sympathetic reasons. That is why the Hong Kong Police have schemes to discharge young offenders and elders with a caution instead of prosecution over minor offences. The intention of these schemes is to exercise leniency, having care and regard for the age of the offenders. In practice, however, this factor is difficult to deliberate, as police officers might be bound to act within the law.

6 Transparency: transparency can facilitate a broader understanding of what the police are doing and thereby give the public the ability to hold the police force accountable (Cheung, 2005). In an open society, the members of the public expect the government to be transparent, they want to be informed as a matter of right of public policies, the rationale behind each official decision, and how civil servants perform. Most members of the public may find police work mysterious, as they usually only gain some idea about police work and operations through the window of the media, which are always keen to report what they think are newsworthy police stories. In Hong Kong, the media expect to be told whom the police have arrested and charged, and the brief facts of such cases, what cases have taken place, etc. In order to cultivate trust and mutual understanding, the police should, if circumstances permit, take the initiative to keep the public informed of their work. To gain understanding and support from society, the police should be as transparent as possible.

Police power and priorities

With so many duties and responsibilities, and a plethora of police powers in hand, the Hong Kong Police should be responsive to the needs of society. However, the police's resources are not unlimited. They do not have the time and manpower sufficient to deal with the many demands they face. Additionally, the public's expectations are always rising, and social demands are always changing and competing.

Furthermore, some sectors of the community may demand the police to step up and own certain types of enforcement, but other sectors may hold an opposing stance. For example, some local community organisations might press the police to eradicate a prostitution problem in their neighbourhood, but other interest groups are more sympathetic towards sex workers and may demand that police stop enforcement, as they often regard such police action as harassment. In a society with so many conflicting political interests, the police must adopt a neutral stance, free from political considerations. It is incumbent upon them to concentrate on more pressing and threatening challenges. They should police wisely and be prepared to justify their priorities. Public interests should always be their main concern.

In practice, the Hong Kong Police each year promulgate the Commissioner's Operational Priorities (COP), setting out a blueprint of what the whole force should follow and focus on. The operational priorities are worked out annually after carefully considering social forces like crime trends, the general law and order situation, public concerns and sentiments, and other relevant factors that threaten the public safety of Hong Kong. The COP serve as a compass, providing enforcement directions. We may expect that police officers will be more devoted to target their work according to these priorities, and exercise their police powers in a manner that relates more to their operational priorities.

The COP is published annually around January. The commissioner of police usually personally communicates this to the public through the media. For 2015, the priorities of the Hong Kong Police were to combat:

- Violent crimes
- Triads, syndicated and organised crime
- Dangerous drugs
- Quick cash crime
- Cyber security and technology crime
- Terrorism

And to uphold:

- Public safety

(The Hong Kong Police's official website: www.police.gov.hk)

Police power and accountability

Who polices the police?

The question 'who polices the police?' is among the oldest of political philosophy. The concern of police accountability is as old as the formation of the police itself (Morton, 1999). Police accountability is a longstanding concern in public administration worldwide. Holding themselves accountable to the public for what they do has important implications for their legitimacy. Robert Mark (1977: 56), a former commissioner of the Metropolitan Police Service of London, UK put it this way: 'The fact that the British police are answerable to the law, that we act on behalf of the community and not under the mantle of government, makes us the least powerful, the most accountable and therefore the most acceptable police in the world.' This stated the central role played in official ideology by the notion of police accountability to the law.

The Hong Kong Police possess a massive amount of police powers which are expansive and pervasive (Wacks, 1993). Therefore dealing with and preventing abuse of power should not be done reactively but proactively. It is important that both the police and the public have a common understanding and acceptance of what 'accountability' entails.

What is accountability?

Max Weber may be one of the earliest well-known sociologists who advocated accountability of the public services. He suggested bureaucracy control through adherence to hierarchical structures and compliance to the legal rational principles (Weber, 2009), but it was not until the middle of the last century when the needs of democracy and control for bureaucracies were raised. Finer (1941) believed that if there was a lack of external control through political means to ensure administrative responsibility, there could be abuses of power. His ideology was complemented by Friedrich (1940), who advocated that bureaucrats should not only rely on traditional controls within the hierarchy, but also respond to the public needs. Accountability was then regarded as a moral responsibility of the public services. Mosher (1968) summed up previous advocacies and advanced that there should be 'objective responsibility' where public services must be obliged to meet the policies, rules and regulations imposed on them, and 'subjective responsibility' where bureaucrats should act according to their consciences and loyalty. This set a good inspiring foundation to the subsequent values that the public service is expected to perform their duties both professionally and ethically.

Accountability is still a complex concept. It has been interchangeably interpreted widely as 'responsibility', 'responsiveness' and 'answerability'. Parker (1976) brought up the four dimensions of accountability: Who is accountable? Accountable to whom? Accountable for what? And how can accountability be enforced? Cheung (2005) opined that police officers are first accountable at the individual level for their own acts while on duty. They have to fulfil their obligations that are laid down by law and internal orders. This is the 'objective responsibility', and officers may face disciplinary or criminal sanctions for failure. Furthermore, the whole police force may be subject to criticism by the media, politicians and the community, when their 'subjective responsibility' is questioned.

Being accountable should not only be a required and established practice, but also a mindset instilled and internalised, as a matter of obligation by society at large. Ultimately, the police must be prepared to give an account, no matter if called upon or not, to the public of how they exercise the powers entrusted to them by society.

The Hong Kong Police accountability system

Internally, the Hong Kong Police have a set of strict disciplinary codes written within the Police General Order. Officers are also subject to *Police (Discipline) Regulations* (Cap. 232A). Apart from 'objective responsibility', the force also has a basket of initiatives to enhance the officers' 'subjective responsibility', such as through corruption prevention studies, healthy lifestyle promotion and integrity management. Externally, there is a two-tier police complaints mechanism. All complaints against the police are referred to the Complaints Against Police Office (CAPO) for handling and investigation. When CAPO has completed the inquiry, the investigation reports will be referred to the Independent Police Complaints Council (IPCC) for scrutiny. The IPCC is an independent statutory body, functioning under the *Independent Police Complaints Council Ordinance* (Cap. 604). The IPCC's mission is to ensure that police complaints are handled in a fair, impartial, effective and transparent manner, and advise on improvement to police procedures to enhance service quality and public accountability of the Hong Kong Police (IPCC, 2014: 3). The CAPO has to address any queries raised by the IPCC and re-investigate cases if requested by the IPCC. These measures provide effective checks and balances to ensure that complaints are handled thoroughly, fairly and impartially (Hong Kong Police, 2013: 6).

Although the CAPO's work is overseen by the IPCC, their fairness and impartiality have always been subject to question, as all investigators working in the CAPO are police officers. The number of reportable complaint cases against the police, categorised by the nature of complaint, received from 2010 to 2014 can be seen in Table 9.3. Reportable complaints refer to complaints, lodged by members of the public, that are not vexatious or frivolous, and are made in good faith, relating to the conduct of police officers while on duty or who identify themselves as police officers whilst off duty (IPCC, 2014: 20).

One may always criticise the low substantiation rate. The substantiation rate of complaint cases in 2012/13 was 2.07% and in 2013/14 was 1.81% (derived from IPCC, 2014: 35), but this phenomenon is also common in Western societies (Box and Russell, 1975; Goldsmith and Lewis, 2000; Smith, 2001),

Table 9.3 Number of reportable complaints and allegations against police received in 2010–14

	2010	*2011*	*2012*	*2013*	*2014*
Neglect of duty	1,650	1,395	1,272	1,393	1,288
Misconduct/improper manner	900	787	638	578	477
Assault	350	251	256	236	299
Threat	142	127	98	96	89
Fabrication of evidence	92	82	61	64	48
Unnecessary use of authority	64	63	48	32	43
Offensive language	68	55	39	21	24
Police procedures	2	0	0	0	2
Others	3	2	1	1	5
Total	3,271	2,762	2,373	2,421	2,275

Source: Service Quality Wing, Hong Kong Police.

attributed to the 'low visibility' of most practical police work (Goldstein, 1960). Obviously this is attracting scepticism. Not many academic studies have been done to assess the accountability system of the Hong Kong Police. One of the very few studies was conducted by Wong (2010: 20), who in his conclusion found that '[o]verall, the police accountability system and process in Hong Kong, in the guise of IPCC and CAPO, is very well-established and functions adequately'. He also opined that '[t]here is room for improvement, such as improvement in the case substantiation rate'.

The police must be mindful of the need to uphold the integrity of all their accountability system and complaint mechanism. As Cheung (2005) suggested, the goal of the system should be towards improved police performance, increased public satisfaction and, above all, earning more trust and cooperation from the community. The police should adopt a constructive and learning approach to accountability, to guard themselves against abuse of power. Under the current political climate in Hong Kong, police accountability in Hong Kong is certainly becoming a very topical and controversial subject. Further updated and in-depth studies are needed to address these issues of public concern.

Police power and future challenges

Policing problems are quite similar around the world, but as has been pointed out in the early part of this chapter, the situation of Hong Kong has a certain uniqueness. During the change of sovereignty in 1997, this city transformed overnight from a British colonial capitalist society to a Special Administrative Region of the communist People's Republic of China, although promised a lot of autonomy. Under these special circumstances, the nature of police work is not getting easier or simpler. Rather, the social, economic and political environment the Hong Kong Police face is only getting more complicated and unforgiving. In setting their directions, strategies and priorities, the Hong Kong Police must be more mindful of public perception and public sentiments.

Under 'One Country, Two Systems', 'human rights' and 'democracy' will continue to be proclaimed as the most important 'core values' of the society of Hong Kong. In fact, they are not only being proclaimed, but are also being politically campaigned for. A low crime rate in Hong Kong is now being taken as a matter of course. Comparing the overall crime rates and crime rates of selected key crimes such as murder, robbery and burglary, Hong Kong is lower than many other major cosmopolitan cities like New York, London, Paris and Tokyo (these figures and comparisons may be found on the Hong Kong Police website: www.police.gov.hk.) With little or no fear of crime, some people have even asked whether Hong Kong needs the size of police force it has. It appears that the problems the Hong Kong Police face today are less associated with crime reductions and more related to dealing with the many politically connected public order activities and incidents. Indeed, handling civil and political events can be much more complicated and difficult than dealing with criminals in such a politically divided society. In recent years, the Hong Kong Police have been criticised for high-handed policing in managing some large-scale public protests and political events. They must not only live with these challenges positively, but also be prepared to deal with the political challenges strategically and sensitively.

Whilst some politicians may be keen to see police powers curbed, the Hong Kong Police are at the same time facing increasing demands for them to tackle newer threats locally and globally. To name just a few, these include the heightening of terrorism, money-laundering activities, cyber security and more complex white-collar crimes. Indeed, many of these problems are taking place across different countries and jurisdictions. The police need the necessary powers, even more new powers, to enable them to tackle the new threats posed against the society of Hong Kong. Political issues considered, the Hong Kong Police should robustly defend and uphold the powers necessary for them to maintain the safety, law and order of Hong Kong, as the general public at large still relies on them for protection.

Nowadays, popular mobilisation and collective action constitute important components of social life in Hong Kong (Lui and Chiu, 1999: 102). With the sophistication of social media, mobilisation powers for public order events are massive. Moreover, the Hong Kong Police are well aware that on top of dealing with many difficult tasks, they are also working in a very transparent and high-tech society. Most people are carrying at least one mobile phone with a recording device. People enjoy their freedom to capture what the police do in a public place and share it on the Internet. These pictures or clips may be unedited, but they may also be edited and not show the whole truth. The media also receive many of these pictures and clips from the public and the source and authenticity of these materials may be hard to verify. So in exercising their police powers, the police will find dealing with this contextual transparency a significant extra concern and burden.

Conclusion

Police power has been a subject of longstanding research interest around the world by social scientists, philosophers, lawyers and politicians, amongst others, all with a different perspective. The discussions relating to police powers in this chapter have only grazed the surface of so many of the contentious issues. It cannot be emphasised more that the concept of police power needs to be considered with breadth and depth. Looking at the relationship between society, law and the police at the beginning of this chapter is a good starting point for us to understand the subject, as police power originates from the people, and is entrusted by society. The police are given a wide range of duties and they need the necessary powers to fulfil their functions effectively.

The sociological and political debates in Hong Kong often revolve around, on one side, whether police officers have sufficient legal powers to deal with the challenging and ever changing problems of crime, law and order that the society is facing, whilst on the other side the question is whether these police powers are excessive. Some may support law and order and favour more power for the police to contain a law-abiding society, but some antagonists may fight to restrict the power of the police in order to uphold human rights. This dilemma is universal. A conflicting society may be said to structure the police and the people in opposite corners of a boxing ring.

In Hong Kong, we may expect the police powers to continue to be challenged. Until the political divisions within society are reduced and the governance of the Hong Kong Special Administrative Region is more widely stabilised, the situation can hardly change. We can only hope that the society of Hong Kong will soon minimise political disputes, and discover the 'fundamental balance', along its own historical, cultural, social and political development. In Western societies, the 'fundamental balance' refers to the equilibrium between police powers and procedural safeguards for citizens, for example, the emphasis in the *Police and Criminal Evidence Act* (PACE) 1984 of the UK, or the Due Process Clause guaranteed under the Fifth and 14th Amendments of the American Constitution.

The truth must still be realised: police power is not owned by police officers; rather, police power is entrusted by society with important responsibilities, through a law enactment process by legislators elected directly and indirectly by people of Hong Kong. The police must exercise their powers not to their personal preferences, but for social justice and the overall benefits of society. The Hong Kong Police are not there to propitiate the government, political parties or interest groups. They have to use their powers legally, reasonably and fairly. They have to work hard to uphold the rule of law of Hong Kong and make sure that they are politically neutral. Working in a political society, they have to be politically sensitive to eschew being dragged into political entanglements.

A good and widely accepted accountability system must be in place not only to police the police, but also to foster public trust. Monitoring efforts against the police cannot be relaxed so as to maintain public confidence, in particular under the current political climate in Hong Kong. On the other hand, to ensure the police work effectively, society needs to afford them adequate support and protection. Laws exist in Singapore (e.g. Miscellaneous Offences in Singapore – section 13D of the *Public Order and Nuisance Act*, Cap. 184) and the UK (e.g. Harassment, Alarm or Distress Offences in the United Kingdom – section 5 of the *Public Order Act 1986*, Cap. 64), for instance, to protect police officers from being abused and insulted. These two countries are widely recognised as modern and developed. Introducing the same protection for police officers in Hong Kong should be seriously considered and discussed, as some protesters are adopting tactics of increasingly abusive behaviour. Respecting and supporting the police in rightfully exercising their duties is in a way supporting society.

Throughout the world today, we are seeing more political movements against governments. Many of them have the nature of generating large crowds of protesters, and hence policing public protests is only getting more difficult and controversial. Scholars of policing perhaps should explore further in this area for the benefit of all.

Review questions

1. What are the unique challenges that the Hong Kong Police are facing?
2. How much power should be given to the police? Why?
3. Do you think the Hong Kong Police have too much power?
4. What is the relationship between society, police power and accountability? Discuss this in the context of the current political climate of Hong Kong.
5. 'Hong Kong should introduce legislation, like Singapore and Britain, against abusing and insulting behaviour against the Police.' To what extent do you agree or disagree with this statement?

References

Beetham, D. (2013) *The Legitimation of Power*, 2nd edn, Basingstoke: Palgrave Macmillan.

Blagden, N. (2012) *Policing and Psychology*, London: Sage.

Box, S. and Russell, K. (1975) 'The politics of discredibility', *Sociological Review*, 23(2): 315–346.

Cheung, A.B.L. (2005) 'Hong Kong's post-1997 institutional crisis: Problems of governance and institutional incompatibility', *Journal of East Asian Studies*, 5(1): 135–167.

Cheung, J. (2005) 'Police accountability', *Police Journal*, 78(1): 3–36.

Chiu, S. and Lui, T.L. (2009) *Hong Kong: Becoming a Global City*, Abingdon: Routledge.
Chui, W.H. and Lo, T.W. (2008) 'Introduction and overview', in W.H. Chui and T.W. Lo (eds) *Understanding Criminal Justice in Hong Kong* (pp. 1–13), Cullompton: Willan.
Cohen, L.E. and Felson, M. (1979) 'Social change and crime rate trends: A routine activity approach', *American Sociological Review*, 44(4): 588–608.
Cross, I.G. (2008) 'Prosecuting crime', in W.H. Chui and T.W. Lo (eds) *Understanding Criminal Justice in Hong Kong* (pp. 115–130), Cullompton: Willan.
Edwards, C. (2011) *Changing Policing Theories for the 21st Century Societies*, Annandale, Sydney: The Federation Press.
Finer, H. (1941) 'Administrative Responsibility in Democratic Government', *Public Administration Review* 1(4): 335–350.
Friedrich, C.J. (1940) 'Public policy and the nature of administrative accountability', in C.J. Friedrich and E. Mason (eds) *Public Policy: A Yearbook of the Graduate School of Public Administration* (pp. 3–24), Boston, MA: Harvard University Press.
Goldsmith, A. and Lewis, C. (eds) (2000) *Civilian Oversight of Policing*, Oxford: Hart Publishing.
Goldstein, J. (1960) 'Police discretion not to invoke the criminal process: Low visibility decisions in the administration of justice', *Yale Law Journal*, 69(4): 543–594.
Hong Kong Police (2013) *Complaints Against Police Office Annual Report*, Hong Kong: Government Printer.
Independent Police Complaints Council (IPCC) (2014) *2013/14 Report*, Hong Kong: Government Printer.
Jeffries, J. (1952) *The Colonial Police*, London: Max Parrish.
Koffman, L. (1985) 'Safeguarding the rights of the Citizen', in J. Baxter and L. Koffman (eds) *Police: The Constitution and the Community: A Collection of Original Essays on Issues Raised by the Police and Criminal Evidence Act 1984* (pp. 11–37), London: Professional Books.
Lau, S.K. (1984) *Society and Politics in Hong Kong*, Hong Kong: The Chinese University Press.
Lea, J. and Young, J. (1993) *What is to Be Done about Law and Order?* London: Pluto Press.
Lo, S.H.C. and Chui, W.H. (2012) *The Hong Kong Legal System*, Singapore: McGraw-Hill.
Lui, T.L. and Chiu, S. (1999) 'Social movements and public discourse on politics', in T.W. Ngo (ed.) *Hong Kong History: State and Society under Colonial Rule* (pp. 101–118), London: Routledge.
Lui, T.L. and Wong, T. (2000) 'Chinese entrepreneurship in context', in S.K. Lau (ed.) *Social Development and Political Change in Hong Kong* (pp. 33–60), Hong Kong: The Chinese University Press.
Mark, R. (1977) *Policing a Perplexed Society*, London: Allen and Unwin.
Morton, J. (1999) *Bent Cooper*, London: Warner Books.
Mosher, F.C. (1968) *Democracy and the Public Services*, New York: Oxford University Press.
Parker, R. (1976) 'The meaning of responsible government', *Politics*, 11(2): 178–184.
Reiner, R. (2010) *The Politics of the Police* (4th edn), Oxford: Oxford University Press.
Rowe, M. (2014) *Introduction to Policing*, London: Sage.
Skogan, W. and Frydl, K. (2004) *Fairness and Effectiveness in Policing: The Evidence*, Washington, DC: National Academies Press.
Smith, G. (2001) 'Police complaints and criminal prosecutions', *Modern Law Review*, 64(3): 372–392.

Stith, S.M. (1990) 'Police response to domestic violence: The influence of individual and familial factors', *Violence and Victims*, 5(1): 37–49.
Stockdale, J.E. and Gresham, P.J. (1995) *Presentation of Police Evidence in Court*, London: Home Office Policing and Reducing Crime Unit.
Wacks, R. (ed.) (1993) *Police Powers in Hong Kong*, Hong Kong: Faculty of Law, University of Hong Kong.
Weber, M. (2009) 'Bureaucracy', in H.H. Gerth and C.W. Mills (eds) *From Max Weber: Essays in Sociology* (pp. 196–244), London: Routledge.
Wong, K.C. (2010) 'Police powers and control in Hong Kong', *International Journal of Comparative and Applied Criminal Justice*, 34(1): 1–24.
Worrall, J.L. and Schmalleger, F.J. (2015) *Policing* (2nd revised edn), Upper Saddle River, NJ: Pearson Education.

Legislation cited

Dangerous Drugs Ordinance (Cap. 134)
Independent Police Complaints Council Ordinance (Cap. 604)
Police and Criminal Evidence Act (PACE) 1984 (UK)
Police Force Ordinance (Cap. 232)
Police (Discipline) Regulations (Cap. 232A)
Public Order Act 1986 (Cap. 64) (UK)
Public Order and Nuisance Act (Cap. 184) (Singapore)
Public Order Ordinance (Cap. 245)
Road Traffic Ordinance (Cap. 374)
Societies Ordinance (Cap. 151)
Summary Offences Ordinance (Cap. 228)

Cases cited

Leung Kwok-hung & others v HKSAR (CFA FACC Nos. 1 & 2 of 2005, 2)
Yeung May-wan & others v HKSAR (CFAFACC No. 19 of 2004)

Useful websites

Department of Justice, HKSAR www.doj.gov.hk
Hong Kong Police www.police.gov.hk/index.html
Independent Police Complaints Council www.ipcc.gov.hk/en/home/index.html
Information on Complaints Against Police www.police.gov.hk/ppp_en/11_useful_info/cap.html
Legislative Council, HKSAR www.legco.gov.hk/index.html

10

ANTI-CORRUPTION

Cora Y.T. Hui and T. Wing Lo

Introduction

Hong Kong is a story of immense changes. Just half a decade ago, Hong Kong society was filled with corruption and organised crime, and bribery was regarded as folklore. In the 1960s and 1970s, the colonial government began to better understand that in order to curb corruption in Hong Kong, a package of radical reform was required. Lo (2003) highlighted a blanket of strategies, including strong political will, powerful anti-corruption ordinance, absolute independence, a three-pronged attack, draconian powers of the Independent Commission Against Corruption (ICAC), high remuneration in the civil service (to maintain integrity), and a declared investment and integrity check of all civil servants. The success of the reform was globally recognised, and Transparency International has consistently ranked Hong Kong one of the cleanest cities in Asia since 1995.

As can be seen in Figure 10.1, the number of prosecution cases has remained fairly steady, at around 300 to 600 cases per year, since 1980. Occasional increases took place in 1993 and in the early 2000s as a result of political uncertainty and economic downturn. Furthermore, although a high level of corruption existed in government departments and the police force in the 1970s, an image of a clean government began to emerge as the number of prosecutions against civil servants decreased in the early 1980s. Since 1982, the number of prosecutions against civil servants has remained lower than that of agents in the private sector, meaning that this pattern persisted following Hong Kong's return to Chinese sovereignty in 1997. Since the early 2000s, the number of persons prosecuted for corruption-related offences has been in decline.

Corruption reform is a continuous trial-and-error process, and Hong Kong has learnt many lessons regarding which measures are effective and which are not over the last few decades. This chapter aims to deconstruct the package of strategies that helps control corruption in Hong Kong. Five main groups of strategies will be discussed: effective legislation enacted within the rule of law, the establishment of the ICAC, the necessity for strong political will, the emergence of a watchdog culture, and civil service reform.

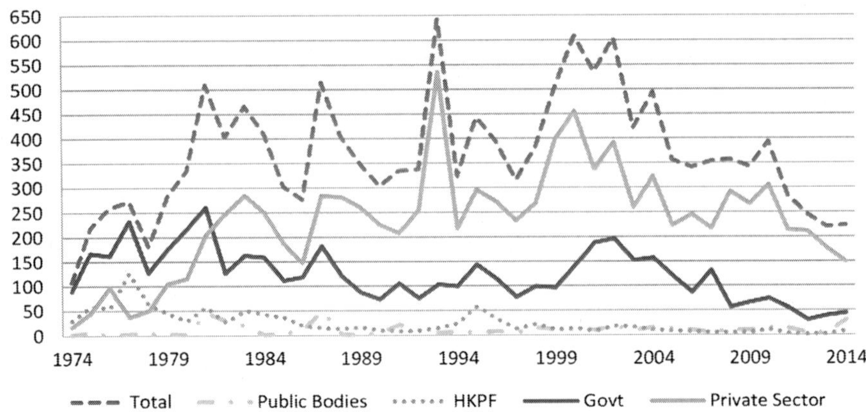

Figure 10.1 Number of persons prosecuted for corruption-related offences, 1974–2014

Effective legislation enacted within the rule of law

Hong Kong has a long history of reforming its legislation to tackle corruption: the *Misdemeanours Punishment Ordinance* (hereafter MIPO) in 1898, the *Prevention of Corruption Ordinance* (hereafter POCO) (Cap. 215) in 1948 and the *Prevention of Bribery Ordinance* (hereafter POBO) (Cap. 201) in 1971. Each new ordinance allowed for an expansion in the legal definition of corruption, a reduction in the burden of proof required to prosecute, and an increase in the maximum penalty.

Expansion in the legal definition of corruption

POCO broadened the legal definition of corruption in two ways. First, corrupt conduct was not only punishable for civil servants, but also for persons employed in private firms. Second, the law began to view an accused's unexplainable wealth as corroborating evidence of corruption, an important innovation that eventually formed the basis of the powerful section 10 offence in the later POBO. According to the famous section 10, once the prosecution proves beyond reasonable doubt that an accused official has maintained a disproportionate standard of living or has been in control of pecuniary resources, the onus is on the accused official to provide a satisfactory explanation.

Kuan (1981) noted that this law aimed to remedy the practical difficulty of securing evidence. Receivers of substantial bribes could now be successfully prosecuted under this law, even when their gains could not be linked to any specific corruption transaction. The theory behind this law is 'to prevent not a single act of temptation but the delicate and graduate process of cultivating friendship between the donor and a civil servant' (Kuan, 1981: 42). The court also acknowledged in *Attorney General v. Hui Kin-hong* [1995] 1 HKCLR 227, that perhaps the even greater value of section 10 was its general deterrent effect.

Reduction in the burden of proof

To establish a corruption charge successfully, both MIPO and POCO required the prosecution to prove that the perquisite accepted/offered was intended to lure the public servant to act (or omit to act) contrary to his or her duty as a public servant. In other words, 'the *mere* acceptance or offering of gratification', according to these provisions, did not constitute an offence (Kuan, 1981: 18, emphasis in original). The burden of proof on the prosecution was greatly reduced in the subsequently enacted POBO to send a strong message of the anti-corruption determination of the colonial government. Section 3 of POBO, which only applies to government officials, is a blanket prohibition against all acts of solicitation and acceptance of advantages (Lo and Ngan, 2009). The prosecution no longer bears the burden of proving any intent, as the *mere* solicitation or acceptance of an advantage exceeding the stipulated standard now constitutes an offence. Once charged, the accused official bears the burden of proving that special permission from the relevant authority has been attained.

Increase in maximum penalty

The maximum penalty stated in MIPO was two years of imprisonment and a fine of HK$500. The maximum penalty was increased to five years of imprisonment (or seven years in certain cases) and a fine of HK$10,000 in POCO. Most importantly, courts could now order the amount of the bribe to be forfeited. Offenders were able to enjoy their ill-gotten wealth after paying the fine and serving their prison sentence prior to POCO, and hence this forfeiture greatly increased the severity of the punishment (Kuan, 1981). The maximum penalty was further increased to a fine of HK$1 million and ten years of imprisonment in POBO.

Recent challenges to the law

Traditional forms of corruption typically involve receiving an immediate advantage, mostly in the form of cash. Recent years have, however, seen the growth of corruption in a more subtle form, as evidenced by the number of senior government officials being implicated in cases of serious conflicts of interest (Li, 2014). Misconduct in public office, an age-old common law offence, has been revived in recent years and has become an important legal weapon in the fight against this new form of corruption. This common law offence enables an even broader definition of corruption that punishes conduct that subordinates public interests to private gain. Misconduct in public office finds it an offence for a public official to wilfully misconduct himself/herself in a serious manner during (or in relation to) his or her public office (*Sin Kam-wah & Another v. HKSAR* [2005] 2 HKLRD 375). As highlighted by the history of the three ordinances and the revival of an age-old common law offence, the law covering corruption in Hong Kong has been modified many times to keep up with the dynamic trend of corruption.

The rule of law

It is important to note, however, that no legislation is effective unless rule of law and judicial independence are firmly upheld. The attorney-general/secretary for justice may be pressured to drop charges and judges may feel pressured to reach verdicts based on political considerations in situations where the executive branch influences the appointment and promotion of prosecutors and judges. Fortunately, the judiciary in Hong Kong has remained virtually incorruptible – even during the 1970s when corruption was particularly rampant (Blair-Kerr, 1973).

The *Basic Law* and the *Hong Kong Bill of Rights Ordinance* (Cap. 383) guarantee equality before the law, the provision of a fair trial and a presumption of innocence. As stated in the *Basic Law*, the appointment of judges in Hong Kong is made based on the recommendations of an independent commission (comprising judges, the legal profession and other eminent persons). Judges enjoy immense job security and can only be removed on the recommendation of an independent commission. The rule of law index, published annually by the World Justice Project since 2011, regards absence of corruption as a strong factor that affects rule of law. Since 2011, Hong Kong has ranked in the top ten regions in terms of guaranteeing order and security, effectiveness of the criminal justice system, absence of corruption, and open government (Agrast et al., 2011; Agrast et al., 2012–13; World Justice Project, 2014).

Formation of the ICAC

POBO is no doubt a powerful law, yet any law is only as effective as the level of its enforcement. The powerful anti-corruption law was only able to exert its power when the ICAC was established to enforce it. In this section, specific emphasis is placed on the various factors that helped establish the ICAC during its first few years.

Pre-ICAC days

The police have been tasked with investigating corruption among public servants since the enactment of MIPO in 1898. Given the syndicated corruption that existed within the police force, the police (both the Anti-Corruption Branch and the later Anti-Corruption Office) had been ineffective in their investigations of corruption cases for over 70 years. The Godber escape in 1973 marked an end to the era of police investigation. Peter Godber, chief police superintendent and suspect in a corruption investigation, managed to slip out of Hong Kong without detection and take refuge back home in England.

Unsurprisingly, the scandal provoked a massive outcry by the public. To restore public confidence in the colonial government, the ICAC was established on 15 February 1974.

Independence and accountability

The ICAC was organised in such a way as to be independent in terms of structure, resource allocation (manpower and finance) and power (Wong, 1981).

- Structure: the ICAC was formed as an independent commission directly responsible to the governor (now Chief Executive). Since the civil service was one of the major targets of corruption investigation, the ICAC could not have come under its wing. With appointments to the post being endorsed by Beijing, the Chief Executive appoints the commissioner and various other senior officers. Article 57 of the *Basic Law* guarantees that the ICAC will function independently and be accountable to the Chief Executive.
- Manpower: ICAC staff members are recruited separately from staff for the civil service, and their posts are not subject to transfer to other government departments (Wong, 1981). Similar to the police, the commissioner and ICAC staff are not subject to the purview of the Public Services Commission.
- Power: ICAC's power is granted by the *Independent Commission Against Corruption Ordinance* (hereafter ICAC Ordinance) (Cap. 204), POBO and the *Elections (Corrupt and Illegal Conduct) Ordinance* (Cap. 554) (enacted in 2000).

An elaborate checks and balances system has been designed to ensure a high degree of accountability and transparency. Since its initial establishment, four civilian advisory committees have been set up to advise on, and supervise the work of, the ICAC (ICAC, 1974; Lo, 1994). The Advisory Committee on Corruption advises the commissioner on aspects of corruption in Hong Kong, and each department (Operations, Community Prevention and Community Relations) also has its own advisory committee.

A charismatic institution

Sir Murray MacLehose and Sir Jack Cater (the first commissioner of the ICAC) understood that the ICAC needed to be backed up by instant victory in order to win the support, awe and respect of the people. The first task was to achieve what the police had failed to accomplish: extradite and prosecute the much-demanded Godber. As such, Godber was returned to Hong Kong by the ICAC in early 1975 and sentenced to four years' imprisonment in a much-publicised 'show trial' (Lethbridge, 1985: 114). Godber was the highest-ranked government servant since 1956 to be prosecuted for corruption, and the conviction of this 'big tiger' was an instant boost to the people's confidence in the ICAC.

Between 1974 and 1977, the ICAC submitted 857 cases for prosecution (around 30% of which were made against police officers – see Figure 10.1), more than five times the total number for the four years preceding the introduction of the ICAC (Blair-Kerr, 1973; ICAC, 1974, 1977). The diligence of the ICAC greatly promoted notions of social justice and equality: 'the view that any person, irrespective of his class, status, rank, occupation, or race, is potentially subject to its jurisdiction' (Lethbridge, 1976: 177).

The support of the public was evident from the number of reports received. In its first year of operation, the ICAC received 3,189 reports of alleged corruption, more than twice the number received by the old police Anti-Corruption Office in 1972 (Blair-Kerr, 1973; ICAC, 1974). A more significant indicator of public trust was the increase in non-anonymous reports, from 35.0% in 1974 to 47.0% in 1976, and then to 56.1% in 1980 (ICAC, 1974, 1976, 1980).

Capable leadership

MacLehose understood the importance of appointing persons of high integrity and regard to lead the crusade and had his eyes set on Cater. Cater had garnered a reputation for integrity and competence during his 30 years in the civil service and was 'an excellent choice as the first man to head the innovative organisation' (Lethbridge, 1985: 106). Even 30 years after his service at the ICAC, the public still remain grateful for the contributions made by Cater (South China Morning Post, 2006). Sir John Prendergast, founding director of operations, was an experienced investigator and intelligence officer. Lethbridge (1985) commended Prendergast for being responsible for branding the ICAC an elite crime-fighting force. He noted that ICAC 'was most fortunate in attracting such an experienced investigator' (ibid.: 109).

Staff with high integrity

All new recruits are subject to integrity checking, which includes ICAC internal checks and checks with the police (ICAC, 1980; Legislative Council Panel on Security, 2004). Home visits and interviews with family members are also undertaken in respect of part of the check of potential candidates. In addition, ICAC has maintained an internal monitoring ('L group') system since its inception. All allegations of corruption against ICAC staff are referred immediately to the attorney-general/secretary for justice (ICAC, 1974; Lo, 1994). The ICAC also placed a high priority on recruiting officers with a sense of mission in the early days. According to our interview with a former principal investigator of the ICAC on 5 May 2015, ICAC officers need to be willing to treat anti-corruption work as a career, not just as a job.

A realistic attitude that corruption is a 'dirty game'

Blair-Kerr (1973) noted that one of the reasons the Corrupt Practices Investigation Bureau (CPIB) in Singapore had been successful in controlling corruption is that they had 'a realistic attitude that corruption is a "dirty game"', and understood that 'unorthodox' methods have to be employed to counter it (ibid.: 45). Corruption is notoriously difficult to detect: both parties to the corrupt deal are frequently satisfied parties. Furthermore, since the law punishes both sides of the corrupt transaction (the giver and receiver), both sides have a reason to remain silent. Unlike other crimes, typically no immediate victim is involved in a corrupt deal, making it less likely that someone will report the case. If we were to compare corruption to cancer, the government, legislators and judiciary in Hong Kong have all agreed that the heaviest possible dose of medicine must first be administered to kill and suppress all the bad cells, before the disease becomes terminal.

The power of the ICAC was regarded as draconian prior to the 1990s (Lo and Yu, 2000). The ICAC held more investigative powers than were held by the police. When the ICAC was first established, the commissioner was empowered to authorise the entry (by force, if necessary) and search of any premises (section 17(1) of the 1987 revised edition), the detention of anyone on the premises for up to three hours (section 17(1A) of the 1987 revised edition), the seizing of a suspect's passport for up to six months during the investigation process (an obvious lesson learnt from the Godber incident) (section 17A), and the examination of any accounts and company books (investment accounts, bank accounts, purchase accounts, share accounts, safe-deposit boxes, etc.) (section 13(1)(a) of the 1987 revised edition).

Defiance of the investigator's requests and the provision of false information are both offences. POBO even forbids anyone (most likely the media) from disclosing the identities of suspects prior to laying charges (section 30(1)). These powers, albeit sweeping and intrusive, were useful in corruption investigations (Lo and Yu, 2000) but they have since been significantly confined as a result of the *Hong Kong Bill of Rights Ordinance* and the subsequent review of the ICAC in 1994 (ICAC Review Committee, 1994; Lo, 1995).

Tainted witnesses

It is perhaps not an overstatement to say that ICAC would not have achieved the success it has without the effective yet controversial use of tainted witnesses. The use of tainted witnesses was neatly demonstrated in the Godber case. The extradition of Godber was justified as the ICAC presented evidence that he had accepted a bribe from Superintendent Cheng Hon-Kuen in return for appointing Cheng as the divisional chief of Wanchai District (Lethbridge, 1985). The two key witnesses were Cheng himself and Ernest Hunt, an even more corrupt officer who admitted to pocketing HK$8 million (double the amount received by Godber). The tainted witnesses received immunity deals and substantially reduced sentences in return. Courts in general have endorsed the use of tainted witnesses (ICAC, 1976; Lo, 2003).

MacLehose understood that the sweeping powers offered to the ICAC were quite 'unusual' (Hong Kong Legislative Council, 1973: 17). He was, however, convinced that unusual measures were needed to win back people's confidence in this grave situation. Indeed, the ICAC was able to pronounce, after four years of forceful actions, that major corruption syndicates within the civil service had been eradicated (ICAC, 1978; Lo, 1993; Kwok and Lo, 2014). Even former Police Commissioner Dick Lee (who worked in the police force from 1972 to 2007) recalled: 'The speed with which syndicated corruption was eradicated has few parallels in the history of law enforcement' (South China Morning Post, 2004).

A three-pronged approach

When the ICAC was conceived in 1973, Cater realised that corruption had to be simultaneously tackled via a three-pronged approach: deterrence, prevention and education. The three-division structure of the ICAC is an attempt to execute this idea. Helen Yu, founding director of the Community Relations Department, noted that the three goals of ICAC were to make people feel that they dare not (*bu gan*), cannot (*bu neng*) and would not (*bu xiang*) engage in corruption (Cheung, 2010). People 'dare not' engage in corruption as a result of the general deterrence effect of the Operations Department; they 'cannot' engage in corruption because the Corruption Prevention Department had plugged the loopholes in the system; and they 'would not' engage in corruption because of the education of the Community Relations Department.

The Operations Department is the largest department among the three and has been allocated the most resources. The Operations Department has broad anti-corruption jurisdiction: section 12(b) of the ICAC Ordinance requires investigations into 'any' suspected corruption offences under the ICAC Ordinance, POBO and the *Elections (Corrupt and Illegal Conduct) Ordinance*, and 'any' common law corruption-related offences (misconduct in public office). In other words, the Operations Department is required to pursue *all* corruption, large or small, with no discretion, in the private and public sectors. Lethbridge (1985) noted, however, that the commissioner was able to select which cases were given priority in practice.

Lethbridge (1976) posed the timeless question: Why do only some people break the law and not everyone? His own response was: 'The answer supplied by control theory is "we all would, if only we dared"' (ibid.: 157). To deter the public from corruption, a culture of zero tolerance must be cultivated. A powerful Operations Department was essential to the survival of the ICAC and in gaining public confidence in the early days.

ICAC regularly publishes cases of successful prosecutions and convictions to remind the public of its effectiveness, and continues to do so to this day. Such publicity serves as a deterrence effect – a regular reminder to the general public that corruption will be effectively punished. Furthermore, the Operations Department's pursuit of cases, especially in the early days, resembles the 'broken window' theory of policing. The term 'broken window' is an analogy used to describe the escalation from disorder to serious crime: an unattended broken window is a signal that no one cares, and soon the remaining windows in the building will be broken (Wilson and Kelling, 1982). The broken window model of policing stresses the importance of early intervention while fighting the spread of disorder: monitoring and pursuing relatively minor crimes creates a norm of law and order and could prevent the occurrence of more serious crimes. In the early days of the ICAC, the agency took measures, albeit extreme at times, to pursue large and small cases.

As suggested by the Situational Crime Prevention literature, managerial and environmental changes can reduce opportunities for crimes to occur (Clarke, 1997). The focus is on changing the settings and situations that give rise to crime. The ICAC Ordinance states that the responsibility of the Corruption Prevention Department (CPD) is to examine procedures and practices of all government departments and public bodies in order to remove any corruption opportunities – 'plugging loopholes'. To execute its statutory function, the CPD provides advisory services, monitors newly enacted procedures and provides training. The CPD carefully examines the systems and policies within an agency to reduce or even eliminate opportunities conducive to corruption.

The CPD also adopts a 'partnership approach' with government departments and relies on their knowledge of departmental matters to identify flaws in procedures and practices (Tong, 2007). In the bad old days, for example, it is a well-known fact that learners could never pass a driving test without providing 'tea money' to the instructor (Tong, 2007). In the first year of inception, the Operations Department prosecuted a former driving test examiner for amassing assets exceeding HK$1 million. Immediately, the CPD began reviewing the procedures and practices involved in the issuing of driving licences (ICAC, 1974).

Private businesses could also request assistance from the CPD to examine their own procedures and practices. The Advisory Services Group was established by the CPD in 1985 to provide free and tailor-made recommendations to private companies on how to prevent corruption (Lo, 2001; ICAC, 2015a).

The Community Relations Department (CRD) has the statutory responsibility to 'educate the public against the evils of corruption' and 'enlist and foster public support in combatting corruption' (sections 12(g) and (h) of the ICAC Ordinance). The CRD has been using two complementary strategies to preach its messages: bottom-up, face-to-face interactions for depth, and top-down media dissemination for breadth (Mu, 2008). When the ICAC was first established, CRD officers conducted 'door-to-door, factory-to-factory, and even boat-to-boat' visits to introduce the anti-corruption legislation and work of the ICAC to a sceptical crowd (Mu, 2008). The CRD also places heavy emphasis on moral education for young people, targeting young people from primary schools to tertiary institutions. The CRD has collaborated with the Education Department since 1977 in the design of teaching kits for use by primary and secondary school teachers (ICAC, 1977; Lo, 1998).

Regional offices opened for 14 hours a day (8am to 10pm) when the ICAC was first established, and there were nine regional offices by 1980 (ICAC, 1980). This strong local-level presence has three advantages (Scott, 2013a). First, fundamental tasks of the centralised agency could be carried out more effectively, e.g. complaints lodged more conveniently and continuous liaison with civil societies and local-level institutions. Second, regional offices could ensure that the prevailing community attitudes towards corruption were not discrepant with those the ICAC was attempting to preach. Third, regional offices could support local initiatives to combat corruption.

Cater saw education via multi-media as the 'ultimate quiet revolution' (China Daily Asia, 2013a). The Press Information team was one of the first units set up in the CRD to maintain a timely news enquiry service and hold regular briefings for the news media (ICAC, 1975). The CRD also designs and produces radio programmes, educational television programmes, advertisements, posters, pamphlets, etc. to spread the seeds of anti-corruption.

The Quiet Revolution – the CRD's first drama production – was broadcast in 1976. The CRD has since then produced 14 dramas, all of which have been based on real cases handled by the Operations Department. The CRD adjusts its media strategy according to the immediate socio-political conditions (Lai, 2000). The Community Research Unit (now placed under the Administrative Branch) was established in 1977 to survey and analyse public attitudes to corruption and community responses to ICAC activities (ICAC, 1977).

Necessity for strong political will

The obdurate and consistent political will to prioritise corruption prevention is a prerequisite for any anti-corruption reform to succeed. The government must recognise two realities of radical reform: it is expensive and it is a continuous process. One-off, superficial and top-down anti-corruption campaigns have little chance of success. The government in Hong Kong has invested heavily in corruption prevention in terms of the annual ICAC budget, adequate remuneration packages for civil servants, time and money spent on monitoring the civil service administration to ensure it is corruption-proof, etc. (Scott, 2013b).

Reform is a continuous process, in which the whole community is required to participate actively. Furthermore, the government will consistently face resistance from other power blocs because their interests are at stake (Lo, 1993). Examples of resistance in Hong Kong include opposition from London regarding the reverse onus clause in POBO, the business sector fighting for the necessity of offering commissions when doing business, and the ICAC–police clash that forced the governor to grant a partial amnesty (Lo, 1993; Yep, 2013).

Partial amnesty

The hostile ICAC–police clash in October 1977 forced Governor MacLehose to grant a partial amnesty, stating, 'the ICAC will not normally act on complaints or evidence relating to offences committed before 1 January, 1977' (Hong Kong Legislative Council, 1977: 157). It was important to MacLehose and Cater that the government did not appear to be bowing down to corruption (Yep, 2013). They decided that three criteria must be satisfied before partial amnesty was granted. First, the amnesty was not subject to further negotiation. Second, the leaders of the police mutiny must not be let off the hook. Third, the *Police Force Ordinance* (Cap. 232) should be amended to give the police commissioner the power to summarily dismiss disobedient officers.

Despite these criteria, the immediate damage to the morale and credibility of the ICAC was obvious. The Operations Department had to terminate 83 investigations of offences committed prior to 1 January 1977. The number of complaints reported to the ICAC dropped 27.4% in 1978 when compared to the year before, and 49% when compared to 1976 (ICAC, 1978). Even a year after granting the partial amnesty, MacLehose acknowledged that 'the question in many minds has been whether things would slip back into the bad old ways' (Hong Kong Legislative Council, 1978: 12).

Surviving the partial amnesty

Fortunately, the government did not retreat after losing this battle, instead remaining determined to prioritise the fight against corruption. Three factors helped restore public confidence in the ICAC and government after the partial amnesty. First, the ICAC concluded the investigation of the Yau Ma Tei fruit market drug syndicate case and prosecuted 26 serving or former officers (18 were eventually convicted) in 1978. The fruit market case – the largest inquiry to have been carried out by the ICAC at that time – was the immediate trigger of the ICAC–police clash. Second, the government dismissed another 119 officers in accordance with *Colonial Regulation* 55 for their suspected involvement in the fruit market case (Litton, 1978). *Colonial Regulation* 55 empowered the government to dismiss civil servants 'at the pleasure of the Crown' (i.e. dismissal without reason). Third, the government continued to provide generous support to the ICAC. By 1980, the ICAC had expanded into a force of 1,099, almost a threefold expansion from 1974 (ICAC, 1980). The *ICAC Ordinance* and POBO were also amended by the Legislative Council in 1980 to give ICAC investigators additional powers.

With the benefit of hindsight, at least two benefits came about as a result of the partial amnesty. First, the ICAC could focus all resources on investigating corruption taking place at present and preventing future corruption (ICAC, 1978). Second, the partial amnesty signified a cut-off line and offered many, by then honest, civil servants a new lease on life (Lo, 1993). Prior to the establishment of the ICAC, syndicated corruption was the norm within the civil service. As one of our interviewees, a former ICAC principal investigator, contended, almost the entire civil service felt uneasy about the ICAC. Any petty one-off corrupt act in the past could be a ticking time bomb for them: they could never know if someone would someday report their act to the ICAC. As MacLehose phrased it, the partial amnesty thus put the minds of by then honest people at ease, as it 'removed all cause for fear from all who keep straight' (Hong Kong Legislative Council, 1977: 157).

Breaking the police–triad connection

Prior to the late 1970s, the police and triad societies were business partners: the police protected triad-operated vice trade and establishments (e.g. prostitution, drug-trade, gambling) in return for substantial bribes. The ICAC described the police and triads as feeding off each other and growing fat together (ICAC, 1976: 2). The crackdown on syndicated police corruption eliminated this protective umbrella and substantially weakened the power of triads (Kwok and Lo, 2014).

Furthermore, various ordinances have been used to prosecute triad-related crime. The *Societies Ordinance* (Cap. 151) declares triad societies unlawful and criminalises triad membership. The *Organized and Serious Crimes Ordinance* (Cap. 455) targets the laundering of illegal proceeds and granted the police greater powers of investigation. The *Drug Trafficking (Recovery of Proceeds) Ordinance* (Cap. 405) targets perpetrators of drug offences (Kwok and Lo, 2013). Once the power of triad societies is weakened, the 'bullets' they use to bribe law enforcers are restricted too.

Emergence of a watchdog culture

Free press and public vigilance are powerful tools in ensuring government transparency and accountability. Between the 1950s and 1970s, Hong Kong, being a migrant city, had been regarded as a low-participation society (Lau, 1982), where integration and interaction between the government and its people was low. Blair-Kerr (1973) also attributed the widespread corruption of the 1950s and 1970s to citizen apathy. He wrote that the vast majority of immigrants from Mainland China were accustomed to a government that was 'riddled with corruption'. They had no 'real roots' or 'true sense of belonging' to this borrowed place living on borrowed time – rather, immigrants arrived in Hong Kong because of an 'overwhelming desire to make money quickly' (ibid.: 22–23).

By the 1970s, a civil society began to emerge in line with the rise of a new generation of people who had transformed the migrant Hong Kong society into their own home (Lo, 1993). Unlike their parents, young people in the 1970s were born and raised in Hong Kong and had not been brainwashed by negative experiences in Mainland China to accept corruption and oppression as a way of life. Instead, they had been under heavy Western influences by way of education, television, newspapers, films, etc. when growing up. Lee (1981) found that younger and better-educated Chinese have a lower level of Chinese traditionalism and are less tolerant of corruption. The 'Catch Godber, Fight Corruption' campaign that eventually led to the formation of the ICAC showed that young people believed they had a role in building a corruption-free future.

The democratisation of legislature as a result of the Sino-British negotiation of Hong Kong's future further fostered people's political awareness and participation in the 1980s. Civic organisations and political parties were formed. Various student and social movements that have occurred during the last few decades have also strengthened the foundation of an emerging civil society (Lui and Chiu, 1999).

The case of 'structural defects in 26 public housing blocks' best illustrates the fact that the media and citizens can act as powerful watchdogs to ensure government accountability (Lo, 1993). As the problematic housing blocks were built between 1964 and 1973, the ICAC 'normally' would not act upon pre-1977 cases as required by the partial amnesty. However, mounting pressure from residents, the press, civil society groups and politicians eventually forced the governor to order the ICAC investigation of this corruption case (Lo, 2001; ICAC, 2015b).

Mass media

News media, frequently considered the fourth estate in a democratic society, is vital in upholding the checks and balances of the three branches of government. The watchdog role is particularly important in Hong Kong due to the limited democracy enjoyed throughout the colonial era, until after the return to Chinese sovereignty (Weisenhaus, 2007). Freedom of expression is guaranteed in the *Basic Law* (Article 27) and the *Hong Kong Bill of Rights Ordinance* (Article 19, section 8). In the 1970s, commercial newspapers, both privately owned and publicly traded, began to flourish (Weisenhaus, 2007). Privately owned media companies have greater autonomy from the government and are less politically connected. Their main goals are competing for market share and maximising profit.

Competition is a facilitating factor for watchdog reporting in Hong Kong, as newspapers are more willing to invest in exposé news if it enables them to outsell their rivals (Coronel, 2009). Once a newspaper starts reporting on a popular exposé, other newspapers will naturally follow suit and reveal more information that concerns the public. Since the return to Chinese sovereignty, the commercial press in Hong Kong has produced thorough and extensive coverage of the Severe Acute Respiratory Syndrome (SARS) crisis, the attempt to pass Article 23 legislation, the melamine-tainted dairy scandal in Mainland China, conflicts of interest and the illegal building structure of candidates during the chief executive election in 2012, and protests in response to the moral and national education curriculum. Timothy Tong, former commissioner of the ICAC, was also the subject of intense media scrutiny regarding his lavish spending of public funds.

Citizen engagement

The ICAC does not proactively seek out corruption cases; it reactively responds to reports of corruption. Citizens have to report instances of corruption in order for the ICAC to take action. This reactive type of policing ensures that the ICAC does not discriminate among cases. Two tactics need to be highlighted that have encouraged citizens to report instances of corruption. First, the CRD has successfully used fear appeals by way of posters and advertisements to encourage support and action from the general public. In the case of ICAC advertisements, personally relevant and likely consequences of corruption are depicted to viewers (e.g. the fear of unjust competition, fear of economic setback, fear of punishment if caught, etc.) (ICAC, 2015c). ICAC advertisements then offer viewers a straightforward and effective response to remove the source of fear: support the ICAC and report corruption.

Second, the seemingly indiscriminate approach to investigation is instrumental in encouraging reports of corruption (de Speville, 1999). The ICAC assures citizens that every complaint, whether large or small, will be handled. This trust that ICAC will pursue their complaints perhaps leads to more non-anonymous reports from the public. Non-anonymous reports have greater investigative success because investigators can return to the complainant to gather further information when needed.

Civil service reform

It was syndicated corruption in the civil service and the police that forced the public to fight back. A clean civil service is therefore necessary to maintain the legitimacy and political authority of the colonial government.

Using a high remuneration package to 'nourish integrity' (*yang lian*) is an age-old Chinese concept. Chung-li Chang explained: 'This allowance, which was many times the amount of the regular salary, was given in recognition of the effect that the regular salary was too low for positions with so much responsibility and so much opportunity for financial gain' (cited by Lethbridge, 1985: 13). Cater believed that public officers carrying authority, especially the police, would face a great deal of temptation if they were not sufficiently remunerated (*China Daily Asia*, 2013b). He was instrumental in raising the pay of police officers following the 1967 riots (ibid.). He also introduced a generous special monthly allowance for ICAC staff (Standing Commission on Civil Service Salaries and Conditions of Service, 1980).

Civil servants in Hong Kong in the 1980s were adequately compensated with a base salary, housing benefits, medical benefits, dental benefits and a pension (Standing Commission on Civil Service Salaries and Conditions of Service, 1987). This remuneration package offered civil servants peace of mind that they and their loved ones would have a comfortable living for life. The package was credited for preventing corruption motivated by need among junior and mid-level officials.

A rule-based administrative system

The government of Hong Kong has adopted a three-pronged approach to ensuring good conduct within the civil service – namely, prevention, education and sanctions (Civil Service Bureau, 2015).

- Prevention: rules guiding appropriate behaviour. A number of agencies in Hong Kong play a role in reviewing and monitoring the civil service administration, including the Civil Service Bureau, the ICAC, the Public Service Commission, the Audit Commission and the Ombudsman (Scott, 2013b). Scott (2013b) notes that corruption prevention in Hong Kong makes a distinction between corruption cases that result from systematic flaws and cases that result from individual action.

  a Departmental level: the CPD of the ICAC has been tasked with identifying systematic flaws within the civil service that are conducive to corruption. As a result of these CPD reports, the hierarchical structure within the civil service has been strengthened to better monitor performance, and the control system has been tightened to limit discretion (Scott, 2013b).

  b Personal level: civil servants in Hong Kong are required to observe more stringent rules than employees in the private sector. All candidates undergo various types of integrity checks during their civil service career. Three levels of checks are undertaken by the police and the ICAC (Legislative Council Panel on Security, 2005). Strict regulations are imposed by the Civil Service Bureau, restricting the acceptance of gifts and loans. Since 1998, posts at directorate level and above have been required to declare their global investments at least biennially, in addition to the occupations of their spouses (Legislative Council Panel on Public Service, 2000). Investments that need to be declared include securities, shareholdings, interests in companies and land property, gifts, sponsorships, etc. Disclosure of investments prevents officers from taking up certain posts or projects that might constitute a conflict of interest and is a measure designed to uphold civil service impartiality. As of March 2000, around 3,000 officials were required to declare their investments.

- Education: a value-based approach. Scott (2013b) notes that the rule-based administrative system has been supplemented by value-based measures to counter new forms of anti-corruption since 1997. Anson Chan, former chief secretary for administration, proclaimed six core values of the civil service less than one year after the return of Hong Kong to Chinese sovereignty (Chan, 1998). The six values are commitment to the rule of law, honesty and integrity above private interests, accountability and openness in decision making, political neutrality, impartiality, and dedication and diligence in serving the community. The emphasis on integrity management could also be seen in the introduction of the Ethical Leadership Programme and the Civil Service Code.

- Sanctions: failure to comply with the rules governing appropriate civil service behaviour holds officers liable to disciplinary action, dismissal from the service and even criminal proceedings. The ICAC reasserted that public service remained its first priority in enforcement and that they would prosecute public servants for breaches of POBO or for misconduct in public office (ICAC, 1994). The ICAC also forwards cases of suspected misconduct to the secretary for the civil service/Civil Service Bureau for disciplinary action.

Conclusion

The United Nations Convention against Corruption asserts that the international community has formally acknowledged the pervasive and destructive consequences of corruption, and has legally pledged to bring corruption under control. Nevertheless, despite this legal pledge and the efforts of the countries involved, Transparency International noted that two-thirds of these countries scored below the midpoint of 50 on the Corruption Perceptions Index 2014. On the other hand, Hong Kong has consistently been rated as one of the cleanest cities, year after year. The success in Hong Kong demonstrates that the radical package of reform has been effective in curbing corruption.

The most significant lesson seen in the history of anti-corruption in Hong Kong is perhaps this: 'Where there's a will, there's a way.' Over the last few decades, the political will to combat corruption has enabled laws to be changed, an independent agency to be established solely for the purpose of fighting corruption, and administration systems to be changed. Minds, attitudes, cultures, behaviours and practices have also been altered. However, an effective ICAC alone is not sufficiently powerful to curb corruption. The support of other political, legal and social systems is required to form the pillars of a society of integrity. The present chapter highlighted the importance of effective legislation enacted within the rule of law, the necessity for strong political will, the emergence of a watchdog culture and civil service reform.

However, with the 'Sinofication' or 'mainlandisation' of the political, economic, social, cultural and criminal justice systems of Hong Kong following China's resumption of sovereignty of Hong Kong in 1997, its unique model of anti-corruption has been challenged (Lo, 2012). This is reflected in the recent corruption- and integrity-related scandals of former Chief Executive Donald Tsang, former Chief Secretary for Administration Rafael Hui Si-Yan, and former ICAC Commissioner Timothy Tong. Further research is required to examine the current legal and political barriers to maintaining the practices and effectiveness of the fight against corruption.

Review questions

1 What were the major strategies enacted to help build a corruption-free culture since the 1960s and 1970s?
2 How do the five main groups of strategies relate to each other in tackling corruption?
3 What factors contributed to how ICAC gained legitimacy and its unique nature as an independent commission against corruption?

References

Agrast, M., Botero, J., Martinez, J., Ponce, A. and Pratt, C. (2012–13) *WJP Rule of Law Index 2012–2013*, Washington, DC: The World Justice Project.

Agrast, M., Botero, J. and Ponce, A. (2011) *WJP Rule of Law Index 2011*, Washington, DC: The World Justice Project.

Blair-Kerr, Sir A. (1973) *Second Report of the Commission of Inquiry under Sir Alastair Blair-Kerr*, Hong Kong: Government Printer.

Chan, A. (1998, May 21). *Opening Remarks of the Chief Secretary for Administration – Seminar on Hong Kong into the 21st Century: Maintaining Integrity in the Civil Service*, Hong Kong: Civil Service Bureau, www.csb.gov.hk/hkgcsb/rcim/pdf/english/conference_meterials/1998_anson.pdf (accessed 15 February 2016).

Cheung, C.F. (2010) *Fantan Tingbuliao: Lianzhenggongshu Qishilu (Anti-Corruption Efforts Must Continue: Lessons from ICAC)*, Hong Kong: Joint Publishing (in Chinese).

Civil Service Bureau (2015) *Conduct and Discipline*, Hong Kong: Civil Service Bureau, www.csb.gov.hk/english/admin/conduct/134.html (accessed 15 February 2016).

Clarke, R.V. (1997) *Situational Crime Prevention: Successful Case Studies* (2nd edn), New York: Harrow and Heston.

Coronel, S. (2009) 'Corruption and the watchdog role of the news media', in P. Norris (ed.) *Public Sentinel: News Media & Governance Reform*, Washington, DC: World Bank, www.hks.harvard.edu/fs/pnorris/Acrobat/WorldBankReport/Chapter%205%20Coronel.pdf (accessed 15 February 2016).

de Speville, B.E.D. (1999) 'The experience of Hong Kong, China, in combatting corruption', in R. Stapenhurst and S.J. Kpundeh (eds) *Curbing Corruption: Toward a Model for Building National Integrity* (pp. 51–58), Washington, DC: World Bank.

Hong Kong Legislative Council (1973) *The Legislative Council Debates Official Report in the Session of the Legislative Council of Hong Kong which opened 17th October 1973 in the Twenty-Second Year of the Reign of Her Majesty Queen Elizabeth II*, Hong Kong: Hong Kong Legislative Council.

Hong Kong Legislative Council (1977, November 11) *Official Report of Proceedings*, Hong Kong: Hong Kong Legislative Council.

Hong Kong Legislative Council (1978, October 11) *Official Report of Proceedings*, Hong Kong: Hong Kong Legislative Council.

Independent Commission Against Corruption (ICAC) (various issues, 1974–94) *Annual Report on the Activities of the Independent Commission Against Corruption*, Hong Kong: ICAC.

Independent Commission Against Corruption (ICAC) (2015a) *Corruption Prevention Department*, Hong Kong: ICAC, www.icac.org.hk/en/corruption_prevention_department/index.html (accessed 15 February 2016).

Independent Commission Against Corruption (ICAC) (2015b) *Landmark Cases: 26 Public Housing Blocks Case*, Hong Kong: ICAC, www.icac.org.hk/new_icac/eng/cases/26p/26p.htm (accessed 15 February 2016).

Independent Commission Against Corruption (ICAC) (2015c) *Audio-visual Products*, Hong Kong: ICAC, www.icac.hk/en/acr/avp/index.html (accessed 15 February 2016).

Independent Commission Against Corruption (ICAC) Review Committee (1994) *Report of the ICAC Review Committee*, Hong Kong: Government Printer.

Kuan, H. (1981) 'Anti-corruption legislation in Hong Kong – A history', in R.P.L. Lee (ed.) *Corruption and its Control in Hong Kong: Situations Up to the Late Seventies* (pp. 15–43), Hong Kong: Chinese University Press.

Kwok, S.I. and Lo, T.W. (2013) 'Anti-triad legislations in Hong Kong: Issues, problems and development', *Trends in Organized Crime*, 16(1): 74–94.

Kwok, S.I. and Lo, T.W. (2014) 'Crime and its control in Hong Kong', in L. Cao, I. Sun and B. Hebenton (eds) *The Routledge Handbook of Chinese Criminology* (pp. 284–294), New York: Routledge.

Lai, A.N. (2000) *A Quiet Revolution: The Hong Kong Experience*, Hong Kong: ICAC, www.icac.org.hk/en/acr/sa/qrhke/index.html (accessed 15 February 2016).

Lau, S.K. (1982) *Society and Politics in Hong Kong*, Hong Kong: Chinese University Press.

Lee, R.P.L. (1981) 'Incongruence of legal codes and folk norms', in R.P.L. Lee (ed.) *Corruption and its Control in Hong Kong: Situations Up to the Late Seventies* (pp. 75–104), Hong Kong: Chinese University Press.

Legislative Council Panel on Public Service (2000, March 20) *Declaration of Investments by Civil Servants* (meeting on March 20, 2000), Hong Kong: Legislative Council Panel on Public Service.

Legislative Council Panel on Security (2004, May 13) *Integrity Checking of ICAC Personnel* (LC Paper No. CB(2)2270/03-04(05)), Hong Kong: Legislative Council Panel on Security.

Legislative Council Panel on Security (2005, July) *Integrity Checking for Disciplined Forces* (CB(2)2395/04-05(01)), Hong Kong: Legislative Council Panel on Security.

Lethbridge, H.J. (1976) 'Corruption, white collar crime and the I.C.A.C.', *Hong Kong Law Journal*, 6: 150–178.

Lethbridge, H.J. (1985) *Hard Graft in Hong Kong: Scandal, Corruption, the ICAC*, Hong Kong: Oxford University Press.

Li, L. (2014) *Senior Officials' Corruption-Related Malpractice in Hong Kong after 1997*, unpublished doctoral dissertation, Hong Kong: The City University of Hong Kong.

Litton, H. (1978) 'Colonial Regulation 55: The fragile rice-bowl [Editorial]', *Hong Kong Law Journal*, 8: 137–142.

Lo, T.W. (1993) *Corruption and Politics in Hong Kong and China*, Buckingham: Open University Press.

Lo, T.W. (1994) 'The Independent Commission Against Corruption', in M. Gaylord and H. Traver (eds) *Introduction to the Hong Kong Criminal Justice System* (pp. 63–77), Hong Kong: Hong Kong University Press.

Lo, T.W. (1995) 'Anti-corruption', in S.Y.L. Cheung and S.M.H. Sze (eds) *The Other Hong Kong Report 1995* (pp. 87–101), Hong Kong: Chinese University Press.

Lo, T.W. (1998) 'Pioneer of moral education: Independent Commission Against Corruption', *Trends in Organized Crime*, 4(2): 19–30.

Lo, T.W. (2001) 'Anti-corruption strategies and housing scandals in Hong Kong', in A.C. Pedro, Jr (ed.) *Combating Corruption in East Asia* (pp. 17–40), Manila: De La Salle University Press.

Lo, T.W. (2003) 'Minimizing crime and corruption in Hong Kong', in R. Godson (ed.) *Menace to Society: Political-criminal Collaboration around the World* (pp. 231–256), London: Transaction Publishers.

Lo, T.W. (2012) 'Resistance to the mainlandization of criminal justice practices: A barrier to the development of restorative justice in Hong Kong', *International Journal of Offender Therapy and Comparative Criminology*, 56(4): 627–645.

Lo, T.W. and Ngan, P. (2009) 'Restricting loans of money to Hong Kong civil servants: Social censure or violation of human rights?', *Crime, Law and Social Change*, 52(4): 385–403.

Lo, T.W. and Yu, R.C.C. (2000) 'Curbing draconian powers: The effects of Hong Kong's graft-fighter', *The International Journal of Human Rights*, 4(1): 54–73.

Lui, T.L. and Chiu, S.W. (1999) 'Social movements and public discourse on politics', in T.W. Ngo (ed.) *Hong Kong's History: State and Society under Colonial Rule* (pp. 101–118), New York: Routledge.

Mu, J. (2008) *Community Support – The Key to Fight Corruption*, Hong Kong: ICAC, www.icac.org.hk/en/acr/sa/oc6pcc/index.html (accessed 15 February 2016).

Scott, I. (2013a) 'Engaging the public: Hong Kong's Independent Commission Against Corruption's community relations strategy', in J.S.T. Quah (ed.) *Different Paths to Curbing Corruption: Lessons from Denmark, Finland, Hong Kong, New Zealand and Singapore* (Research in Public Policy Analysis and Management Volume 23) (pp. 79–108), Bingley: Emerald Group Publishing.

Scott, I. (2013b) 'Institutional design and corruption prevention in Hong Kong', *Journal of Contemporary China*, 22(79): 77–92.

Standing Commission on Civil Service Salaries and Conditions of Service (1980) *Report on the Pay of Staff of the Independent Commission Against Corruption*, Hong Kong: Standing Commission on Civil Service Salaries and Conditions of Service.

Standing Commission on Civil Service Salaries and Conditions of Service (1987) *The Second and Final Report on 1986 Pay Level Survey*, Hong Kong: Standing Commission on Civil Service Salaries and Conditions of Service.

Tong, T. (2007) *Building a Public Sector Integrity System for Effective Governance: The Hong Kong Experience*, Hong Kong: ICAC, www.icac.org.hk/en/acr/sa/bpsis/index.html (accessed 15 February 2016).

Weisenhaus, D. (2007) *Hong Kong Media Law: A Guide for Journalists and Media Professionals*, Hong Kong: Hong Kong University Press.

Wilson, J.Q. and Kelling, G.L. (1982) 'The police and neighborhood safety: Broken windows', *Atlantic Monthly*, 127 (March): 29–38.

Wong, J. K. H. (1981) 'The ICAC and its anti-corruption measures', in R.P.L. Lee (ed.) *Corruption and its Control in Hong Kong: Situations Up to the Late Seventies* (pp. 45–72), Hong Kong: Chinese University Press.

World Justice Project (2014) *WJP Rule of Law Index 2014*, Washington, DC: The World Justice Project.

Yep, R. (2013) 'The crusade against corruption in Hong Kong in the 1970s: Governor MacLehose as a zealous reformer or reluctant hero?', *China Information*, 27(2): 197–221.

Newspapers articles cited

China Daily Asia (2013a) 'Timely vigilance reminder', 4 October, www.chinadailyasia.com/opinion/2013-10/24/content_15094401.html (accessed 15 February 2016).

China Daily Asia (2013b) 'LETTERS: Elsie Tu appears rather off track', 6 November, www.chinadailyasia.com/opinion/2013-11/06/content_15096740.html (accessed 15 February 2016).

South China Morning Post (2004) '30 years of hard graft', 1 February, www.scmp.com/article/442896/30-years-hard-graft (accessed 15 February 2016).

South China Morning Post (2006) 'The man who ran corrupt officials out of city', 17 April, www.scmp.com/article/545049/man-who-ran-corrupt-officials-out-city (accessed 15 February 2016).

Legislation cited

Basic Law of the Hong Kong Special Administrative Region of the People's Republic of China
Colonial Regulation 55
Drug Trafficking (Recovery of Proceeds) Ordinance (Cap. 405)
Elections (Corrupt and Illegal Conduct) Ordinance (Cap. 554)
Hong Kong Bill of Rights Ordinance (Cap. 383)
Independent Commission Against Corruption Ordinance (Cap. 204)
Misdemeanours Punishment Ordinance
Organized and Serious Crimes Ordinance (Cap. 455)
Police Force Ordinance (Cap. 232)
Prevention of Bribery Ordinance (Cap. 201)
Prevention of Corruption Ordinance (Cap. 215)
Societies Ordinance (Cap. 151)

Cases cited

Attorney General v. Hui Kin-hong [1995] 1 HKCLR 227
Sin Kam-wah & Another v. HKSAR [2005] 2 HKLRD 375

Useful websites

Civil Service Bureau www.csb.gov.hk
Hong Kong Legislative Council www.legco.gov.hk
Independent Commission Against Corruption www.icac.org.hk

11

PROSECUTING CRIME

I. Grenville Cross SC

Introduction

In 2000, when the former South African President, Nelson Mandela, was awarded the Medal of Honour of the International Association of Prosecutors, he described the duty of the prosecutor as being to 'prosecute fairly and effectively, according to the rule of law, and to act in a principled way, without fear, favour or prejudice'. Much is expected of the modern prosecutor, and great care must be taken over prosecutorial decisions. Suspects must not be prosecuted unless this is fully justified, and the interests of victims and witnesses must be safeguarded. Wrong decisions can have serious consequences, and may even undermine public trust in the criminal justice system. If victims feel they have not received justice, they may be tempted to take matters into their own hands, and the prosecutor must try to ensure that confidence in the legal system is maintained. The prosecutor must act honestly and independently at all times, and within the parameters of prosecution policy guidelines.

Article 63 of the *Basic Law*

The *Basic Law of the Hong Kong Special Administrative Region* (hereafter the *Basic Law*), came into effect on 1 July 1997. Article 63 provides that the Department of Justice shall control criminal prosecutions, free from any interference. It is reassuring that this principle, long recognised in colonial times as a convention, now has an entrenched status. This means, in practice, that prosecutors are able to discharge their duties to the public from a secure base. At times of controversy, the prosecutor can take refuge within a constitutionally guaranteed position.

It is noteworthy that Article 63 vests control of prosecutions in the Department of Justice, and not in a particular individual. The department, however, has construed Article 63 as vesting control in the secretary for justice personally, as departmental head, rather than in the director of public prosecutions, as head of the Prosecutions Division. This has proved controversial, given that the secretary is a political appointee who sits in the Executive Council and serves as legal adviser to the chief executive. Some people have argued that prosecution control should be vested instead in an independent director, as elsewhere in the common law world.

The Hong Kong Basic Law Institute has, moreover, explained that not only is an independent director constitutionally permissible, but that for the secretary to be involved in public prosecutions is, of itself, contrary to Article 63, given his or her political role. A strong case undoubtedly exists for the secretary handing over the control of prosecutions to the director of public prosecutions, either in whole or in part, as in England and Wales, given that the director is, unlike the secretary, a politically neutral figure without ministerial responsibilities. A campaign for an independent director controlling prosecutions was launched in 2011 (Cross, 2011), and continues to gain support, particularly in light of developments attendant upon the street protests that occurred in parts of Hong Kong in late 2014.

Prosecutors and investigators

In many jurisdictions, including the mainland of China, the Macao Special Administrative Region (SAR) and Taiwan, the prosecutor not only prosecutes cases but also investigates them. In those places, the prosecutor is closely involved in the investigation of cases of corruption and of misconduct in public office. In Hong Kong, the prosecutor has no such investigative function. Whereas general crime is investigated by the Hong Kong Police Force, offences of corruption are investigated by the Independent Commission Against Corruption, and customs crime is investigated by the Customs and Excise Department (ICAC). Of course, the prosecutor can advise the investigator upon lines of enquiry which can profitably be pursued and upon the admissibility of evidence, but the investigation of crime is, ultimately, a matter for the law enforcement agencies themselves.

The Department of Justice has the responsibility for the conduct of prosecutions, without the power to control or direct the investigation, as set out in *The Prosecution Code* (Department of Justice, 2013). However, the lack of any such power in Hong Kong by no means undermines effective law enforcement. Were police to ignore legal advice to conduct the investigation in a particular way, the prosecutor holds the trump card. He or she can decline to prosecute. Alternatively, he or she can discontinue a prosecution that is in progress, if the investigator does not pursue the enquiries which are deemed necessary. This separation of the prosecutorial and investigatory functions works well in practice, and facilitates the application of an independent and dedicated perspective to each function. In practice, the prosecutor and the investigator invariably cooperate harmoniously in pursuit of shared objectives.

When the investigator prepares a case, he or she will, if necessary, consult the prosecutor, on legal and evidential issues, actual or potential. He or she may also require advice on undercover operations and the legitimacy of particular areas of investigation. It is in the interests of the investigator to prepare a case that satisfies the threshold test for prosecution, and which will not collapse in court when tested by the defence. This means that while the investigator is not strictly required to accept the advice of the prosecutor, he or she will, in practice, usually do so. The interests of the prosecutor and the investigator invariably converge in a shared desire to assemble a case that is watertight and will withstand close forensic scrutiny.

The Prosecutions Division is the largest legal division in the Department of Justice. Headed by the director of public prosecutions, who in turn is superintended by the secretary for justice, it comprises approximately 135 government counsel and 102 court prosecutors (Department of Justice, 2015). The role of the division is to prosecute trials and appeals at all levels, to provide legal advice to law enforcement agencies and others in government, and to review the operation of criminal law. The division itself is divided into four sub-divisions, concerned with management and case preparation, trial advocacy, appellate advocacy, and commercial crime and corruption. In recent years, the division has developed its capacity to prosecute transnational and organised crime, as well as to handle specific types of offences, such as copyright piracy, technology crime and money laundering. In addition, a dedicated unit advises on, and conducts, criminal cases that engage *Basic Law* and human rights issues.

Qualities of the prosecutor

The prosecutor occupies a formidable position in the criminal justice system. His or her responsibilities are awesome (Department of Justice, 2012). The decisions he or she takes can profoundly affect the lives of others. In each case, the prosecutor must carefully evaluate the evidence, apply the law and decide if a prosecution is appropriate. A decision to prosecute must be taken with the keenest appreciation of the ordeal involved in a trial, as well as with full awareness of the trauma and stigma that can be caused to the accused and his or her family, even if, ultimately, there is an acquittal. At the same time, difficult decisions cannot be sidestepped. The prosecutor must possess judgement and good sense in abundance, and have the courage of his or her convictions.

Of the many qualities that the prosecutor needs to possess, fearlessness is perhaps the most important. Sometimes he or she will be criticised for prosecuting, but more often for not prosecuting. The decisions he or she has to take are inherently controversial. Provided the prosecutor has acted conscientiously and correctly, he or she must not be deflected from the most appropriate course, even if this attracts unpopularity. This requires strength of character, to resist criticism from whatever quarter, no matter how strident or painful. Never must the prosecutor's judgement be overborne by political, media or public pressure or censure. The profession of prosecutor is often stressful but ultimately, satisfying, and is certainly not one for the faint-hearted.

Protection of the suspect

It can be far easier for the prosecutor to decide to prosecute a suspect than to decide not to prosecute. Once criminal proceedings have begun, the issues move from the domain of the prosecutor to that of the court. Questions about the case can be avoided on the basis of the *sub judice* rule, which, quite simply, means that since the case is before the courts for trial there cannot be any public discussion of the issues, as this might prejudice the fairness of the trial. However, in a matter as important as the liberty of the suspect, no responsible prosecutor can avoid his or her duty to properly assess the evidence. After all, the prosecutor is a gatekeeper, charged with the duty of ensuring that only meritorious cases proceed to trial. Just as the judge must scrupulously protect the interests of the accused who stands trial, so should the prosecutor be vigilant in defence of the rights of the suspect who does not. Once the trial starts, the suspect enjoys certain fundamental rights, including the right to question the witness who accuses him or her, to know exactly what the prosecution case is, and to give and call evidence in his or her own defence.

Evidential test for prosecution

No citizen should ever be subjected to a criminal trial unless the evidence warrants that course. Prosecuting, after all, is the art of the possible. A suspect can only ever properly be prosecuted if there is sufficient evidence to justify that course. Prosecution policy in this area is clear and unambiguous. Those who prosecute in Hong Kong apply the guidance contained in *The Prosecution Code* (Department of Justice, 2013), which, in turn, reflects the English approach and that of the wider common law world.

The Department of Justice does not support the proposition that a mere prima facie case suffices to ground a prosecution. In deciding whether to start proceedings, the single most important consideration for the prosecutor is the likelihood of conviction. However, a conviction can never be guaranteed, and the system of justice could not operate effectively if the prosecutor pursued only those cases where there was an absolute certainty of conviction. At the same time, the enforcement of the law would be brought into disrepute if there were an inordinate number of failed prosecutions. This could also affect public confidence in the efficacy of the criminal process.

The job of the prosecutor is to institute criminal proceedings against a suspect in accordance with prosecution policy guidelines. It is then for the court, if guilt is disputed, to decide if the charge has been proven beyond reasonable doubt. A prosecution may properly be started once it is decided that the evidence is capable of proving the guilt of the suspect. The decision to prosecute has usually to be taken by the prosecutor without the opportunity of seeing or hearing the witnesses, and is based invariably upon an assessment of the papers submitted by the investigator and the advice of the case officer. The prosecutor must be satisfied that there exists at least a reasonable prospect of conviction. Mere suspicion, no matter how great, falls well short of what is required.

A suspect should not be prosecuted on the basis of what lawyers sometimes call 'a bare case', by which is meant a case that proceeds on no more than the basis of a 51% prospect of conviction. Just as the prosecutor will wish to see that those against whom the evidence is compelling face trial, so also will he or she wish to avoid unnecessary proceedings. A proper evaluation of the case will involve an assessment of the evidence as well as of the law. It is also necessary to take account of such matters as the availability, competence and credibility of witnesses, their likely impression on the court, and the prospects for the admissibility of evidence implicating the accused, such as an alleged confession. The prosecutor should also consider any defences that are plainly open to the accused, such as alibi evidence, by which is meant evidence that puts the accused somewhere else when the crime occurred, and which may affect directly the prospects of conviction.

Article 87 of the *Basic Law* recognises the right of those accused of crime to be presumed innocent. It is only if the court is satisfied of guilt beyond reasonable doubt that the prosecutor will secure a conviction. Even if the prosecution fails, it by no means follows that the case ought not to have been brought. Prosecutions fail for all sorts of reasons. Witnesses may not come up to proof, or may be shaken in cross-examination, or may even fail to appear. The judge may sometimes exclude crucial items of evidence on legal grounds, such as an admission allegedly made by the accused. Such factors are imponderables, and cannot be predicted with certainty prior to trial.

Public interest factors

If a proposed prosecution satisfies the evidential test, the prosecutor must then assess the impact of the public interest factors, if any. In general, the more serious the offence, the more likely is it that the public interest will require a prosecution. Factors which might suggest to the prosecutor that proceedings are inexpedient include the triviality of the offence; the medical condition of the suspect, his antecedents, and his age, whether very young or very old; the viability of any alternative to prosecution, such as a discretionary warning from a superintendent of police; the likelihood of a nominal penalty upon conviction; the staleness of the offence; any assistance that has been provided by the suspect to the authorities; the attitude of the victim, most obviously if it is forgiving; and the indicia of remorse, if any, such as the payment of compensation by the suspect to the victim.

Alternatively, factors may exist that aggravate the seriousness of the offence and emphasise the public interest in the prosecution of the suspect. Into this category fall such considerations as an abuse of trust by someone in authority; premeditation; the use of a weapon or the threat of violence; the prevalence of the offence; the role played in the offence, particularly if the suspect was a ringleader; any element of corruption; the criminal record of the suspect; and the prospects of repetition. If any of these factors is combined with others, the case for prosecution may become overwhelming, but that of itself does not absolve the prosecutor of the duty to evaluate the significance of each factor in the overall scheme of things.

Prosecutor at court

At court, the prosecutor represents the Hong Kong SAR. He or she is not the representative of the government or the law enforcement agency. The prosecutor is as independent as the judge, and his or her interest throughout is the just disposal of the issues joined. The prosecutor has no client in the conventional sense, and his or her duty is to act impartially and objectively in the public interest. He or she operates not as an adversary, but as a minister of justice. Rightly has it been said that the prosecutor secures no victories and sustains no defeats.

When he or she prosecutes a suspect, the prosecutor is on trial. The public perception of the administration of justice may be affected if he or she badly manages the case, displays discourtesy or is deficient in advocacy. Fairness by the prosecutor does not, however, make him or her some sort of 'soft touch'. The prosecutor must be vigorous in prosecuting the case, but restrained and courteous throughout. He or she may strike hard blows, but not foul ones. Evidence should be efficiently marshalled and cogently adduced.

The duty of the prosecutor is to call evidence that is relevant to prove the case, and to present it with appropriate fairness. The prosecutor should not advance submissions to the court in which he or she does not truly believe, and material that may benefit the accused must be disclosed, not concealed. The function of the prosecutor is to ensure that every material point is made which supports the prosecution case or undermines the defence case. At the same time, he or she should not press for a conviction at all costs.

Properly seen, the interest of the prosecutor is to ensure that the right person is convicted and that the truth emerges. If it becomes apparent to the prosecutor during the course of the trial that a reasonable prospect of securing a conviction no longer exists, he or she should acquaint the court with this view and seek to terminate the proceedings. In such a scenario, the sooner the ordeal the accused is undergoing is ended, the better it will be for him or her, as well as for the public purse.

Duty of disclosure

The right of the accused to a fair trial is enshrined in Article 87 of the *Basic Law*. No trial can be fair if the prosecutor does not observe his or her disclosure obligations, a point fully examined by the Court of Final Appeal in *HKSAR v Lee Ming Tee* (2003) 6 HKCFAR 336. The general duty upon the prosecution is to provide the defence in advance of trial with the evidence upon which reliance is intended to be placed. This ensures that the accused is aware of the case he will be required to meet, and enables him or her to prepare his or her position accordingly. Also disclosable, and often more problematic, is material upon which the prosecution does not intend to rely, but which might undermine the prosecution case or advance the defence case. The duty to disclose applies not only to previous convictions of a prosecution witness, but also to discreditable conduct by the witness which might affect his or her credibility. This, for example, might include disciplinary proceedings against an investigator. This duty is continuing, and matters not previously disclosable may have to be revealed in consequence of developments at trial. If there is a dispute as to whether evidence is in fact disclosable, it is for the court to resolve the issue, not the prosecution.

Victims and witnesses

Both at trial and before the case begins, the prosecutor should safeguard the interests of victims of crime and witnesses. The cooperation of such people is essential if offenders are to be brought to justice. They must have faith in the system, and the prosecutor should uphold their rights. These rights are reflected in *The Statement on the Treatment of Victims and Witnesses* (Department of Justice, 2009), which the director of public prosecutions issued to prosecutors in 2009, as well as in *The Victims of Crime Charter* (Department of Justice, 2015). The rights of victims and witnesses include:

- the right to witness protection,
- the right to information throughout proceedings,
- the right to liaison at each stage,
- the right to assistance at court,
- the right to seek compensation or restitution,
- the right to protection from unjust criticism,
- the right to have the court appraised of the consequences of crime,
- the right to seek witness expenses,
- the right to information on appeals or reviews, and
- the right to have property disposed of appropriately once proceedings conclude.

Prosecutor and sentence

Once an accused has been convicted, the prosecutor plays an important role in the sentencing process, not least in ensuring that the exercise proceeds on a correct factual basis. He or she has the right to alert the court to guideline and tariff cases, including those that prescribe relevant sentencing principles. If requested, the prosecutor should be in a position to advise the court of the prevalence of the offence, and of the broad range of sentences passed generally for a particular offence. The prosecutor should ensure that any sentence that is in contemplation is in fact within the jurisdiction of the court, and an accurate record of previous convictions should be supplied. The court should be advised if the accused has assisted the authorities, and also if he or she faces satellite proceedings in other courts. In some situations, the prosecutor will be entitled to seek an enhanced sentence under the provisions of the *Organized and Serious Crimes Ordinance* (Cap. 455), most notably if the offence involves an organised crime. If a dispute arises over matters asserted in mitigation of sentence by the defence, the court should be alerted so that it may, if necessary, conduct an inquiry to resolve the issue. In essence, the duty of the prosecutor at the point of sentence is to assist the court to achieve a correct disposal, and to avoid appealable error. At the same time, it is no part of his or her function to press by advocacy for a more severe sentence.

Appeal against conviction and sentence

Article 39 of the *Basic Law* stipulates that the *International Covenant on Civil and Political Rights* (ICCPR) as applied to Hong Kong shall remain in force, and shall be implemented through the laws of the Hong Kong SAR. Article 14(5) of the ICCPR provides that everyone 'convicted of a crime shall have the right to his conviction and sentence being reviewed by a higher tribunal according to law'. When those convicted of offences exercise their rights of appeal against conviction or sentence, or both, much is required of the prosecutor in the determination of the case before the appellate tribunal.

If there is an appeal against conviction, the duty of the prosecutor is to assist the court to achieve a just disposal of the case. To succeed, an accused must be in a position to show that his or her conviction is unsafe or unsatisfactory, or that the judgment of the trial court involves a wrong decision on a question of law, or that there was a material irregularity at trial. If an accused relies on any such grounds of appeal, the prosecutor must evaluate it, settle his or her response and identify relevant case law to assist the court. If he or she sees a basis for appeal that has not hitherto been noticed, the prosecutor should alert the court. Although the prosecutor will generally seek to uphold a conviction, if he or she concludes that the appeal is meritorious, the court should be informed, with the reasons for the concession being explained. If the court disagrees with the reasoning, the prosecutor is entitled to adhere to his or her view of the merits and is not required to proceed in a manner that in any way conflicts with the assessment made.

If an accused appeals against sentence, he or she will generally need to demonstrate that the penalty imposed was unlawful, wrong in principle or manifestly excessive. If the prosecutor decides that on the facts and the authorities the sentence does in fact fall into one of those categories, it is not his or her function to seek to uphold it. However, once the prosecutor decides that the sentence is legitimate and falls within an acceptable range, he or she should settle the submissions accordingly, and fortify them, if necessary, by reference to case law and, on occasion, to statistics that illustrate such things as prevalence or the customary range of sentence for the offence in question. The prosecutor must also be aware of the jurisdiction of the court when it disposes of an appeal.

Review of sentence

In some situations, it is open to the secretary for justice to apply to the Court of Appeal for leave to challenge a particular sentence (section 81A, *Criminal Procedure Ordinance*, Cap. 221). Whilst this power is only invoked in exceptional cases, it is deployed most commonly where the sentence is considered to be manifestly inadequate, wrong in principle or contrary to law. Every application is carefully vetted by the director of public prosecutions, who must usually be satisfied not only that the sentencing court has committed a serious error, but also that it is in the public interest for the matter to be corrected. In practice, the situation in which a review is most usually pursued is where a sentence has been imposed that is unduly lenient, by which is meant that it falls outside the range of sentences that in all the circumstances could reasonably be regarded as appropriate.

If leave is granted to the secretary for justice to seek a review of sentence, the duty of the prosecutor at the hearing is to identify for the Court of Appeal the precise nature of the error alleged to have been made. If the application is based on an error of law or principle, the prosecutor should indicate the substance of the complaint, making reference as required to relevant authority. If the sentence is said to be unduly lenient, the prosecutor will refer to guideline or tariff cases, if any, and to cases that establish points of principle. He or she may also indicate the approach that the sentencing court ought to have applied, perhaps by reference to material that illustrates the prevalence or heinousness of the offence. The prosecutor may draw attention to matters appearing on the court record, although it is not open to him or her to rely on new evidence as a basis for a higher sentence. Just as at trial, the prosecutor must be restrained and balanced at a review hearing, ever mindful of his or her role as a minister of justice.

Private prosecution

If the citizen is aggrieved by the decision of the prosecutor not to bring a prosecution, he or she may institute a private prosecution, a point acknowledged in *Ma Pui Tung v Department of Justice* CACV 64/2008. The *Magistrates Ordinance* (Cap. 227), moreover, enables a complainant or informant to conduct a prosecution, either in person or by counsel (section 14, Cap. 227). In *Gouriet v Union of Post Office Workers* [1978] AC 435, Lord Wilberforce described the right of the citizen to start a prosecution as 'a valuable constitutional safeguard against inertia or partiality on the part of authority'. This device provides a remedy to the individual who wishes to see the law enforced. At common law, every citizen has exactly the same right to institute proceedings as the public prosecutor. The right originated in the Middle Ages, and it continues, subject to certain restrictions, to enjoy a respectable position in modern schemes of criminal justice.

The right of private prosecution is not absolute. A private prosecutor has two hurdles to surmount. He or she must first persuade a magistrate to issue a summons. Then, if he or she wishes to retain control of the case, and not everyone does, for it can be an expensive process, he or she may have to persuade the Department of Justice not to take it over. The criteria will be different.

The magistrate has discretion whether to issue a summons. Before so doing, the magistrate should ascertain: 1 whether the allegation is of an offence known to law and, if so, whether the essential ingredients of the offence are prima facie present; 2 whether the time limits have been complied with; 3 whether the court has jurisdiction; and 4 whether the informant has the necessary discretion to prosecute (*R v West London Metropolitan Stipendiary Magistrate, ex p Klahn* [1979] 1 WLR 933). The magistrate should also consider if the allegation is vexatious, and before issuing a summons he must be satisfied that this is a proper thing to do (*R v Bros* (1901) 85 LT 581).

Once a private prosecution has started, it is open to the secretary for justice to intervene. Such intervention may be with a view to continuing or terminating the private prosecution. In *Dowson v R* (1983) 62 CCC (2) 286, Howland CJO recognised the right of a private citizen to lay an information, and added that the 'right and duty of the Attorney General to supervise criminal prosecutions are both fundamental parts of our criminal justice system'. As indicated, the *Basic Law* vests the ultimate control of prosecutions in the Department of Justice. However, as acknowledged in *Ng Chi Keung v Secretary for Justice* [2014] 5 HKC 89, there are two competing interests at play which need to be reconciled, involving, on the one hand, the right of access to the courts by citizens and, on the other, the Department of Justice's control of prosecutions.

The taking over of a prosecution is exceptional, but if the right of private prosecution is abused, intervention may be unavoidable. The procedure is open to the intrusion of improper personal or other motives. It may be used to bring groundless, oppressive or frivolous prosecutions. The state of the evidence may be such that there will clearly be no case to answer if the case is pursued. There may be a duplication of proceedings. The prosecution may be contrary to the public interests, included in which is a consideration of the likelihood of conviction, and of the appropriateness of proceedings. In any such situation the power and the duty of the secretary for justice will be to take over the conduct of the case and to offer no evidence. Whilst this is a sensitive area, section 14 of the *Magistrates Ordinance* recognises that the secretary 'may at any stage of the proceedings before the magistrate intervene and assume the conduct of the proceedings'.

Judicial review of prosecution decisions

Although great deference must, on constitutional grounds, always be accorded to decisions reached on prosecutions by the Department of Justice, particularly in light of Article 63 of the *Basic Law*, the courts, in some circumstances, are prepared to intervene and to hold the prosecutor to account if there is irregularity in the decision-making process. In *R v Director of Public Prosecutions, ex p Kebilene* [2002] 2 AC 326 (HL), Lord Steyn indicated that if a prosecution decision was reached by dishonesty or in bad faith, it would be amenable to judicial review. Quite clearly, if the prosecutor acts corruptly or out of some base motive an aggrieved party ought to have a means of redress, a point recognised in *Re C (A Bankrupt)* [2006] 4 HKC 582. Equally, if a prosecution decision runs contrary to prosecution policy in a particular area it may be judicially reviewed, as in *Iqbal Shahid & Others v Secretary for Justice* [2010] 5 HKC 51.

In *Keung Siu Wah v Attorney General* [1990] 2 HKLR 445, Fuad VP said it was '*a constitutional imperative*' that the courts would not interfere with the discretion of the attorney-general to prosecute. This, however, did not mean that there was no remedy if the discretion to prosecute was improperly exercised, as the court 'retained an inherent jurisdiction to prevent an abuse of process'. This, presumably, referred to the power of the court to order the stay of proceedings which were improperly instituted. In *RV v Director of Immigration* [2008] 2 HKC 209, it was acknowledged that judicial review may lie if the prosecutor has acted in bad faith, or acted corruptly, or has not acted independently but in obedience to a political instruction.

If the judicial review of a prosecution decision is granted, it has the effect of requiring a reconsideration of the original decision, and the court cannot substitute its own view of the matter for that of the prosecutor. Nor can the court require the prosecutor to change his or her view. The court may, however, express an opinion, which may assist the prosecutor who has to decide on the next step.

Guidelines on the role of prosecutors

In 1990, in Havana, Cuba, the Eighth United Nations Congress on the Prevention of Crime and the Treatment of Offenders adopted 'The Guidelines on the Role of Prosecutors' (see Appendix I of *The Prosecution Code*, Department of Justice, 2013). These affirm the important responsibilities of the prosecutor in the administration of justice. At paragraph 12, they state:

> Prosecutors shall, in accordance with the law, perform their duties fairly, consistently and expeditiously, and respect and protect human dignity and uphold human rights, thus contributing to ensuring due process and the smooth administration of the criminal justice system.

Human rights of the accused

In any criminal case, the human rights of the accused are engaged, and these include the right to liberty and the right to a fair trial. In the course of a trial, it is the prosecutor who must supply the perspective which may sometimes be lacking. The prosecutor, after all, has no vested interest of his or her own to pursue, and no client to serve. This means that he or she is well placed to ensure that the court is in a position to make decisions that take full account of the rights of the accused and serve the wider public interest. The prosecutor will, for example, need to disclose to the court that a witness is testifying pursuant to an immunity from prosecution, for this may mean that the witness has an interest of his or her own in testifying against the accused. If the prosecutor becomes aware of the existence of a witness who can help the defence case, this also should be revealed.

Conclusion

The prosecutor is an integral part of the means by which our society maintains personal liberty as well as law and order. He or she should be seen as the public prosecutor, not because he or she prosecutes the public, but because he or she prosecutes on behalf of the community. The prosecutor is uniquely placed to protect human rights, and in the course of a trial, he or she must behave in a way that takes account of the rights of the accused as well as those of the public. Rights, that is, may be either personal or public in nature. Just as it is important that an individual should not be wrongly prosecuted, convicted or punished, so also must members of the public be free to walk the streets, to live in their homes without fear of violation, and to enjoy their rights as citizens. Justice belongs to everyone.

Review questions

1 What criteria must the prosecutor apply before deciding to start a prosecution?
2 In what circumstances will the Department of Justice intervene in a prosecution brought by a private prosecutor?
3 When may a prosecution decision be challenged by means of a judicial review?
4 What types of material is the prosecutor obliged to disclose to the defence as part of the duty to ensure that the accused receives a fair trial?
5 Is it constitutionally permissible for the control of prosecutions to be vested in the director of public prosecutions rather than the secretary for justice?

References

Cross, I.G. (2011) 'Let the public prosecutor decide, not the political appointee', *Hong Kong Lawyer* (19 March), Hong Kong: Legal Business on Asia.

Department of Justice (2009) *The Statement on the Treatment of Victims and Witnesses*, Hong Kong: Department of Justice.
Department of Justice (2012) *Department of Justice*, Hong Kong: Department of Justice.
Department of Justice (2013) *The Prosecution Code*, Hong Kong: Department of Justice.
Department of Justice (2015) *The Victims of Crime Charter*, Hong Kong: Department of Justice.
Department of Justice (2015) *TDepartment of Justice*, Hong Kong: Department of Justice.

Legislation cited

Basic Law of the Hong Kong Special Administrative Region of the People's Republic of China
Criminal Procedure Ordinance (Cap. 221)
International Covenant on Civil and Political Rights
Magistrates Ordinance (Cap. 227)
Organized and Serious Crimes Ordinance (Cap. 455)

Cases cited

Dowson v R (1983) 62 CCC (2) 286
Gouriet v Union of Post Office Workers [1978] AC 435
HKSAR v Lee Ming Tee (2003) 6 HKCFAR 336
Iqbal Shahid & Others v Secretary for Justice [2010] 5 HKC 51
Keung Siu Wah v Attorney General [1990] 2 HKLR 445
Ma Pui Tung v Department of Justice CACV 64/2008
Ng Chi Keung v Secretary for Justice [2014] 5 HKC 89
R v Bros (1901) 85 LT 581
R v Director of Public Prosecutions, ex p Kebilene [2002] 2 AC 326 (HL)
R v West London Metropolitan Stipendiary Magistrate, ex p Klahn [1979] 1 WLR 933
Re C (A Bankrupt) [2006] 4 HKC 582
RV v Director of Immigration [2008] 2 HKC 209

Useful websites

The *Basic Law of the Hong Kong Special Administrative Region* www.info.gov.hk/basic_law/flash.html
The Code for Crown Prosecutors (UK) www.cps.gov.uk/publications/code_for_crown_prosecutors/index.html
Crown Prosecution Service (UK) www.cps.gov.uk
Customs and Excise Department, HKSAR www.customs.gov.hk
Department of Justice, HKSAR www.doj.gov.hk
Hong Kong Police Force, HKSAR www.police.gov.hk
Independent Commission Against Corruption, HKSAR www.icac.org.hk
The Prosecution Code (2013) www.doj.gov.hk/eng/public/pubsoppaptoc.html
Public Prosecution Service (UK) www.ppsni.gov.uk

Part III

TRIAL STAGE

12

LEGAL PROFESSION AND REPRESENTATION

Eric C. Ip

Introduction

The legal profession of Hong Kong is arguably the oldest continuously functioning one in East Asia, and has been an unquestioned fixture of the former British Crown Colony's criminal justice system since its inception in the mid-19th century. Hong Kong's common law system predates the current legal systems in force in the East Asian jurisdictions of Mainland China, Japan, the Koreas, Mongolia and Taiwan (Ip, 2014: 3). An organised legal profession emerged in Macau only in 1992 with the establishment of the Lawyer's Association (Ip, 2013: 821). The British Hong Kong legal system operated on a limited basis even during the Japanese Occupation (Birch, 1973). Notwithstanding the transfer of sovereignty to the People's Republic of China in 1997, the Hong Kong Bar Association and the Law Society of Hong Kong have both retained their constitutional separation from the government, together with full competences to manage their own affairs in accordance with their own professional codes (Tam, 2013) – in stark contrast to their counterpart in Mainland China, the All-China Lawyers' Association, which to this day remains a 'subordinate unit' of the Ministry of Justice (Wang, 2011: 55). The independence of the legal profession is an important bulwark of constitutionalism. As the then Chief Justice (CJ) Li remarked, it is 'of crucial importance to the functioning of an independent Judiciary' (*Farewell Sitting for the Honourable Mr Justice Andrew Li CJ* (2010) 13 HKCFAR 128, 130).

In criminal trials, which invariably involve the state as a party, representation by a qualified lawyer is in many ways prerequisite if an accused person is to obtain objective, unprejudiced legal advice and fearless advocacy, even in the most unpopular cases (Partington, 2014). The ideals of the rule of law will descend to empty promises without competent professional lawyers accessible to the ordinary citizen to serve as pathfinders through the complex maze that is today's law (Wacks, 2008: 108). Failure to supply defendants with adequate legal representation has led to acquittals upon appeal on the basis of the lack of a fair trial (e.g. *Chan Fat Chu Raymond v HKSAR* (2009) 12 HKCFAR 775, 781). Article 35 of the *Basic Law of the Hong Kong Special Administrative Region* (hereafter the *Basic Law*) thus guarantees 'the right to confidential legal advice, access to the courts, choice of lawyers for timely protection of their lawful rights and interests or for representation in the courts, and to judicial remedies'. The right to legal representation even in criminal cases is, however, neither absolute nor illimitable, even if '[c]ompelling reasons would generally be required to satisfy an appellate court [that] a defendant had not been prejudiced to some degree' by the wrongful denial of legal representation (*HKSAR v Wong Chi Kwong* [2011] 1 HKLRD 843, 855).

This chapter introduces the reader to significant aspects of the legal profession and of legal representation in Hong Kong. It is organised as follows. The first section outlines the history, structure and regulation of, and the latest developments in the legal profession. The second section examines four thematic issues in legal representation: criminal legal aid; duty lawyers; free legal advice schemes; and legal professional privilege. The third section sums up the main points of the chapter.

The legal profession in Hong Kong

Overview

Hong Kong's legal profession mainly comprises solicitors (including solicitor advocates), barristers and registered foreign lawyers, all of whom are regulated by the *Legal Practitioners Ordinance* (LPO) (Cap. 159). One may be a solicitor or barrister but not both at the same time, although it is possible for a solicitor to turn barrister and vice versa. As at September 2014, there were 8,123 practising solicitors, 1,294 practising barristers and 1,340 registered foreign lawyers, as well as 825 local law firms, 79 non-local law firms and 36 registered associations between non-local and local law firms in Hong Kong (Information Services Department, 2015). These two branches of the legal profession are not the only providers of legal services, if we factor in those such as the tax departments of accounting firms, construction claims consultancies, and compliance officers in investment fund management companies (Levin, 2009). Moreover, not all members of the legal profession are involved in private practice; many work for private companies, law schools, non-governmental organisations, the Legislative Council, the government's Department of Justice and Legal Aid Department, and public bodies such as the Equal Opportunities Commission and the Competition Commission.

Solicitors

Historically, the rank of solicitor developed out of three kinds of English lawyers who were not barristers: attorneys, solicitors and proctors. Attorneys date back to the 13th century and specialised in what would now be regarded as the work of criminal solicitors, such as briefing counsel on behalf of client prisoners and pleading before the junior criminal courts known as Courts of Quarter Sessions (Bentley, 1998). Solicitors originated in the 16th century as professionals who petitioned or 'solicited' on behalf of their clients in the Court of Chancery, the fountainhead of equity (Rivlin, 2012). Proctors litigated in the ecclesiastical and admiralty courts (Baade, 2001). With solicitors in the ascendency after their reorganisation under the *Judicature Act 1873*, the English Bar were finally persuaded to give up conveyancing and eschew seeing clients directly in exchange for the continuation of their preferment as candidates for judicial appointment and as advocates before the superior courts (Zander, 2007).

Solicitors generally spend less time on advocacy than barristers, preferring to advise clients, write briefs and draw up legal documents, wherein they are assisted by paralegals and legal executives. They manage the gamut of pre-appellate cases, from conveyancing, probate and matrimony to corporate finance, contracts and intellectual property. Although having rights of audience (that is, the right to advocate for clients before courts) in the Magistrates' Courts, the District Court, and in 'chambers hearings' of the Court of First Instance and Court of Appeal, solicitors, with the notable exception of solicitor advocates, are debarred from pleading in open court before the Court of First Instance, the Court of Appeal or the Court of Final Appeal. On the other hand, solicitors are not bound by the cab-rank rule, but may pick and choose their clients (*Rondel v Worsley* [1967] 1 QB 504), and may be sued for professional negligence, whence the *Solicitors' (Professional Indemnity) Rules* (Cap. 159M) compel them to maintain insurance to indemnify civil liability arising from their work in private practice. Solicitors generally charge hourly rates for their work. Unlike barristers, solicitors are allowed to form partnerships called 'law firms'. Law firms in Hong Kong include international firms, such as the 'Magic Circle' firms, and local firms of various sizes, specialising in market niches.

Barristers

Barristers-at-law, or 'counsel', have been in existence ever since the phasing-out of priests from the English legal profession in the 13th century (Hirschel et al., 2007). Upon earning their qualifications, barristers are 'called to the bar', a locution adopted in view of the traditional set-up of English courtrooms, which were fitted with a bar to separate courtroom players from the spectating public. Only barristers were allowed to approach the bar and plead their clients' cases (Rivlin, 2012). In *Rondel v Worsley* [1967] 1 QB 502, Lord Denning MR called the ideal barrister 'a minister of justice' who 'owes allegiance [to] the cause of truth and justice' – a status which dictates that 'he must disregard the most specific instructions of his client' in case of conflict with 'the rules of the profession [if he or she wishes to remain] subject to its discipline'.

Between the 14th to the 17th centuries, barristers established professional associations known as Inns of Court in London, eventually winning the exclusive right to practise in the common law courts. As at the present day, counsel in England must still be affiliated with one of the following Inns of Court: Gray's Inn, Inner Temple, Lincoln's Inn or Middle Temple, arenas where they both study and socialise with each other. Before the 20th century, barristers were arranged in three ranks: serjeants-at-law, King's/Queen's Counsel, and barristers. Up until 1868, serjeants, the most senior rank, monopolised the right to plead before the Court of Common Pleas (Bentley 1998). With the extinction of serjeants-at-law by the end of the 19th century, Queen's Counsel (QC), who had originated in the 17th century as aides to the Crown in matters of law (Zander, 2007), took up the mantle of the British Empire's pre-eminent lawyers.

In contemporary Hong Kong barristers act as advocates at all levels of the courts system and write legal opinions on difficult issues of law. They still wear gowns, wigs and bands in the Court of Final Appeal, the Court of Appeal, the Court of First Instance and the District Court. Barristers are normally self-employed and may not form partnerships, according to Paragraph 28 of the *Code of Conduct of the Bar of the Hong Kong Special Administrative Region*, adopted by the Bar Council on 20 November 1997, effective from May 1998, and updated as of 5 August 2013 (Bar Code of Conduct). They are considered independent, individual practitioners who are bound to take full responsibility for their work (Zander, 2007: 752). However, an employed barrister who holds a current employed barrister's certificate is entitled to instruct a practising barrister (without retaining a solicitor) for the sole purpose of obtaining a legal opinion (section 31C(5), LPO). Barristers organise themselves into 'chambers', where they pay rent and a portion of their income to cover chambers expenses as 'tenants'. Barristers' clerks often play pivotal roles in negotiating fees and distributing work (Fisher, 2010). Barristers charge according to their seniority and the nature of the matter, with reference to the days or hours spent.

A barrister does not enter into a contract with the client or instructing solicitor, following a tradition that a barrister is paid an 'honorarium' instead of a fee; this effectively immunises barristers from suit for breach of contract or negligence (Fisher, 2010). Note that the immunity of barristers was abolished in England and Wales – but not Hong Kong – by the decision of the Appellate Committee of the House of Lords in *Arthur JS Hall v Simons* [2002] 1 AC 191. Honoraria are at times difficult for barristers to recover from solicitors. What is more, a barrister may not meet his lay client without the presence of the instructing solicitor or his or her representative, on the theory that a barrister's detachment from his or her client is essential to the objectivity of his or her professional opinion (Slapper and Kelly, 2014: 686).

Pursuant to the cab-rank rule, 'a practising barrister is bound to accept any brief to appear before a Court in the field in which he professes to practice at his usual fee having regard to the type, nature, length and difficulty of the case' (paragraph 21, Bar Code of Conduct). This means that a barrister may not insist that he or she will only act as defence counsel and never represent plaintiffs (Gillespie, 2012). The barrister is under a further duty to defend a case regardless of any belief he or she may have formed of the defendant's guilt (paragraph 148, Bar Code of Conduct). The cab-rank rule does provide for several exceptions; for instance, a barrister may refuse a brief where there is 'a conflict of interest or the possession of relevant and confidential information' (paragraph 21, Bar Code of Conduct).

Regardless of age or year of admission to the bar, all practising barristers are known as Junior Counsel unless and until appointed to the 'inner bar' as Senior Counsel (SC) – the highest rank of advocate in Hong Kong and the local equivalent to QC. Eligibility for appointment requires a barrister to possess, in the opinion of the chief justice, 'sufficient ability and standing as a barrister [as well as] sufficient knowledge of the law' (section 31A(2)(a), LPO) in addition to at least ten years' experience, in the aggregate, as an advocate (section 31A(3)(a), LPO). A barrister on the faculty of a Hong Kong law school may be appointed as an Honorary Senior Counsel if he has 'provided distinguished service to the law of Hong Kong', in the opinion of the chief justice (section 31A(4), LPO), but this does not necessarily entitle the appointee to advocate before the courts (section 31A(5), LPO). As at February 2016 there were 96 Senior Counsel, including one Honorary Senior Counsel, of whom 84 were male and 12 were female (Hong Kong Bar Association, 2016).

Senior Counsel are appointed by the chief justice of the Court of Final Appeal after consultation with the chairman of the Bar Council and the president of the Law Society (section 31A(1), LPO). The process of becoming a Senior Counsel is known as 'taking silk', after their court dress made of silk rather than stuff, to be worn over a court jacket (Gillespie, 2012: 281–283); hence they are known as 'silks'. Silks are entitled to wear full-bottomed wigs on ceremonial occasions, like those worn by judges of the Court of First Instance or justices of appeal, to symbolise their professional eminence. Before the 1997 handover, Senior Counsel were styled 'Her Majesty's Counsel learned in the law' or simply 'the Queen's Counsel' (QC). They were appointed by the Queen of the United Kingdom by letters patent on the advice of the chief justice of Hong Kong. Whilst no longer formally required, Senior Counsel (called the 'leader') is customarily accompanied by Junior Counsel when appearing in court hearings.

As a thoroughly internationalised jurisdiction heavily reliant on transnational common law principles and international jurisprudence, Hong Kong frequently admits overseas counsel to the bar on a temporary basis. The LPO vests in the Court of First Instance discretion to admit overseas counsel if 'a fit and proper person' who has acquired a qualification and engaged in work 'similar to that undertaken by a barrister in the course of ordinary practice in the High Court and the Court of Final Appeal' (section 27(4), LPO). The chief judge of the High Court must strike a balance between expertise gained from overseas counsel versus the detrimental impact they have on the local bar, especially the junior bar, which comprises 90% of all Hong Kong barristers (*Re Bratza* [1986]

HKLR 763; see also *Re Flesh QC* [1999] 1 HKLRD 506; *Re McGregor* QC [2003] 3 HLRD 585). Nevertheless, in criminal cases the director of public prosecutions' professional view on what constitutes the best legal team available must be accorded due weight, and this consideration may outweigh the negative repercussions on the local junior bar (*Re Mably* [2013] 3 HKLRD 738; *Re Mably* [2014] 1 HKLRD 627).

Registered foreign lawyers

Lawyers employed by foreign law firms in Hong Kong after recruitment from foreign jurisdictions, whether common law or civil law, are required to register with the Law Society each year in order to practise foreign law. Registered foreign lawyers, generally speaking, cannot practise Hong Kong law (*Voce v Henley Group Ltd* [2008] 5 HKLRD 429), advise on Hong Kong legal matters (rule 12 of the *Foreign Lawyers Registration Rules* (Cap. 159S)), or form partnerships with local solicitors. Like local solicitors, they are regulated by the Law Society and subject to the jurisdiction of the Solicitors' Disciplinary Tribunal to answer for allegations of professional misbehaviour (section 9A, LPO).

Qualifying as solicitors and barristers

To qualify as a solicitor or barrister in Hong Kong, a prospect usually passes through three stages of training: academic, vocational and on-the-job. A qualifying law degree is required, such as Bachelor of Laws (LLB) or Juris Doctor (JD) from an accredited university in Hong Kong or other common law jurisdiction. Having passed certain specified subjects, one then pursues a Postgraduate Certificate in Laws (PCLL) from a local law school. Lawyers from overseas common law jurisdictions are permitted to qualify as either barristers or solicitors by sitting the Barristers Qualification Examination or the Overseas Lawyers Qualification Examination, respectively, subject to the conditions in the LPO and relevant subsidiary legislation, such as the *Barristers (Qualification for Admission and Pupillage) Rules* (Cap. 159AC) and the *Overseas Lawyers (Qualification for Admission) Rules* (Cap. 159Q).

Prospective solicitors must serve a two-year traineeship attached to practising solicitors called 'principals'. Trainees are paid a monthly salary. They may apply to the Court of First Instance for admission to practise only after the completion of their traineeship, and then to the Law Society for a practising certificate, which must be renewed annually. Prospective barristers must serve a one-year pupillage, normally unpaid, attached to practising barristers known as 'pupil masters'. Following the first six months of his or her pupillage, a prospect may apply to the Court of First Instance for admission as a barrister-at-law, and then obtain a limited practising certificate. Upon finishing his or her pupillage, a barrister may apply to the Bar Council for a certificate granting unrestricted rights of audience at all levels of court.

Professional regulation

The Law Society of Hong Kong, an incorporated company limited by guarantee, functions as the professional association for solicitors. The Law Society Council, chaired by the president of the Society, is its executive committee. The society has powers to certify the admission of solicitors; issue annual practising certificates and certificates of registration (section 6, LPO); investigate professional misconduct allegations and refer appropriate cases to the Solicitors' Disciplinary Tribunal (section 9A, LPO); intervene in solicitors' practice in case of dishonesty, bankruptcy or death (sections 26A, 26B, 26C, and 26D, LPO); establish rules of professional conduct; and provide for the training as well as continuing education of solicitors (section 73, LPO).

The Panel for the Solicitors' Disciplinary Tribunal is made up of practising solicitors, foreign lawyers and lay persons appointed by the chief justice (section 9, LPO). The tribunal convener, appointed by the chief justice (section 9(4), LPO), chooses members from the panel to inquire into submissions made by the Law Society Council arising from investigations or complaints (section 9A(1), LPO). The tribunal has power to inquire into the conduct of any person in respect of which it was appointed and to make orders at the conclusion of an inquiry, which include striking the name of the solicitor from the roll of solicitors, suspending him or her from practice and imposing fines (section 10, LPO).

Practising barristers must join the Bar Association, an unincorporated professional body set up in 1949 to set rules regulating professional conduct, discipline and etiquette (section 2(e) of the Rules, Regulations and By-laws of the Hong Kong Bar Association (1998)). The Bar Council, presided over by the chairman of the Bar Association, is the executive committee of the association. The panel for the Barristers' Disciplinary Tribunal consists of Senior Counsel, Junior Counsel and lay persons appointed by the chief justice (section 34(1), LPO). The tribunal convener, also appointed by the chief justice (section 34(4), LPO), is tasked with choosing members from the panel to inquire into submissions made by the Bar Council. In case the Bar Council refuses to submit a complaint to the tribunal convener, the chief judge of the High Court may in his or her own discretion submit it to the tribunal convener within the next six months (section 35, LPO). The tribunal is competent to censure barristers, suspend their practice of law for a specific period, order their names struck off the roll of barristers, award to the complainant an amount not exceeding the sums paid to the offending barrister, order an offending barrister to pay into the general revenue penalties not exceeding HK$500,000, pay the costs of any prior inquiry or investigation relating to matters before the tribunal, and so on (section 37, LPO).

Fusion of solicitors and barristers

Nowadays many solicitors specialise, while some barristers choose general practice and eschew advocacy (Fisher, 2010: 150). This has raised questions as to whether the current split in the legal profession is still justified under today's circumstances. This question is in fact not a new one. As early as 1858 Hong Kong Attorney-General T.C. Anstey, responding to a call from local barristers, convened a meeting of the entire legal profession to debate the unification of barristers and solicitors into one profession (Wesley-Smith, 1992). Their fusion under the *Amalgamation Ordinance* of 1858, fiercely opposed by the Law Society, did not last. Strong opposition from new Attorney-General John Smale, who was destined to become one of Hong Kong's greatest pre-handover chief justices, prevailed to repeal the *Amalgamation Ordinance*.

Barristers' and solicitors' attitudes to fusion are now reversed (Wesley-Smith, 1992: 268). In 1993 the Law Society put forth a proposal to merge the two branches by permitting barristers direct access to lay clients and solicitors rights of audience in the superior courts (Ho, 1994). The society justified its proposal as follows: first, the total fees chargeable to the client would be reduced if all legal practitioners had unlimited rights of audience and worked hand in hand in fully integrated teams; second, clients would have a wider choice of advocates to represent them if solicitors had rights of audience in the superior courts; and third, legal services would no longer be segregated into paperwork and advocacy – the same lawyer(s) could represent a client from beginning to end (Wong, 1994). The improved continuity in handling cases would reduce the miscommunications and duplication of work that currently bedevil a split profession. Intuitively, legal costs are bound to be reduced if only one lawyer, rather than two, is required for a case (Gillespie, 2012).

The Bar articulated in 1994 its position that a professional merger is unnecessary, justifying it as follows. First, fusion would lead to the evaporation of the Bar's independence: barristers are self-employed legal practitioners who do not normally maintain long-standing relationships with lay clients, as do many solicitors, who often depend on regular clientele for conveyancing or commercial work. On this view, barristers are freer from conflicts of interest. Second, the cab-rank rule would be suspended, undermining the procedural rights of unpopular defendants. Third, clients would no longer be able to make an informed choice of advocates: the current split of the profession incentivises solicitors to make an informed, conscientious choice of barrister on behalf of the client, as the solicitor is barred from selecting himself/herself or his/her colleagues from the same firm without due regard to relevant factors like experience of advocacy. Fourth, fusion would result in the loss of an independent assessment mechanism for the competence of barristers: assessment of the ability of barristers to argue cases before the superior courts depends in large part on solicitors, which serves as a competitive vetting mechanism ensuring that those vetted actually deserve higher rights of audience (Wong, 1994).

Despite the Bar's eventual victory in conserving the split, the chief justice established a Working Committee in 2004 '[t]o consider whether solicitors' existing rights of audience should be extended and, if so, the mechanism for dealing with the grant of extended rights of audience to solicitors'. This led to the enactment of the *Legal Practitioners (Amendment) Ordinance* (No. 2 of 2010) six years later, on 28 January 2010, to amend the *Legal Practitioners Ordinance* with effect from 1 July 2010. Thereafter, qualified solicitors have been vested higher rights of audience 'before the High Court and the Court of Final Appeal, whether in civil proceedings, criminal proceedings, or both' (section 39H(3), LPO). This step, which imported the solicitor advocate qualification from Britain, is seen by some as the pretext of fusing the two branches of the legal profession (Kaur, 2011: 378).

To accede to higher rights of audience, a prospective solicitor advocate must have practised law for at least five years in a common law jurisdiction, including at least two years in Hong Kong (section 39I, LPO). In the three years immediately before application he or she must have acquired sufficient litigation experience and suitability for the qualification (section 39L(1)(b), LPO). Such applications are made to the Higher Rights Assessment Board, consisting of three superior court judges, three litigation solicitors, three Senior Counsel, a Department of Justice official, and a lay person (section 39E, LPO). The *Higher Rights of Audience Rules* (Cap. 159AK), drawn up by the board, entered into force on 22 June 2012. In the first round of assessments in February 2013, 15 solicitors were granted higher rights of audience in either criminal or civil matters (Hughes, 2014). As at June 2015, there were only 31 solicitor advocates in Hong Kong (Conventus Law, 2015). Solicitor advocates are bound by a Code of Conduct independent of and in addition to the *Hong Kong Solicitors' Guide to Professional Conduct* (section 39R, LPO).

Themes in legal representation

The mere existence of competent lawyers is insufficient to guarantee the right of independent legal representation, hence the system includes further safeguards which relate to funding, professional legal advice and lawyer–client communications in order to ensure that competent lawyers are also independent and accessible.

Criminal legal aid

Legal aid is government-provided funding for legal services by which eligible applicants may receive financial support to instruct lawyers to represent them in legal proceedings. It is a relatively new concept in the English common law tradition and is traceable only back to the Second World War (Gillespie, 2012). Currently, legal aid is administered by the Legal Aid Department, a government agency affiliated since 2007 with the Home Affairs Bureau. The director, the deputy directors and the assistant directors of Legal Aid, as well as the several Legal Aid officers, are civil servants appointed by the chief executive according to section 3, *Legal Aid Ordinance* (Cap. 91), originally enacted in 1966. The Legal Aid Services Council is an independent statutory agency set up under the *Legal Aid Services Council Ordinance* (LASCO) (Cap. 489) and tasked with superintending the Legal Aid Department. It is also the 'Chief Executive's advisory body on the policy of the government concerning publicly funded legal aid services provided by the Department', and is mandated to advise on 'the feasibility and desirability of the establishment of an independent legal aid authority' (section 4(5)(b), LASCO).

Hong Kong has three Legal Aid schemes: Ordinary Legal Aid, Supplementary Legal Aid and Criminal Legal Aid. A solicitor owes a professional duty, under the *Hong Kong Solicitors' Guide to Professional Conduct*, to take steps to 'give his client the best information he can under the circumstances about the likely costs of the matter ... discuss with the client how the costs and disbursements are to be met [and] consider whether the client ... may be eligible and should apply for legal aid (including legal advice and assistance) or the assistance of the Duty Lawyer Service' (paragraph 4.01, *Hong Kong Solicitors' Guide to Professional Conduct*).

Legal aid is recognised as a fundamental right in the context of criminal justice. Article 11(2)(d) of the *Hong Kong Bill of Rights Ordinance* (Cap. 383) provides that, with regard to 'any criminal charge', every person is entitled to 'minimum guarantees', including but not limited to the right 'to defend himself in person or through legal assistance of his own choosing' and 'to be informed, if he does not have legal assistance, of this right'; and to be assigned legal assistance 'in any case where the interests of justice so require, and without payment by him in any such case if he does not have sufficient means to pay for it'. There is, however, no general right to legal aid; no scheme aids eligible persons unconditionally. 'Reasonable constraints' may be imposed by the director of Legal Aid on 'the provision of financially assisted legal representation' even if applicant defendants are 'impecunious' or 'claim to be such' (*HKSAR v Wong Chi Kwong* [2011] 1 HKLRD 843, 850).

Criminal Legal Aid is available for committal proceedings – but not trials – in the Magistracies; trials in the District Court and the Court of First Instance; appeals from the Magistracies and the Court of Appeal; and reviews of sentence by the Court of Appeal. Legal aid may be granted to a criminal defendant if the director is satisfied that the means test and merits test have both been passed. The means test is satisfied if the applicant's 'financial resources' do not exceed the financial eligibility limit, currently fixed at HK$269,620. The merits test requires the director to consider whether it is 'in the interests of justice' to provide aid in light of the 'Widgery Criteria', *viz.* the consequences to the accused's liberty, livelihood and reputation; the legal significance of the issues involved; the accused's ability to understand the proceedings; the need to interview or cross-examine witnesses; and the interests of relevant third parties. The means test may be waived if the director believes it is in 'the interests of justice' to grant the application regardless of the accused's financial assets. For appeals, the merits test requires the director to be convinced of the existence of meritorious grounds for proceeding and a reasonable prospect of success.

Criminal Legal Aid is governed by the *Legal Aid in Criminal Cases Rules* (LACCR) (Cap. 221D), subsidiary legislation promulgated by the Criminal Rules Committee pursuant to section 9A of the *Criminal Procedure Ordinance* (Cap. 221). In an appellate case, a judge may grant the accused an appeal aid certificate notwithstanding the director's decision to the contrary. The director is then obliged to assign a solicitor and at most two counsel to represent the appellant (Section 12(3), LACCR). A judge of the Court of First Instance may overrule the director's denial of legal aid in cases involving an accusation of murder, treason or piracy (Section 13(1)(2), LACCR). Additionally, the director's decision to refuse legal aid is an administrative act susceptible to judicial review. In *Z v Director of Legal Aid* [2011] 4 HKLRD 362, the Court of First Instance quashed as irrational a decision of the director to refuse legal aid to a refugee awaiting resettlement for failing to comply with the Widgery Criteria.

Duty lawyers

The Duty Lawyer Service is subvented by the government and administered by a committee consisting of representatives from the Bar Association and the Law Society, among others. Every Magistrates' Court has a Duty Lawyer Service Court Liaison Office, which rosters private legal practitioners to represent defendants, to be continually available for those who satisfy a means test (a gross annual income of no more than HK$175,220) and a merits test ('in the interests of justice' with reference to the Widgery Criteria). Defendants pay a handling charge of HK$500 once granted representation. Subject to qualifying provisions, the service also offers duty lawyer representation to those at risk of criminal prosecution for giving incriminating evidence in a coroner's inquest; hawkers appealing to the Municipal Services Appeals Board against decisions denying hawkers' licences; and persons facing extradition proceedings. The service's 1,632 duty lawyers assisted 27,201 adult and juvenile defendants in 2014 (The Duty Lawyer Service, 2015a).

Legal advice schemes

The Free Legal Advice Scheme, providing free legal advice regardless of the seeker's financial worth, is funded by the government and administered by the Duty Lawyer Service. It has over 900 volunteer lawyers holding 11 advisory sessions per week at evening centres in the nine District Offices of the government. It is supported by 28 referral agencies with 153 branches, which assist the scheme with arranging meetings between prospective users and volunteer lawyers. As at 2014, there were 1,107 volunteer lawyers on the scheme's panel, of whom 824 contributed actively to the processing of 6,727 cases (The Duty Lawyer Service, 2015b). Today, the scheme teams up with other institutions, such as the Hong Kong Federation of Women's Centres, the Family Welfare Society (Mediation Centre), and the University of Hong Kong, to deliver comparable free legal advice services.

The Community Legal Information Centre (www.clic.org.hk) is an informative online platform managed by the University of Hong Kong, providing Internet users since 2007 with free legal information in both English and Chinese. Between 2012 and 2014 the government contracted with the university to develop special topics relating to young people, the elderly and the family.

The Convention Against Torture Scheme offers legal assistance to eligible persons who have made claims under the United Nations *Convention Against Torture and Other Cruel, Inhuman or Degrading Treatment or Punishment* 1984, or under the non-refoulement principle pursuant to the *Convention Relating to the Status of Refugees* (Persecution) 1951. The scheme allows eligible claimants access to 414 lawyers (288 barristers and 126 solicitors) from the Duty Lawyer Service: in 2014, it handled 7,547 claims.

The Tel-Law Service (25213333 and 25228018) operates eight telephone lines 24 hours a day, giving taped information on 80 legal topics in English, Cantonese and Mandarin. These topics include family law; land law, landlord and tenant; criminal law; employment law; commercial, banking and sale of goods law; administration and constitutional law; environmental law and tort; and general legal information. In 2014 the service received 23,692 calls (The Duty Lawyer Service, 2015c).

Legal professional privilege

Legal professional privilege, also known as the right to confidential legal advice (see Article 35 of the *Basic Law*), encompasses all confidential communications and documents passing between a lawyer and his client, as well as potential witnesses, provided that the communications are made in regard to or in anticipation of litigation (see Chan, 2011). As such, legal professional privilege can be further subdivided into legal advice privilege and litigation privilege (see *CITIC Pacific Ltd v Secretary for Justice and Commissioner of Police* CACV 7/2012 (29 June 2015)).

Significantly, legal professional privilege cannot be overridden by a court or by 'some supposedly greater public interest' (*HKSAR v Wong Chi Wai* (2013) 16 HKCFAR 539, 557). Without the client's consent a lawyer has no right to disclose materials that form the subject matter of the legal professional privilege. The wilful infringement of the privilege by a law enforcement agency may be considered an abuse of process and result in a stay of proceedings by the court (*Secretary for Justice v Shum Chiu* [2008] 1 HKLRD 155, but compare with *HKSAR v Ng Chun To Raymond* [2013] 5 HKC 390). Legal professional privilege shields legal advice given by a registered foreign lawyer on issues of foreign law as well as advice given by an in-house company lawyer (Hughes, 2014).

The classical justification for legal professional privilege offered by Lord Taylor of Gosforth in the English case *R v Derby Magistrates' Court, ex p B* [1996] AC 507, is that 'a man must be able to consult his lawyer in confidence, since otherwise he might hold back half the truth', and that 'the client must be sure that what he tells his lawyer in confidence will never be revealed without his consent', for these two principles constitute 'a fundamental condition on which the administration of justice as a whole rests'. In *Pang Yiu Hung v Commissioner of Police* [2003] 2 HKLRD 134, Hartmann J styled legal professional privilege 'a fundamental human right' protected by international conventions and 'long established in the common law', as well as 'a necessary corollary of the right of any person to obtain skilled advice about the law'. The constitutional status of legal professional privilege has thereafter been repeatedly affirmed by the Court of Final Appeal (see *Solicitor v Law Society of Hong Kong* (2006) 9 HKCFAR 175; *Secretary for Justice v Florence Tsang Chiu Wing* (2014) 17 HKCFAR 739).

Conclusion

Access to the legal profession and legal representation is vital to the safeguard of legal rights in an ever more complex criminal justice system (Ip, 2014: 221–247). The independence of the legal profession reinforces judicial independence and ensures that the constitutional right of access to legal services can be exercised free of arbitrary political interference. Hong Kong's legal profession is currently split into two branches: solicitors and barristers. Unlike barristers, solicitors have direct access to lay clients, may form partnerships, are not bound by the cab-rank rule, and lack higher rights of audience before the superior courts in open court hearings. The solicitor advocate qualification opened up higher rights of audience to select solicitors. Barristers are self-employed advocacy specialists working in chambers, and their highest rank in Hong Kong is known as Senior Counsel. Foreign lawyers registered with the Law Society may advise on foreign law.

Several institutions exist to guarantee the accessibility and quality of legal representation in Hong Kong. The Bar Association and Law Society are the independent professional and regulatory bodies for barristers and solicitors, respectively. Members of the Barristers' Disciplinary Tribunal Panel and Solicitors' Disciplinary Tribunal Panel are appointed by the chief justice rather than by a politician from the Executive Branch or the Legislative Council. Criminal Legal Aid may be provided by the Legal Aid Department and is superintended by the Legal Aid Services Council. The Duty Lawyers Service provides legal representation to eligible defendants in the Magistrates' Courts. Free legal advice schemes are subvented by the government to disseminate legal knowledge across the community and promote better access to justice. Finally, legal professional privilege protects the rights of lay clients to receive objective, full and frank legal advice from lawyers without prejudice to their case.

Review questions

1 Should the two branches of the Hong Kong legal profession merge?
2 Should the merits test of the criminal legal aid scheme be abolished?

3 In what ways is legal professional privilege important to the constitutional right to legal representation?

References

Baade, H.W. (2001) 'The education and qualification of civil lawyers in historical perspective: From jurists and orators to advocates, procurators and notaries', in J.W. Cairns, A. Watson and O.F. Robinson (eds) *Critical Studies in Ancient Law, Comparative Law and Legal History* (pp. 213–234), Oxford: Hart Publishing.

Bentley, D. (1998) *English Criminal Justice in the 19th Century*, London: Bloomsbury Publishing.

Birch, A. (1973) 'Confinement and constitutional conflict in occupied Hong Kong 1941–1945', *Hong Kong Law Journal*, 3(3): 293–318.

Chan, J.M.M. (2011) 'Right to fair hearing in non-criminal process', in J.M.M. Chan and C.L. Lim (eds) *Law of the Hong Kong Constitution* (pp. 581–604), Hong Kong: Sweet & Maxwell.

Conventus Law (2015) *Phillip Rompotis Appointed Solicitor Advocate in Hong Kong* (1 June), www.conventuslaw.com/archive/phillip-rompotis-appointed-solicitor-advocate-in-hong-kong/ (accessed 15 February 2016).

The Duty Lawyer Service (2015a) *Annual Report 2014: Duty Lawyer Scheme*, Hong Kong: The Duty Lawyer Service, www.dutylawyer.org.hk/en/annual_14/scheme.asp (accessed 15 February 2016).

The Duty Lawyer Service (2015b) *Annual Report 2014: Free Legal Advice Scheme*, Hong Kong: The Duty Lawyer Service, www.dutylawyer.org.hk/en/annual_14/advice.asp (accessed 15 February 2016).

The Duty Lawyer Service (2015c) *Annual Report 2014: Tel-Law Scheme*, Hong Kong: The Duty Lawyer Service, www.dutylawyer.org.hk/en/annual_14/tel-law.asp (accessed 15 February 2016).

Fisher, M.J. (2010) *The Legal System of Hong Kong*, Hong Kong: Blue Dragon.

Gillespie, A. (2012) *The English Legal System*, New York: Oxford University Press.

Hirschel, D., Wakefield, W. and Sasse, S. (2007) *Criminal Justice in England and the United States* (2nd edn), London: Jones and Bartlett Publishers.

Ho, J.D. (1994) 'The legal system: Are the changes too little, too late?', in D.H. McMillen and S. Man (eds) *The Other Hong Kong Report 1994* (pp. 9–22), Hong Kong: The Chinese University Press.

Hong Kong Bar Association (2016) *Senior Counsel*, barlist.hkba.org/hkba/Seniority/seniority.htm (accessed 15 February 2016).

Hughes, M. (2014) 'Hong Kong', in J. Cotton (ed.) *The Dispute Resolution Review* (6th edn) (pp. 307–331), London: Law Research Business Limited.

Information Services Department (2015) *Hong Kong: The Facts, Legal System*, Hong Kong: Information Services Department, Hong Kong Special Administrative Region.

Ip, E.C. (2013) 'The evolution of constitutional adjudication in the Chinese special administrative regions: Theory and evidence', *The American Journal of Comparative Law*, 61(4): 799–829.

Ip, E.C. (2014) *Law and Justice in Hong Kong*, Hong Kong: Sweet & Maxwell.

Kaur, P. (2011) 'Legal developments in Hong Kong in 2009–2010: Something for everyone', *City University of Hong Kong Law Review*, 2(2): 369–382.

Levin, A. (2009) 'Professional bodies and professional regulation in Hong Kong', in H.F. Siu and A.S. Ku (ed.) *Hong Kong Mobile: Making a Global Population* (pp. 247–292), Hong Kong: Hong Kong University Press.

Partington, M. (2014) *Introduction to the English Legal System* (9th edn), Oxford: Oxford University Press.

Rivlin, G. (2012) *Understanding the Law* (6th edn), Oxford: Oxford University Press.

Slapper, G. and Kelly, D. (2014) *The English Legal System, 2014–2015* (15th edn), Abingdon: Routledge.

Tam, W. (2013) *Legal Mobilization under Authoritarianism: The Case of Post-Colonial Hong Kong*, Cambridge: Cambridge University Press.

Wacks, R. (2008) *Law: A Very Short Introduction*, Oxford: Oxford University Press.

Wang, J.Y. (2011) 'China: Legal reform in an emerging socialist market economy', in E.A. Black and G.F. Bell (eds) *Law and Legal Institutions of Asia: Traditions, Adaptations and Innovations* (pp. 24–61), Cambridge: Cambridge University Press.

Wesley-Smith, P. (1992) 'Nineteenth-century fusion of the legal profession in Hong Kong', *Hong Kong Law Journal*, 22: 257–268.

Wong, R.F.H. (1994) *Right of Audience*, Hong Kong Bar Association's Letter to the Chief Justice of Hong Kong (16 September 1994).

Zander, M. (2007) *Cases and Materials on the English Legal System* (10th edn), Cambridge: Cambridge University Press.

Legislation cited

Amalgamation Ordinance 1858
Barristers (Qualification for Admission and Pupillage) Rules (Cap. 159AC)
Basic Law of the Hong Kong Special Administrative Region of the People's Republic of China
Convention Against Torture and Other Cruel, Inhuman or Degrading Treatment or Punishment 1984
Convention Relating to the Status of Refugees (Persecution) 1951
Criminal Procedure Ordinance (Cap. 221)
Foreign Lawyers Registration Rules (Cap. 159S)
Higher Rights of Audience Rules (Cap. 159AK)
Hong Kong Bill of Rights Ordinance (Cap. 383)
Judicature Act 1873 (UK)
Legal Aid in Criminal Cases Rules (Cap. 221D)
Legal Aid Ordinance (Cap. 91)
Legal Aid Services Council Ordinance (Cap. 489)
Legal Practitioners (Amendment) Ordinance (No. 2 of 2010)
Legal Practitioners Ordinance (Cap. 159)
Overseas Lawyers (Qualification for Admission) Rules (Cap. 159Q)
Solicitors' (Professional Indemnity) Rules (Cap. 159M)

Cases cited

Arthur JS Hall v Simons [2002] 1 AC 191
Chan Fat Chu Raymond v HKSAR (2009) 12 HKCFAR 775
CITIC Pacific Ltd v Secretary for Justice and Commissioner of Police CACV 7/2012 (29 June 2015)

Farewell Sitting for the Honourable Mr Justice Andrew Li CJ (2010) 13 HKCFAR 128
HKSAR v Ng Chun To Raymond [2013] 5 HKC 390
HKSAR v Wong Chi Kwong [2011] 1 HKLRD 843
HKSAR v Wong Chi Wai (2013) 16 HKCFAR 539
Pang Yiu Hung v Commissioner of Police [2003] 2 HKLRD 134
R v Derby Magistrates' Court, ex p B [1996] AC 507
Re Bratza [1986] HKLR 763
Re Flesh QC [1999] 1 HKLRD 506
Re Mably [2013] 3 HKLRD 738
Re Mably [2014] 1 HKLRD 627
Re McGregor QC [2003] 3 HLRD 585
Rondel v Worsley [1967] 1 QB 504
Secretary for Justice v Florence Tsang Chiu Wing (2014) 17 HKCFAR 739
Secretary for Justice v Shum Chiu [2008] 1 HKLRD 155
Solicitor v Law Society of Hong Kong (2006) 9 HKCFAR 175
Voce v Henley Group Ltd [2008] 5 HKLRD 429
Z v Director of Legal Aid [2011] 4 HKLRD 362

Useful websites

Community Legal Information Centre www.clic.org.hk
Duty Lawyer Service www.dutylawyer.org.hk
Free Legal Advice Scheme www.dutylawyer.org.hk/en/free/free.asp
Higher Rights Assessment Board www.hrab.org.hk
Hong Kong Bar Association www.hkba.org
Law Society of Hong Kong www.hklawsoc.org.hk
Legal Aid Department www.lad.gov.hk
Legal Aid Services Council www.lasc.hk

13

GUILTY PLEAS AND PLEA BARGAINING

Kevin Kwok-yin Cheng

Introduction

Article 87(2) of the *Basic Law of the Hong Kong Special Administrative Region* guarantees that: 'Anyone who is lawfully arrested shall have the right to a fair trial by the judicial organs without delay and shall be presumed innocent until convicted by the judicial organs.' However, a small proportion of cases actually result in contested trials before the courts. Like many other jurisdictions including England, Canada and the USA, most criminal cases in Hong Kong are resolved by guilty pleas. As illustrated in Table 13.1, most cases that appear in the District Court and Court of First Instance conclude with defendants pleading guilty (on average a guilty plea rate of 76% and 77%, respectively). In the Magistrates' Courts, while statistics show a much lower ratio of guilty plea rates, the official figures include bind over orders as an acquittal. This is a point that will be returned to later in the chapter. Excluding bind over orders, Cheng (2013) found an approximately 60% guilty plea rate in Court No. 1 by defendants appearing in the Magistrates' Courts.

The frequency of guilty pleas is so high that some commentators have suggested that the criminal justice system is geared towards the mass production of guilty pleas (Sanders et al., 2010). Others have asserted that there is a discrepancy between the due process protections stated in the law and the actual daily functions of the criminal justice system which systematically encourages guilty pleas (McConville and Mirsky, 1993). This chapter begins by outlining the law with respect to guilty pleas. Then it will move on to examine the sentence discount and factors that affect guilty pleas. Finally this chapter will conclude with a discussion on the controversial practice of plea bargaining.

Table 13.1 Number of people who plead guilty in Hong Kong

	Total no. of accused	*No. of accused who pleaded guilty*	*No. of accused who pleaded not guilty**	*% of accused who pleaded guilty***
Magistrates' Courts				
2009	14,546	6,656	7,890	46%
2010	12,594	5,781	6,813	46%
2011	11,398	5,383	6,015	47%
2012	11,071	5,422	5,649	49%
2013	9,786	4,663	5,123	48%
District Court				
2009	1,586	1,190	396	75%
2010	1,421	1,056	365	74%
2011	1,757	1,352	405	77%
2012	1,577	1,238	339	79%
2013	1,452	1,115	337	77%
Court of First Instance				
2009	422	321	101	76%
2010	454	355	99	78%
2011	524	399	125	76%
2012	488	353	135	72%
2013	534	436	98	82%

Source: 2009 figures are from the Department of Justice, 2010; 2010 figures are from the Department of Justice, 2012; 2011 figures are from the Department of Justice, 2013; 2012 and 2013 figures are from the Department of Justice, 2014.

Notes: * This number includes bind over orders and cases where the prosecution 'offered no evidence'. It is a contentious point whether a bind over order ought to be considered a plea of not guilty since the accused in most cases must admit to wrongdoing in accordance with the prosecution's facts before being bound over. ** The rates were calculated by the author.

Law on guilty pleas

Turner *guidelines*

The decision of whether to plead guilty or not guilty rests with the defendant. The defendant must be given a freedom of choice in his or her plea decision. A guilty plea that was made involuntarily or is equivocal or ambiguous is a nullity. A guilty plea may be considered as equivocal if the defendant pleads guilty but during plea mitigation contends that there was an absence of *mens rea*. A guilty plea may be considered to be made involuntarily if it was made because of undue pressure. Hong Kong continues to follow the *Turner* guidelines set out in the English case of *R v Turner* [1970] 2 WLR 1093. In this case, during the course of trial, counsel advised the accused that a change to plea of guilty might result in a non-custodial sentence whereas if he was convicted post-trial the deendant would risk imprisonment. Counsel's advice was repeated after the matter was discussed privately with the trial judge. Counsel said that 'in his personal opinion', the defendant would likely get imprisonment if the case lost at trial and not if he pleaded guilty. The accused was told that the choice was his but he had believed his counsel to be repeating the judge's view. Turner entered a guilty plea. The English Court of Appeal ordered a new trial because it was seen that Turner's plea was made involuntarily. Turner may have concluded that his counsel was echoing the view of the trial judge. In this way, it cannot be said that the accused had a free choice in his plea. The court also took the opportunity to lay down some guidelines in this matter. The key points are:

1 Counsel must be completely free to give the accused the best advice, including the advice to plead guilty. Such advice may need to be given in strong terms.
2 The accused, after considering counsel's advice, must have a complete freedom of choice in terms of plea decision.
3 There must be freedom of access between counsel and the judge. Any discussion must take place with both the defence counsel (and solicitor if desired) and prosecution present.
4 Counsel should seek the judge privately only when it is felt necessary. As far as possible, justice should be administered in open court.
5 The judge, subject to one exception, should never indicate the sentence that he or she is minded to impose. The judge should not indicate that he or she would impose one sentence on a guilty plea but following conviction after trial a more severe sentence.
6 The only exception is that it would be permissible for a judge to state that regardless of plea the sentence would not take a particular form, e.g. a custodial sentence.

These guidelines underscore how judges should not provide sentence indications in order to preserve the accused's freedom of choice in plea. Otherwise it may be seen as undue pressure.

It should be pointed out that in England and Wales, the *Turner* guidelines were replaced by *R v. Goodyear* [2005] EWCA Crim. 888. Advanced sentence indications by the trial judge are now permissible in England. The new guidelines are summarised as follows:

1 The principle that the defendant's plea must be voluntary is not to be watered down.
2 However, for judges to respond to an indication of sentence would not constitute improper pressure.

3 Judges are restricted to indicating the maximum possible level of sentence if a plea of guilty was tendered at the stage at which the indication is sought.
4 Judges are free to indicate that the type of sentence would be the same regardless of the plea.
5 Judges can remind counsel in open court that the defendant can seek a sentence indication.
6 Judges should, however, not insist on giving an indication.
7 Judges can decline to give an indication if asked by the defence.
8 Any sentence indication by the judge binds both the judge and any other judge responsible for the case. This ceases to have an effect if the defendant fails to plead within a reasonable time.
9 The request for sentence indication should be made in open court.

In short, the idea that an advanced sentence indication by the judge would amount to improper pressure on the accused has been overturned. Hong Kong continues to follow the previous *Turner* guidelines.

Plea arraignment

If a case is to be dealt with at the magistracy level, for administrative purposes, all cases first appear in Court No. 1 of the particular Magistrate's Court. This is also known as the Principal Magistrate's Court or the plea court. As its name suggests, this is where defendants are first provided the opportunity to enter their pleas. The case number and the defendant's name will be called by the court. The accused will go forth from the public gallery and stand behind the bar table to face the magistrate. If the accused is remanded in custody, he or she will be brought from the cells to the court dock. The court ascertains that the individual charged is the person before the court. The prosecution asks the court to take a plea.

The court determines the language and dialect of the accused and determines if an interpreter is required. In situations where the defendant neither speaks Chinese nor English, a freelance interpreter would usually be employed. The interpreter would take the interpreter's oath or affirmation. The charge(s) is/are read to the accused and the accused is asked whether he or she understands the charge(s). If yes, then he or she is asked whether the plea is guilty or not guilty. The accused must clearly state his or her plea by using the words 'guilty' or 'not guilty'. Nodding or shaking of the head is not accepted as a plea. If a plea is not clearly made, the magistrate will have to enter a plea of not guilty on the defendant's behalf.

If the accused pleads guilty, a document known as the brief facts of the case is usually read out. The accused is then asked to confirm the truth of the facts. If the magistrate is satisfied, then the magistrate will record the plea. It is the duty of the solicitor to ensure that the charge(s) is/are understood by the defendant. Greater care must be taken by the court if the accused appears unrepresented to ensure that all elements of the offence(s) are understood.

If the accused pleads not guilty, then a court date is fixed. The average waiting time for trial in the Magistrates' Courts is around 41 days for defendants in custody and 49 days for defendants on bail (Hong Kong Judiciary, 2015). The trial, unless it is short and uncomplicated, will not take place in Court No. 1 but in one of the side courts. The magistrate, when fixing a date for trial, will ask the prosecution how long the case is estimated to take, how many witnesses will be called, and whether the prosecution will rely on recorded interviews with the accused.

The plea arraignment procedure is similar in the District Court (DC). Before or on the date of transfer from the Magistrates' Courts, the prosecution serves the bundle of statements and documentary exhibits on the accused. On first appearance in the DC, if the accused indicates a plea of guilty, the case will be remanded to a later date in order for the prosecution to prepare a written summary of facts. For cases in the Court of First Instance (CFI), the magistrate will appoint a return day. The return day must be no fewer than ten days and no more than 42 days starting from when the prosecution asks the magistrate to appoint a return day. On the return day, if the accused pleads guilty, he or she will be committed to the CFI for sentence. If not, there will either be a preliminary inquiry or the accused will be committed to trial in the CFI without an inquiry. In the case of a guilty plea, the accused must have read and agreed to the contents of the summary of facts obtained from the prosecution. If the magistrate is satisfied that the accused fully understands the charge(s) and that the plea was made voluntarily then the plea is accepted and recorded (for more details on the procedure, see Knight and Upham, 2011).

Cracked trials

Cracked trials occur when on the day of trial (or before verdict is passed) it is unable to proceed because of the prosecution withdrawing the charge(s), offering no evidence, or the defendant making a late guilty plea. This contributes to the phenomenon called 'cracked trials' because the trial has been rendered obsolete. Mainly cracked trials refer to late guilty pleas by defendants either to the original charge(s) or alternative charges(s). This is also known as 'pleading at the door of the court'. Cracked trials are regarded as a problem since the time and effort that court personnel have put in – judges, prosecutors, defence lawyers, and even law clerks and bailiffs, and witnesses who have been summoned to appear – are wasted.

Sentence discount

The law in Hong Kong encourages guilty pleas by guilty defendants (*R v Yu Man-wu* [1995] HKLY 481). One of the strongest encouragements to plead guilty comes from the sentence discount. A guilty plea normally attracts a one-third sentence discount as it is considered a strong mitigating factor. Plea mitigation occurs when the defence, either through the defence lawyer or by the defendant, raises mitigating factors to urge the court to impose a more lenient sentence in the circumstances of the offence or of the offender's background before the court passes sentence. For example, if a sentence would result in nine months' imprisonment following conviction at trial, then by pleading guilty, the accused would only receive six months' imprisonment. The magistrate or judge should clearly indicate the starting point of the sentence and the reduction following a guilty plea. A guilty plea may also lead the court to impose a non-custodial sentence as opposed to a custodial one. For more serious offences, where the sentences are substantial, the sentence discount makes a large difference. A 21-year sentence may be reduced to 14 years, a reduction of seven years' imprisonment. The discount is applicable to fines as well.

Traditionally, a guilty plea is seen as an indication of remorse. Even if the accused is not seen as remorseful, the sentence discount is still deemed justified because of its utilitarian benefits. For the state, the rationale behind the sentence discount is that guilty pleas save the courts time and expense. Trials inevitably take longer than having defendants plead guilty at first opportunity. Given the long court lists, guilty pleas assist in the effective operation of the criminal court system. The discount of one-third would only be withheld if exceptional circumstances existed – for instance, if the accused absconded from bail or a change of plea was made after a failure to challenge a confession statement during trial. At the same time, the one-third discount is considered a 'high watermark' and the discount should not exceed one-third unless there are good reasons to do so (Cross et al., 2015).

In Hong Kong, a one-third discount is customarily awarded even if the accused makes a late plea on the day of trial. In England and Wales, this has been changed in recent years through the implementation of a sliding scale. The traditional one-third discount is still awarded to defendants who plead guilty at the first available opportunity. A one-quarter discount is awarded to defendants who change their pleas to guilty after a trial date has been set. For defendants who plead guilty at the door of the court, only a one-tenth sentence discount is awarded (Sentencing Guidelines Council, 2007). The reason for the sliding scale is to reduce the amount of cracked trials by late guilty pleas.

There are a number of criticisms against the sentence discount. The discount has been described as a blatant attempt to induce a guilty plea (Sanders et al., 2010). Defendants are aware, or made aware, that by pleading guilty, they will be assured a lower sentence compared to a sentence received after conviction at trial. Lawyers are able to advise their clients on potential starting points of sentences by reviewing sentencing guidelines in tariff cases, other precedents, and through their own experience. As noted above, this can mean substantial reductions and the difference between a custodial or community sentence. This is argued to place enormous pressure on the accused to plead guilty. As a result, it may lead innocent defendants to plead guilty in order to secure the discount and avoid the risks of losing at trial. Therefore it serves to discourage defendants from putting the prosecution's case to the test in a contested trial. In principle, the sentence discount is a reward of leniency to defendants who plead guilty, but it can be interpreted as a penalty for those who plead not guilty and elect for trial.

Another argument against the sentence discount is that the sentence does not reflect the criminality or the seriousness of the offence. Two defendants who commit identical crimes will receive different sentences if one pleads guilty and the other is convicted at trial. The sentence discount is not supported by any sentencing principles. It goes against the principle of retribution, for instance, which contends that defendants ought to receive punishment based on the gravity of the offence and the conduct of the accused. It is also difficult to see how the discount enhances the goal of rehabilitation since the sentence is not based on the defendant's characteristics or social circumstances. Instead, the sentence discount is awarded based on the costs and benefits to the criminal justice system (Mack and Roach Anleu, 1995).

Factors affecting guilty pleas

There are numerous factors that may encourage defendants to plead guilty, the most obvious of which is the likelihood of conviction at trial, assessed by measuring the strength of the prosecution's evidence. The prosecution has the burden to prove the state's case beyond a reasonable doubt before a conviction can be secured in trial. If the prosecution's case is strong, and if the defence's case is weak, then it may be more beneficial for the accused to plead guilty and receive the one-third sentence discount. Cheng (2013), through courtroom observations of over 1,000 cases in the Magistrates' Courts, found an admission under caution by defendants to be positively associated with the likelihood of guilty pleas. This is due to the difficulty in challenging admissions obtained by the police in court (Cheng, 2014). Hence admissions are powerful incriminating evidence.

Empirical studies have found various factors, both legal and extra-legal, that affect the likelihood of guilty pleas. It is beyond the scope of this chapter to examine all factors. Here several intriguing factors are highlighted.

Defence lawyers

The classic study is derived from Baldwin and McConville (1977) who surprisingly discovered that the main source of why defendants plead guilty is because of their legal representatives. Through interviews with 121 defendants who made late guilty pleas (cracked trials) in Birmingham, it was discovered that defendants changed their minds with respect to their pleas because of pressure from defence lawyers. Defendants asserted that they were not given many alternatives but to comply in pleading guilty. In a subsequent study by McConville and colleagues (1994), where lawyer–client interactions in law firms were 'shadowed' by the research team, it was found that publicly funded lawyers hurry their legally aided clients to plead guilty. It was argued that these defence lawyers perceived their clients to be factually guilty and undeserving of a contested trial.

Tague (2007) disagrees and argues that barristers have selfish incentives to prefer trials over guilty pleas. By going to trial, barristers can maximise their remuneration since more effort and time will be needed to prepare for trial, they will be able to put their advocacy skills on display which helps to attract briefs in the future, and they risk sanction if they are seen to sacrifice clients.

In Hong Kong, there are some indications that publicly funded lawyers adopt a mentality that defendants are factually guilty even before they are convicted by the courts (Cheng et al., 2015). Overall, there were no differences found between the types of legal representation, privately or publicly funded, with the likelihood of defendants pleading guilty. Instead, defendants who are self-represented were far more likely to plead guilty at the first opportunity (Cheng, 2013).

Defence lawyers do, however, play an important role in terms of defendants' plea decisions since it is their duty to advise their clients on this crucial choice. *The Hong Kong Solicitors' Guide to Professional Conduct* (Law Society of Hong Kong, 2013) reminds litigation solicitors that defendants possess two fundamental rights: the right to choose to plead guilty or not guilty, and the right to choose whether or not to give evidence (principle 10.16). Furthermore, the commentary to this principle echoes the guideline in *Turner*:

> Advice may be given in a strong and persuasive manner but the client must be left with the clear understanding that he has the right to choose how to plead and whether to give evidence.
>
> (Principle 10.16 Commentary 2)

Similarly, the Hong Kong Bar Association *Code of Conduct* (2012) states:

> It is the duty of defending Counsel to advise his client generally about his plea to the charge. It should be made clear that whether he pleads 'not guilty' or 'guilty', the client has the responsibility for and complete freedom of choice in his plea. For the purposes of giving proper advice, Counsel is entitled to refer to all aspects of the case and where appropriate he may advise his client in strong terms that he is unlikely to escape conviction and that a plea of guilty is generally regarded by the Court as a mitigating factor.
>
> (Paragraph 150(a))

In short, both solicitors and barristers may advise their clients to plead guilty in strong terms but defendants must understand that they have a freedom of choice to accept or reject that advice.

Bail status

Another variable that affects plea decisions is bail status. Defendants appear before court either on bail or remanded in custody. The decision to grant the accused bail or not depends on several factors. First is the risk of the accused absconding before he or she appears in court. The accused may have little attachment to Hong Kong and may flee the region to avoid criminal sanction. Second, there is a risk that the accused may commit another offence while on bail. Third, the accused may interfere with witnesses or pervert the course of justice if granted bail. The accused may be denied bail simply because he or she is unable to post the bail money. Defendants may be remanded in custody if they have breached a condition of bail. In theory, whether the accused is remanded or not is separate from the decision to plead guilty. However, past empirical studies note a direct correlation.

In observations of criminal cases in a Toronto court, Kellough and Wortley (2002) found defendants remanded in custody to be more than twice as likely to plead guilty than defendants who were on bail. Similarly in Hong Kong, remanded defendants were found to plead guilty at a higher rate compared with defendants on bail (Cheng, 2013). Remanded defendants wanted to avoid serving 'dead time', the time in which they are held in custody without being convicted yet. Many offences may not entail any incarceration and by pleading guilty, remanded defendants may be immediately released. Furthermore, they may receive time served if they plead guilty and their sentence of imprisonment will be reduced. This could also lead to an immediate release. Conditions in remand centres are often unpleasant where overcrowding is a norm (Kellough and Wortley, 2002). Given all these reasons, it is not surprising how guilty pleas are a tempting option for defendants remanded in custody.

Stress and costs

Getting caught up in the criminal justice process is a stressful situation for many. There is the uncertainty of conviction and the prospect of sanction. Family members, friends and co-workers may add pressure to already nervous defendants. When asked about the mindset of defendants, one criminal barrister in Hong Kong had this to say:

> Any defendant is like this, when they are charged, it's already stressful, and this stress will only increase and not decrease. The second thing is if you have a positive defence case where you have to build a defence, you will have extra stress. And there's more stress to perform on the spot to persuade the judge. I must say this, the pressure is not easy. Even in cases even where the defendant has failed, a lot of times you see that he feels released, and that's very important. The case has been

> decided and you need no longer worry about it; for better or for worse, it's decided.
>
> (cited in Cheng and Chui 2015: 407)

A guilty plea is an option for defendants to end their cases quickly and avoid the stress of preparing and going through a trial.

As the case drags on, the costs of criminal proceedings add up. These include: legal costs to lawyers, time spent in custody as described above, and other opportunities lost. If the accused is privately represented, it is not difficult to see that the legal costs will mount up as the case goes on. Even if the accused is represented by a duty lawyer or a legal aid lawyer, he or she will still have to make an application, go through a financial means test and schedule meetings with his or her legal representatives. There are also costs associated with being on bail. Often, besides having to put up bail money, there are conditions imposed on bail such as having to surrender travel documents, report to police stations and abide by curfews. Time spent at conferences with lawyers and waiting in court means opportunities lost in other activities such as employment. Defendants need to take time off work and other events to attend case-related matters.

Feeley (1979) famously underscored how 'the process is the punishment'. The costs of being caught up in the criminal justice process may outweigh the criminal sanction imposed upon conviction. Feeley (1979) in addition noted that these costs apply to everyone, as he asserts:

> The time, effort, money, and opportunities lost as a direct result of being caught up in the system can quickly come to outweigh the penalty that issues from adjudication and sentence. Furthermore, pre-trial costs do not distinguish between innocent and guilty; they are borne by all …
>
> (Feeley, 1979: 31)

This is particularly true in the lower courts where sanctions are relatively more lenient. The guilty plea is the most direct way for defendants to dispose of their cases as quickly as possible.

Plea bargaining

Plea bargaining refers to some concessions made by the prosecution to the accused in return for the accused pleading guilty. While plea bargaining is a common feature of the criminal justice system across many jurisdictions, it remains one of the most controversial practices in the criminal process. In Hong Kong, plea bargaining occurs in the background between the prosecution and defence as it is very rarely directly referred to in open court. Mainly it is the defence that initiates plea bargaining offers either through writing a letter to the

Department of Justice or engaging in face-to-face interactions with prosecutors. The latter usually occurs when duty lawyers meet their clients on the day of court and they must quickly reach out to the prosecution before the accused's appearance and plea arraignment. It is up to the prosecution to accept or reject the offer. Plea bargaining takes several forms, and not all of them exist in Hong Kong.

Charge bargaining

Charge bargaining is the most common form of plea bargaining in Hong Kong. The prosecution has the discretion to decide which charges to lay. Charge bargaining takes place in two ways. In multiple charge cases, the accused may plead guilty to some charges if the prosecution agrees to drop the others. This mainly occurs when the defence deems the prosecution's evidence for certain charges are weaker, and proposes to plead guilty to the other charges in return for the prosecution dropping the weaker charges. For the prosecution, there are incentives to agree since it would be more difficult for them to prove the weaker charges anyway. In this way they can secure conviction for the other charges. For the accused, convictions on a lower number of charges mean a more lenient sentence overall.

The other way that charge bargaining occurs, is for the prosecution to reduce a particular charge to a lesser charge. Many criminal offences are organised on a spectrum of seriousness. For example, for the accused pleading guilty, the prosecution may reduce a charge of drug trafficking to drug possession or a charge of assault occasioning actual bodily harm to common assault. A lesser charge would inevitably mean a lower sentence for the accused.

Sentence bargaining

Another type of plea bargaining, which does not occur in Hong Kong, is sentence bargaining. Sentence bargaining takes place when the accused is guaranteed a reduced sentence in return for pleading guilty. In Hong Kong, prosecutors cannot guarantee sentences as the sentence is up to the court to decide. As noted above, Hong Kong magistrates and judges are prohibited from indicating to the defence that if the accused pleads guilty, he or she will receive one sentence, but if the accused is convicted after trial, then a more severe sentence will be imposed.

Fact bargaining

This type of plea bargaining occurs when the defence negotiates with the prosecution regarding how the facts against the accused are presented. In return for a guilty plea, the prosecution will agree to amend the facts of the case to minimise aggravating factors. For instance, the injury suffered by the victim may be minimised and the prosecution may not mention the involvement of other persons, such as the accused's spouse or friend in the offence. Because sentencing is based in part on the prosecution's set of facts, by reducing its seriousness, the accused will receive a more lenient sentence.

Bind over order

Traditionally, the bind over order is not considered a type of plea bargaining. As pointed out above, official statistics record bind overs as acquittals. Technically, bind overs are acquittals because the prosecution either does not charge the accused or offers no evidence for a particular charge if the accused accepts to be bound over. Acquitted defendants or even witnesses can be bound over. Here, the focus is on defendants who enter into their recognisance to keep the peace and be of good behaviour. The defence may go to the prosecution in search for the prosecution agreeing to offer no evidence and pursue a bind over order, known as an ONE bind over. In turn, the accused admits to wrongdoing in accordance with the prosecution's facts. Given that the accused does in fact admit to wrongdoing, they are not fully off the hook for the crime as in an acquittal.

The court will stipulate the behaviour from which the accused is prohibited once bound over. For instance, if the case involved violence of some form, the court will indicate to the accused that he or she is prohibited from engaging in acts of violence including the threat of violence. A time period will also be set, usually 12 months. The accused will moreover be bound over for a sum of money. This sum does not have to be paid unless the accused breaches the order. If the order is breached, not only will the accused likely have to pay the amount of recognisance but he or she will be sentenced for the new offence as well. Bind over orders are attractive to defendants because they do not receive criminal records if bound over. The purpose of the bind over order is not to sanction past behaviour but to prevent future breaches of the peace (see *Lau Wai-wo v HKSAR* (2003) 6 HKCFAR 624).

Criticisms against plea bargaining

Like the sentence discount, there are a number of criticisms levied against the practice of plea bargaining. Here some of these criticisms are outlined.

Undermines adversarial system

The adversarial system in Hong Kong as in other common law jurisdictions is based on the notion of two opposing sides, the prosecution and defence, acting as adversaries before a neutral tribunal. The prosecution, on behalf of the state, has the burden to prove through admissible and reliable evidence, beyond a reasonable doubt, that the accused committed all elements of the offence(s).

The presumption of innocence is regarded as the 'golden thread' of common law and it is guaranteed constitutionally in Hong Kong as well. At the same time, the defence is not required to put forth any evidence. It is up to the defence to choose to call witnesses or have the accused testify. All it has to do is raise a reasonable doubt.

A rationale for this is to close the gap between the wide power disparity between the state and the accused. The state possesses enormous resources such as the police force and legal counsel employed by the Department of Justice. The police are trained to investigate crimes and collect evidence. The prosecution decides which charges to bring forth. The accused, even those who are very wealthy, do not possess such resources and expertise.

Plea bargaining absolves the prosecution of its burden to prove its case. It no longer has to convince the court that the accused is guilty. It need not question witnesses nor produce admissible evidence. The court likewise does not have to hear evidence from both sides. A guilty plea leads directly to a conviction, and the court's role is only to determine the appropriate sentence (McConville, 2002).

Overcharging

As discussed, the prosecution has the discretion to decide whether to prosecute or not, and if so, which charges are brought against the accused. There is concern that through the frequent use of plea bargaining, the prosecution may be tempted to overcharge in order to enhance its bargaining position. In charge bargaining, the prosecution will drop certain charges if the accused pleads guilty to the remaining charges. The prosecution may put forth charges where there is weak evidence so that they can drop them later in hopes that the accused will plead guilty to the rest.

Non-transparent

Plea bargaining is distasteful to many because it operates in a non-transparent fashion. Unlike trials where most are open to the public to sit in or allow the media to report on them, plea bargaining is hidden from public view. This goes against the cardinal maxim that justice must be seen to be done. In trials where the evidence is tested, potential abuses or procedural irregularities are brought to light. Plea bargaining is a deal struck between the prosecution and the defence. There is a sense that justice is being circumvented.

Justifications for plea bargaining

While there are certainly arguments in favour of plea bargaining, for those who do not think plea bargaining is ideal, there are justifications for this controversial practice.

Expediency

The most obvious argument for plea bargaining is that in reality, it would not be practical for every criminal case to go to trial. The court system would simply be unable to cope with the large amount of cases. Hong Kong is already faced with a shortage of magistrates and judges (Reyes, 2014). The time waiting for trial would be exacerbated, and justice delayed is justice denied. For the state, plea bargaining not only reduces the time and resources needed to dispose of cases, but also asserts that the prosecution can devote their attention to more complex cases that do require trials. For the accused, plea bargaining averts the costs of criminal proceeding and leads to a lesser sentence. Witnesses and victims are also spared from having to testify in court.

Avoids risk of trial

Trials are inherently unpredictable. The outcome depends on many factors such as whether certain evidence is made inadmissible or what witnesses say in court. The outcome for plea bargaining is easier to predict. Although prosecutors cannot guarantee sentences, defence lawyers are able to advise based on the charges and sentencing guidelines.

Voluntariness preserved

Defence lawyers contend that the voluntariness of defendants whether to plead guilty is preserved in plea bargains. Lawyers only advise clients and it is up to the latter to decide. It is not up to defence lawyers to determine whether the accused is indeed guilty or not, although they may have their own personal opinions. Defence lawyers emphasise that they are only advisers and they follow the instructions of their clients (Cheng, 2014).

Conclusion

Guilty pleas are an integral part of the criminal justice system in Hong Kong. This chapter has discussed the importance of giving defendants the freedom of choice in deciding to plead guilty or not as stipulated in the law. However, empirical studies have also highlighted the discrepancy between the law in the books and the daily practices of the criminal process. There are strong incentives for the accused to plead guilty, including the one-third sentence discount and other costs such as bail status, legal costs and the overall stress in being caught up in the criminal justice system. This chapter also examined the controversial practice of plea bargaining as well as criticisms against it and justifications for it. It is important for policymakers to weigh the advantages and disadvantages of the guilty plea process carefully in order to ensure that the criminal justice system fulfils its role in effectively convicting the guilty and safeguarding that the innocent are acquitted.

Review questions

1 What are the benefits of guilty pleas for the state and for defendants?
2 Should the courts in Hong Kong be allowed to provide advanced sentence indications?
3 Does the one-third sentence discount undermine the accused's voluntariness in making his or her plea decision?
4 Should plea bargaining be abolished, maintained or promoted?

References

Baldwin, J. and McConville, M. (1977) *Negotiated Justice: Pressures to Plead Guilty*, London: Martin Robertson.

Cheng, K.K. (2013) 'Pressures to plead guilty: Factors affecting plea decisions in Hong Kong's magistrates' courts', *British Journal of Criminology*, 53(2): 257–275.

Cheng, K.K. (2014) 'The practice and justifications of plea bargaining by Hong Kong criminal defence lawyers', *Asian Journal of Law and Society*, 1(2): 395–412.

Cheng, K.K. and Chui, W.H. (2015) 'Beyond the shadow-of-trial: Decision-making behind plea bargaining in Hong Kong', *International Journal of Law, Crime and Justice*, 43(4): 397–411.

Cheng, K.K., Chui, W.H. and Ong, R. (2015) 'Providing justice for low-income youths: Publicly funded lawyers and youth clients in Hong Kong', *Social & Legal Studies*, 24(4): 577–593.

Cross, I.G., Cheung, P.W.S. and Tsui, E.Y.L. (2015) *Sentencing in Hong Kong* (7th edn), Hong Kong: LexisNexis.

Department of Justice (2010–14, various issues) *Yearly Review of the Prosecutions Division*, Hong Kong: Department of Justice.

Feeley, M. (1979) *The Process is the Punishment: Handling Cases in a Lower Criminal Court*, New York: Russell Sage Foundation.

Hong Kong Bar Association (2012) *Code of Conduct*, Hong Kong: Hong Kong Bar Association.

Hong Kong Judiciary (2015) *Hong Kong Judiciary Annual Report 2014*, Hong Kong: Hong Kong Judiciary.

Kellough, G. and Wortley, S. (2002) 'Remand for plea: Bail decisions and plea bargaining as commensurate decisions', *British Journal of Criminology*, 42(1): 186–210.

Knight, C. and Upham, A. (2011) *Criminal Litigation in Hong Kong* (3rd edn), Hong Kong: Sweet & Maxwell.

Law Society of Hong Kong (2013) *The Hong Kong Solicitor's Guide to Professional Conduct*, Hong Kong: Law Society of Hong Kong.

Mack, K. and Roach Anleu, S. (1995) *Pleading Guilty: Issues and Practices*, Carlton South: Australian Institute of Judicial Administration Incorporated.

McConville, M. (2002) 'Plea bargaining', in M. McConville and G. Wilson (eds) *The Handbook of the Criminal Justice Process* (pp. 353–377), Oxford: Oxford University Press.

McConville, M., Hodgson, J., Bridges, L. and Pavlovic, A. (1994) *Standing Accused: The Organisation and Practices of Criminal Defence Lawyers in Britain*, Oxford: Clarendon Press.

McConville, M. and Mirsky, C. (1993) 'Looking through the guilty plea glass: The structural framework of English and American state courts', *Social & Legal Studies*, 2(2): 173–193.

Reyes, A. (2014) 'The future of the judiciary: Reflections on present challenges to the administration of justice in Hong Kong', *Hong Kong Law Journal*, 44(2): 429–446.

Sanders, A., Young, R. and Burton, M. (2010) *Criminal Justice* (4th edn), Oxford: Oxford University Press.

Sentencing Guidelines Council (2007) *Reduction in Sentence for a Guilty Plea: Definition Guidelines*. London: Sentencing Guidelines Secretariat.

Tague, P.W. (2007) 'Barristers' selfish incentives in counselling defendants over the choice of plea', *Criminal Law Review*, January: 3–23.

Legislation cited

Basic Law of the Hong Kong Special Administrative Region

Cases cited

Lau Wai-wo v HKSAR (2003) 6 HKCFAR 624
R v Goodyear [2005] EWCA Crim. 888
R v Turner [1970] 2 WLR 1093
R v Yu Man-wu [1995] HKLY 481

Useful websites

Hong Kong Bar Association www.hkba.org
Hong Kong Department of Justice www.doj.gov.hk/eng/index.html
Hong Kong Judiciary www.judiciary.gov.hk/en/index/index.htm
The Law Society of Hong Kong www.hklawsoc.org.hk/pub_e/default.asp

14

THE CRIMINAL COURT SYSTEM

Stefan H.C. Lo

Introduction

Defendants or accused persons who are prosecuted for commission of an offence are tried before the courts. The courts determine the guilt or innocence of defendants in the eyes of the law. If the defendant is found to be guilty, the courts also decide on the sentence to be imposed on the convicted person. This chapter outlines the system and structure of the criminal courts in Hong Kong.

Judicial power of the courts in Hong Kong is derived from section 4 of Chapter IV of the *Basic Law of the Hong Kong Special Administrative Region* (hereafter the *Basic Law*). The *Basic Law* came into effect on the resumption of sovereignty by China on 1 July 1997, but the provisions of the *Basic Law* seek to provide continuity in the court system that existed in Hong Kong under British rule. Article 81 provides that the judicial system previously practised in Hong Kong shall be maintained except for those changes consequent upon the establishment of the Court of Final Appeal. Article 86 provides that the principle of trial by jury previously practised in Hong Kong shall be maintained. Also, the principles previously applied in criminal (or civil) proceedings in Hong Kong and the rights previously enjoyed by parties to proceedings shall be maintained (article 87). Despite the change in sovereignty, the common law and other laws previously in force in Hong Kong continue to apply in Hong Kong in accordance with articles 8 and 18.

Article 81 specifies the courts in Hong Kong: the Court of Final Appeal, the High Court (composed of the Court of Appeal and the Court of First Instance), District Courts, Magistrates' Courts and other special courts. The structure, powers and functions of the courts are prescribed by law (article 83). Accordingly, each of the courts in Hong Kong is established pursuant to specific ordinances, with their powers and functions specified in their respective ordinances and the court rules made under the relevant ordinance. The High Court and the Court of Final Appeal are established as 'superior courts' (see *High Court Ordinance* (Cap. 4) sections 3, 12, 13; *Hong Kong Court of Final Appeal Ordinance* (Cap. 484) section 3), which means they also have what are referred to as inherent powers, which are derived from common law. Also relevant is the *Criminal Procedure Ordinance* (Cap. 221) which sets out certain rules on procedure and other matters in the criminal courts.

Categories of offence and the trial court

The procedure and the court in which the trial of a defendant takes place may differ depending on whether the offence is a summary offence or an indictable offence. Generally, summary offences are tried in the Magistrates' Court while indictable offences are tried in the District Court or Court of First Instance.

Summary offences are less serious offences, such as touting (*Summary Offences Ordinance* (Cap. 228) section 6A) and unlawful gambling (*Gambling Ordinance* (Cap. 148) section 13). Indictable offences are more serious, such as robbery (*Theft Ordinance* (Cap. 210) section 10) and indecent assault (*Crimes Ordinance* (Cap. 200) section 122). A statutory offence is an indictable offence if the statutory provision so provides; otherwise it is a summary offence (*Criminal Procedure Ordinance* (Cap. 221) section 14A). Common law offences are indictable offences (for example, see *Waroquiers v Marsden* [1950] 2 KB 1).

Certain statutory offences expressly state that the offence can be tried either way, namely either summarily or on indictment. Such offences are in the middle range of seriousness. The prosecutor decides whether to try the defendant summarily or on indictment, depending on factors such as the gravity of the allegations and general circumstances of the case. The prosecution also takes into account the maximum penalties that the particular court can impose so that an adequate sentence (subject to the statutory maximum for the particular offence) can be imposed: see the *Prosecution Code* of the Department of Justice (2013), paragraph 8.4. The maximum prison sentence in the Magistrates' Court is generally two years and in the District Court seven years. There is no maximum in the Court of First Instance (though this is still subject to the limit specified for the offence in question).

Most indictable offences can also be tried summarily, pursuant to the *Magistrates Ordinance* (Cap. 227) section 91, 92 or 94; however, consent of the prosecutor is required (section 94A). Certain offences can only be tried on indictment. These include treasonable offences (*Crimes Ordinance* sections 2 and 3) and offences that are punishable by imprisonment for life, such as rape (*Crimes Ordinance* section 118) and murder or manslaughter (sections 2 and 7, *Offences Against the Person Ordinance* (Cap. 212)).

In practice, the great majority of criminal cases are dealt with in the Magistrates' Court. In 2014, there were 322,964 criminal cases before the Magistrates' Court (99.5%), 1,079 before the District Court (0.3%) and 545 before the Court of First Instance (0.2%) (The Judiciary, 2014).

Adversarial system

The court system in Hong Kong, as is the case in common law jurisdictions generally, adopts an adversarial system as opposed to an inquisitorial system. The latter is adopted in civil law jurisdictions where the judge has an active role in the pre-trial investigation of the matter and has a more interventionist role in court proceedings through the asking of questions and directing of counsel on legal matters (Lo and Chui 2012). By contrast, in an adversarial system, the judge is not involved in the collection of evidence before the trial and is impartial and largely passive throughout the proceedings. It is the task of the prosecution and defence counsel to be 'adversaries' and to argue their respective cases before the court. In coming to its decision, the court would generally only consider issues and arguments that are raised by the parties in the proceedings.

However, even within an adversarial system, judges do have some powers of intervention. For example, judges may exercise powers in pre-trial case management. In court, judges have powers not only to ask counsel to rephrase questions or to restrict certain questions, but also to ask questions themselves to clarify the evidence. However, judges do not take on an inquisitorial role by marginalising counsel and taking over questioning of witnesses (Henderson, 2015). In the adversarial system, the judge still has a role to ensure the fair and orderly unfolding of the parties' cases in accordance with the practice and procedure of the court (Devlin, 1979).

Magistrates' Courts

Magistrates are appointed pursuant to the *Magistrates' Ordinance* (Cap. 227) (MO). There are currently seven Magistrates' Courts: Eastern, Kowloon City, Kwun Tong, Tsuen Wan, Fanling, Shatin and Tuen Mun Magistrates' Courts. All criminal cases start in the Magistrates' Court (MC) and most are wholly dealt with there as well, with only the more serious cases referred to the District Court or Court of First Instance. Apart from hearing and determining prosecutions for offences, magistrates also have power in relation to, for example, the issuing of search or arrest warrants (MO sections 9, 72) and granting of bail (*Criminal Procedure Ordinance* (Cap. 221) Part IA).

Magistrates are appointed as permanent magistrates or special magistrates (MO section 5). Permanent magistrates must have the requisite legal professional qualifications and at least five years' relevant professional experience as a legal practitioner as stipulated in MO section 5AA. Persons with such qualifications and experience can also be appointed as special magistrates. In addition, legally qualified persons without such experience can be appointed as special magistrates if they have at least five years' experience as a court prosecutor, court interpreter or judicial clerk in the government (MO section 5AB). Special magistrates deal with relatively minor offences, such as hawking, traffic violations and littering.

Commencement of criminal proceedings

All criminal proceedings are commenced before a magistrate. Generally a defendant is brought to the court by summons or by arrest. For cases dealt with on summons, a magistrate may issue the summons to the defendant (after a complaint is made or information laid before the magistrate), requiring the defendant to appear at the specified time at the MC to answer to the complaint or information (MO sections 8, 72). For littering and similar offences, apart from the procedure on a summons, specified public officers have power to serve a notice requiring a defendant to appear before a magistrate (MO section 8A).

In the case where the defendant is first arrested and charged, the defendant may be released on bail by the police to appear before a magistrate at a later specified time (usually the next day). Where the offence is of a serious nature, the police may detain the defendant in custody instead, in which case the defendant must be brought before a magistrate as soon as practicable, which means not later than the next sitting of the MC (*Police Force Ordinance* (Cap. 232) section 52; *Police General Orders* 49-01(13); see Hong Kong Police Force, 2016).

The first appearance of the defendant in court is in Court No. 1 (also referred to as the Plea Court or the Principal Magistrate's Court) of the particular magistracy.

Offence tried summarily

At the first appearance before the magistrate, the defendant may enter a plea or the matter may be adjourned. If adjourned, the magistrate may grant the defendant bail or commit him or her to prison (MO section 20). Defendants are granted bail unless there are substantial grounds for believing that the defendant would abscond, commit an offence while on bail, or interfere with a witness or pervert or obstruct the course of justice (*Criminal Procedure Ordinance* (Cap. 221) sections 9D, 9G).

If the defendant pleads guilty, the prosecutor hands a brief statement of facts to the magistrate. If the magistrate is satisfied that the facts establish the offence charged and if the defendant agrees with the statement of facts, then the magistrate convicts the defendant. The magistrate may then proceed to sentencing or the sentencing hearing may be adjourned.

If the defendant pleads not guilty, the case is listed for trial at a subsequent date in one of the trial courts of the particular magistracy. Proceedings before a magistrate are heard by the magistrate sitting alone, and there is no jury involved. The prosecution presents its case first. Prosecution witnesses are called to provide their evidence via examination in chief by the prosecutor. They may be cross-examined by the defence (through the defence counsel) and then re-examined by the prosecutor. After the prosecution has called all its evidence, the prosecution closes its case.

If the prosecution evidence taken at its highest is insufficient to establish commission of the offence, the magistrate will rule that there is no case to answer and acquit the defendant.

If there is a case to answer, the defendant may give evidence in the witness box by being examined in chief by defence counsel. Alternatively the defendant may choose to remain silent and not give evidence. If the defendant does give evidence, he or she can be cross-examined by the prosecutor and then re-examined by the defence counsel. The defence may also call its own witnesses, who are examined in chief, cross-examined and re-examined in the same manner. After the defence has called all its evidence, the prosecution and defence then provide their closing addresses.

Upon consideration of all the evidence and the submissions of the parties, the magistrate decides on the verdict (MO section 19(2)). If the defendant is found guilty, the magistrate may proceed to sentencing, or there may be adjournment to a later date for the sentencing hearing. If adjourned, the defendant may be remanded in custody or granted bail pending sentencing.

The maximum sentence that can be imposed is as provided for in the relevant statutory provision that sets out the offence. Subject to those limits, the maximum sentence that can be imposed by a special magistrate is six months' imprisonment and a fine of HK$50,000 (MO section 91; but this is also subject to certain exceptions where a higher sentence can be imposed: MO sections 57, 94); and by a permanent magistrate two years' imprisonment and a fine of HK $100,000 (MO section 92; but again a higher sentence can be imposed in certain cases: see, for example, MO section 57; *Dangerous Drugs Ordinance* (Cap. 134) section 8(2)(b)).

Review of a magistrate's decision and appeals

Section 104 of the MO allows a magistrate to review his or her own decision on either the verdict or the sentence, upon application by either the prosecution or the defendant or upon the magistrate's own initiative. This procedure provides for a relatively simple way to correct errors such as where a relevant case or statutory provision has been overlooked which may affect the correctness of the decision. If an appeal is made (as discussed below), then it is no longer permissible for a review under section 104 unless the appeal is abandoned.

A defendant who has been convicted may appeal against the conviction or sentence pursuant to MO section 113, under what is referred to as the 'alternative procedure'. This right of appeal can be relied upon whether or not an application had been made for review under section 104. The appeal is to the Court of First Instance. The appeal can challenge both findings of fact and decisions on the law made by the magistrate.

Apart from section 113, there is also the 'case stated procedure' in section 105, which allows appeals to the Court of First Instance on points of law. Appeal under section 105 can be made by either the prosecution or the defence.

As regards sentence, the prosecution can also rely on section 81A of the *Criminal Procedure Ordinance* (Cap. 221) to apply to the Court of Appeal for review of the sentence.

Offence tried on indictment

Where the prosecution of an offence is to be proceeded by way of indictment, the matter may be transferred to the District Court (MO Part IV). The prosecutor asks the magistrate not to take a plea and makes the application to the magistrate for the transfer pursuant to MO section 88.

Where an indictable offence is to be tried in the Court of First Instance (CFI), committal proceedings are held before the magistrate first (MO Part III). The prosecution would request the magistrate to set a 'return day', which is usually not fewer than ten days nor more than 42 days from the day on which the return day is appointed (MO section 80A). On the return day (see MO section 80C), the defendant may enter a guilty plea, in which case the defendant is committed to the CFI for sentence. If the defendant pleads not guilty, then the magistrate commits the defendant to trial. This is referred to as a 'paper committal'. Alternatively the defendant may elect to have the charge heard at a preliminary inquiry, wherein the magistrate determines whether there is sufficient evidence to commit the defendant to trial.

A preliminary inquiry may take place in a closed court. That is, the magistrate may restrict public access to the hearing (see MO section 80). At a preliminary inquiry, the prosecution puts forward its evidence by witness statements or by oral testimony in the case of witnesses whom the defence wish to have called (so that the witness can be cross-examined). After the prosecution evidence has been presented, the magistrate determines whether there is a case to answer. If so, the defence may then give evidence from the defendant or other defence witnesses. Usually the defence chooses not to provide any evidence at this stage though. After hearing all the evidence of the prosecution and any evidence of the defence, the magistrate decides whether there is sufficient evidence to put the defendant on trial (MO section 85). If so, the magistrate makes an order for the defendant to stand trial at the CFI. If not, the defendant is discharged, but the discharge does not prevent the prosecution from re-commencing a prosecution by a subsequent complaint or information in respect of the same facts.

The current provisions in the MO for a paper committal, which provide for an automatic committal, were introduced with effect in 1984. Prior to that, all committal proceedings involved a preliminary inquiry, subject to the possibility of witness statements being admissible without calling the witness. Since 1984, the use of 'old-style' committals in the form of a preliminary inquiry has become uncommon.

Juvenile Court

The Juvenile Court (JC) is established under section 3A of the *Juvenile Offenders Ordinance* (Cap. 226) (JOO) to deal with prosecutions of children and young persons. For the purposes of the JOO, a child means a person under 14, and a young person means a person aged 14 or above but below 16. No child under the age of ten can be guilty of an offence (JOO section 3), and hence the JC deals with cases involving juveniles ten or above but below 16. Permanent magistrates sit in the JC. The JC has jurisdiction to determine and hear a charge against a child or young person for any offence except homicide.

The JC has all the powers of a permanent magistrate and, subject to the JOO, the MO applies to proceedings before the JC as it applies to proceedings before the MC (JOO section 3A(4)). There are various differences in the proceedings, as set out in the JOO, to protect the interests of the juvenile. For example, the JC sits in private in that only officers of the court, parties to the case and their solicitors and counsel, witnesses and other persons directly concerned in the case may be present in court (JOO section 3D). Journalists may be present but the court has power to exclude their presence if it is necessary in the interests of the child or young person. Section 20A also imposes restrictions on media reporting that could reveal the identity of the child or young person. Before deciding how to deal with a child or young person who is brought before the JC, the court must obtain such information as may be readily available as to his or her general conduct, home surroundings, school record and medical history, in order to enable the court to deal with the case in the best interests of the child or young person (JOO section 8(8)).

The approach to sentencing of juveniles found guilty can be different from that for adults. No child can be sentenced to imprisonment, while a young person can only be sentenced to imprisonment if he or she cannot be suitably dealt with in any other way (JOO section 11). There is a focus on rehabilitation, though custodial sentences can still be required, for example for serious offences (*HKSAR v Law Ka Kit* [2003] 2 HKC 178).

District Court

The District Court (DC) is established pursuant to the *District Court Ordinance* (Cap. 336) (DCO). The court has both civil and criminal jurisdiction. For a person to be appointed as a judge in the DC, the person must be qualified to practise as a barrister, solicitor or advocate in a court in Hong Kong or any other common law jurisdiction having unlimited jurisdiction, and have at least five years' relevant experience as specified in DCO section 5(1).

Criminal jurisdiction

Part 5 of the DCO sets out the criminal jurisdiction of the DC. The criminal jurisdiction mainly covers indictable offences transferred to the DC by a magistrate under Part IV of the MO. However, certain indictable offences cannot be transferred to the DC under the MO (and would need to be tried in the Court of First Instance instead). These include offences punishable with life imprisonment (subject to certain exceptions), treason, blasphemy and genocide (MO section 88 and Second Schedule, Part III). The DC also has criminal jurisdiction over indictable offences transferred from the Court of First Instance under section 65F of the *Criminal Procedure Ordinance* (Cap. 221), though this is not common.

The DC does not have power to impose a sentence of imprisonment of greater than seven years (DCO section 82).

Procedure

Upon a magistrate making an order for transfer of a charge or complaint in respect of an indictable offence to the DC under MO section 88, the magistrate must appoint a day on which the defendant is to appear before the DC (MO section 90(1)(a)). The magistrate either remands the defendant in prison custody or grants bail to the defendant (MO section 90(1)(b)).

The procedure and practice of the Court of First Instance in relation to criminal proceedings apply in the DC, but this is expressly subject to the provisions of the DCO (section 79). An important difference is that there is no jury in trials in the DC (DCO section 79(5)). The case is heard by a judge sitting alone (DCO section 6). The process of giving evidence by the prosecution and defence is largely similar to that in the MC, but there is a greater degree of formality in the DC.

A DC judge must give reasons for both the verdict and for the sentence (if any) that is handed down (DCO section 80). The reasons must be reduced to writing within 21 days.

Appeals

Sections 80 to 83Y of the *Criminal Procedure Ordinance* (Cap. 221) (CPO), dealing with appeals, apply to criminal proceedings in the DC (DCO section 83). A convicted person may appeal to the Court of Appeal (CA) against a conviction (CPO section 82) or against the sentence (CPO sections 83G, 83I).

The prosecution has a right to appeal to the CA against an acquittal on matters of law only. This is pursuant to the case stated procedure in DCO section 84. As to sentence, the prosecution may apply to the CA for the review of the sentence (CPO section 81A).

Court of First Instance of the High Court

The Court of First Instance (CFI) of the High Court of the Hong Kong Special Administrative Region (HKSAR) is established pursuant to the *High Court Ordinance* (Cap. 4) (HCO). The CFI has both civil and criminal jurisdiction, and is the highest criminal trial court in Hong Kong. Prior to the transfer of sovereignty from the UK to China in July 1997, the High Court was named the Supreme Court, which was originally established in 1844.

A person can only be appointed as a judge of the High Court if he or she satisfies the professional requirements as set out in section 9 of the HCO.

Persons who have practised as a barrister or advocate in a court in Hong Kong or any other common law jurisdiction having unlimited jurisdiction for at least ten years are eligible. A solicitor of the High Court with ten years' experience is also eligible. There are also alternative bases for satisfying the eligibility requirements, as set out in HCO section 9.

Criminal jurisdiction

The High Court is a superior court, and as such, has unlimited jurisdiction, subject to the provisions of the HCO (see HCO section 3(2)). The criminal jurisdiction of the CFI consists of original jurisdiction of a like nature and extent as that held and exercised in criminal matters by the High Court of Justice and the Crown Court in England, respectively, as well as any other jurisdiction, whether original or appellate, conferred on it by any law (HCO section 12(3)).

Although the High Court is said to have unlimited original jurisdiction, it only deals with the more serious criminal cases in practice. These are cases transferred to the CFI following committal of a defendant to trial under MO Part III. There are a number of offences that can only be proceeded by way of indictment and which must be dealt with in the CFI. These are listed in Part III of the Second Schedule to the MO, and include treason, blasphemy, genocide and offences punishable with imprisonment for life (subject to exceptions). Examples of offences punishable with life imprisonment which can only be tried in the CFI include murder and manslaughter (*Offences Against the Person Ordinance* (Cap. 212) sections 2, 7), rape (*Crimes Ordinance* (Cap. 200) section 118), hostage taking (*Internationally Protected Persons and Taking of Hostages Ordinance* (Cap. 468) section 4) and certain terrorism-related offences (for example, *United Nations (Anti-Terrorism Measures) Ordinance* (Cap. 575) sections 11B, 14).

For those indictable offences that can also be tried before the DC, the prosecution may elect to have the matter dealt with in the CFI if the sentence sought would be more than seven years' imprisonment. The CFI can impose any sentence up to the maximum prescribed for the offence in the relevant ordinance that sets out the offence. Apart from cases of murder, manslaughter and rape, other types of offences usually dealt with in the CFI include armed robbery, trafficking in large quantities of dangerous drugs, and complex commercial fraud.

The CFI also has appellate jurisdiction covering appeals from the decisions of magistrates (MO sections 105, 113).

Pre-trial procedures and arraignment of the accused

Where there was a paper committal pursuant to MO section 80C(4), the prosecution initiates proceedings in the CFI by delivering a signed indictment to the

Registrar of the High Court within seven days of such committal (CPO section 14(1)(a)). Where there was a preliminary inquiry, then the prosecution files the indictment upon receipt of the documents relating to the case following committal (CPO section 14(1)(b)).

The indictment contains a statement of the specific offence with which the accused person is charged describing the offence, together with such particulars as may be necessary for giving reasonable information as to the nature of the charge. The form and requirements for the indictment are set out in the *Indictment Rules* (Cap. 221C).

The Registrar files the indictment in the court (CPO section 26) and endorses on the indictment a notice of trial specifying the date on which the accused is required to attend before the court to answer to the indictment (CPO section 27). A copy of the indictment is delivered to the bailiff for service on the accused (CPO sections 28, 29).

Certain pre-trial case management procedures are set out in *Practice Direction 9.3 – Criminal Proceedings in the Court of First Instance* (The Judiciary, 1998). For example, the prosecution may serve on the accused or his solicitor a notice to admit facts, and the solicitor for the accused may serve a notice in reply stating which facts are admitted. Not fewer than four days before the date fixed for trial, the judge may require counsel for the prosecution and the defence to attend a meeting in chambers before the judge for a pre-trial review. At the pre-trial review, counsel would be expected to inform the judge of various matters, including the pleas to be tendered at trial, which prosecution witnesses are to be called, whether expert testimony is to be called, any alibi of the accused (if not already disclosed pursuant to CPO section 65D), and any point of law that may arise in the trial.

On the trial day (the date appointed for the arraignment), the accused appears before the court to plead to the indictment. Arraignment consists of the reading of the indictment to the accused and asking the accused whether he or she pleads guilty (*R v Ellis* (1973) 57 Cr App R 571; CPO section 49). If the accused pleads guilty, then the judge may proceed to deal with sentencing or there may be an adjournment for the sentencing hearing to be conducted on a later day. If the accused pleads not guilty, then the jury is empanelled in order for the trial to commence.

Jury system

Criminal trials in the CFI are conducted before a judge and jury (CPO section 41(2)). The judge decides on questions of law, while the jury decides on questions of fact. Jurors are private citizens and are selected randomly to act pursuant to the *Jury Ordinance* (Cap. 3) (JO). In determining the guilt or innocence of the accused, the judge directs the jury on the relevant law and the jury then decides whether the accused is guilty in light of the facts as ascertained in the trial.

The system of trial by jury was introduced in Hong Kong in 1845 in the early years of the establishment of Hong Kong as a British colony (Duff et al., 1992). The principle of being tried by a jury of the defendant's peers under English common law was reflected in Magna Carta, though the concept can be traced back to even earlier times (Devlin, 1966; Davies, 2004).

It has been said that '[t]he purpose of a jury is to guard against the exercise of arbitrary power – to make available the common sense judgment of the community as a hedge against the overzealous or mistaken prosecutor and in preference to the professional or perhaps over-conditioned or biased response of a judge' (*Taylor v Louisiana* 419 US 522, 530 (1975)). Thus, in addition to its role in deciding on the facts of a case, the jury can also act as a check against the power of the state. As Lord Devlin has observed: 'No tyrant could afford to leave a subject's freedom in the hands of twelve of his countrymen. So that trial by jury is more than an instrument of justice and more than one wheel of the constitution: it is the lamp that shows that freedom lives' (Devlin, 1966).

The jury is able to take on the above role because an acquittal of a defendant by the jury cannot be appealed against by the prosecution. A jury's acquittal stands even if it is contrary to the evidence or the directions of the judge on the applicable law. A juror who decides contrary to the judge's directions could be in contempt of court if the juror acted dishonestly, namely with an intention to impede or create a real risk of prejudicing the administration of justice. However, the function of deciding the facts and on the verdict is placed on the jury and not the judge, and a juror cannot be punished for contempt merely because the judge considers that the jury's decision was wrong (*Bushell's Case* (1670) Vaugh 135, 124 ER 1006; *R v Schot* [1997] 2 Cr App R 383; Crosby, 2012). In practice, dishonesty on the part of a juror may be difficult to prove, especially since the jury does not give reasons for its verdict and no records are kept of the jury's deliberations. Disclosure of the deliberations of a jury can itself amount to a contempt of court if the disclosure tends or would tend to imperil the finality of jury verdicts, or to affect adversely the attitude of future jurors and the quality of their deliberations (*Attorney-General v New Statesman and Nation Publishing Co Ltd* [1980] 2 WLR 246).

Notwithstanding the above, it seems that in practice juries do not often reach verdicts against the evidence or the law (Koo, 2010). This is appropriate if the laws in a society are by and large just.

In Hong Kong, a jury consists of seven persons, though it is also possible for the court to make an order for the jury to consist of nine persons (JO section 3). The court might make such an order, for example, if the trial is expected to be long, so that the trial can continue even if a member of the jury withdraws. In all cases, a jury can continue to act if it consists of no fewer than five persons (JO section 25(4)).

Hong Kong residents who are 21 years of age or above, but below 65, are liable to serve as a juror as long as they are of sound mind and not afflicted by blindness, deafness or other disability preventing the person from serving as a juror, are of good character, and have sufficient knowledge of the language in which the proceedings are to be conducted to be able to understand the proceedings (JO section 4). Certain categories of persons are exempted from service as juror, as set out in JO section 5. These include legal practitioners, medical practitioners, full-time students, pilots and air crew, police, and others. Such persons are exempted because, for example, they are themselves involved in the administration of justice (such that unfairness may result or may be perceived to result), or there may be undue hardship or substantial inconvenience caused to the person or to the public if they were required to serve as juror (Law Reform Commission of Hong Kong, 2008). In England, the list of exempted persons is much narrower (*Juries Act 1974*, as amended by the *Criminal Justice Act 2003*).

By 1 October every two years, the registrar of the High Court compiles a provisional list of jurors (JO sections 7, 9). Persons who are to be newly added to the list are notified by the registrar. If a person is exempt, he or she can write to the registrar stating the grounds of the exemption claimed. The registrar publishes the final list of jurors by 1 February of the following year (JO section 10).

Whenever it is necessary to summon a jury, the registrar randomly selects, by ballot or by any other random means, a certain number of jurors to form a panel of jurors (JO section 13). The registrar then issues a summons to the selected persons requiring their attendance at court on the specified day (JO section 17).

The jury is formed by selection from the panel of jurors. The panel is brought before the court if the accused has pleaded not guilty. Each panel member is allocated a number, and the numbers are printed on separate cards and put in a box. The registrar or a clerk of the court then, in open court, draws from the box (JO section 21).

After a name is drawn, the defence may challenge the selected juror – that is, object to the selected person from being on the jury in the case. The defence may challenge up to five jurors without cause (that is, without any reason being given), and any number of jurors for cause (JO section 29). A challenge could be made, for example, if the person is unqualified (*R v Tremearne* (1826) 5 B & C 254, 108 ER 95) or is biased or prejudiced (*R v Martin* (1848) 6 State Tr NS 925). The prosecution may also ask for any selected juror to 'stand by' and not be included in the jury without the need for any reason to be given. If the panel has been exhausted of potential jurors, then the prosecution can still challenge selected jurors for cause (Whitford 2012). The prosecution's right to challenge is provided for under common law (for example, see *R v Swain* (1838) 2 Mood & R 112, 174 ER 232).

After the jurors are selected, they take their seats in the jury box and are sworn in by taking an oath or affirmation.

The trial

The trial procedure is largely the same as in the DC, but with some differences to take into account the presence of a jury. The prosecution gives its opening address and there is then examination in chief and cross-examination (and re-examination, if necessary) of each prosecution witness.

At the end of the prosecution case, the judge considers whether there is a case for the accused to answer. The jury should not be present when submissions are made on whether there is a case to answer since this is a legal question for the judge to determine (*Crosdale v R* [1995] 1 WLR 864). There is no case to answer if there is no evidence that the accused had committed the crime or if the evidence is tenuous and, taken at its highest, is such that a properly directed jury could not properly convict on it (*R v Galbraith* [1981] 1 WLR 1039). In such a situation, the jury returns to court and would be directed by the judge to return a not guilty verdict.

If there is a case to answer, the defence then presents its case. The accused may, if he or she chooses, give evidence and other defence witnesses may also be called. Any witnesses (including the accused) called to give evidence are examined in chief, cross-examined and may also be re-examined. At the end of the defence case, the prosecution and defence each give their closing addresses.

After the closing address for the defence, the judge sums up to the jury. The judge sums up the facts and gives the jury directions as to the law that they must apply in deciding on the verdict (for example, see *HKSAR v Lung Cheuk Tong* [1999] 4 HKC 179).

The verdict

Following the completion of the summing up, the jury retires to the jury room to consider its verdict. Jurors can only discuss the case amongst themselves. During the course of the trial, jurors are not permitted to discuss the case with others; otherwise they commit contempt of court (*Ellis v Deheer* [1922] 2 KB 113, 118). The jury must make their decision solely on the basis of the evidence and the arguments presented in court. Jurors who conduct their own research on the case, such as in visiting the crime scene or researching information from the Internet, commit contempt (*Attorney-General v Dallas* [2012] 1 WLR 991) and any guilty verdict that results is liable to be set aside on appeal (*R v Karakaya* [2005] 2 Cr App R 5; *HKSAP v Chan Huandai* [2016] 2 HKLRD 384). However, a conviction would not be set aside merely because there has been publicity about the accused and the case in the media, as jurors can generally be expected to comply with the judge's directions to disregard anything that they may have read or heard about outside court (*Hughes v R* [2015] NSWCCA 330).

If the jury requires further assistance, then the jury foreman can put a question in writing to the judge. Both the prosecution and defence would be notified of the request and may be given an opportunity to make submissions to the judge on the appropriate answer. The jury is then brought back to court for the judge to give directions in answer to the question.

If the jury cannot reach a verdict in one day, they will be given accommodation in rooms in the High Court building and would resume their deliberations in the jury room the next day. The jurors are not permitted to speak to others in order to avoid their decision being affected by outside influences.

If a unanimous decision of the jurors cannot be reached, then after reasonable consultation, it is possible for a verdict to be decided upon by a majority in accordance with JO section 24. Decisions on the verdict can be made by a majority of 5:2 if the jury is composed of seven members. Where there is a jury of nine persons, then it is necessary for a majority of 7:2. If a nine-member jury is reduced to eight persons (where a juror had been discharged prior to the verdict pursuant to JO section 25, such as where a juror suffered from serious illness that rendered him or her incapable of continuing as juror), then the required majority is 6:2. If a jury is reduced to six members, the verdict must be by a majority of 5:1; and if the jury is reduced to five, the decision must be unanimous.

The trial judge should not give directions that place undue pressure on the jury to reach a verdict (*Cai Zong Gang v HKSAR* (2009) 12 HKCFAR 494). When it sufficiently appears to the court that no majority for either a guilty or not guilty verdict can be reached by the jury, then the jury must be discharged (JO section 27). A new jury is empanelled and the trial is re-commenced before the new jury. However, where the jury was unable to reach a verdict, it is possible for the prosecution to take the option of offering no further evidence, in which case the jury would be directed to acquit. There is a practice, but not a rule of law, for the prosecution to offer no evidence if the accused has been tried twice and both juries were unable to reach a verdict, but whether that is appropriate would depend on the circumstances of the case (*HKSAR v Hau King Yeung* [2006] HKEC 2070).

If the jury convicts the accused, then sentencing is dealt with by the judge. The jury is not involved in sentencing. The CFI has power to impose the maximum sentence as prescribed for the offence under the law.

Appeals against verdict and/or sentence

A convicted person may appeal to the Court of Appeal (CA) against a conviction on a question of law or fact (CPO section 82(2)). The defendant may also seek to appeal against the sentence to the CA (CPO sections 83G, 83I).

The prosecution does not have a right of appeal against an acquittal by a jury. The prosecution may refer to the CA a question of law that arose in the case, but such a reference does not affect the acquittal (CPO section 81D). The prosecution may seek to apply to the CA for a review of the sentence (CPO section 81A).

Appeals to CFI from magistrate's decision

As discussed earlier, decisions from the MC can be appealed to the CFI on questions of law under the case stated procedure in MO section 105 by either the prosecution or the defendant. The defendant can also use the alternative procedure in MO section 113 to appeal against both findings of fact and decisions on the law.

The application for an appeal by way of case stated must be made to the magistrate within 14 days of the magistrate's determination (MO section 105). The magistrate then states and signs a case setting forth the facts and the grounds for the conviction or determination for the opinion of the CFI. Within 14 days of the delivery of the case from the magistrate to the applicant, the applicant is required to transmit the case to the registrar of the High Court and to give written notice of the appeal to the other party (MO section 106).

In the case of the alternative procedure, the convicted person must also lodge the appeal within 14 days of the day of the conviction (MO section 114(a)). The application is made to the magistrate's clerk, and the magistrate must then prepare a signed statement of his or her findings on the facts and other grounds of his decision and cause a copy to be served on each of the parties within 15 days of the day on which the notice of appeal was given (MO section 114(b)).

The following applies for appeals under both section 105 and section 113, pursuant to sections 118 and 119. The appellant is heard first in support of the appeal, and the respondent may then be heard against the appeal. The depositions taken earlier in the trial before the magistrate are admissible as evidence before the CFI, but the CFI may also receive additional evidence in the form of oral testimony or by way of documentary evidence or any other exhibit (MO section 118(1)(a), (b); CPO section 83V).

The judge in the CFI may confirm, reverse or vary the magistrate's decision or may direct that the case shall be heard *de novo* by a magistrate or may remit the matter with his or her opinion to a magistrate (MO section 119(1)(d)). The judge can exercise any power that the magistrate might have exercised, and any decision or order made by the judge has the same effect as if it had been made by the magistrate (MO section 119(1)(d)).

The judge may reserve the appeal, or any point in the appeal for the consideration of the Court of Appeal (CA), or may direct the appeal, or point in the appeal, to be argued before the CA (MO section 118(1)(d)).

A decision of the CFI on appeal from the Magistrate's Court may be further appealed to the Court of Final Appeal at the instance of any party to the appeal, subject to leave being granted (*Hong Kong Court of Final Appeal Ordinance* (Cap. 484) section 31).

Court of Appeal of the High Court

Introduction

The Court of Appeal (CA) exercises the appellate jurisdiction of the High Court in relation to both civil and criminal matters. The CA's powers are set out in the *High Court Ordinance* (Cap. 4) (HCO) and the court also has inherent powers as a superior court. The provisions on appeals from the DC and CFI to the CA are mainly dealt with under CPO sections 80–83Z.

The eligibility requirements to be appointed as a judge of the CA are the same as in the CFI, pursuant to HCO section 9.

In the hearing of an appeal, there are generally three judges sitting in the CA, but there can be more, as long as there is an uneven number of judges (HCO section 34).

Jurisdiction

The CA has criminal jurisdiction to hear appeals and reviews as follows:

- Appeal from the MC to the CFI which is referred by the CFI to the CA (MO section 118(1)(d)).
- Appeal by the defendant against a conviction made in either the DC or the CFI (CPO section 82; DCO section 83).
- Appeal by the defendant against sentence imposed either in the DC or the CFI (CPO section 83G; DCO section 83).
- Appeal by the prosecution against an acquittal in the DC on questions of law (DCO section 84).
- Reference of question of law by prosecution following acquittal by a jury in the CFI (CPO section 81D).
- Review of sentence on application by the prosecution whether the sentence was handed down in the MC, DC or CFI (CPO section 81A).

Appeal against a magistrate's decision

If the CFI has reserved an appeal against a magistrate's decision for consideration by the CA pursuant to MO section 118(1)(d), then the CA has power to hear and determine such appeal, and in doing so, may exercise any of the powers conferred on a judge of the CFI by MO Part VII, which includes the power to hear new evidence and to exercise any of the powers exercisable by the magistrate in deciding the case afresh (MO section 118(1)(d)). Alternatively, the CA may remit the matter to the CFI with the opinion or decision of the CA and may also make any other order in relation to the matter and orders as to costs as the CA deems fit.

Appeal against convictions made in the DC or CFI

A person convicted in the DC or CFI may appeal to the CA without the need to obtain the leave of court if the appeal is on a ground that involves a question of law only (CPO section 82(2)(a)). An appeal may also be made on grounds involving questions of fact, or of mixed law and fact, or on any other ground that appears to the CA to be a sufficient ground of appeal (CPO section 82(2)(b)).

Leave is required under section 82(2)(b) unless, where the appeal is on a question of fact or mixed law and fact, the trial judge has granted a certificate that the case is fit for appeal.

Appeals on questions of law involve disputes over, for example, whether the court had correctly interpreted a legal rule or principle that was relevant to the case. An appeal on a question of fact involves a dispute over whether the judge (in a DC trial) or the jury (in a CFI trial) had correctly ascertained the facts of what happened. Questions of mixed law and fact involve both interpretation or application of a legal rule and the determination of fact. For example, it has been held that whether a signalling kit consisting of flares and a hand-held discharger was a firearm within the meaning of section 57(1) of the *Firearms Act 1968* (UK) was a question of mixed law and fact to be determined by reference to the statutory definition of 'firearm' and the factual material concerning the item in question (*R v Singh* (1989) Times, 29 May).

A convicted person who seeks to appeal must make the application within 28 days of the date of the conviction (CPO section 83Q).

In hearing an appeal, the CA does not try the case afresh, but deals with the grounds of appeal raised by the appellant. The CA may admit new evidence (whether oral testimony or evidence in the form of a document or other exhibit) if the court thinks it necessary or expedient in the interests of justice (CPO section 83V(1)). Where new evidence is tendered to the CA, then, unless the evidence would not afford any ground for allowing the appeal, the CA must allow the evidence to be admitted if: 1 the evidence is likely to be credible and would have been admissible in the proceedings from which the appeal lies on an issue that is the subject of the appeal; and 2 there is a reasonable explanation for the failure to adduce the evidence in the trial proceedings (CPO section 83V(2)). However, section 83V(2) does not apply if the fresh evidence is called to advance a completely fresh line of argument on which no issue had been taken in the trial court (*HKSAR v Lam Chun Wah* [1999] 2 HKC 731), though it is still possible for the CA to exercise its discretion to admit the evidence under section 83V(1).

For an appeal to succeed, the appellant must establish that:

- the conviction should be set aside on the ground that under all the circumstances of the case it is unsafe or unsatisfactory;
- the judgment of the trial court should be set aside on the ground of a wrong decision on any question of law; or
- there was a material irregularity in the course of the trial (CPO section 83(1)).

However, even if the appellant succeeds on a point raised in the appeal, the appeal will still be dismissed if the CA considers that no miscarriage of justice actually occurred (CPO section 83(1)).

In assessing whether a conviction is unsafe and unsatisfactory, the CA must ask itself whether it is content to let the matter stand as it is, or whether there is some lurking doubt that makes the court wonder whether an injustice has been done (*R v Cooper* (1968) 53 Cr App R 82, 86). However, since the witnesses do not ordinarily give their evidence afresh in the appellate court, with the court needing to rely on the transcripts of the oral evidence, the appellate court must bear in mind that it does not have the advantage of seeing the witnesses in person so as to be able to assess their credibility in the way that the jury or the trial judge is able to do. Thus 'lurking doubt' means a 'substantial remaining doubt' and not an 'insubstantial doubt' (*Tang Wai-tong v R* [1979] HKLR 479, 486). The conviction is not unsafe and unsatisfactory if there was evidence upon which a properly directed jury could conscientiously have convicted (*Kwong Kin Hung v R* [1997] HKLRD 15).

An example of where a conviction was set aside on the above ground is *HKSAR v Ling Kam Wah* [2002] 3 HKC 297, where the jury returned a verdict of guilty for the charge of manslaughter. The CA quashed the conviction, stating that '[i]n the present case, we have concluded that the number of conflicts [in the evidence] and the important nature of many of them, coupled with the improbabilities which we have itemised, were such that it is not possible to say that this conviction was safe'.

As for the ground of a wrong decision on a question of law, see for example *HKSAR v Sze Mei Mun* [2014] 5 HKC 513, where the CA held that the trial judge incorrectly interpreted the meaning of a statutory provision but where (applying the 'proviso' in CPO section 83(1) where there is no miscarriage of justice) the CA did not set aside the conviction because the erroneous determination of law was not applied by the judge to his analysis of the facts and there was overwhelming evidence to support the conviction.

On the third ground (namely, material irregularity), an example is *HKSAR v Chan Hoi Wing* [2015] 1 HKC 522. The CA noted that the right of the prosecution to make a closing speech differs depending on whether the defendant is legally represented. In order for the defendant to receive a fair trial, the rule is that where a defendant is not legally represented and called no witnesses, then even though he gave evidence for himself, the prosecution is not entitled to make a closing speech. In this case, the prosecution was improperly allowed to make a closing speech, which amounted to a material irregularity sufficient for the CA to allow the appeal against conviction.

Where the CA allows an appeal, the conviction is quashed and the trial court is required to enter a verdict of acquittal (CPO section 83(2), (3)). However, the CA may substitute a conviction of an alternative offence (CPO section 83A) instead, or order a retrial of the defendant if the interests of justice so require (CPO section 83E). For example, a retrial was ordered in the above case of *HKSAR v Chan Hoi Wing* [2015] 1 HKC 522.

Appeal against a sentence by the defendant

A convicted person may appeal against a sentence imposed in the DC or CFI, but only with leave of the CA (CPO sections 83G, 83I).

The grounds for such an appeal are: where the sentence is wrong in principle (for example, wrong as a matter of law); where the sentence is manifestly excessive; or where the sentence is based on a wrong factual premise or matters were wrongly taken into account or the circumstances have changed significantly since the imposition of the sentence (Whitford 2012).

For example, in *Mahal v HKSAR* [2012] 1 HKC 146, the defendant was convicted of rape and indecent assault and sentenced to seven and a half years' and six years' imprisonment, respectively (to be served concurrently). The CA accepted that there were certain aggravating factors which justified a longer period of imprisonment than would otherwise be the case (including using deception to trick the victim and excessive force in carrying out the rape, and abandoning use of a condom), but the resulting sentences were still manifestly excessive. The CA substituted sentences of six and a half years' and five years' imprisonment for the two offences (to be served concurrently).

Appeal by prosecution against acquittal in the DC

Under DCO section 84, the prosecution may appeal to the CA against a verdict of acquittal handed down in the DC. The appeal can only relate to matters of law. At the hearing of the appeal, the CA must dismiss the appeal if it is satisfied that there is no sufficient ground for interfering. If the CA allows the appeal, the CA reverses the verdict and may direct that the accused be retried. Alternatively, the CA may find the accused guilty and record a conviction and pass such sentence on the accused as might have been passed on him or her by a judge (DCO section 84(c)).

Reference by prosecution on a question of law following jury acquittal

Although the prosecution cannot appeal against a jury's decision to acquit a defendant made in the CFI, the prosecution can, following an acquittal, rely on CPO section 81D to refer a question of law that arose in the case to the CA to seek the CA's opinion on the matter. The reference does not affect the trial nor the acquittal (CPO section 81D(4)), and hence the acquittal by the jury must stand. Section 81D can be relied upon not only for heavy questions of law but also short but important points which require a quick ruling of the court before a potentially false decision of law has too wide a circulation in the courts (*Attorney-General's Reference (No. 1 of 1975)* [1975] QB 773, 776).

Review of sentence on application by prosecution

Under CPO section 81A, the prosecution may, with leave of the CA, apply to the CA for the review of a sentence on the grounds that the sentence is not authorised by law, is wrong in principle, or is manifestly excessive or manifestly inadequate. If any of these grounds are established, the CA may quash the original sentence and pass a new sentence in substitution as the court thinks ought to have been passed (CPO section 81B(1)). The substituted sentence may be more or less severe than the original sentence.

For example, in *Secretary for Justice v Chau Tsz Tim* [2015] 2 HKC 88, sentences for detention at a training centre handed down to the defendants (who were 17 and 18 at the time of the offences) for convictions for serious drug trafficking (0.14 kg of ketamine and 35.05 g of cocaine) were held to be manifestly inadequate. The CA held that although young age is often a mitigating factor and rehabilitation is important, it is necessary to impose a sentence to deter others for serious drug trafficking cases. The court held that the training centre orders were unduly lenient and fell outside the range of sentences that a judge could reasonably consider appropriate. The CA substituted sentences of four years' imprisonment each for the defendants.

Court of Final Appeal

The Court of Final Appeal (CFA) was established pursuant to *Basic Law* article 81 and the *Hong Kong Court of Final Appeal Ordinance* (Cap. 484) (HKCFAO) section 3. The CFA is a superior court of record, and (upon the transfer of sovereignty in 1997) replaced the UK Privy Council as the highest court in Hong Kong, being vested with the final power of adjudication in the HKSAR under article 82. The CFA has both civil and criminal jurisdiction. In the case of criminal matters, appeals from the CA (and in certain situations from the CFI) lie with the CFA, at the CFA's discretion (HKCFAO section 31).

The CFA, in hearing an appeal, is to consist of the chief justice, three permanent judges of the court, and either one non-permanent Hong Kong judge or one judge from another common law jurisdiction (HKCFAO section 16). Under HKCFAO sections 7–9, there must be at least three permanent judges appointed to the court and there must also be kept a list of non-permanent Hong Kong judges and a list of judges from other common law jurisdictions. The possibility of inviting judges from other common law jurisdictions to sit on the CFA is enshrined in article 82 of the *Basic Law*. This was proposed to ensure that there would be available judges of the highest calibre to replace the Privy Council, and to enhance the prospects of the court maintaining its independence (Ghai, 1999; Lo and Chui, 2012). A number of pre-eminent Law Lords of the former House of Lords and the present Supreme Court in the UK and former justices of the High Court of Australia (the highest court in Australia) have, for example, been appointed as non-permanent judges to the CFA.

HKCFAO section 12 sets out the qualifications for appointment to the CFA. A person may be appointed as the chief justice or a permanent judge of the CFA if he or she is a judge of the High Court or a barrister who has practised as a barrister or solicitor in Hong Kong for a period of at least ten years. Retired chief justices and retired permanent judges of the CFA, retired judges of the High Court, and barristers with the above-mentioned experience can be appointed as non-permanent Hong Kong judges. The following persons can be appointed as a non-permanent judge from another common law jurisdiction: judges or retired judges of a court of unlimited jurisdiction in another common law jurisdiction who are ordinarily resident outside Hong Kong and who have never been a judge or magistrate in Hong Kong.

Criminal jurisdiction

Under HKCFAO section 31, an appeal lies, at the discretion of the CFA, in any criminal case, at the instance of any party to the proceedings, from: 1 any final decision of the CA; or 2 any final decision of the CFI (not being a verdict or finding of a jury) from which no appeal lies to the CA. Appeals from the MC which are heard in the CFI can accordingly be further appealed to the CFA under section 31(b).

Leave to appeal

Pursuant to HKCFAO section 32, there are two grounds for seeking leave to appeal: 1 that a point of law of great and general importance is involved; or 2 that substantial and grave injustice has been done.

Where an application involves the first ground, the applicant should first seek a certification from the CA or the CFI, as the case may be (depending on whether the appeal is from the CA or the CFI), that a point of law of great and general importance is involved in the decision. Leave to appeal must then be obtained from the CFA (HKCFAO section 32(1)). Even if the lower court has certified a point of law, the CFA has discretion whether or not to grant leave (*HKSAR v VW-Ves (HK) Ltd* (2015) 18 HKCFAR 84). If the CA or the CFI, as the case may be, declines to certify as mentioned above, application may be made to the CFA for certification and the granting of leave (HKCFAO section 32(3)).

Where an application involves the second ground (namely 'substantial and grave injustice'), there is no need to seek certification from the lower court, and the application for leave should be addressed directly to the CFA (*Zeng Liang Xin v HKSAR* (1997–98) 1 HKCFAR 12).

The application to the CFA for leave must be made within 28 days of the date of the decision of the CA or the CFI, as the case may be (HKCFAO section 33(1)).

Role of the CFA in hearing appeals

The thresholds in section 32 mean that it is not always possible for the matter to be taken to the CFA. As stated by Bokhary PJ in *So Yiu Fung v HKSAR* (1999) 2 HKCFAR 539, 541–542:

> This Court's primary role in the administration of criminal justice is to resolve real controversy on points of law of great and general

> importance. For this Court does not function as a court of criminal appeal in the ordinary way. However the 'substantial and grave injustice' limb of s. 32(2) exists as a residual safeguard to cater for those rare and exceptional cases in which there is a real danger of something so seriously wrong that justice demands an enquiry by way of a final criminal appeal despite the absence of any real controversy on any point of law of great and general importance.

In the above case, the CFA further held that where the appellant was granted leave to appeal on the basis that it is reasonably arguable that substantial and grave injustice has been done, then in order for the appellant to succeed at the substantive hearing of the appeal, the appellant must show that there has been to the appellant's disadvantage a departure from accepted norms that is so serious as to constitute a substantial and grave injustice. This is more difficult to establish than simply showing that the conviction is unsafe or unsatisfactory.

The prosecution can also appeal against acquittals on the ground of substantial and grave injustice within section 32(2) but, like all appeals on that ground, it will be rare for leave to be granted. In *HKSAR v To Chak Hang* (2015) 18 HKCFAR 541, the CFA declined leave in relation to an application to appeal a decision of the CFI under which a conviction in the magistracy of causing death by dangerous driving was quashed but where the CFI declined to substitute a conviction of careless driving.

Powers of the CFA in hearing an appeal

Under HKCFAO section 17(1), the CFA may confirm, reverse or vary the decision of the court from which the appeal lies or may remit the matter with its opinion to that court, or may make such other order in the matter, including any order as to costs, as it thinks fit. The CFA may exercise any powers of the court from which the appeal lies (including the power to order a retrial), or may remit the case to that court (HKCFAO section 17(2)).

Conclusion

This chapter has outlined the system of criminal courts in Hong Kong. Criminal prosecutions of persons alleged to have committed an offence start in the MC. The trial is conducted in the MC if the offence is dealt with summarily. If an offence is to be dealt with on indictment, then the matter is transferred to either the DC or the CFI. Only the most serious cases are heard in the CFI.

Cases heard in the MC are dealt with by a magistrate, and cases in the DC are heard by a judge sitting alone. By contrast, trials in the CFI are heard before a judge and jury. In the CFI, the judge decides on questions of law while the jury determines the facts and decides whether the accused is to be convicted or is to be acquitted.

A person who is convicted has the right to appeal against the conviction and/or the sentence. A conviction in the MC may be appealed by the convicted to the CFI (on the ground of error in the magistrate's determination of either the law or facts), and the CFI's decision may be appealed further to the CFA subject to the CFA granting leave. A convicted person may appeal from decisions of the DC or CFI to the CA (on either questions of law or fact), though leave of the CA (or certification from the trial judge) is required unless the matter involves a question of law only. A further appeal from the decision of the CA to the CFA may be possible, subject to leave granted by the CFA.

The prosecution has more limited rights of appeal where the defendant is acquitted. The prosecution may appeal acquittals in the MC (to the CFI) or the DC (to the CA) on questions of law only. Further appeal to the CFA from the decision of the appellate court may be possible, but leave of the CFA is required. The prosecution cannot appeal an acquittal by the jury in the CFI, though it can seek an authoritative decision of the CA on questions of law that arose in the case. As for sentencing, it is possible for the prosecution to seek a review of a sentence in the CA, whether handed down in the MC, DC or CFI.

Review questions

1. What is the difference between a summary offence and an indictable offence?
2. What factors determine whether an accused person would be tried in the Magistrates' Court, District Court or Court of First Instance? In which court are most criminal cases heard?
3. What is the role of the jury in criminal trials?
4. Rick has been charged with murder. In which court would his trial be heard and why?
5. If Rick is found guilty and is convicted for murder, can he challenge either the conviction or the sentence, and if so, how and on what grounds?
6. Why are the rights of appeal of the prosecution more limited compared with the rights of appeal of a convicted person?
7. What are the differences between the appellate role of the Court of Appeal and the Court of Final Appeal?

References

Crosby, K. (2012) 'Bushell's case and the juror's soul', *Journal of Legal History*, 33(3): 251–290.

Davies, C. (2004) '"A jury of peers": A comparative analysis', *Journal of Criminal Law*, 68(2): 150–159.

Department of Justice (2013) *The Prosecution Code*, Hong Kong: Department of Justice.

Devlin, P. (1966) *Trial by Jury*, London: Stevens & Sons.

Devlin, P. (1979) *The Judge*, Oxford: Oxford University Press.

Duff, P., Findlay, M., Howarth, C. and Chan, T-f. (1992) *Juries: A Hong Kong Perspective*, Hong Kong: Hong Kong University Press.

Ghai, Y. (1999) *Hong Kong's New Constitutional Order: The Resumption of Chinese Sovereignty and the Basic Law* (2nd edn), Hong Kong: Hong Kong University Press.

Henderson, E. (2015) 'Theoretically speaking: English judges and advocates discuss the changing theory of cross-examination', *Criminal Law Review*, 12: 929–948.

Hong Kong Police Force (2016) *Police General Orders Available to the Public*, Hong Kong: Hong Kong Police Force, www.police.gov.hk/ppp_en/11_useful_info/pgo.html (accessed 15 February 2016).

The Judiciary (1998) *Practice Direction 9.3 – Criminal Proceedings in the Court of First Instance*, Hong Kong: The Judiciary.

The Judiciary (2014) *Hong Kong Judiciary Annual Report 2014*, Hong Kong: The Judiciary.

Koo, F. (2010) 'Power to the people: Extending the jury to the Hong Kong's District Court', *City University of Hong Kong Law Review*, 2: 301–329.

Law Reform Commission of Hong Kong (2008) *Criteria for Service as Jurors: Consultation Paper*, Hong Kong: Law Reform Commission of Hong Kong.

Lo, S. and Chui, W.H. (2012) *Hong Kong Legal System*, Singapore: McGraw-Hill.

Whitford, A. (2012) *Criminal Procedure in Hong Kong* (2nd edn), Hong Kong: LexisNexis.

Legislation cited

Basic Law of the Hong Kong Special Administrative Region
Crimes Ordinance (Cap. 200)
Criminal Justice Act 2003 (UK)
Criminal Procedure Ordinance (Cap. 221)
Dangerous Drugs Ordinance (Cap. 134)
District Court Ordinance (Cap. 336)
Firearms Act 1968 (UK)
Gambling Ordinance (Cap. 148)
High Court Ordinance (Cap. 4)
Hong Kong Court of Final Appeal Ordinance (Cap. 484)
Indictment Rules (Cap. 221C)
Internationally Protected Persons and Taking of Hostages Ordinance (Cap. 468)
Juries Act 1974 (UK)
Jury Ordinance (Cap. 3)
Juvenile Offenders Ordinance (Cap. 226)
Magistrates' Ordinance (Cap. 227)
Offences Against the Person Ordinance (Cap. 212)
Police Force Ordinance (Cap. 232)
Summary Offences Ordinance (Cap. 228)
Theft Ordinance (Cap. 210)
United Nations (Anti-Terrorism Measures) Ordinance (Cap. 575)

Cases cited

Attorney-General v Dallas [2012] 1 WLR 991
Attorney-General v New Statesman and Nation Publishing Co Ltd [1980] 2 WLR 246

Attorney-General's Reference (No. 1 of 1975) [1975] QB 773
Bushell's Case (1670) Vaugh 135, 124 ER 1006
Cai Zong Gang v HKSAR (2009) 12 HKCFAR 494
Crosdale v R [1995] 1 WLR 864
Ellis v Deheer [1922] 2 KB 113
HKSAR v Chan Hoi Wing [2015] 1 HKC 522
HKSAR v Chan Huandai [2016] 2 HKLRD 384
HKSAR v Hau King Yeung [2006] HKEC 2070
HKSAR v Lam Chun Wah [1999] 2 HKC 731
HKSAR v Law Ka Kit [2003] 2 HKC 178
HKSAR v Ling Kam Wah [2002] 3 HKC 297
HKSAR v Lung Cheuk Tong [1999] 4 HKC 179
HKSAR v Sze Mei Mun [2014] 5 HKC 513
HKSAR v To Chak Hang (2015) 18 HKCFAR 541
HKSAR v VW-Ves (HK) Ltd (2015) 18 HKCFAR 84
Hughes v R [2015] NSWCCA 330
Kwong Kin Hung v R [1997] HKLRD 15
Mahal v HKSAR [2012] 1 HKC 146
R v Cooper (1968) 53 Cr App R 82
R v Ellis (1973) 57 Cr App R 571
R v Galbraith [1981] 1 WLR 1039
R v Karakaya [2005] 2 Cr App R 5
R v Martin (1848) 6 State Tr NS 925
R v Schot [1997] 2 Cr App R 383
R v Singh (1989) Times, 29 May
R v Swain (1838) 2 Mood & R 112, 174 ER 232
R v Tremearne (1826) 5 B & C 254, 108 ER 95
Secretary for Justice v Chau Tsz Tim [2015] 2 HKC 88
So Yiu Fung v HKSAR (1999) 2 HKCFAR 539
Tang Wai-tong v R [1979] HKLR 479
Taylor v Louisiana 419 US 522, 530 (1975)
Waroquiers v Marsden [1950] 2 KB 1
Zeng Liang Xin v HKSAR (1997–98) 1 HKCFAR 12

Useful websites

Bilingual Laws Information System (BLIS) (Hong Kong) www.legislation.gov.hk/eng/index.htm
Department of Justice, HKSAR www.doj.gov.hk
Duty Lawyer Service www.dutylawyer.org.hk
Hong Kong Bar Association www.hkba.org
Hong Kong Legal Information Institute www.hklii.hk/eng/
The Judiciary www.judiciary.gov.hk/en/index/index.htm
Law Society of Hong Kong www.hklawsoc.org.hk
Legal Aid Department www.lad.gov.hk

15

SENTENCING

Simon N.M. Young

Introduction

Sentencing is one of the most important aspects of the criminal process. The sentencing judge must take into account a multitude of factors including the interests of the offender, the victim and society in arriving at a just and appropriate sentence. Errors made in the sentencing process can result in the excessive detention of an individual, the premature release of a dangerous offender, aggrieved victims who feel justice has not been done, and other issues. Sentencing can also be highly political, with governments using sentencing reform as a way to curry favour with voters attracted to 'get tough on crime' policies. In Hong Kong, however, with its developing state of democracy, the politicisation of sentencing has not been seen, and indeed one might criticise the legislature for giving insufficient attention to the topic generally.

This chapter outlines the main sentencing options currently available in Hong Kong before discussing the various purposes and principles of sentencing that the judge or magistrate must consider and apply in determining the punishment to be given in a particular case.

Punishment and sentencing

Every child knows (or should know) that doing something 'bad' or 'wrong' will usually be met by 'punishment' of some form from one's parents. In this everyday sense, punishment is a response from an authority figure to misbehaviour. In law, the word 'punishment' is reserved for the category of misconduct that constitutes a criminal offence. Punishment is the response of a court to a person's criminal conduct. By contrast, if a person is ordered to pay damages in a civil lawsuit or subject to discipline by a professional body, these measures are not typically described as punishment. Thus the word punishment carries with it a special meaning and signifies censure from a court for breaching criminal laws (von Hirsch, 1993). Easton and Piper (2005: 4) note that punishment 'rests on a moral foundation' and 'stems from an authoritative source, usually the state'.

Sentencing is the legal process by which a person is punished by a court. The law of sentencing is concerned with how and how much a person should be punished for the criminal offence(s) he or she has committed. In every case, the court balances the purposes of sentencing and applies established sentencing principles in accordance with the law to reach a just and appropriate sentence given the circumstances of the offence and the offender.

Before moving on, a word should be said about the classical debate over the theories and justification of punishment. Punishment theories generally fall within two schools of thought. The *utilitarian* school justifies punishment as a means to achieving the greatest good for the greatest number. While punishment is a source of unhappiness for the offender, it is nevertheless able to bring about a greater good in its direct and indirect consequences, e.g. deterring the offender and others from causing further harm in society. The competing school of thought is concerned more with the particular offender and his or her criminal offence. Punishment is justified as *just desert* for the crime committed by the offender. In other words, a person who commits a criminal offence deserves to be punished and how much he or she deserves is measured by the extent of the offender's wrongdoing and blameworthiness. The essential difference between the two schools is that the former treats the offender and his or her punishment as a means to a greater end while the latter respects the autonomy of the offender and treats his or her punishment as an end in and of itself. As will be seen, Hong Kong's system of sentencing may appear incoherent at times as it reflects elements of both schools of thought.

Sentencing options

Sentencing options lie along a spectrum of severity and can serve different purposes. The range of options changes with time and place. As you read about the different sentencing options, reflect upon why certain options exist and the purposes they are meant to achieve. Describing them as options is not meant to suggest that the court can freely choose any option to apply in a given case. Both the law and sentencing principles will constrain the range of options on the basis of the circumstances of each case.

Death and corporal punishment

The death penalty in Hong Kong was abolished in 1993, and the last execution by hanging took place in 1966 (Cross and Cheung, 1994: 32). Death was the punishment for the offences of murder, treason and piracy with violence (Liu, 1992). In the period before the formal abolition of the death penalty, death sentences imposed were commuted to sentences of life imprisonment. Corporal punishment, although it once existed in Hong Kong primarily in the form of caning, was abolished in 1990 (Cross and Cheung, 1994: 20). While both these sentencing options are now part of Hong Kong's criminal justice history, it should not be forgotten that they remain popular sentencing measures in many other Asian jurisdictions. For example, a Singapore court recently upheld the constitutionality of the use of caning in that jurisdiction (see *Yong Vui Kong v Public Prosecutor* [2015] 2 SLR 1129 (CA)).

Imprisonment

Jail is the typical sentencing option in the mind of most people. Jail sentences can range from a term as short as 'to the rising of the court' (see *White v Brown* (2003) 175 FLR 325), to one as long as life imprisonment, the most severe sentence available in Hong Kong. Statutory offences will normally specify a maximum term of imprisonment, and very few offences in Hong Kong carry a minimum term. When a judge orders different terms of imprisonment for several offences, he or she must specify whether the terms are to run at the same time (i.e. concurrent terms) or one after another (i.e. consecutive terms). It is a constitutional principle that a person who is imprisoned must 'be treated with humanity and with respect for the inherent dignity of the human person': Article 6(1) of the *Hong Kong Bill of Rights Ordinance* (Cap. 383).

Murder is the only offence that must be punished by life imprisonment, and a small category of serious offences, such as manslaughter, rape and robbery, can attract discretionary life sentences. When the judge sentences someone to a discretionary life sentence, the judge must also specify a minimum term in years that the person will have to serve before he or she can be released. There is no guarantee that the person will in fact be released after he or she has served the minimum term. Decisions concerning the release of such persons are made by the Long-term Prison Sentences Review Board (LTPSRB) and the chief executive (CE) in accordance with the *Long-term Prison Sentences Review Ordinance* (Cap. 524). A person who receives a mandatory life sentence for murder is not given a minimum term by the judge. Instead, his or her sentence is reviewed by the LTPSRB after five years of the sentence and every two years thereafter until he or she is released under the terms of the ordinance. Hong Kong courts have held this detention review mechanism to be constitutional.

Fine

The sentencing court has a discretionary power to impose a fine in lieu of or in addition to other forms of punishment. A fine serves a punitive purpose but should only be given if the offender is in a position to pay the fine. To enforce the fine, a default period of imprisonment up to 12 months may have to be served by the offender if he fails to pay the fine. Fines can range from HK$1 to HK$100,000 according to Schedule 8 in the *Criminal Procedure Ordinance* (Cap. 221); however, other ordinances may provide for much higher upper limits. For example, the indictable offence of making child pornography carries with it a maximum fine of HK$2,000,000. For some offences, the fine is at large, and there is no ceiling, although regard will be had to the capacity of the offender to pay in the calculation of the amount.

Suspended sentence

A person who receives a suspended sentence gets a chance to keep his or her freedom and to demonstrate his or her potential to rehabilitate. This option is only reserved for less serious wrongdoing, i.e. when the court orders a jail term of two years or less. Schedule 3 of the *Criminal Procedure Ordinance* lists a number of excluded offences including indecent assault and manslaughter for which no suspension is possible, even if the actual sentence is a term of jail within the two-year period. In February 2014, the Law Reform Commission of Hong Kong, persuaded by the findings of a report prepared by the University of Hong Kong's Centre for Comparative and Public Law and commissioned by the Law Society of Hong Kong, recommended that the list of excluded offences be abolished. The commission believed that 'judges and magistrates should not be restricted from exercising their discretion to achieve a just and appropriate sentence depending on the circumstances of the offence and the offender' (see Law Reform Commission of Hong Kong, 2014). Before suspending a sentence, a court should first decide that a term of imprisonment is required, and then satisfy itself that exceptional circumstances exist to justify its suspension (Cross et al., 2015: 541).

For a period of at least one year and up to three years, the offender must not commit another offence in Hong Kong punishable by imprisonment. Otherwise he or she may have to serve the original sentence, which had been suspended, along with any other sentence he or she might receive for the subsequent offence; however, at the court's discretion the two sentences may be ordered to be served concurrently either in whole or in part. When imposing a suspended sentence the court may also impose reasonable conditions to which the offender must adhere during the period of suspension, but it is rare for conditions to be imposed. Breach of a condition is tantamount to recommitting a further offence and can result in having to serve the original sentence. As conditions can attach to suspended sentences, the imposition of a simultaneous probation order for other offences is not allowed: section 109B(2) of the *Criminal Procedure Ordinance*. This prohibition does not, however, extend to the making on a later occasion of a probation order for some other offence (see *R v Tarry* [1970] 2 QB 560 (CA)).

Probation

A probation order requires the offender to be under the supervision of a probation officer and to adhere to certain conditions during the period of the order which must be at least one year in duration but no more than three years (see section 3 of the *Probation of Offenders Ordinance* (Cap. 298)). The conditions aim at securing the good conduct of the offender or to prevent re-offending by the offender. They can provide that the offender reside at a particular residence or approved youth institution but cannot require the offender to pay compensation (as compensation orders are provided for separately). The probation officer plays an important supervisory role in respect of the discharge, amendment and review of probation orders.

Like the suspended sentence, the probation order has rehabilitative aims and is a measure that gives the offender a second chance, albeit with some restrictions on his or her liberty. It is not available for offences whose sentence is fixed by law (e.g. murder), and when the judge orders probation he or she is not allowed to sentence the offender any further (see *R v Isherwood* (1974) 59 Cr App R 162 (CA)). Thus, probation is only an option for less serious offending and will not be available for serious offences, even if the offender has an impeccable background. It is a common method of dealing with juvenile offenders.

A probationer who breaches a condition of his or her probation order is required to return to court where he or she may be cautioned, fined up to HK $500, or in serious cases re-sentenced for the original offence as if he or she had just been convicted of it. If the probationer commits another offence during the period of the probation order, he or she will also be liable to be re-sentenced for the original offence in addition to any sentence received for the new offence (see Chapter 16 of this edited volume).

Community service

In 2002, the then young actor Nicholas Tse Ting-fung received a controversial community service order for perverting the course of justice by trying to conceal his responsibility for a vehicle accident. A community service order requires the offender to perform unpaid work in the community up to a maximum of 240 hours: *Community Service Orders Ordinance* (Cap. 378). Such orders can only be given to an offender of or over 14 years of age who consents to the order, and only after conviction for an offence punishable with imprisonment. The order will not be made if the judge finds that the offender is not a suitable person to perform work under such an order.

As with probation and suspended sentences, the community service order serves the primary purpose of rehabilitation with a meaningful degree of liberty restriction to convey a punitive message. This sentencing option was first introduced in 1984 following a study and report on the topic by the Law Reform Commission of Hong Kong (1983; see Chapter 16 of this edited volume).

Discharge

Where an offender is convicted of an offence, he may receive a conditional or absolute discharge by a magistrate (section 36 of the *Magistrates' Ordinance* (Cap. 227)) or a conditional discharge by the Court of First Instance or District Court (section 107 of the *Criminal Procedure Ordinance*). An absolute discharge is reserved for wrongdoing of a very low order, while conditional discharges serve a similar purpose to probation orders. Absolute discharges are typically not appropriate for shoplifting cases given the offender's moral blameworthiness (*Secretary for Justice v Tse Sheung Kai & Others* [2001] 3 HKLRD 487 (CA)).

When a person is discharged he or she cannot be given a custodial sentence, fine or community service order. Before ordering a discharge, the court must find that it is 'inexpedient to inflict any punishment or any other than a nominal punishment' on the offender having regard to 'the character, antecedents, age, health, or mental condition of the person charged, or to the trivial nature of the offence, or to the extenuating circumstances under which the offence was committed' (section of 36 of the *Magistrates Ordinance*; section 107 of the *Criminal Procedure Ordinance*).

Binding over

The power to bind over an individual is a non-custodial measure that helps to keep the peace in a potentially violent context and/or to ensure good behaviour from that individual. 'The making of binding-over orders is sometimes explained as constituting "preventive" justice' (*HKSAR v Lau Wai Wo* (2003) 6 HKCFAR 624 at para. 39, applied in *David Morter v HKSAR* (2004) 7 HKCFAR 53).

Under section 109I of the *Criminal Procedure Ordinance*, the judge or magistrate has the power to bind over a person who or whose case was before the court irrespective of whether he or she has been convicted of an offence. However, where the court proposes to bind over an acquitted person, the court must give him or her fair notice of this proposal and an opportunity to make representations. The power obligates the person to enter into his or her own recognisance or to find sureties or both, and for the duration of the recognisance (usually one year but not more than three years) to keep the peace and/or be of good behaviour. Failure to enter into the recognisance can result in contempt proceedings against the person who has been bound over. In fixing the amount of the recognisance, the judge or magistrate should try to satisfy him- or herself that the amount is such that the person could reasonably be expected to be able to pay (*Lau Wai Wo* at para. 55). If the recognisance is breached then the amount may be forfeited.

Restitution and compensation

In recent times, victims of crime have been given a greater role in the trial of persons accused of crime. It has been recognised that victims should not have to bring their own legal proceedings (and suffer all the costs of doing so) to obtain either the return of property from the offender or compensation for harm caused by the offender. The restitution order and compensation order are two different orders available to the sentencing judge in order to bring corrective justice to the victim (sections 73 and 84 of the *Criminal Procedure Ordinance*). Both orders are made in addition to the sentence that the offender receives.

Forfeiture and confiscation

Forfeiture and confiscation orders aim at depriving the offender of property related to crime. Such crime-related property is of three kinds: 1 property that is in itself illegal to possess (i.e. contraband); 2 property used in the commission of the offence (i.e. an instrument of crime); and 3 property derived directly or indirectly from crime (i.e. proceeds of crime). In respect of contraband and instruments of crime, there are a number of disparate provisions which allow the court to forfeit property ranging from dangerous drugs, counterfeit goods to detained property used in the commission of an offence.

In respect of proceeds of crime, there exists a complex legal regime in the *Drug Trafficking (Recovery of Proceeds) Ordinance* (Cap. 405) and *Organized and Serious Crimes Ordinance* (Cap. 455) that allows the sentencing court to order the offender to pay a confiscation order in an amount equivalent to the degree to which the offender has benefited from drug trafficking and/or serious crime. If the offender fails to pay the confiscation order, he may be liable to serve an additional term of imprisonment up to ten years.

Other orders

Disqualification orders prohibit the offender from engaging in certain activities as a preventative measure to possible re-offending. Such orders include disqualifying the offender from driving, or in cases of white-collar crime from being a company director, for a fixed period of time. A criminal bankruptcy order, which can only be made by the District Court or Court of First Instance, can force the offender's bankruptcy and assist in ensuring that the proceeds of crime are returned to victims. A judge or magistrate can also order a hospital order for an accused where there is medical evidence that the person is mentally disordered and the nature and degree of the mental disorder from which the person is suffering warrants his or her detention in a mental hospital for medical treatment (section 54(3) of the *Mental Health Ordinance* (Cap. 136)).

Sources of purposes and principles under the *Basic Law*

Surprisingly, while most of the above sentencing options are clearly spelled out in legislation, the statutes are silent when it comes to the purposes and principles of sentencing. In other words, the Hong Kong ordinances contain no express guidance on when a certain sentencing option should be given and on how much a person should be sentenced. This of course does not mean that there are no rules that govern a judge's exercise of his or her sentencing powers in a particular case. Rather, the purposes and principles of sentencing are found in the common law and have been developed over the years by judges in England and Hong Kong.

In 1991, Hong Kong passed the *Hong Kong Bill of Rights Ordinance* (Cap. 383) (BORO) as the means to implement the UK's international treaty obligations in respect of Hong Kong under the *International Covenant on Civil and Political Rights*. After 1997, China allowed the BORO to continue alongside the many human rights protections under Hong Kong's constitution, the *Basic Law of the Hong Kong Special Administrative Region* (hereafter the *Basic Law*). As will be seen, both the BORO and the *Basic Law* contain very important constitutional principles relevant to sentencing.

In the constitutional framework of the *Basic Law*, courts have recognised the operation of the principle of separation of powers. The independence of the judiciary is protected in Article 85. Courts have also held that judicial powers, including those that relate to sentencing, cannot be conferred on the executive or legislative authorities. In *Yau Kwong Man & Another v Secretary for Security* [2002] 3 HKC 457 (CFI), Mr Justice Hartmann found that the old scheme whereby the chief executive would fix the minimum term of imprisonment for a young person convicted of murder was unconstitutional as it infringed on the principle of separation of powers. The scheme infringed on the *Basic Law* as it conferred what amounted to a judicial power on the executive and according to the judge this was not permitted under the constitution. However, it is clear that under the *Basic Law*, the administration of a sentence and the granting of a pardon or commutation of penalties are matters within the authority of the executive (see Articles 48(12) and 62(2) of the *Basic Law*).

The purposes of sentencing

There are many varied sentencing purposes which express themselves more or less strongly in any given case. It would be incoherent if all the sentencing purposes were to have full expression in every case. Instead, the relative emphasis given to the different purposes varies depending on the nature of the criminal offence of which the offender is convicted, its prevalence in a particular community, public attitudes to that offence, the harm caused to the particular victim, and the moral culpability and background of the offender (see the discussion in *R v Sargeant* (1974) 60 Cr App R 74).

While sentencing purposes can explain what the sentence is trying to achieve, they are poor indicators of how much punishment should be given in a particular case. For this, it is necessary to apply established sentencing principles which provide greater guidance on the quantum of punishment. Even greater precision comes from the development of case law by appellate courts establishing certain guidelines and precedents as to sentences for certain types of cases.

Public protection

It is uncontroversial that one of the main purposes of sentencing is to protect the public. Imprisoning the offender is not the only means to protect the public but can be an effective one. Any measure, including a binding over order, which can prevent the offender from re-offending would also achieve the purpose. In cases of habitual offenders whose criminal records show an escalation of seriousness in offending, the purpose of public protection will find strong emphasis in the sentence.

Deterrence: general and specific

Deterrence sees punishment for a particular offence as a means to lower the incidence of that offence. In this respect, deterrence has much in common with public protection since lowering the incidence of crime has the effect of protecting the public. General deterrence uses the offender as an example to deter others from committing the same or a similar offence. Specific deterrence punishes the offender to deter him or her from recommitting offences.

At a theoretical level, deterrence 'works' because of the notion that humans are rational beings who will choose to avoid conduct that can result in a deprivation of liberty or other personal discomfort. In respect of imprisonment, however, this theory breaks down for two categories of offenders: rational decision makers, often motivated by profit, who are prepared to take the risk of non-apprehension; and those with mental disorders or substance abuse problems who do not think rationally before committing an offence. For these offenders, other sentencing purposes and options may need to find more prominent expression in the sentence.

When sentencing judges have regard to the prevalence of the offender's offence in the community, they are giving effect to the purpose of general deterrence. In Hong Kong, section 27 of the *Organized and Serious Crimes Ordinance* allows the court to take into consideration admissible evidence concerning the prevalence of the offence committed by the offender to order a more severe sentence than it would have ordered had it not considered this evidence. For example, in *HKSAR v Ma Suet Chun & Others* [2001] 4 HKC 337, the Court of Appeal approved an enhancement of sentence in a case concerning street deception. The prosecution had called three police officers to testify to the increasing number of street deception complaints made in the New Territories and West Kowloon region. The court held that in future cases of this kind the enhancement could be as great as 50%. While there has yet to be a constitutional challenge to section 27, courts will need to be wary that giving general deterrence such great emphasis could well put the sentence in conflict with other established sentencing purposes and principles. In a serious case concerning high-volume sales of pirated compact discs, the Court of Appeal thought the 50% enhancement was too great given that the judge had already used a high starting point; the enhancement was reduced to one-third, recognising that 'restraint should be exercised by the court when passing sentences and the sentencing guidelines should be followed' (see *HKSAR v Chan Cheong Kit* [2010] 2 HKLRD 636 at para 30 (CA)).

Retribution

If public protection and deterrence were the only sentencing purposes then long custodial sentences would be the norm. Retribution reins in excessive punishments by ensuring that the offender is only punished for what he or she deserves. There is a misconception that retribution is the same as vengeance. This passage from a Canadian judgment explains the difference (see *R v M(CA)* [1996] 1 SCR 500, para. 80, per Lamer CJC):

> Vengeance ... represents an uncalibrated act of harm upon another, frequently motivated by emotion and anger, as a reprisal for harm inflicted upon oneself by that person. Retribution in a criminal context, by contrast, represents an objective, reasoned and measured determination of an appropriate punishment which properly reflects the moral culpability of the offender, having regard to the intentional risk-taking of the offender, the consequential harm caused by the offender, and the normative character of the offender's conduct. Furthermore, unlike vengeance, retribution incorporates a principle of restraint; retribution requires the imposition of a just and appropriate punishment, and nothing more.

This was cited with approval by Mr Justice McWalters in *HKSAR v Lee Yau Wing* [2013] 1 HKC 572 at para 34 (CA). Retribution is closely related to the principle of proportionality, which is a fundamental principle that informs all sentences.

Denunciation

There are times when the circumstances of the offence are so aggravating in terms of the harm done to the victim and society that it calls for denunciation by the court. See recent references to the purpose of denunciation in *HKSAR v Tsang Pui Yu, Shirlina* [2014] 5 HKC 111 at para 45 (CA), and *HKSAR v Ma Tik Lun Dicky* [2015] 1 HKLRD 380 at para 40 (CA). To achieve this purpose, the court denounces the offender and his or her crime in the public forum of the courtroom and orders a severe sentence to reflect the denunciation. Thus there is a strong communicative element when giving effect to the purpose of denunciation. The court sends a message voicing the sentiments of the victim and community that the offender's conduct is wrong and must be sharply condemned. The 'sentencing principle of denunciation brings home to the offender, those affected by his conduct and the public generally that the punishment that is meted out ... is because by their conduct they have fallen below the values that society has imposed on them' (*HKSAR v Lee Yau Wing* [2013] 1 HKC 572 at para 37 (CA)).

Denunciation was voiced in the case concerning the infamous Mr Yip Kai Foon, who, after escaping from jail, led a criminal gang armed with assault rifles and explosives in a street battle with the police. He was sentenced to 30 years' imprisonment on top of the 11 years and three months he had left to serve when he escaped custody. As a result of the shoot-out with the police, Yip became paralysed from the waist down. The Appeal Committee of the Court of Final Appeal (by majority) refused to hear Yip's appeal and held that even if appropriate weight was given to Yip's paralysed condition, his offences were so extremely grave that they deserved the sentence given (albeit reduced slightly by the Court of Appeal) (*HKSAR v Yip Kai Foon* (2000) 3 HKCFAR 31). The Appeal Committee described the actions of Yip and his gang as coming 'very close to declaring war on society' and approved of the Court of Appeal's statement in this case that '[s]entences must be imposed which, to use the words of Lord Denning, express the emphatic denunciation by the community of such crimes' (cited in the committee's determination at page 37).

Rehabilitation

Rehabilitation aims to address the underlying causes of the offender's criminal behaviour and thereby serves to prevent a recurrence of the offending. Rehabilitative aims are often served by non-custodial orders such as the suspended sentence, community service order, probation, discharge and binding over order. If the offender has a drug or alcohol addiction problem which caused him or her to commit the crime, rehabilitation would require the offender to be treated for this substance abuse problem.

Long terms of imprisonment are often perceived as being inconsistent with achieving rehabilitative aims. Article 6(3) of the Hong Kong Bill of Rights requires that custodial institutions 'comprise treatment of prisoners the essential aim of which shall be their reformation and social rehabilitation'. This, however, relates not to the appropriateness of the sentences passed, but to the treatment of offenders who are detained (*R v Chu Man Chiu*, Cr App 198/1991 (CA)). In Hong Kong, specialised custodial settings have been established to pursue specific rehabilitative aims. For example, young offenders can be sentenced to serve a term in a reformatory school or training centre. Those with drug problems can be sentenced to a term in a drug addiction treatment centre. In one case of serious drug trafficking by offenders aged 17 and 18 years old, the Court of Appeal held that it was too lenient to send the young offenders to a training centre (where the detention period averages from 18 months to two years), when the appropriate sentence was four years' imprisonment on a plea of guilty (see *Secretary for Justice v Chau Tsz Tim* [2015] 1 HKLRD 853 (CA)).

Reparation for victims

While the victim is not a formal party to criminal proceedings, modern criminal justice systems have accorded the victim a greater role, particularly in the sentencing stage. Some jurisdictions use victim impact statements to convey the victim's views to the sentencing judge. In *HKSAR v Tsoi Chi Ming*, unreported HCCC308/2014, 28 November 2014, CFI, Mr Justice Zervos called for the greater use of such statements in Hong Kong courts:

> A victim impact statement plays a vital role in assisting the court in imposing a just and appropriate sentence on the offender. Its function is to help the sentence understand the impact of a crime on the victim which is an important consideration when sentencing someone.

The restitution and compensation orders are two mechanisms by which the sentencing court can achieve a degree of civil justice as between the victim and the wrongdoer. The availability of such orders at sentencing saves the victim time and money from having to bring his or her own lawsuit.

There are, however, limits to the ability of the sentencing court to make full reparation to the victim(s). Sentencing proceedings are typically held immediately after conviction and, once commenced, are expeditiously completed; they are not supposed to be long drawn-out hearings in which complex factual and legal issues are decided. Ultimately it is at the discretion of the sentencing judge to decide whether and how much reparation should be made for victims. Where the issues are likely to distort and delay the sentencing process (e.g. many victims, each raising contested factual and liability issues), the judge may decide not to order restitution or compensation and to leave such issues for a civil court to resolve.

Restoration

A separate but related sentencing purpose to reparation is restoration, sometimes known as restorative justice. Where all parties are willing, restorative justice aims to reintegrate the offender back into the community by having him or her accept responsibility for his or her wrongdoing and make amends to the victim for the harm caused. The process by which this is achieved typically involves the offender and victim agreeing to meet in mediation conducted by a neutral mediator. While achieving acknowledged responsibility and reintegration is an end in itself, restorative justice can also protect the public by lowering the risk of re-offending by the offender. While much literature now exists on restorative justice, it has yet to be generally accepted in Hong Kong sentencing law, nor has the legislature enacted provisions aimed at furthering restorative justice.

The principles of sentencing

It is imperative that the courts apply the correct principles of sentencing in every case as an error of principle is a recognised ground of appeal. Where an appeal court has found an error of principle in the reasons for sentence, the appeal court will sentence the offender afresh, applying the correct principles. Some of the major sentencing principles are discussed below.

Proportionality

The principle of proportionality requires that the sentence and punishment be calibrated according to the seriousness of the offence and the circumstances of the offender. Seriousness of the offence will depend on the nature of the offence, the gravity of the harm caused to individual victims and society generally, and the degree of moral culpability of the offender. The maximum sentence for the offence is often a reliable indicator of the relative seriousness of different offences. The circumstances of the offender, including his or her criminal history and the consequential hardship that the sentence will have on him or her, are all relevant to the application of the proportionality principle. However, in general, a person with a long criminal record should have already received proportionate punishment for all of his or her past crimes and should not be punished again for them. That said, a recidivist on deterrence grounds must expect to receive a longer sentence than a first offender (*HKSAR v Chan Pui Chi* [1998] 2 HKLRD 830 (CA)).

Proportionality is a fundamental principle since all sentences are liable to be altered on appeal if they are manifestly excessive or inadequate. A good illustration of the application of this principle is found in *HKSAR v Wong Chun Cheong* (2001) 4 HKCFAR 12. Wong, who was aged 16 at the time of the offence, pleaded guilty to participating in a lion dance in a public place without a permit. The magistrate sentenced Wong to be detained in a training centre where the period of detention would range from a minimum of six months up to a maximum of three years. However, the maximum sentence for the offence for which Wong was convicted was only a HK$2,000 fine and imprisonment for six months. In allowing the appeal and substituting a fine of HK$100 (Wong had already served four months in the training centre), the court found that detention in a training centre for the period allowed by the legislation would be a 'wholly disproportionate period given the triviality of the offence' (p. 25). This was true even if Wong was a suitable candidate for rehabilitation in a training centre. The case stands for the proposition that a person should not lose his or her liberty in the name of rehabilitation if it would be disproportionate to do so.

Proportionality in the sentence is also a constitutional principle. Article 28 of the *Basic Law* protects individuals from 'arbitrary or unlawful ... detention or imprisonment', and Article 3 of the Hong Kong Bill of Rights provides that '[n]o one shall be subjected to torture or to cruel, inhuman or degrading treatment or punishment'. In *HKSAR v Lau Cheong & Another* (2002) 5 HKCFAR 415, the Court of Final Appeal held that a sentence would give rise to arbitrary imprisonment if it was 'manifestly disproportionate' (at para. 110). In relation to Article 3 of the Bill of Rights, the court held that the threshold test for determining whether a sentence constituted cruel, inhuman or degrading punishment was either the same test ot one involving a higher threshold. *Lau Cheong* was concerned with a challenge to the mandatory life imprisonment sentence for murder. In rejecting all the constitutional arguments, the court noted the 'inherent and unique gravity of the offence' and the 'legislative judgment' to have the mandatory sentence together with a statutory regime for review of all life sentences by an independent board (at paras. 123–125).

Totality

The principle of totality ensures proportionality when the offender is sentenced, whether at the same time or different times, for multiple offences. In *HKSAR v Ngai Yiu Ching* [2011] 5 HKLRD 690 at para 22 (CA), Stock VP wrote that the principle was there:

> to ensure not only fairness to the offender, in the sense that he is not punished twice for the same offence and, further, that the sentence is not an unduly crushing punishment, but it is also a tool by which to ensure that 'the overall effect of the sentence is sufficient having regard to the usual principles of deterrence, rehabilitation and denunciation': *R v KM* [2004] NSWCCA 65 at para 55.

In practice, the court 'should fix appropriate sentences for each offence, then consider the application of the totality principle, and, in particular, whether any adjustment needs to be made to any of the sentences to achieve the total effective sentence which is consistent with the application of the principle' (Cross et al., 2015: 562).

The principle was applied in *HKSAR v Chung Yiu Ming* [2003] 3 HKLRD K14 (CA), where the offender was sentenced to five years' imprisonment for drug trafficking to be served consecutively to a sentence of three and a half years' imprisonment he was already serving, also for drug trafficking. The Court of Appeal held that the total eight and a half-year term was excessive and had the judge properly applied the totality principle the total custodial sentence should have been seven years. The principle was applicable because the offence for which he was being sentenced related to the previous charges which concerned drug trafficking in the same premises and were closely related in time. The court looked to see what the appropriate sentence would have been had all the charges been dealt with at the same time.

Parity of sentencing

Another important principle of sentencing requires parity of sentencing as between offenders. In theory, this principle requires that two offenders with similar backgrounds committing the same offence receive the same sentence. In practice, this position is rarely seen since the circumstances in any two given cases invariably differ in some respect. Nevertheless, the principle, like the principle of *stare decisis*, still holds to ensure that like cases are decided alike and any material differences in two similar cases are reflected in the difference between the two sentences.

The sentencing of co-accused in the same case will usually put this principle to the test. Two co-accused whose degree of involvement in the crime is the same and whose backgrounds are similar should in principle receive the same sentence. However, if different sentences are accorded to the co-accused it must be justified according to the gravity of their role in the offence and/or their backgrounds, particularly in terms of their criminal record.

Aggravating and mitigating factors

It is a basic principle that the presence of aggravating factors will tend to make the sentence more severe while mitigating factors will lighten the sentence. From time to time, appellate courts in Hong Kong will provide guidelines on sentencing for a given offence having certain factual characteristics. For example, in *Secretary for Justice v Ho Mei Wa* [2004] 3 HKLRD 270 (CA), the court set a new starting point sentence of three months' imprisonment in cases where an employer knowingly or recklessly employed an employee who was not lawfully employable. This sentence applied where there was casual employment and no aggravating factors. The case was important because a previous appellate authority had set the starting point at 15 months' imprisonment but magistrates had for many years not followed this guideline. In *HKSAR v Tsang Chiu Tak* [2013] 1 HKLRD 422 (CA), the court laid down guidelines on sentencing principles for cases involving sexual assaults by adults on children.

Aggravating factors are those that highlight the seriousness of the offence and the criminal record of the offender. Circumstances such as the planning and premeditation of the offender, a breach of trust owed to the victim and the degree of violence involved are some aggravating factors pertaining to the offence. Where the offence is possession of dangerous drugs, it is an aggravating factor if the circumstances in which the drugs were found, e.g. in multiple small bags, indicated a risk of dissemination; this was not the same as imputing an unproven intent to traffic to the defendant (see *HKSAR v Minney, John Edwin* (2013) 16 HKCFAR 26). Commission of an offence while on bail is also regarded as an aggravating factor (see *HKSAR v Leung Ting Fung* [2015] 1 HKC 290 at para 29 (CA)).

Mitigating factors are generally those concerning the background of the offender, the remorse of the offender, and consequential hardship of the sentence on the offender. In 2001–02, there was a lively debate on whether the fact that the offender was a foreigner could constitute a mitigating factor given the hardship of serving the sentence in an alien jail in Hong Kong. Despite one appellate judgment showing sympathy for this position, the prevailing position was that for serious offences, particularly drug trafficking, the element of foreignness will carry little if any weight (see *HKSAR v Rohrer* [2001] 3 HKC 371 (CA), and *HKSAR v Hong Chang-chi* [2002] 1 HKC 295 (CA), which are discussed by Young, 2001). A well-recognised mitigating factor is where the offender provides assistance to the authorities. 'Its object is to provide an incentive for offenders to co-operate with the authorities' (see *Z v HKSAR* (2007) 10 HKCFAR 183, para 11). A discount of up to two-thirds the starting point sentence may be granted.

No retrospective punishment

It is a constitutional principle that an offender shall not be sentenced retrospectively to a heavier penalty than the one that was applicable when the offence was committed (Article 12(1) of the Hong Kong Bill of Rights). For example, if at the time the offence was committed, the maximum sentence for the offence was ten years' imprisonment and by the time the offender was sentenced the maximum had been increased by the legislature to 14 years, it would offend the principle if the judge imposed a jail sentence of 12 years under the new law.

The principle does not apply in respect of a lighter penalty applied retrospectively (Article 12(1) of the Hong Kong Bill of Rights). If, in the same example, the law was changed by lowering the maximum sentence to five years' imprisonment, at the time of sentencing the offender would be entitled to benefit from this change in the law as it could result in a lighter penalty. This principle of benefiting from a change in the law that results in a lighter penalty applies even if the change is by way of a reformulated offence with a lower maximum sentence (*R v Chan-Chi Hung* [2005] 2 HKCLR 50 (PC)). In *Seabrook v HKSAR* (1999) 2 HKCFAR 184, the court held that the principle also applied to judge-made changes in the law so that an accused could benefit from a change that lowered the guideline sentences for a particular offence.

Rehabilitation of juvenile offenders

In Hong Kong, the current minimum age of criminal responsibility is ten years of age (section 3 of the *Juvenile Offenders Ordinance* (Cap. 226)). In the *Juvenile Offenders Ordinance*, a child is defined as a person under the age of 14 years and a young person is defined as a person 14 years of age or upwards and under the age of 16 years. There is a general principle that in the sentencing of children and young persons, rehabilitation above all other purposes of sentencing should be emphasised (see *HKSAR v Law Ka Kit & Others* [2003] 2 HKC 178 (CA)). There are at least two reasons for this.

First, young offenders who commit the same crime as an adult will generally do so with a lower degree of moral culpability since their mental faculties have not been fully formed. Second, and perhaps more importantly, even if the young offender acts with full moral culpability, the principle reflects the policy that one's misdeeds in childhood should not haunt one's future as an adult, and thus there should be a clean break as one makes the transition from being a young person to an adult. For these reasons a sentence that emphasises rehabilitation will generally be a more lenient sentence, attentive to the needs and problems of the individual young person. The juvenile offender is to be 'accorded treatment appropriate to their age and legal status' (Article 6(3) of the Hong Kong Bill of Rights). However, if the principle could result in an excessive deprivation of liberty, the principle of proportionality will step in to limit the rehabilitative measures, as was seen in *Wong Chun Cheong*'s case.

In giving effect to this principle, legislation prohibits imprisoning children in default of payment of fines, damages or costs (section 11(1) of the *Juvenile Offenders Ordinance*). No young person is to be sentenced to imprisonment if he or she can be suitably dealt with in any other way (section 11(2) of the ordinance). For persons 16 years or over and under 21 years of age, the court must not sentence the person to imprisonment unless it is of the opinion that no other method of dealing with such person is appropriate (section 109A(1) of the *Criminal Procedure Ordinance*). Thus, imprisonment is a last resort. This rule, however, does not apply to a list of serious offences including murder, manslaughter, rape, serious drug offences and so on (see Schedule 3 of the *Criminal Procedure Ordinance*). In February 2014, the Law Reform Commission of Hong Kong recommended repealing this list of excepted offences as part of its recommendations for removing the list of excepted offences for suspended sentences. A person who was under the age of 18 years when he or she committed murder may be sentenced to imprisonment for life or a lesser period at the discretion of the court (section 2 of the *Offences Against the Person Ordinance* (Cap 212)).

A related principle is the one found in the Hong Kong Bill of Rights and elsewhere that juvenile accused and offenders shall be segregated from adults (Article 6(3) of the Hong Kong Bill of Rights; sections 6 and 11(3) of the *Juvenile Offenders Ordinance*).

Conclusion

It must always be remembered that the purposes and principles of sentencing operate in the real world of criminal proceedings. Thus efficiency and judicial economy are also important considerations that can affect the sentence and punishment of an offender. These considerations are the basis for the rule which reduces an offender's sentence up to as much as one-third from the starting point if he or she pleads guilty without going to trial (see *Yu Fai Tat v HKSAR* (2004) 7 HKCFAR 293, para 9). Similarly, another rule exists to disallow the offender from counting the time that he or she spends in jail pending the determination of his or her application for leave to appeal as part of his or her sentence if the application was totally without merit (*HKSAR v Hau Kin & Others* (2005) 8 HKCFAR 63, applying *Nauthum Chau Ching Kay v HKSAR* (2002) 5 HKCFAR 540, para 56). However important these considerations may be, though, the constitutional safeguards in Hong Kong ensure that the offender's dignity and liberty interest will be of paramount importance in the law of sentencing.

Review questions

1 Why is it said that the purposes of sentencing are often in conflict?
2 What are the constitutional principles of sentencing that exist in Hong Kong?
3 What sentencing purpose was emphasised in Yip Kai Foon's case?
4 Why should juvenile offenders be sentenced differently from adult offenders?
5 Is remorse an aggravating or mitigating factor on sentence? Why?

References

Cross, I.G. and Cheung, P.W.S. (1994) *Sentencing in Hong Kong*, Hong Kong: Butterworths Asia.

Cross, I.G., Cheung, P.W.S. and Tsui, E.Y.L. (2015) *Sentencing in Hong Kong* (7th edn), Hong Kong: LexisNexis Butterworths.

Easton, S. and Piper, C. (2005) *Sentencing and Punishment: The Quest for Justice*, Oxford: Oxford University Press.

Law Reform Commission of Hong Kong (1983) *Report – Community Service Orders (Topic 7)*, Hong Kong: Law Reform Commission of Hong Kong.

Law Reform Commission of Hong Kong (2014) 'LRC report proposes removing sentencing restrictions in Criminal Procedure Ordinance', Press Release (25 February), www.info.gov.hk/gia/general/201402/25/P201402250275.htm (accessed 15 February 2016).

Liu, A. (1992) 'The right to life', in R. Wacks (ed.) *Human Rights in Hong Kong* (pp. 264–300), Hong Kong: Oxford University Press.

von Hirsch, A. (1993) *Censure and Sanctions*, Oxford: Clarendon Press.

Young, S.N.M. (2001) 'Justifying sentencing discounts for foreigners', *Hong Kong Law Journal*, 31(3): 369–379.

Legislation cited

Basic Law of the Hong Kong Special Administrative Region
Community Service Orders Ordinance (Cap. 378)
Criminal Procedure Ordinance (Cap. 221)
Drug Trafficking (Recovery of Proceeds) Ordinance (Cap. 405)
Hong Kong Bill of Rights Ordinance (Cap. 383)
International Covenant on Civil and Political Rights

Juvenile Offenders Ordinance (Cap. 226)
Long-term Prison Sentences Review Ordinance (Cap. 524)
Magistrates Ordinance (Cap. 227)
Mental Health Ordinance (Cap. 136)
Offences Against the Person Ordinance (Cap. 212)
Organized and Serious Crimes Ordinance (Cap. 455)
Probation of Offenders Ordinance (Cap. 298)

Cases cited

David Morter v HKSAR (2004) 7 HKCFAR 53
HKSAR v Chan Cheong Kit [2010] 2 HKLRD 636 (CA)
HKSAR v Chan Pui Chi [1998] 2 HKLRD 830 (CA)
HKSAR v Chung Yiu Ming [2003] 3 HKLRD K14 (CA)
HKSAR v Hau Kin & Others (2005) 8 HKCFAR 63
HKSAR v Hong Chang-chi [2002] 1 HKC 295 (CA)
HKSAR v Lau Cheong & Another (2002) 5 HKCFAR 415
HKSAR v Lau Wai Wo (2003) 6 HKCFAR 624
HKSAR v Law Ka Kit & Others [2003] 2 HKC 178 (CA)
HKSAR v Lee Yau Wing [2013] 1 HKC 572 (CA)
HKSAR v Leung Ting Fung [2015] 1 HKC 290 (CA)
HKSAR v Ma Suet Chun & Others [2001] HKEC 1190 (CA)
HKSAR v Ma Tik Lun Dicky [2015] 1 HKLRD 380 (CA)
HKSAR v Minney, John Edwin (2013) 16 HKCFAR 26
HKSAR v Ngai Yiu Ching [2011] 5 HKLRD 690 (CA)
HKSAR v Rohrer [2001] 3 HKC 371 (CA)
HKSAR v Tsang Chiu Tak [2013] 1 HKLRD 422 (CA)
HKSAR v Tsang Pui Yu, Shirlina [2014] 5 HKC 111 (CA)
HKSAR v Tsoi Chi Ming, unreported HCCC308/2014, 28 November 2014, CFI
HKSAR v Wong Chun Cheong (2001) 4 HKCFAR 12
HKSAR v Yip Kai Foon (2000) 3 HKCFAR 31
Nauthum Chau Ching Kay v HKSAR (2002) 5 HKCFAR 540
R v Chan-Chi Hung [2005] 2 HKCLR 50 (PC)
R v Chu Man Chiu Cr App 198/1991 (CA)
R v Isherwood (1974) 59 Cr App R 162 (CA)
R v KM [2004] NSWCCA 65
R v M(CA) [1996] 1 SCR 500
R v Sargeant (1974) 60 Cr App R 74 (Eng CA)
R v Tarry [1970] 2 QB 560 (CA)
Seabrook v HKSAR (1999) 2 HKCFAR 184
Secretary for Justice v Chau Tsz Tim [2015] 1 HKLRD 853 (CA)
Secretary for Justice v Ho Mei Wa [2004] 3 HKLRD 270 (CA)
Secretary for Justice v Tse Sheung Kai & Others [2001] 3 HKLRD 487 (CA)
White v Brown (2003) 175 FLR 325
Yau Kwong Man & Another v Secretary for Security [2002] 3 HKC 457 (CFI)
Yong Vui Kong v Public Prosecutor [2015] 2 SLR 1129 (CA)
Yu Fai Tat v HKSAR (2004) 7 HKCFAR 293
Z v HKSAR (2007) 10 HKCFAR 183

Useful websites

The *Basic Law of the Hong Kong Special Administrative Region* www.info.gov.hk/basic_law/flash.html

Community Justice & Reconciliation www.restorativejustice.org

Community Legal Information Centre, Law and Technology Centre, The University of Hong Kong www.clic.org.hk

Department of Justice www.doj.gov.hk

Sentencing Law and Policy, Law Professors Blog Network sentencing.typepad.com/sentencing_law_and_policy/

Part IV

POST-TRIAL STAGE

16

PROBATION AND COMMUNITY SERVICE ORDERS

Wing Hong Chui

Introduction

This chapter examines various issues surrounding the use of community sentences for juvenile and adult offenders. Issues such as the rationale for community sentences and the effectiveness of these sentences for offenders will be discussed. Broadly speaking, there are two main types of community sentence in Hong Kong, namely the probation order and community service order. In contrast to other non-custodial sentences such as fines, disqualification and compensation, both probation and community service orders involve an element of active participation by the offender and close supervision or monitoring by a designated authority figure from the state. The intended goal of these two community-based supervised sentences is to 'help [offenders] reintegrate into the community as law-abiding citizens' through proper supervision, counselling, and academic, pre-vocational and social skills training (Director of Social Welfare, 2015).

What is central to community sentences is the emphasis of social work approaches to rehabilitate offenders, encourage their pro-social behaviours and equip them with necessary skills to deal with life demands. Registered social workers are employed to supervise all offenders on probation and community service orders that are administered by the Social Welfare Department (Chui, 1999, 2002, 2003a, 2004, 2011). Whilst proponents of the criminal justice social work intervention for offenders firmly believe that 'a highly motivated individual can change into a productive and law-abiding citizen if he or she is given the right counselling (non-judgmental, empathetic, confrontative, reality-oriented, strengths-based, and cognitive-behavioural), as well as academic, vocational, and social education opportunities' (Brownell and Roberts, 2002: 2; see also Barry, 2000; Taylor, 2001; Reynolds et al., 2004), others believe that the state should be tough on the convicted and they should be deterred and incapacitated from further offending by imposing heavy penalties on them. For instance, in England and Wales, in order to give community sentences a new face, the probation order and community service order was once named the community rehabilitation order and community punishment order, respectively (Nellis, 2000). One major reason for renaming was largely driven by political reasons. The policymakers and politicians intended to convey to the public that these sentences were no longer 'soft' options and measures were taken to ensure community sentences were enforced (Raynor and Vanstone, 2002; Worrall and Hoy, 2005). Noted by Chui and Nellis (2003) is that probation training in England and Wales is no longer part of generic social work training and has become more criminologically focused since the early 2000s (see also Nellis, 2003; Whitehead and Thompson, 2004; Gregory, 2007). In this respect, the chapter will also speculate why the social work model of community sentences in Hong Kong has been able to preserve its social work identity, and discusses what should be done to improve the quality and effectiveness of these sentences.

This chapter consists of three main sections. The first section discusses the various justifications for community sentences such as diversion or deinstitutionalisation, reintegration (or rehabilitation) and reparation. The second section describes the operation of community sentences, and relevant sections of the ordinances will be cited to examine their operations. The third section examines the ingredients of effective intervention with offenders. In line with the 'What Works' movement, the chapter points to the importance of developing a more systematic and evidence-based criminal justice social work intervention for offenders.

The justifications for community sentences

Community sentences are formal control or penal measures to deal with certain selected offenders who are mostly first and second offenders. These offenders are not considered to pose any undue risk to the public for whom the increasing use of community sentences is appropriate. Community-based disposals are able to divert low-risk offenders from being incarcerated, help with their personal and social problems and, most importantly, prevent them from causing further harm to society. However, in terms of media coverage and empirical research conducted, it appears that community sentencing does not have a high profile in the field of criminal justice, especially when compared with the attention that police, courts and prisons have (Chui, 2002). Pollock (2004: 349) comments:

> Community corrections has a more positive and helpful image than does institutional corrections. However, even in this subsystem of the criminal justice system, the ideals of justice and care become diluted by bureaucratic mismanagement and personal agendas. Professionals in the community corrections do not have the same power as police or correctional officers to use physical force, but they do have a great deal of non-physical power over the clients they control.

While this chapter does not examine why community sentences have a low profile within the criminal justice system, it attempts to outline what community sentences can offer.

Diversion from custody

One justification for community sentences is diversion from custody which is based on policy and practical consideration. Putting all criminals in prison is unlikely because of the huge costs involved, and some crimes are simply not serious enough to justify imprisonment. There are different kinds of diversion programmes available, primarily for juvenile offenders in Hong Kong, and some examples are 'diversion from arrest' and 'diversion from prosecution' (Lo et al., 2006). As argued by Klapmuts (1976), another type of diversion from the criminal justice system for adult offenders is 'associated with the movement away from the incarceration of offenders in penal institutions and their ostracism upon release, receiving impetus from the same pressures that account for the immense popularity of alternatives to incarceration and community-based treatment' (ibid.: 222). A specific example of the diversionary programme is the use of community sentences as an alternative to some shorter custodial sentences (Ashworth, 2007). According to section 2(2) of the *Community Service Orders Ordinance* (Cap. 378), this order is suitable for those guilty of an offence to be treated as punishable with imprisonment.

With reference to section 109A of the *Criminal Procedure Ordinance* (Cap. 221), imprisonment is considered the last resort for young offenders between 18 and 21 years of age in both the Magistrates' Court and District Court:

> No court shall sentence a person of or over 16 and under 21 years of age to imprisonment unless the court is of opinion that no other method of dealing with such person is appropriate; and for the purpose of determining whether any other method of dealing with any such person is appropriate the court should obtain and consider information about the circumstances, and shall take into account any information before the court which is relevant to the character of such person and his physical and mental condition.

However, the above section shall not apply to a person who has been convicted of any of ten exempted offences in Schedule 3 to the ordinance, for example, manslaughter, rape or attempted rape, affray, any offence against section 4, 5 or 6 of the *Dangerous Drugs Ordinance* (Cap. 134), and any offence under section 4 or 10 of the *Weapons Ordinance* (Cap. 217).

Reintegration

One important role of penal sentences is to assist offenders in reintegrating into the community. Reintegration has a strong theoretical root in the rehabilitative theories of punishment (Miller and Gaines, 2016). The rehabilitation model is based on the premise that an individual's offending is related to a wide range of personal and social factors such as personality problems, poor schooling, lack of parental supervision, and community disorganisation, and the removal of these factors will bring about his or her positive changes. The model also places great emphasis on the treatment, welfare and therapy of the individual offender. The ultimate goal of community sentences is to strengthen the ties between an offender and the community, and to integrate the offender into community life by helping him or her to assume normal social roles. Supporters would see the probation and community service programmes being conducive to provide help with offenders to become law-abiding citizens. While the effect of incarceration on prisoners is primarily negative, the community correctional approaches are more reintegrative and cause less stigmatisation than imprisonment to encourage pro-social behaviour (Pollock, 2004).

Reparation

Reparation or restoration is another justification for the use of community sentences as opposed to custodial sentences (see Chapters 4 and 15 of this edited volume). Community service orders can provide general reparation to the community whereas probation sentences and custody cannot. The community is a symbolic victim in need of reparation (McDonald, 1986). On the one hand, the activities carried out during a community service order should deliberately be unpleasant in the expectation that this will deter the offender (that is specific deterrence) and other potential offenders (that is general deterrence). On the other, the convicted offender should make amends to society for his or her wrongdoing by performing unpaid manual labour or working with disabled or elderly people. While acknowledging this as a punishment, they are treated as volunteers to improve the environment or to help people in their communities.

Types of community sentences

In this chapter the operation of two community sentences is considered, including probation orders and community service orders. Tables 16.1 and 16.2 show the number of persons who are put on probation orders and community service orders, respectively. The official statistics show that there has been a continued reduction in the number of persons on probation orders since 2004/05 while the number of community service orders granted has remained relatively stable.

Table 16.1 Probation orders by type of offence and age of offender

Type of offence/ age group	*Number of persons*						
	2004/ 2005	*2009/ 2010*	*2010/ 2011*	*2011/ 2012*	*2012/ 2013*	*2013/ 2014*	*2014/ 2015*
Against lawful authority							
Under 16 years	33	21	22	12	12	13	9
16–20 years	69	47	49	81	46	36	27
21 years or over	33	52	46	39	38	26	18
Against public morality							
Under 16 years	28	27	22	24	10	20	11
16–20 years	60	65	58	80	54	36	53
21 years or over	42	43	62	65	63	48	52
Against the person							
Under 16 years	124	126	87	97	58	57	32
16–20 years	136	76	79	83	67	75	58
21 years or over	96	160	121	103	97	77	98
Against property							
Under 16 years	393	227	188	221	145	95	73
16–20 years	379	220	170	228	166	122	96
21 years or over	483	430	354	316	351	274	352
Other serious offence							
Under 16 years	25	58	17	33	23	22	13
16–20 years	161	244	149	161	76	65	37
21 years or over	101	280	201	260	155	145	88
Minor offences							
Under 16 years	99	130	76	82	42	35	23
16–20 years	220	272	209	128	139	135	87
21 years or over	380	446	341	338	344	326	324
Total	2,862	2,924	2,251	2,351	1,886	1,607	1,451
Under 16 years	702	589	412	469	290	242	161
16–20 years	1,025	924	714	761	548	469	358
21 years or over	1,135	1,411	1,125	1,121	1,048	896	932

Source: Census and Statistics Department, 2015: Table 15.13.

Table 16.2 Community service orders by type of offence and age of offender

Type of offence/ age group	*Number of persons*						
	2004/05	*2009/10*	*2010/11*	*2011/12*	*2012/13*	*2013/14*	*2014/15*
Type of offence							
Against lawful authority	93	131	88	96	59	72	61
Against public morality	91	126	87	87	95	80	85
Against the person	262	330	229	249	228	183	223
Against property	587	712	624	652	581	486	523
Other serious offences	345	344	280	202	143	168	170
Minor offences	358	464	429	418	332	349	492
Age group							
Under 16 years	15	18	5	10	4	5	1
16–20 years	262	190	157	133	105	107	107
21 years or over	1,459	1,899	1,575	1,561	1,329	1,226	1,446
Total	1,736	2,107	1,737	1,704	1,438	1,338	1,554

Source: Census and Statistics Department, 2015: Table 15.14.

Probation orders

The emergence of probation orders

Probation was introduced in Hong Kong on a formal statutory basis right from its beginning and was basically an overseas import during colonial times. The historical roots of the system can be traced to the penal practice in the UK in the early 20th century. Its inception was due to the belief that in giving the offender a chance to reform through welfare advice, education and counselling. The offender is allowed to return to the community to resume normal work and could then be an asset to the society as a whole from an economic point of view. Also the offender is helped to obey the law under the supervision of a probation officer, and thus saving the government any expense involved in holding the offender in an institution (Mak, 1973; Lee, 1973).

The first step towards putting the probation system into effect was the *Juvenile Offenders Ordinance* in 1933 under which juvenile offenders may be placed on probation at the direction of the court. The probation officers were attached to the police force until 1938 when the service was taken over by the Prisons Department. A further change took place in 1948 when the Probation Service was grouped under the Social Welfare Office established as a branch of the Secretariat for Chinese Affairs in post-war Hong Kong. The Probation Service was also upgraded to professional status upon the appointment in 1950 of the late Donald Peterson, a trained social worker from Australia, who headed the development of the Probation Section of the Social Welfare Office. By law, he was gazetted as Principal Probation Officer, the first one ever appointed in the history of Hong Kong (Chan, 1996). All this indicated a recognition by the government of the importance of the Probation Service as a field of social work practice for offenders in the community since the early 1950s. The final Probation of Offenders Bill was passed in 1956, which extended the probation system to adult offenders (Huang, 1970; Mak, 1973; Lee, 1973; Chan, 1996).

Details of probation orders

The *Probation of Offenders Ordinance* (POO) (Cap. 298) as revised and amended details the responsibilities and core tasks of probation officers, and how an offender should be supervised in legal terms. By definition, 'probation officer' is a person appointed under Section 9 of POO and 'probationer' denotes a person who is under supervision by virtue of a probation order. The order applies to all those aged ten or above. It must clearly specify the period of probation which should not be less than one year and no longer than three years. Probation orders are issued after the court has considered carefully the circumstances leading to the offence, the nature of the offence, the character of the offender, and the recommendation of the probation officer in the social enquiry report. A basic probation order requires the offender to keep in touch with the probation officer in person regularly and inform the officer of any change of address. If at any time during the probation period it appears that a probationer has failed to comply with any of the requirements of the order or has committed another offence, he or she is liable to be brought back to the court for re-sentencing in the light of both new and old offences.

To address special circumstances in a case, added conditions can be imposed on the standard probation. They are required to: 1 work and place of residence as directed (such as living at an approved institution for a period of time); 2 abstain from dangerous drugs; 3 submit a urine sample for drug testing; 4 attend drug treatment programmes; 5 receive psychological treatment; 6 obtain psychiatric treatment; 7 comply with the curfew order (that is remaining at home from 11:00 pm to 6:00 am); 8 attend the court usually half way through the sentence in order to demonstrate improvement in behaviour (that is the progress report court attendance); and 9 attend group and rehabilitative programmes (such as the Community Support Service Scheme). Probation officers in Hong Kong usually recommend additional conditions with reference to the needs and problems of offenders identified in the social enquiry report. In effect, the liberty of the offenders would be restricted by attaching added conditions on the sentence. However, the recommendations are subject to the approval of the court.

As a statutory requirement, a probation officer will endeavour to 'advise, assist, and befriend' a probationer under section 19 of the POO. It is the duty of the supervising officer to reform an offender by virtue of his or her specialised social work knowledge and practical experience in the treatment of offenders and by arranging special services felt necessary for the successful offender rehabilitation within the community such as employment, schooling and accommodation (Yip, 1973; Corrections Section, 1994). In other words, the medical or rehabilitative model of probation is still existent with an emphasis on careful case planning and intervention in order to help probationers to improve their individual and social adjustment during the period of supervision.

The medical or treatment model emphasised the need 'to diagnose, treat and cure criminals', thereby reintegrating offenders into the community (Davies et al., 2015). This led to a growing involvement of professional social work that overtly supported the use of casework counselling for offenders on probation supervision. The dominant approach in supervising probationers in the 1960s and early 1970s in the UK was to 'advise, assist and befriend' them with the aim of enhancing their ability to avoid committing further offences (Willis, 1986). Given the penological optimism allied to the ethos of rehabilitation, McWilliams (1987) noticed the expansion of the probation caseload and the increasing number of probation staff between the 1960s and 1970s in the UK. In line with this development, Chan also reports that '[s]tarting in the 60s, the total number of probationers had been on the rise, and was almost double in the early 70s as documented in the 1973 White Paper *The Way Ahead* [in Hong Kong]' (Chan, 1996: 102). In addition, during this period, three approved institutions for juvenile and young offenders were established in Hong Kong with the aim of providing residential treatment programmes on top of the probation orders. The use of social work approaches to rehabilitate offenders was formally and explicitly spelt out in the 1973 White Paper (Lee, 1973).

Pre-sentence investigation

There are two major functions of probation, namely pre-sentence investigation and supervision of offenders. One of the official aims of probation is to give recommendation to the court on the suitability of offenders to be put on probation order or community service order in the form of social enquiry report or pre-sentence report. In this respect, the probation officer is the servant of the court and the magistrate or judge will take the recommendation from the report into account when sentencing an offender. It should be noted that the pre-sentence investigation is needed upon the request from the magistrate or judge following the offender's conviction. These reports are often requested when dealing with juvenile offenders to assess basic background information and their suitability to be put on a community sentence.

The nature of the social enquiry report is to give a detailed account of the offence and the offender, but not to determine guilt or otherwise. By assessing the circumstances of the crime and the personal, family and social background of the offender, the report proposes a recommendation with justification to the court in regard to the sentence (Clear and Dammer, 2003). Several sources of information are relied upon by the probation officer to prepare the report. An in-depth interview with the individual offender and often with his or her family members or guardians is conducted. Those whose bail application was denied will be interviewed in the remand centre or in custody. Additionally, official records and reports on the arrest records, previous conviction and sentence are consulted. Regardless of the brevity of the report, it must be succinct and contain facts and evidence to justify the perspectives about defendants in terms of their risk of reoffending or the likelihood of successful completion of the sentence. This information helps the court make its decision.

Supervision and enforcement

The main customers of probation are the offender and the community. Supervision begins as soon as an offender is sentenced to probation. Section 17 of the Rules of the POO requires the probation officer to explain the requirements and conditions of the probation order as clearly as possible. The expectations of the probation supervision should also be discussed between supervising officers and probationers. Clear and Dammer (2003: 275) hold the view that 'the probation supervision process emerges from informal understandings and inter-dependence'. However, it should be emphasised that the way probation officers work with offenders is based on a professional relationship, which ensures the law is enforced in order to protect the interests of society.

An empirical study with 115 adult probationers aged between 18 and 35 found that the probation service in Hong Kong still places a great emphasis on an individualised casework treatment approach to the probationers (Chui, 2003a, 2006). The one-to-one counselling sessions usually took place in the probation offices, and the three most commonly discussed topics during the sessions were issues related to 'personal problems', 'problems with family' and 'employment' of the offenders. A considerable number of probationers who misused drugs mentioned that they were asked to submit urine samples for drug testing. Those who were unemployed while on probation were asked to look in the newspapers for a job during the sessions. This confirms that probation officers tend to discuss the topics and design tasks to be done according to the characteristics and problems of offenders. This probation practice in Hong Kong has been guided by a casework-type philosophical ideology that was dominant in the 1960s in the USA (Sluder et al., 1994) and UK (Bottoms and McWilliams, 1979).

Apart from having regular face-to-face sessions, other means of contact with probationers that were rendered include family interviews during home visits and telephone interviews. Family interviews were usually arranged with the aim of assessing the family dynamics and interactions well before the probation officers have to prepare the social enquiry reports. It is not uncommon for family members to be involved in the treatment process with the offenders, especially for those who are still young. As might be expected, those who were given an added condition of a curfew order were more likely to receive telephone calls from the probation officers than those who were not in order to monitor whether they were at home after 11:00 pm as required.

A strong probation service develops close working relationships with a wide range of governmental and non-governmental organisations which can get offenders into education, training and employment. The probationers may be encouraged to contact relevant governmental organisations or social welfare agencies for help. For example, they may be encouraged to participate in social and recreational activities organised by community centres. They may also be asked to contact the Labour Department and the Employment Service of the Hong Kong Council of Social Services for help with their employment. Drug offenders can be referred to non-residential (such as methadone treatment) and residential drug rehabilitation centres in the course of supervision to deal with their drug misuse. They may also be referred to clinical psychologists and psychiatrists to receive some form of psychotherapeutic counselling.

In a recent study conducted by Chui and Chan (2014), a total of 113 male juvenile probationers aged from 14 to 20 were asked how they perceived their probation officers and the probation service. One of the major findings was that these juvenile probationers generally perceived their probation officer as relatively authoritarian or punitive by using two scales, Perceptions of the Assigned Probation Officer and Perceptions of the Job Nature of Probation Officers. Interestingly, juveniles supervised by female probation officers perceived officers to be more authoritarian or punitive than those supervised by a male counterpart. Also, an ordinary least squares (OLS) regression analysis shows that probation officers are perceived to be more authoritarian or punitive by older juveniles and those supervised by females. While acknowledging this study as small in scale, it is the first of its kind to explore the style of probation supervision in Hong Kong.

Outcome of probation orders

Table 16.3 shows the annual success rates of probation supervision for those cases completed from the financial years 2009/10 to 2012/13. Taking the face value of these statistics, close to or more than 84% of probation cases completed their orders satisfactorily. However, care should be taken when interpreting these official figures for two main reasons. First, the compilation of these statistics largely relies on probation officers' detection of and willingness to report further offences. Such rates illustrate probation work as it is seen from the point of view of the probation officer (Maltz, 1984). Harris (1992: 25) contends that: 'No more would there be that awkward thought that, say, probation officers "successes" might reflect no more than the good fortune of the

Table 16.3 Annual success rates of probation orders in the financial years 2009/10 to 2012/13

Year	*Total number of cases closed*	*Total number of satisfactory cases closed*	*Success rate* (%)*
2009/10	3,016	2,550	84.5
2010/11	2,571	2,183	84.9
2011/12	2,176	1,879	86.4
2012/13	2,396	2,036	84.5

Source: Derived data from the departmental *Annual Reports*, Director of Social Welfare, 2009–13.

Note: * The annual success rate is the total number of satisfactory cases closed divided by the total number of cases closed each year.

probationer in not having been caught reoffending.' Second, it is worth giving our attention to the counting rules of these statistics. Even where a probationer's order has been extended for failure to comply with the conditions of probation or for committing some further offence, he or she is still not considered as an unsatisfactory completion. This counting rule therefore may underestimate the actual reoffending rates. Thus, the statistics are only a rough estimation of the effectiveness of the probation.

Chui and Chan (2012) carried out an empirical study to explore the six-month short-term recidivism rate of 92 male juvenile probationers (aged 14 to 20 years), with and without controlling for the type of crime they committed. Based on the self-reported offending behaviour, 30% of the juveniles reoffended within the six-month follow-up period, though most of this self-reported offending was not detected. Their results indicated that type of crime, onset age of delinquent behaviour, frequency of delinquency involvement in the past year, social bond, negative affect, impulsivity and pro-offending attitudes were significant risk factors for recidivism. These findings highlight the need for social workers and other youth justice personnel to prioritise the intervention resources for juvenile probationers to address these risk factors associated with their self-reported reoffending.

Community service orders

The emergence of community service orders

In 1983, community service was first introduced as an additional means of dealing with offenders as a result of a recommendation made by the Law Reform Commission of Hong Kong. A sub-committee was formed to examine this issue in a detailed manner and concluded that community service orders should be available to offenders aged 14 and over for the offences for which the offender is liable to punishment by imprisonment (Law Reform Commission of

Hong Kong, 1983; for detailed accounts of the development of community service orders scheme see Lo and Harris, 2000). In 1984 the *Community Service Orders Ordinance* (CSOO) (Cap. 378) was enacted. The community service orders scheme was launched in 1987 as a pilot in three magistracies, and subsequently has been extended to all courts since 1998 (Harris and Lo, 2002; Lo and Harris, 2004). Since its inception, the community service orders scheme is under the administration of the Probation Service of the Social Welfare Department.

Aims of community service orders

By enjoining an offender to carry out a task within the community for a specified number of hours, community service orders aim at being rehabilitative and reparative. More specifically, these orders are expected to fulfil three penological objectives:

a Rehabilitation – Through structured work/service placement and the guidance of probation officers [POs (CSO)], offenders are helped to observe regulations, take up own responsibility for self-progress, broaden perspective, develop an enriched sense of self-worth, cultivate a more constructive pattern of living and steer away from committing further crime;
b Constructive disposal – Offenders are allowed to remain in the community while serving the sentence; and
c Reparation – Offenders are made a contribution to the community.

(Director of Social Welfare, 2015)

In addition to these three objectives, the order is punitive by depriving the offender of their leisure time to undertake volunteer service experience. Unlike volunteering which is influenced by an individual's altruistic motivation, offenders are coerced to perform this task whilst agreeing to be put on the scheme.

Details of community service orders

Section 4(1) of the CSOO enables the court to impose the order on those convicted of an offence punishable with imprisonment. It should be for any number of hours up to a maximum of 240 within a period of 12 months. Section 4(3) of the CSOO makes it clear that the court shall not make the order against an offender unless the offender consents to the making of such an order, and the court is satisfied after considering a social enquiry report as to the offender's suitability to be made the subject of such an order. Similar to the probation officer's report discussed above, the social enquiry report or the Suitability Report for Community Service Orders provides information to the court to consider which sentence is the most appropriate for sentencing the convicted. The hours of community service work are largely determined by the seriousness of the offence committed. The study conducted by Lo and Harris (2000) indicated that the majority of community service orders required the offender to undertake between 101 and 120 hours of unpaid work in the period 1994/95 to 1997/98.

Section 6 of the CSOO explicitly outlines the obligations of offenders under community service orders: to perform community work as directed by the supervising probation officer in a satisfactory manner, to comply with any conditions and requirements specified in the order with the reasonable direction to enable that supervising probation officer to provide rehabilitative counselling and guidance, and to notify any change of residence. The probation officer is advised to take into account the offender's religious beliefs and practice, employment status and personal circumstances when organising work or placement. Amongst others, two of the most important tasks of the supervising probation officer are to explain the objective of the community service orders to the offender, and assign work placement according to the offender's and community interest. By doing so, it is hoped that the offender not only enjoys the work itself but also finds the experience meaningful, constructive and worthwhile. The mode of community service or work placement includes task-oriented work such as painting, carpentry and gardening, and service-type work such as organising game stalls, escorting the disabled during outings and visiting homes for the elderly. Each work placement normally lasts for about four to eight consecutive hours, and for many it is their first experience of community work. Liaising with prospective voluntary agencies or governmental departments to identify possible suitable placements is indeed one of the core tasks of the probation officer.

Lo and Harris (2000) rightly point out that while the community service practice in Hong Kong is primarily modelled on the British experience, the Hong Kong model places more emphasis on the role of counselling by supervising probation officers. Probation supervision in the form of periodic counselling is an integral component of the order. The supervising officers pay site visits to monitor the performance of the offender and to engage the offender to address offending behaviour. The format in terms of content, frequency and length of the supervisory meeting varies according to the individual, family and social circumstances of the offender. During the course of the order, the supervising officer has regular appointments with the offender to evaluate the experience of community service with the aim of engaging the offender actively to redress the damage done to the community. The officers can also refer the offender and his or her family to participate in the Community Support Service Scheme which consists of counselling services, mutual aid group activities and recreational programmes (Director of Social Welfare, 2015).

Outcomes of community service orders

Previous literature shows that there is considerable support for community service from the offenders themselves and other stakeholders such as non-governmental organisations and governmental departments that provide placement opportunities and on-the-post supervision (Law Reform Commission of Hong Kong, 1983; Lo and Harris, 2000). They genuinely believe that the offender has to make reparation to the public through unpaid work and learn to be responsible for the harm caused to others. As indicated in Table 16.4, the annual success rate is high which means more than 96% of the orders were terminated satisfactorily.

When dealing with a breach of a community service order, the commission of a further offence whilst the order is in force, or revocation of the order, the court may impose a fine not exceeding of HK$1,000, increase the number of hours specified in the order, or re-sentence the offender for the original offence for which the order has been made. The last option may cause the offender to leave the service, which is counted as the case being closed unsatisfactorily.

Elements of successful community sentences intervention for offenders

In contrast to the use of imprisonment, a community approach to deal with criminals is founded on the grounds that a significant proportion of the causes of offending originates in their environment or community. This leads to a common-sense conclusion that it is more effective to devise intervention programmes that work within the given reality of their social environment, especially amongst juvenile offenders. Custody punishes but alienates, whereas community punishes but reintegrates (Vass, 1990). It is not difficult to understand that people end up feeling isolated, resentful and angry if the punishing experience is alienated and meaningless. This may explain why penal custody seems not to be the best way of reintegrating people into the community against which they offend, and where they ultimately must learn to live. For instance, probation supervision with a strong emphasis on social work and counselling attempts to integrate offenders into the community in a positive fashion, overcoming the problems that might exist in relation to school, employment or

Table 16.4 Annual success rates of community service orders in the financial years 2009/10 to 2012/13

Year	*Total number of cases closed*	*Total number of satisfactory cases closed*	*Success rate* (%)*
2009/10	2,175	2,096	96.4
2010/11	1,552	1,525	98.3
2011/12	1,814	1,763	97.2
2012/13	1,616	1,574	97.4

Source: Derived data from the departmental *Annual Reports*, Director of Social Welfare, 2009–13.

Note: * The annual success rate is the total number of satisfactory cases closed divided by the total number of cases closed each year.

family. Community service orders not only provide worthwhile experiences for offenders (McIvor, 1992), but also create opportunities for them to contribute to the community, thus gaining status and approval for their actions. The visibility of community sentences creates advantages for the offender and opportunities for the community to benefit from a service, and strengthen its ties with individuals who might otherwise be excluded and resentful. Another benefit is that it encourages offenders, rather than becoming recipients of a service, to dispense a service in the form of work that tends to be greatly appreciated by its beneficiaries. A community is capable of forgetting and forgiving offenders' past criminal behaviour and this assists in the healing and reintegration process.

Also, being perceived as a kind of humane punishment, community sentences help offenders to remain part of their families, and to retain their schooling and employment. Through their supervised activities, offenders can contribute to their own well-being as well as that of the community. In many respects, probation orders and community service orders can be effective ways to strengthen offenders' links to the community without weakening them. The Probation Service itself makes use of ordinary active citizens as volunteers to befriend offenders and to provide them with informal help and support. Effective links with employment training schemes can enhance an offender's capacity to become a law-abiding citizen. This strengthens offenders' links with the community and gives them a sense of their own worth, thereby improving the likelihood of their success in becoming law-abiding citizens.

Experience to date supports a number of generalisations about the apparent ingredients of effective community sentences. These generalisations are mainly derived from the meta-analytic reviews of interventions with offenders primarily in North America (Bernfeld et al., 2001; McGuire, 2002). The generalisations are also part of the 'What Works' initiative that was initiated jointly by the Home Office Probation Unit, HM Inspectorate of Probation, Association of Chief Officers of Probation and Central Probation Council (but with interest from the Prison Service and other Home Office agencies) in England and Wales (Chui, 2003b, Chui and Nellis, 2003; Whitehead and Thompson, 2004). In one of the earlier reports, the elements of effective interventions with offenders are: risk assessment and management, targeting and addressing the specific factors linked with offenders' offending, relevance to offenders' learning style, using promising intervention approaches with offenders, promoting community reintegration, and maintaining quality and integrity of programme delivery (Underdown, 1998). More specifically, some of the principles are:

- Risk assessment and classification: matching between offender risk level based on criminal history and other variables and level of supervision or degree of service intervention by using existing actuarial assessment tools (Robinson, 2003; Andrews et al., 2006).
- Criminogenic needs: identifying the needs most related to offending by using the risk-need assessment tool and focusing intervention on these

issues during the course of supervision (Ward and Stewart, 2003; Hollin and Palmer, 2006).

- Responsivity: matching learning styles between supervising officers and offenders (Ward et al., 2007).
- Treatment modality: applying a variety of models or approaches such as skills-based training, pro-social modelling and cognitive-behavioural theory to design and implement intervention programmes (see Fleet and Annison, 2003; Cherry, 2005; Trotter, 2014).
- Programme integrity: ensuring that the stated aims of programmes are linked to the theories and methods being used, and that well-trained and well-supported staff deliver the programmes with adequate resources (Andrews and Dowden, 2005).
- Partnerships: encouraging multi-agency collaboration to provide the offender help with employment, health, welfare and accommodation, and address the problems of specific groups of individuals involved in criminal activity in local districts (Rumgay, 2003).

It is important to note that the above principles of effective practice with offenders are primarily the research evidence from the British and North American experience. Whether all these are transferable to the Hong Kong Chinese context is questionable due to the different social, cultural and legal background. However, one lesson learnt from their experience is their commitment to evaluation research, and they see research as a part of accountable criminal justice management to identify good practice as well as room for improvement in the quality of the Probation Service (Chui, 2002; Israel and Chui, 2006; Mair, 2008).

Conclusion

The Social Welfare Department which is responsible for administering the two community sentences maintains a strong and cohesive professional identity as a social work agency. The cornerstone of the practice is to 'advise, assist and befriend' offenders under supervision. It may be true that frontline practitioners still have strong faith in the social work model of probation practice. The official data also confirm that a number of probation and community service orders were closed satisfactorily (see Tables 16.3 and 16.4). However, by using a different outcome measurement, slightly more than one-third of the adult probationers in Chui's (2004) study admitted to committing at least one further offence within one year of the order being awarded. This recidivism rate based on the offender's self-report is higher than the rate of unsatisfactory completion derived from the official records. This further confirms the deficiency of using official data to measure the effectiveness of the sentence.

Vexing questions have as yet remained unanswered, including: Amongst a broad range of social work intervention, what works or otherwise with the Chinese offenders? On what grounds should residential requirement in a probation home be attached to the probation sentence? How do the probation officers deal with revocation of the community sentence? Instead of using the completion rate as a measurement of recidivism, are there other outcome indicators? What is the short-term and long-term impact of the community sentence on offenders and the community? Does probation work better than community service in reducing offending behaviour? Should risk and needs instruments be introduced in Hong Kong? How do the magistrates and judges rate the quality of the social enquiry report? Do the public have confidence in the Probation Service? What sorts of changes should be proposed to improve the effectiveness of community sentences? How can we modernise the probation practice? Can community sentences be a real and effective alternative to short- or medium-term imprisonment for some offenders?

All these questions are difficult to answer at this point. Nevertheless, they point to the importance of moving a social work model of probation practice towards a more empirical-based social work criminal justice practice. Evidence-based practice encourages probation officers or social workers to be critical of their own intervention with offenders and continue to look for better alternatives for the offenders who are often marginalised and excluded from society.

Review questions

1 What are the major justifications for community sentences?
2 To what extent do you agree that qualified social workers should be appointed to deal with offenders in the community? Give reasons to justify your answer.
3 What are the advantages and disadvantages of sentencing offenders to community sentences as opposed to imprisonment?
4 If you were asked to evaluate the effectiveness of community sentences, how would you measure recidivism?

References

Andrews, D.A., Bonta, J. and Wormith, J.S. (2006) 'The recent past and near future of risk and/or need assessment', *Crime and Delinquency*, 52(1): 7–27.

Andrews, D.A. and Dowden, C. (2005) 'Managing correctional treatment of reduced recidivism: A meta-analytic review of programme integrity', *Legal and Criminological Psychology*, 10(2): 173–187.

Ashworth, A. (2007) 'Sentencing', in M. Maguire, R. Morgan and R. Reiner (eds) *The Oxford Handbook of Criminology* (4th edn) (pp. 990–1023), Oxford: Oxford University Press.

Barry, M. (2000) 'The mentor/monitor debate in criminal justice: "What works" for offenders', *British Journal of Social Work*, 30(5): 575–595.

Bernfeld, G.A., Farrington, D.P. and Leschied, A.W. (eds) (2001) *Offender Rehabilitation in Practice: Implementing and Evaluating Effective Programs*, Chichester, West Sussex: John Wiley & Sons.

Bottoms, A.E. and McWilliams, W. (1979) 'A non-treatment paradigm for probation practice', *British Journal of Social Work*, 9(2): 159–202.

Brownell, P. and Roberts, A.R. (2002) 'A century of social work in criminal justice and correctional settings', *Journal of Offender Rehabilitation*, 35(2): 1–17.

Census and Statistics Department (2015) *Hong Kong Annual Digest of Statistics*, Hong Kong: Census and Statistics Department.

Chan, W.T. (1996) 'Social work and services for offenders', in I. Chi and S.K. Cheung (eds) *Social Work in Hong Kong* (pp. 98–111), Hong Kong: Hong Kong Social Workers Association.

Cherry, S. (2005) *Transforming Behaviour: Pro-social Modelling in Practice*, Cullompton: Willan.

Chui, W.H. (1999) 'Residential treatment programs for young offenders in Hong Kong: A report', *International Journal of Offender Therapy and Comparative Criminology*, 43(3): 308–321.

Chui, W.H. (2002) 'Social work model of probation supervision for offenders in Hong Kong', *Probation Journal*, 49(4): 297–304.

Chui, W.H. (2003a) 'Experiences of probation supervision in Hong Kong: Listening to the young adult probationers', *Journal of Criminal Justice*, 31(6): 567–577.

Chui, W.H. (2003b) 'What works in reducing re-offending: Principles and programmes', in W.H. Chui and M. Nellis (eds) *Moving Probation Forward: Evidence, Arguments and Practice* (pp. 56–73), Harlow, Essex: Pearson Education.

Chui, W.H. (2004) 'Adult offenders on probation in Hong Kong: An exploratory study', *British Journal of Social Work*, 34(3): 443–454.

Chui, W.H. (2006) 'Factors associated with the one-year probation outcome: A self-report study in Hong Kong', *Asian Journal of Criminology*, 1(2): 155–171.

Chui, W.H. and Chan, H.C. (2011) 'Baseline findings of a prospective study on pro-offending attitudes and self-reported problems among juvenile probationers', *Hong Kong Journal of Social Work, 45*(1/2): 13–26.

Chui, W.H. and Chan, H.C. (2012) 'Criminal recidivism among Hong Kong male juvenile probationers', *Journal of Child and Family Studies*, 21(5): 857–868.

Chui, W.H. and Chan, H.C. (2014) 'Juvenile offenders' perceptions of probation officers as social workers in Hong Kong', *Journal of Social Work*, 14(4): 398–418.

Chui, W.H. and Nellis, M. (eds) (2003) *Moving Probation Forward: Evidence, Arguments and Practice*, Essex, Harlow: Pearson Education.

Clear, T. and Dammer, H.R. (2003) *The Offender in the Community* (2nd edn), Belmont, CA: Wadsworth.

Corrections Section (1994) *Basic Guide for Practice in Probation Service*. Hong Kong: Social Welfare Department (unpublished).

Davies, M., Croall, H. and Tyrer, J. (2015) *Criminal Justice: An Introduction to the Criminal Justice System in England and Wales* (5th edn), London: Pearson Education.

Director of Social Welfare (various issues, 2009–13) *Annual Report*, Hong Kong: Government Printer.

Director of Social Welfare (2015) *Services for Offenders*, Hong Kong: Social Welfare Department.

Fleet, F. and Annison, J. (2003) 'In support of effectiveness: Facilitating participation and sustaining change', in W.H. Chui and M. Nellis (eds) *Moving Probation Forward: Evidence, Arguments and Practice* (pp. 129–145), Harlow, Essex: Pearson Education.

Gregory, M. (2007) 'Probation training: Evidence from newly qualified officers', *Social Work Education*, 26(1): 53–68.

Harris, R. (1992) *Crime, Criminal Justice and the Probation Service*, London: Routledge.

Harris, R.J. and Lo, T.W. (2002) 'Community service: Its use in criminal justice', *International Journal of Offender Therapy and Comparative Criminology*, 46(4): 427–444.

Hollin, C.R. and Palmer, E.J. (2006) 'Criminogenic need and women offenders: A critique of the literature', *Legal and Criminological Psychology*, 11(2): 179–195.

Huang, T.P. (1970) 'A mini memoir of days gone by', *Hong Kong Probation*, 1(2): 2–9.

Israel, M. and Chui, W.H. (2006) 'If "something works" is the answer, what is the question?: Supporting pluralist evaluation in community corrections in the United Kingdom', *European Journal of Criminology*, 3(2): 181–200.

Klapmuts, N. (1976) 'Diversion from the justice system', in S. Schafer (ed.) *Readings in Contemporary Criminology* (pp. 222–233), Reston, VA: Reston Publishing.

Law Reform Commission of Hong Kong (1983) *Report – Community Service Orders (Topic 7)*, Hong Kong: Law Reform Commission of Hong Kong.

Lee, S.M. (1973) 'The Probation Service in Hong Kong', *International Journal of Offender Therapy and Comparative Criminology*, 17(1): 90–94.

Lo, T.W. and Harris, R. (2000) *Research Report on the Operation of Community Service Orders*, Hong Kong: Youth Studies Net, City University of Hong Kong.

Lo, T.W. and Harris, R. J. (2004) 'Community service orders in Hong Kong, England, and Wales: Twins or cousins', *International Journal of Offender Therapy and Comparative Criminology*, 48(3), 373–388.

Lo, T.W., Wong, D. and Maxwell, G. (2006) 'Community support and diversionary measures for juvenile offenders in Hong Kong: Old legacy, new age', *Asian Journal of Criminology*, 1(1): 9–20.

Mair, G. (2008) 'Research on community penalties', in R.D. King and E. Wincup (eds) *Doing Research on Crime and Justice* (2nd edn) (pp. 399–430), Oxford: Oxford University Press.

Mak, W.H. (1973) 'Reminiscence of the early probation work in Hong Kong', in Social Welfare Department (ed.) *Open Day Special Issue* (pp. 7–9), Hong Kong: Social Welfare Department.

Maltz, M.D. (1984) *Recidivism*, Orlando, FL: Academic Press.

McDonald, D. (1986) *Punishment Without Walls: Community Service Sentences in New York City*, New Brunswick, NJ: Rutgers University Press.

McGuire, J. (ed.) (2002) *Offender Rehabilitation and Treatment: Effective Programmes and Policies to Reduce Re-offending*, Chichester, West Sussex: John Wiley & Sons.

McIvor, G. (1992) *Sentenced to Serve: The Operation and Impact of Community Service by Offenders*, Aldershot: Avebury.

McWilliams, W. (1987) 'Probation, pragmatism and policy', *Howard Journal of Criminal Justice*, 26(2): 97–121.

Miller, R.L. and Gaines, L.K. (2016) *Criminal Justice in Action* (9th revised edn), Belmont, CA: Cengage Learning.

Nellis, M. (2000) 'Re-naming probation', *Probation Journal*, 47(1): 39–44.

Nellis, M. (2003) 'Probation training and the community justice curriculum', *British Journal of Social Work*, 33(7): 943–959.

Pollock, J.M. (2004) *Ethics in Crime and Justice: Dilemmas and Decisions* (4th edn), Belmont, CA: Wadsworth/Thomson Learning.

Raynor, P. and Vanstone, M. (2002) *Understanding Community Penalties: Probation, Policy and Social Change*, Buckingham: Open University Press.

Reynolds, K.M., Dziegielewski, S.F. and Sharp, C. (2004) 'Serving mentally ill offenders through community corrections: Joining two disciplines', *Journal of Offender Rehabilitation*, 40(1/2): 185–198.

Robinson, G. (2003) 'Risk and risk assessment', in W.H. Chui and M. Nellis (eds) *Moving Probation Forward: Evidence, Arguments and Practice* (pp. 108–128), Harlow: Pearson Education.

Rumgay, J. (2003) 'Partnerships in the probation service', in W.H. Chui and M. Nellis (eds) *Moving Probation Forward: Evidence, Arguments and Practice* (pp. 195–213), Harlow: Pearson Education.

Sluder, R.D., Sapp, A.D. and Langston, D.C. (1994) 'Guiding philosophies for probation in the 21st century', *Federal Probation*, 58(2): 3–10.

Social Welfare Department (various issues, 2003–06) *Social Welfare Services in Figures*, Hong Kong: Government Printer.

Taylor, A. (2001) 'Criminal justice social work in prison and community settings', in M. Connolly (ed.) *New Zealand Social Work: Contexts and Practice* (pp. 193–205), Auckland: Oxford University Press.

Trotter, C. (2014) *Working with Involuntary Clients: A Guide to Practice* (3rd edn), London: Routledge.

Underdown, A. (1998) *Strategies for Effective Offender Rehabilitation: Report of the HMIP What Works Project*, London: Home Office.

Vass, A.A. (1990) *Alternatives to Prison: Punishment, Custody and the Community*, London: Sage.

Ward, T., Melser, J. and Yates, P.M. (2007) 'Reconstructing the risk-need-responsivity model: A theoretical elaboration and evaluation', *Aggression and Violent Behavior*, 12(2): 208–228.

Ward, T. and Stewart, C. (2003) 'Criminogenic needs and human needs: A theoretical model', *Psychology, Crime and Law*, 9(2): 125–143.

Whitehead, P. and Thompson, J. (2004) *Knowledge and the Probation Service: Raising Standards for Trainees, Assessors and Practitioners*, Chichester: John Wiley & Sons.

Willis, A. (1986) 'Help and control in probation: An empirical assessment of probation practice', in J. Pointing (ed.) *Alternatives to Custody* (pp. 162–182), Oxford: Blackwell.

Worrall, A. and Hoy, C. (2005) *Punishment in the Community: Managing Offenders, Making Choices*, Cullompton: Willan.

Yip, T.C. (1973) 'The role of a probation officer', in Social Welfare Department (ed.) *Open Day Special Issue* (pp. 8–12), Hong Kong: Social Welfare Department.

Legislation cited

Community Service Orders Ordinance (Cap. 378)
Criminal Procedure Ordinance (Cap. 221)
Dangerous Drugs Ordinance (Cap. 134)
Juvenile Offenders Ordinance (Cap. 226)
Probation of Offenders Ordinance (Cap. 298)
Weapons Ordinance (Cap. 217)

Useful websites

American Probation and Parole Association www.appa-net.org/eweb/
Confederation of European Probation cep-probation.org
Law Reform Commission of Hong Kong www.hkreform.gov.hk/en/index/index.htm
National Probation Service (Home Office, England and Wales) www.justice.gov.uk/offenders/probationservice
Social Welfare Department, HKSAR www.swd.gov.hk

17

PRISON AND CORRECTIONAL SERVICES

T. Wing Lo

Introduction

Custodial sentences are operated by the Correctional Services Department (CSD), formerly the Prisons Department before 1982, which is responsible for the secure, safe and humane custody of all persons detained under the *Immigration Ordinance* (Cap. 115), and persons convicted of a crime and sentenced by the court under the *Criminal Procedure Ordinance* (Cap. 221), *Prisons Ordinance* (Cap. 234), *Detention Centres Ordinance* (Cap. 239), *Drug Addiction Treatment Centres Ordinance* (Cap. 244), *Rehabilitation Centres Ordinance* (Cap. 567), and *Training Centres Ordinance* (Cap. 280). The vision of the CSD is to become an internationally acclaimed correctional service, upholding five core values: integrity, professionalism, humanity, discipline and perseverance (Hong Kong Correctional Services, 2014). While the CSD provides multi-level intervention to correct offenders, its major duties during daily operations are summarised in two main categories: prison management and rehabilitation of offenders.

Radzinowicz and Hood (1990) remarked that the modern prison has emerged as its functions changed from being primarily custodial-coercive to punitive, and offenders are now sent to prison 'as a punishment, not for punishment' (Ruck, 1951: 23). As such, the loss of personal freedom due to incarceration is already a punishment, and the conditions inside prisons should be as humane and rehabilitative as possible to maintain the dignity of individual prisoners. Inside correctional institutions, the CSD provides prisoners with basic necessities, comprehensive medical services and a decent and healthy living environment. Prisoners are allowed to spend time out of their cells for a significant proportion of the time. The CSD maintains order and control to minimise the chance of escapes and acts of indiscipline, and its programmes emphasise self-control and discipline. It was reported that 3,592 cases of violation of prison discipline occurred in 2014, 10% more than in 2013 (Hong Kong Correctional Services, 2014), but there had been 'no escapes for seven years' (Asia and Pacific Conference of Correctional Administrators (APCCA) 2014: 14). In 2013, X-ray body scanners were introduced to replace manual rectal searching, resulting in 'a decrease in the number of seizures of dangerous drugs from 158 in 2012 to 95 in 2013' (APCCA, 2014: 14).

In the domain of rehabilitation, the CSD provides prisoners with a range of psychological and welfare services, and opportunities to engage in useful work. To correct their criminal behaviour, it provides education, vocational training, drug addiction treatment, community reintegration programmes, and aftercare and support services. Operating under a new correctional services integrated management model (CSIM), based on three core concepts – caring for people, caring for the environment, and caring for community – the CSD protects the public and helps reduce crime but simultaneously promotes community acceptance of, and support for, rehabilitated offenders through public education, publicity and community involvement. The CSIM emphasises 'people orientation, operational efficiency, economy of scale, effective resources management, greening concepts, and community networking' (APCCA, 2011: 21).

Overall situation

Variations in the rate of imprisonment can be explained by many factors, such as crime rates, considerations in public policy, the supply of prison places, unemployment, and changing fashions in punishment philosophy, demography and economic activities (Zimring and Hawkins, 1991). In Hong Kong, the prison population was on the rise since the turn of the century. In 1995, the total prison population was 17,631; this number rose to 20,859 in 2001 and reached its peak with 30,070 prisoners in 2004, then declining gradually for ten years to 11,301 prisoners in 2014. Looking at the differences between male and female prisoners, the female population has increased threefold from the mid-1990s to mid-2000s, jumping from 4,015 in 1995 to 13,775 in 2004 (see Figure 17.1). This was largely a result of the influx of illegal immigrants from Mainland China prostituting in Hong Kong. This trend was similar to the rise in the female prison population in England and Wales throughout the 1990s due to the growth in the number of female foreign nationals convicted of drug trafficking (Morgan, 2002).

Overcrowding was common in correctional institutions in the 1990s and 2000s. In the early 1990s, Vagg (1991, 1994) criticised that the correctional system as a whole was holding approximately a third more prisoners than it was designed for. The problem reached its peak in the mid-2000s. The average daily population of prisoners in all CSD institutions was 13,138 in 2004 and the overall occupancy rate was 123.1% (Hong Kong Correctional Services, 2004). The CSD described it as a 'perennial problem' (APCCA, 2005). However, overcrowding was not spread equally across institutions. Some institutions experienced more problems with overcrowding than others. For instance, it was 'highest (at 88%) in the detention centre in 1991' (Vagg, 1991: 143), and some institutions were holding over 50% above their certified capacity (Vagg, 1994).

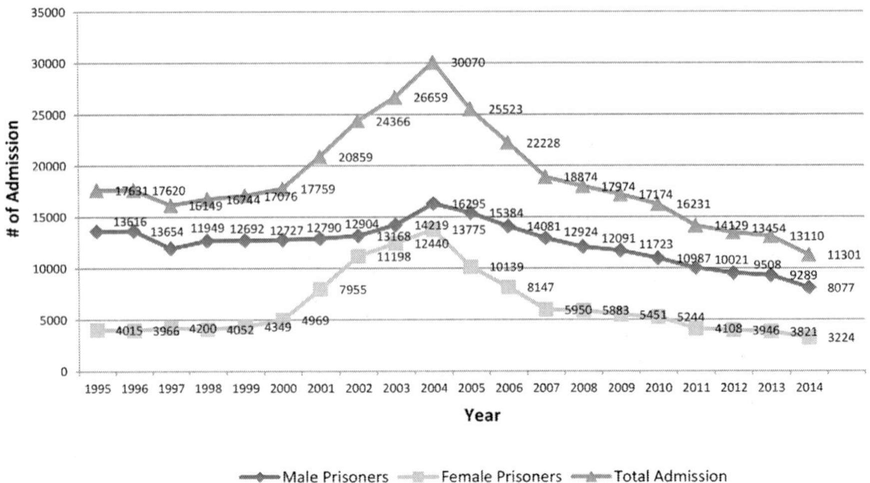

Figure 17.1 Total population of prison, 1995–2014

In 1996, Pik Uk Correctional Institution, with a standard capacity of 385, held over 500 inmates (Lo et al., 1997). Since the number of inmates was far more than the original capacity in some institutions, insufficient space and resources were used to the maximum level, facilities and manpower were thinly spread to meet their needs, and the staff were pressurised.

Hong Kong is a very crowded city and electronic monitoring (Whitfield, 1997) is not a viable option to monitor offenders' activities in the community. As such, the failure to use electronic monitoring, or specifically, incapacitation achieved through electronic tagging, adds to the issues of overcrowding in prisons. In addition, the extensive use of recalls to prisons (Vagg, 1991) for those who breach supervision conditions was another direct cause of overcrowding. In 2005, 791 recall orders were issued (Hong Kong Correctional Services, 2005). In 2009, the percentages of recallees for rehabilitation, detention and training centres were 51%, 46% and 34%, respectively (Lo et al., 2010). They were recalled mainly because of curfew violation.

In particular, overcrowding was more of a serious problem in female institutions. In 1997, Tai Tam Gap Correctional Institution held 81% over its original capacity of 160 (Lo et al., 1997). From 2002 to 2005, the average daily population of female prisoners ranged from 2,507 to 2,821 (see Figure 17.2), and the occupancy rates for female institutions were between 159% and 197% (Hong Kong Correctional Services, 2002, 2003, 2004, 2005), resulting in the conversion of some male prisons to house female prisoners temporarily. The International Centre for Prison Studies discovered that Hong Kong had one of the highest proportions of female prisoners (Walmsley, 2006). They found that female prisoners made up 22.1% of the penal population in Hong Kong, as

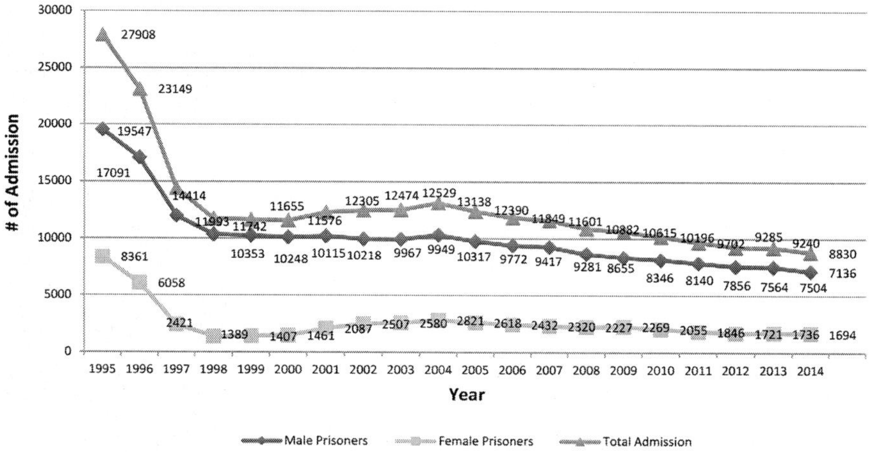

Figure 17.2 Average daily population of prisoners, 1995–2014

against 4.6% in Mainland China, 5.3% in South Korea and 11% in Singapore. From 2000 to 2006, between 70% and 88% of female prisoners in Hong Kong were mainland sex workers. They were imprisoned for soliciting and/or breaching their conditions of stay (Laidler, 2009). Laidler et al. (2007) described this as a 'bureaucratic approach to justice' as the sentence was frequently a result of routine guilty pleas, quick sentencing decisions (three minutes on average) that ignored case characteristics, and standardised sentencing protocols. This bureaucratic routine was criticised as achieving neither deterrence nor rehabilitation of female prisoners.

The year 2004 saw a record high in the imprisonment of female offenders. The overall prison admissions of female offenders began to drop in 2005 and maintained a downward trend over the last decade (dropping from 13,775 in 2004 to 3,224 in 2014) (see Figure 17.1). The exact reason for the decline in imprisonment rates is yet to be determined, but it is speculated that the rising economy on the mainland makes it unattractive for mainland sex workers to work in Hong Kong (*South China Morning Post*, 2014). With the decline in the penal population, the overcrowding situation in prisons has been substantially improved. When compared, however, female institutions have suffered overcrowding more than young male institutions.

In recent years, the overall overcrowding situation in prisons has been substantially improved. In 2014, the average daily population of prisoners dropped to 8,830 from its 2004 peak, and the occupancy rate was only 76.6% (Hong Kong Correctional Services, 2014). Nevertheless, services and facilities for female prisoners continue to be a concern of the CSD administration (APCCA, 2014). The CSD sought long-term solutions to address the issue of overcrowding in female institutions by the redevelopment of Lo Wu Correctional Institution. Completed in 2010, it has a capacity of 1,400 female adult prisoners who are housed in one minimum-security wing and two medium-security wings.

In line with the United Nations' adoption of the Bangkok Rules (*The United Nations Rules for the Treatment of Women Prisoners and Non-custodial Measures for Women Offenders*) in 2010, the CSD has endeavoured to provide quality correctional services for female prisoners. In addition, to alleviate overcrowding in female prisons, the Personal Growth and Emotion Treatment Centre for Women (PSY GYM) was set up in the Lo Wu Correctional Institution in 2011. It provides specialised treatment to handle female prisoners' parenting problems, dysfunctional human relationships, abusive and traumatic experiences, as well as violence committed by/against women (Hong Kong Correctional Services, 2014).

A milestone in the correctional services

In 1996, the government commissioned a research team at City University of Hong Kong to review all the rehabilitation services for young offenders in Hong Kong. The team interviewed over 500 young offenders and 30 staff from the CSD, as well as 38 magistrates who had experience in sentencing young offenders. Based on the findings, the team recommended a number of measures (Lo et al., 1997). The government responded positively by making a number of improvements in correctional services. The following are two significant developments:

Service gaps and the new rehabilitation centres

Some magistrates expressed concerns about young offenders who were not physically fit but where the detention centre was considered the most appropriate sentencing option due to the absence of a suitable alternative. The detention centre requires young offenders to be physically fit in order to undergo the harsh training, such as hard work, physical training and drilling. The research team found some young offenders who were not fit enough to attend detention centre, but for whom community-based treatment programmes were too lenient, were forced to receive long-term rehabilitation in training centres. In addition, the inadequacy of short-term rehabilitative programmes for young female offenders was another issue raised by magistrates. They expressed the need to provide short-term rehabilitative programmes for young people because the detention centre (1–6 months) was not an option available for female offenders and physically unfit male offenders, and the sentencing period in training centres (6–36 months) was too long.

Having identified the service gaps, the research team recommended another form of short-term rehabilitative programme for both young male and female offenders. In addition to the emphasis on discipline, deportment and hygiene, it was recommended that the programme incorporate social training and counselling services for young offenders. The recommendations were accepted by the government and the *Rehabilitation Centres Ordinance* was enacted in 2001 and implemented in 2002, in response to the service gaps identified in the review.

A new division of rehabilitation

The key task of the CSD is correction and rehabilitation of offenders. In the 1980s, the CSD introduced a whole range of rehabilitative programmes, including pre-sentence assessment, education, vocational training, community reintegration programmes, psychological services, aftercare and welfare services, and the Release Under Supervision Scheme. New services developed in the mid-1990s included sentence planning, a post-release supervision scheme, statutory review of long-term prison sentences and so on. However, the research team was concerned with the organisational structure, in that the assistant commissioner (operations) had to direct and oversee all matters relating to penal operations and rehabilitation. This arrangement was viewed as being manifestly inadequate since operations and security concerns would continue to take precedence over rehabilitation matters (Lo et al., 1997). In order to achieve better coordination of policies and programme development related to rehabilitation, the research team recommended a split of Operations and Rehabilitation in the CSD line management, and for the whole area of rehabilitation to be placed under a new Rehabilitation Division headed by a new post of assistant commissioner (Lo et al., 1997).

This recommendation was later fully adopted and the Division of Rehabilitation was formally set up in 1998. It has functioned effectively since its inception, as reflected by the modernisation of vocational training facilities, provision of social work training to frontline staff, and the development of a systematic risk assessment tool and various treatment programmes for inmates. The rehabilitative programmes and functions, previously under the direction of the Operations Division, were restructured or reorganised. Since then, the CSD has gradually made substantial developments in the following strategic areas (Pang, 2007):

- specialisation of treatment services;
- modernisation of educational programmes;
- accreditation of vocational training;
- reinforcement of drug abuse prevention;
- restoration of parent–inmate relationships;
- promotion of cultural activities;
- enhancement of community partnerships; and
- appeal for community support.

Types of institutional regimes

There are five types of regimes – prisons, drug addiction treatment centres, training centres, a detention centre and rehabilitation centres – with the last three types of centre being targeted solely at young offenders (see Table 17.1). The CSD also runs halfway houses, custodial wards in public hospitals, and remand centres that receive offenders from, and deliver them to, the court while they are waiting for assessment reports, trials and sentencing. The CSD and the Social Welfare Department establish the Young Offender Assessment Panel to advise the court in the sentencing of young offenders.

With the exception of prisons, inmates of all the other regimes have undetermined sentences. Their exact date of release is determined by the administration of each institution rather than by the court. Under a progressive system set by each regime, inmates can be promoted through several grades, with the promotion giving inmates more opportunities and fewer restrictions. The point of release is determined by the superintendent or senior superintendent on the advice of a review board of the institutions concerned. The regimes are introduced below.

Detention centre

The US-style boot camp for teenagers has been increasingly used as a sentencing option in its own right (Lee, 2001). The Hong Kong detention centre is an example of such use. It places an emphasis on physical training, where the '3S' ('short, sharp, shock') training is the core element for male offenders who have

Table 17.1 Regimes of correctional services

Programmes	*Age*	*Period of institutionalisation*	*Post-release supervision period*	*Special supervision conditions*
Detention centre (male only)	14–20 21–24	1–6 months 3–12 months	One year	Under curfew and must stay at home overnight
Rehabilitation centre	14–20	3–9 months	One year	Under curfew and must stay at home overnight
Training centre	14–20	6–36 months	Three years	Long-term supervision
Drug addiction treatment centre	14 or above	2–12 months	One year	Must have urine sample checked regularly
Youth Offenders Scheme (youth prison)	14–20	Determined by the court	One year	–
Prison	21 or above	Determined by the court	–	–

never been institutionalised (Chui, 1999, 2001; Lo, 2008). 'Short' refers to the sentencing period: youth offenders aged between 14 and 20 are detained for terms between one and six months, while young adults aged from 21 to 24 are detained for terms of three to 12 months. 'Sharp' refers to the high physical requirements of the training in which inmates are required to do hard labour. 'Shock' refers to the impact of the training aimed to make inmates realise the consequences of committing crimes within the short training period of institutionalisation. Due to the emphasis on strict discipline, hard labour, and body and foot training, offenders must be physically and mentally fit to participate in the vigorous activities. It is expected that after the tough training, offenders will come to understand the consequences of law breaking. The progress of the inmates is regularly monitored by a review committee, which decides when to discharge them. Before release, the inmates need to have found suitable employment or a school placement. Following release, they are subject to one year of aftercare supervision.

Rehabilitation centres

Those young offenders who are not fit enough to endure the harsh training in the detention centre, may be placed in a rehabilitation centre, which adopts a 3R framework: reconstruction, resilience and reintegration (Lo et al., 2010). The whole rehabilitation programme comprises two phases and provides three to nine months' training for inmates. Phase I of the programme is two to five months in duration, with an emphasis on disciplinary training. Inmates attend half-day basic work skills training and half-day educational or counselling programmes. The aim is to develop offenders' ability for self-control and a regular life pattern. Phase II consists of a one- to four-month community-based reintegration programme. Offenders are permitted to go out to work, attend training and education courses, or participate in community service, and are subject to one year of aftercare supervision following release. On average, the inmates spent three and a half months in Phase I and two months in Phase II (Lo et al., 2010).

However, there is a dilemma whether to treat the rehabilitation centres that house Phase II inmates as a rehabilitation venue or a prison (Lo et al., 2010). On the one hand, Phase II allows the young offenders to attend programmes in the community to achieve the purposes of rehabilitation and community reintegration. On the other hand, they are still detained under the *Rehabilitation Centres Ordinance*, under which section 12 states that *Prisons Ordinance* applies 'as if such persons are prisoners and a rehabilitation centre were a prison'. As such, those who breach the ordinance will be handled according to prison rules. Such prison rules may sometimes clash with the young offenders' rehabilitation needs (Lo et al., 2010).

Training centres

Offenders between the ages of 14 and 20 are the target of training centres. The period of training varies from six months to three years, progressing through three stages. All inmates are required to undergo half-day educational training and half-day vocational training every day, commensurate with their previous educational attainment and work experience. The centres also organise various types of activities for inmates who have behaved satisfactorily and are physically fit. Activities such as volunteer service, Boy Scouts and Girl Guides, outreach training and lion dances are all aimed at helping youths reintegrate into society. These activities also serve as incentives for good behaviour. When inmates have satisfied the centres' requirements, and employment or schooling arrangements are in place, a review committee will approve inmates' release. Most inmates with good behaviour are released after serving around 15 to 18 months (Lo et al., 1997). After release, the youths undergo three years of aftercare supervision.

The population for training centres, which provide longer periods of institutionalisation, declined steadily from 443 in 1995 to 187 in 2004 (see Figure 17.3). In contrast, the population of the detention centre rose sharply from 238 in 1999 to 434 in 2002, while the number of inmates in training centres had dropped sharply from 264 in 1999 to 137 in 2003, reflecting the sentencing ideology of the court at that time – that is, favouring shorter sentences. The detention centre was previously the most overcrowded institution in the early 1990s (Vagg, 1991: 143). Since 2002, the population of the detention centre has dropped, primarily due to two factors. First, there has been an increase in the number of drug-using youth offenders who do not meet the 'physically fit' criterion of the detention centre. Second, the launch in late 2002 of rehabilitation centres, which also provide short-term institutionalisation for young offenders, has reduced the potential targets of the detention centre.

The combined population of detention and rehabilitation centres peaked at nearly 600 inmates in 2003, while the population of training centres dropped

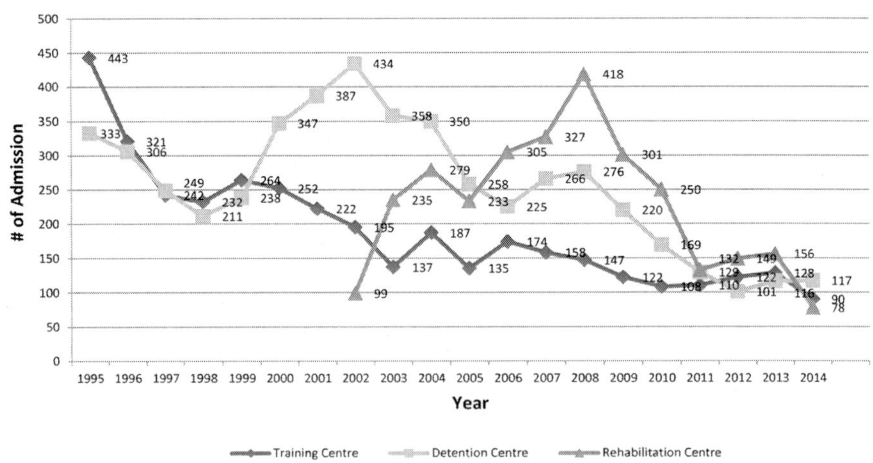

Figure 17.3 Population of detention, rehabilitation and training centres, 1995–2014

below the 200 level, strongly indicating that the court favoured shorter sentences for young offenders. Since 2011, the population of the detention centre, rehabilitation centres and training centres has further declined to a very low level. In 2014, they housed 117, 78 and 90 inmates, respectively. This may reflect the declining youth crime rate in Hong Kong (see Figure 17.4) or the magistrates' reluctance to use custodial sentences for young offenders.

Drug addiction treatment centres

Drug abusers who have been convicted of an offence must undergo compulsory drug treatment at a drug addiction treatment centre run by the CSD. The treatment period lasts from two to 12 months, depending on the progress and improvement of individual offenders. The treatment centres detoxify and restore inmates' physical health. A variety of therapeutic and treatment programmes, including work therapy, personal counselling, outdoor physical activities and discipline training, are provided to wean inmates off drug dependence. Inmates attend a relapse prevention programme to prepare them psychologically for their release. Upon release, inmates must stay in a halfway house for six to eight weeks and receive one year of aftercare supervision (Lo, 2008). In the mid-1990s, the population of drug addiction treatment centres was very high (e.g. 2,650 inmates in 1996), reflecting the alarming number of drug-use offenders at that historical juncture. Alongside the overall decline in penal population, the population of the drug addiction treatment centres dropped to 1,324 inmates in 2004 and further to 1,041 in 2014 (see Figure 17.5).

Prisons/youth prisons

Prisons provide safe and humanitarian confinement of prisoners. The terms of imprisonment are decided by the court. Young inmates aged between 14 and 20

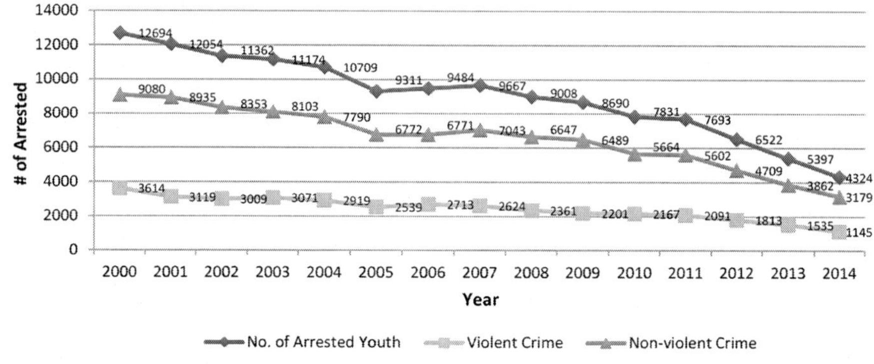

Figure 17.4 Youth crime rate, 2000–14

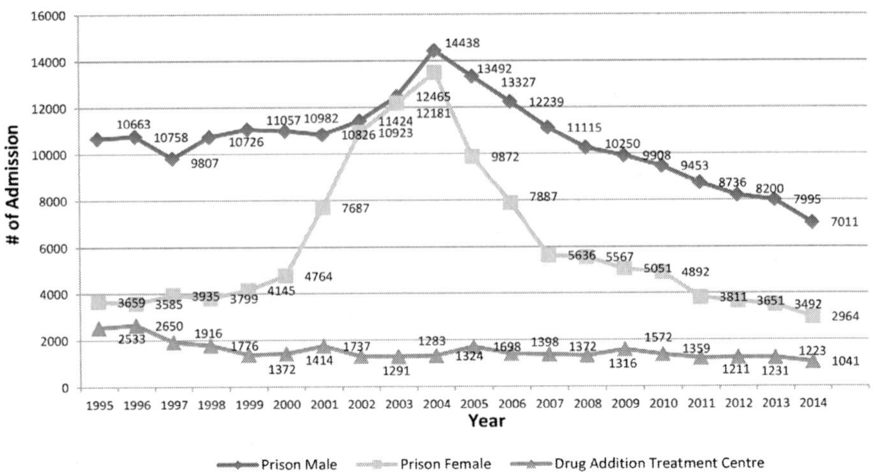

Figure 17.5 Population of prison and drug addiction treatment centres, 1995–2014

are separated from adult prisoners. Although the emphasis is on confinement, those youths who behave well, who have good skills and who have not completed primary education may receive half-day education and half-day vocational training. Vocational training is not aimed at developing offenders' work skills because of the short period of custody, but instead helping them to use their time constructively, to cultivate work habits, and to set positive life goals. Adult male prisons are classified into maximum-, medium- and minimum-security establishments. Prisoners with psychiatric or related problems are housed in the Siu Lam Psychiatric Centre. *Prison Rules* (Cap. 234A) require adult prisoners to work for no more than ten hours a day, six days a week. Rehabilitative programmes previously catering solely for young inmates are now extended to include voluntary adult prisoners aged below 35 who have shown interest in participating in educational programmes and vocational training. Unlike adult prisoners, young inmates are required to receive one year of statutory supervision after release.

Over the last two decades, the prevailing trend of the population of male and female prisoners is quite similar. Being constant for some years in the late 1990s, the population of both groups rose sharply in the first half of the 2000s and peaked in 2004. Since 2005, a sharp fall in the prison population has occurred. In 2014, the population of both groups tumbled to record lows in two decades, with only 7,011 male prisoners and 2,964 female prisoners (see Figure 17.5). However, in line with the ageing population, there is a growing number of elderly prisoners aged 65 or above. It was estimated that the average daily population of this group of prisoners will rise from about 2% in 2015 to approximately 5% in 2023 (Hong Kong Correctional Services, 2014). In response to such an increase, an elderly unit was set up in the Ma Hang Prison with special provisions for elderly prisoners, such as the availability of warm showers throughout the year, barrier-free access and ramps, handrails for support, large-print notices, etc. (APCCA, 2014: 64).

Rehabilitative programmes provided by the regimes

Education

Education is mainly provided to youth inmates, not adult prisoners. Most of them are unmotivated learners, or have gone through frustrating experiences in normal schools, or left school when they were very young (Morgan, 2002). The curriculum is precisely designed to meet with the characteristics of penal education, not only in that inmates have different attainment levels, but in that they are admitted at different times, different rates, stay for different lengths of time, and their social maturity outstrips their education attainment. In view of this diversity, the CSD has to find a balance in achieving three different objectives: skills attainment, knowledge enhancement and moral education. The first objective is to provide inmates with practical subjects so that they can learn useful skills to find employment post-release. The second objective is to enhance inmates' academic knowledge so as to prepare them for public examinations or further studies. Moral education, the third objective, is expected to play a role in reconstructing inmates' characters and life goals (Lo, 2008).

To achieve the first two objectives, classes, with standards ranging from primary to secondary levels, are conducted by qualified schoolmasters, with an inspectorate system run by the CSD itself. The curriculum is close to, but not the same as, mainstream education, modified to suit inmates' needs and academic levels. Time is devoted to the teaching of practical subjects, such as computer application, language, management and accountancy. Teaching materials are tailor-made, using lively teaching styles, such as learning English and Mandarin through listening to pop songs. Inmates dedicated to continuing their studies, or with the will to learn, are helped to fit in the nearest level of normal school. Arrangements are made for able inmates to sit public examinations that can bridge their further studies, such as book keeping and accounts, and international English for speakers of other languages.

It is the strategy of the CSD to achieve the above two objectives in training centres because of the longer period of detention. Since the detention centre emphasises physical training and the period of detention is very short, education is not a primary task. All inmates attend a half-hour remedial class each week, focusing on moral education. At youth prisons, inmates' sentence length varies and education is not mandatory because most inmates have low motivation to study. Having a definite sentence, inmates are not afraid of teachers complaining of class misconduct, and it is difficult for teachers to control class discipline. Nevertheless, education can be provided if requested by inmates, both youth and adult. The main focus of education in youth prisons is on moral education but a small number of able inmates are helped to achieve success in public examinations.

The CSD has set up a number of educational funds, such as the Prisoners' Education Trust Fund, to help prisoners pay for tuition fees, study aids and examination fees. In 2014, adult and young offenders attended public examinations offered by various educational institutions, such as City & Guilds, London Chamber of Commerce and Industry, Hong Kong Management Association, Open University of Hong Kong, and the School of Continuing and Professional Studies of The Chinese University of Hong Kong. They took 763 examination papers, with a pass rate of 72% (Hong Kong Correctional Services, 2014). Volunteer university lecturers have regularly provided continuing education for prisoners since 2004.

Industrial work and vocational training

Research suggests that there is a high correlation between crime and unemployment (Britt, 1995; Collins and Weatherburn, 1995; Raphael and Winter-Ebmer, 2001). In correctional institutions, a variety of industrial activities are offered, such as metalwork, garment making, fibreglass, bookbinding, sign making, carpentry and laundry services. The objectives embodied in industrial work and vocational training are threefold: first, to help inmates cultivate good working habits; second, to gain self-confidence and learn positive working attitudes, such as getting along with others, and following rules and regulations; and third, to help inmates learn specific trade skills to suit their aptitude and capacity, enabling them to experience a sense of achievement and compete for relevant employment upon release (Lo, 2008). It is expected that discharged inmates with stable employment will adjust to society more readily and refrain from a deviant way of life.

Most of the vocational training programmes are carried out in training centres because of the longer period of detention. However, not all inmates can be offered the chance to enrol for special trade skills training within training centres because of limited places, or because the courses demand that inmates possess specific academic attainments. Another consideration is the variation in the length of the sentence. Thus, only those inmates who have performed or behaved well, meet the basic academic requirements; those serving longer sentences have more opportunity to participate in the courses. The reality of the situation in the CSD is that both physical and human resources are always limited, so the CSD gives priority to those inmates best able to benefit from the more favourable training (Lo, 2008). Recently, the chances for training have increased due to the decline in the penal population.

Compared with their counterparts in training centres, inmates in other institutions have fewer opportunities to attend special trade-skills training. For instance, the unique '3S' training in the detention centre does not allow room for vocational training. In rehabilitation centres, although inmates attend half-day basic work skills training, the aim is more on promoting positive work habits and attitudes rather than learning a specific trade because the time of detention is too short. Similarly, the objective of industrial work in youth prisons is mainly to kill time and promote work habits rather than train in job skills. The work programme in drug addiction treatment centres helps addicts to improve their health and develop better work habits. An encouraging development was the launch of the Enhanced Reintegration Programme in the mid-2000s for voluntary male adult prisoners below the age of 30. Inmates can attend full-time vocational training on a voluntary basis if they have completed junior secondary education and have a remainder of six to 18 months in jail. They can attend training programmes, such as Chinese cooking, clerical and office work, hair design, air-conditioning, electrical maintenance and painting.

The CSD actively looks for opportunities for the training courses to be recognised or accredited by external authorities, such as the City & Guilds, Vocational Training Council, Construction Industry Council, Clothing Industry Training Authority, and Employees Retraining Board. For example, after completing a food and beverage course in one of the institutions, inmates will obtain a certificate recognised by Commonwealth countries. Such recognition aims to arouse inmates' interest, enhance self-confidence and increase job opportunities. Moreover, the CSD constantly modifies the course contents to meet market demand. For example, graphic media workshops, travel agent assistant training, care worker training, horticulture assistant training, and professional taxi driver training courses were recently organised for prisoners (Hong Kong Correctional Services, 2014). In 2014, prisoners took 2,649 vocational qualification examination papers and trade tests, with a passing rate of 96%. On daily average, a total of 4,452 prisoners were engaged in 13 trades in about 130 industrial workshops; the rest of the prisoners were assigned to domestic work such as cleaning, kitchen and maintenance work. The total commercial value of products produced was HK$460.6 million (Hong Kong Correctional Services, 2014).

Community reintegration, family and cultural activities

Activities, such as the Hong Kong Award Scheme, Boy Scouts, Girl Guides, adventure-based counselling and Outward Bound, are organised to help inmates develop potential, discipline, leadership and resilience. Other cultural activities such as lion dance classes, marching band, and Chinese orchestra and band are organised for inmates. Coordinated by a full-time chaplain, prisoners' participation in religious activities is highly encouraged. Regular visits to prisons are paid by a number of religious organisations and their volunteers (Chui and Cheng, 2013).

Voluntary work is an effective means to achieve social reintegration. Community service provides opportunities for inmates to connect with people from all walks of life, and helps reduce the social stigma of prisoners. Feeling that they are able to serve society, inmates gain a sense of accomplishment and more positive self-image. Such satisfaction cannot be obtained through committing an offence or in their former life of deviance. When they see the struggle of the deprived and underprivileged, they realise they are not the most unfortunate individuals. This encounter motivates inmates to face personal problems optimistically and appreciate the chances they are given in rehabilitation (Lo, 2008).

However, it is impossible to engage all inmates in such activities because of the limited opportunities provided to inmates by the organising bodies. The financial implications for inmates to participate in costly activities, and the risks and physical demands involved in some activities are also major concerns. Furthermore, not all inmates are entrusted or permitted, on security or medical grounds, to go out of the centres, e.g. those on escapee lists, or on medical officers' lists. Due to limited places, only those with good performance are given a priority to participate in these activities (Lo et al., 1997; Lo, 2008). Thus the activities are seen as an incentive or reward for good behaviour. Inmates have to take turns and very often fair performance does not guarantee a chance, not to mention those with behavioural or adjustment problems.

Family work is regarded as one major means of rehabilitation. Aftercare officers not only provide guidance to inmates but sometimes also to their families, because without adequate family support the rehabilitation inmates have undergone would be in vain. Family contact is a continuous process. Officers normally keep close contact with the inmates' family from immediately after their admission up until just prior to their release. Parents are invited to visit the centre in order to understand its programmes and operation. Family members are invited to attend the inmates' birthday party. Parent groups or inmate–parent programmes are held to improve the relationship and communication between inmates and their family. Inmate–parent centres have been formed (Lo et al., 2010). However, since not all family members are cooperative and supportive, or attend meetings, aftercare officers often encounter difficulties in offering effective services.

Psychological services

Psychological services are provided to inmates and family members who need assistance in coping with emotional, family and behavioural problems. In actual operation, psychological services are provided by small teams, each comprising one clinical psychologist and one officer. The officer is responsible for providing supportive counselling and organising group activities for inmates. In the 1990s, a perpetual shortage of clinical psychologists was a common problem in a variety of disciplines in Hong Kong, and the CSD was no exception. For instance, in 1996, only 60% of clinical psychologist vacancies could be filled (Lo et al., 1997). This shortage issue has been much alleviated today. However, it is still an ideal to achieve the target of one clinical psychologist per institution.

Compared to the 1990s, there has been substantial development in the assessment and treatment programmes in which psychologists play an active and significant role. An integrated procedure for evaluating and managing the risks and needs of offenders has been developed. The Risks and Needs Assessment and Management Protocol for Offenders was implemented to enhance prison management and the quality of rehabilitative programmes (Hong Kong Correctional Services, 2014). A number of quality treatment programmes have been put in place, such as the Sex Offender Evaluation and Treatment Programme, Offending Behaviour Programme, Inmate-Parent Programme for young offenders, Violence Prevention Programme for adult offenders, and Substance Abuse Awareness and Recidivism Prevention Programme for drug addicts. The PSY GYM mentioned above is a gender-specific treatment service for female prisoners (Hong Kong Correctional Services, 2014).

Aftercare services

Discharged inmates of the detention centre, rehabilitation centres, training centres, drug addiction treatment centres, youth prisons and various 'Release Under Supervision' schemes will face a period of statutory supervision provided by aftercare officers. They are recalled if they fail to observe the conditions of supervision. The CSD adopts the principle of 'throughcare' (Lo et al., 1997; Kwok, 2007; Lo et al., 2010). That is, aftercare service begins inside the institutions so that a relationship built on trust can be established between aftercare officers and inmates and their family at an early stage. This includes helping newcomers adjust to the environment of the institution and observe rules and regulations, encouraging inmates to participate in community reintegration activities, and preparing them for release towards the end of custody. Pre-release therapeutic courses and information are provided to help inmates deal with problems they may experience upon release. After release, aftercare officers will visit ex-offenders in their hostel, home or workplace to give further support and guidance.

To facilitate inmates' adjustment into society after a period of incarceration, discharged inmates of the detention centre, rehabilitation centres, training centres or drug addiction treatment centres are placed in a halfway house, such as Phoenix House, Bauhinia House and Pelican House, for a period of six weeks to four months. They either study or work in the community and learn to re-adapt to society. Collaboration between officers of the halfway house and aftercare officers of the discharged inmates' mother institution is in place. The former provides guidance, organises interest and social groups, and encourages inmates to engage in more contact with their family throughout this transitional period. The latter pays regular visits to discharged inmates residing in the halfway house and continues to provide supervision as soon as the discharged inmates move back to stay with family.

Supervision schemes for inmates

The CSD runs five supervision schemes, or parole, for prisoners, largely adults, with the aim of enhancing their reintegration into the community (see Table 17.2). The decision is not solely determined by the CSD, but also involves other departments such as the police and Social Welfare Department. Final approval of application for the schemes rests with independent review boards whose members are appointed by the chief executive of Hong Kong. Operation of the schemes is quite similar to a proposal made in the *Halliday Report* (Home Office, 2001), published in England and Wales, which suggests all custodial sentences should involve discharged prisoners being subject to supervision until the expiry of the sentence, with the possibility of recall to prison in case of breach of supervision conditions. However, the Hong Kong model does not involve all prisoners.

The first two supervision schemes, launched in 1988, aim at helping suitable prisoners serve their sentences in the community. The Release Under Supervision Scheme provides an opportunity for successful applicants who have served half of their sentence of imprisonment of three years or more, or 20 months, whichever is longer, to be discharged from prison and receive aftercare supervision in the community (see *Prisoners (Release Under Supervision) Ordinance* (Cap. 325)). Similarly, the Pre-release Employment Scheme allows those successful applicants, both adult prisoners and youth inmates, who are within six months of the expiry of their imprisonment of two years or more, to have an earlier release on the condition that they engage in appropriate employment. Discharged prisoners of both schemes reside in a halfway house upon release.

Two other schemes target long-term prisoners serving a determinate sentence of ten years or more, prisoners with an indeterminate sentence, juvenile prisoners who have been convicted of murder when they are under 18 years of age, and prisoners detained at Executive discretion. The Conditional Release Scheme allows selected prisoners to be released under supervision for a period of not more than two years before the Long-term Prison Sentences Review Board makes recommendations on whether to convert their indeterminate sentences to determinate ones. Once the sentences are converted, the board may order the prisoners in question to receive post-release supervision under the Supervision After Release Scheme.

The largest scheme, in terms of participant numbers, is the Post-Release Supervision of Prisoners Scheme, launched in November 1996 under the same ordinance passed on 31 May 1995. This scheme involves adult prisoners serving a prison sentence of six years or more, and those sentenced to two years or more for specific offences, such as violent crimes, sexual offences and triad-related crimes. About 35% of adult prisoners were eligible for this scheme in June 2005 (Post-Release Supervision Board, 2005). In making a decision of whether to grant the supervision as well as its length, the Post-Release Supervision Board will consider the prisoner's age, previous convictions, nature of offence, sense of remorse, behaviour in prison, family support, and physical and mental health. Since for prison sentences a system of one-third remission for good behaviour is in place, the supervision period will be no longer than the remitted part of the prisoner's sentence. This normally ranges from six to 24 months and on very rare occasions the board will impose a longer period of supervision. If discharged prisoners breach the supervision conditions regarding residence, employment, good behaviour and meeting with supervising officers, or are likely to commit an arrestable offence, they may be recalled to serve the remainder of the unexpired period in jail.

Previously, prisoners enjoyed one-third automatic remission for good conduct on all determinate sentences. However, since the introduction of the Post-Release Supervision of Prisoners Scheme, discharged prisoners are now required to undergo supervision for a specific period of time decided by the board within the remission period. This controversial move is unwelcome because prisoners believe they are not free after their release. In 1999, the *Post-Release Supervision of Prisoners Ordinance* (Cap. 475) was challenged in court to no avail by a prisoner sentenced before the enactment of the ordinance. The prisoner was given a supervision order which he thought imposed a heavier penalty on him than a treatment given to him at the time he committed the offence. He argued that the ordinance contravened Article 15(1) of the *International Covenant on Civil and Political Rights* (ICCPR) and Article 12(1) of the *Hong Kong Bill of Rights Ordinance* (Cap. 383). The court ruled that the imposition of supervision orders is essentially a rehabilitative measure and does not constitute a 'heavier penalty' within the meaning of Article 15 of the ICCPR or of Article 12(1) of the *Hong Kong Bill of Rights Ordinance*, and the provisions of the ordinance are accordingly not in breach of article 30 of the *Basic Law* (see *Lui Tat Hang Louis v The Post-Release Supervision Board & Another* (1999) HCAL 154/1999). The ordinance was further challenged on similar grounds in 2000 and 2002 but the legality of the application of the scheme to prisoners who were sentenced before the commencement of the ordinance was re-affirmed (see *Chan Chung Kan v The Post-Release Supervision Board* (2000) HCAL 1149/2000; Post-Release Supervision Board, 2003).

Success rates

To measure the recidivism of offenders is a sophisticated issue, involving both static and dynamic factors (Zamble and Quinsey, 1997). The success rates officially published by the CSD are measured by non-conviction of a criminal offence (as well as remaining drug-free for drug addiction treatment centres) within the period of statutory aftercare supervision. Since there is no statutory supervision period following discharge of adult prisoners, no statistics have been published on their success rate. Table 17.2 shows the success rates of different regimes and supervision schemes run by the CSD in 2004 and 2014. Four of the Release Under Supervision Schemes have 100% success rates because of the small number of cases under supervision. When the sample is large, as in

Table 17.2 Success rates of regimes and schemes

Regimes/schemes	*2004 (%)*	*2014 (%)*
Detention centre (non-conviction one year after discharge)	96	95
Rehabilitation centres (non-conviction one year after discharge)	97	95
Training centres (non-conviction three years after discharge)	68	67
Drug addiction treatment centres (non-conviction and drug-free one year after discharge)	64	51
Young prisons (non-conviction one year after discharge)	85	91
Release Under Supervision Scheme (non-conviction until latest date of discharge)	100	100
Pre-Release Employment Scheme (non-conviction until earliest date of discharge)	100	100
Post-Release Supervision Scheme (non-conviction during supervision period)	89	90
Conditional Release Scheme (non-conviction during supervision period)	100	100
Supervision After Release Scheme (non-conviction during supervision period)	100	100
All programmes	77	67

Source:Hong Kong Correctional Services, 2004, 2014.

the case of the Post-Release Supervision Scheme, the success rate drops to about 90%. For the five correctional regimes, the detention centre and rehabilitation centres have the highest success rate (95%–97%) followed by youth prisons (85%–91%), mainly because the period of aftercare supervision is shorter (one year), compared to the three-year supervision period for discharged inmates of training centres, which have lower success rates (67%–68%). The regimes' success rates in 2004 and 2014 are comparable, except for drug addiction treatment centres, whose success rates are 64% in 2004 and 51% in 2014. The overall success of all programmes has dropped from 77% in 2004 to 67% in 2014.

Overall, the success rates achieved are relatively high throughout the different regimes and schemes. Vagg (1991) suggested that the high success rates were attributed in part to the extensive use of recall to prison. However, there is a difference between overall success rate and overall recidivism rate, which 'declined from 39 per cent to 29 per cent in the past decade' (APCCA, 2014: 13). The latter is measured by the percentage of readmission of local offenders to a CSD facility within a two-year period from release, excluding convictions resulting in probation or fines. Such recidivism rates are lower than those reported in Western studies; for instance, a 31% one-year failure rate found by Harris et al. (1993); a 70.1% two-year failure rate found by Mulder et al.

(2011); and a 67.5% three-year reoffending rate, with 73.8% of property offenders by Langan and Levin (2002).

Similar to Western research (Caulkins and Reuter, 1998), many of those who reoffend are related to the availability of drugs and price variations in the drug market (Pang, 2007). It was found that the strongest predictors of self-anticipated reoffending are offenders' criminogenic exposure, negative self-image, detachment from family, illicit drug use and pro-offending attitudes (Chan et al., forthcoming). Another study also found that offending history, psychological attributes, interpersonal relationships and environmental influences are significant reoffending risk factors (Chan et al., 2015). Lo and associates (2008) noted that the common factors associated with reoffending include crime opportunities in the community, undesirable friends, triad influences, social labelling and so on. The above findings suggest that the aforementioned rehabilitative and community approaches run by the CSD are appropriate in targeting the risk factors of reoffending.

Community partnerships and service initiatives

In recent years, the CSD has been proactive in strengthening community partnerships with non-governmental organisations (NGOs) and in developing various service initiatives for the community. The Committee on Community Support for Rehabilitated Offenders was formed to provide guidance for the CSD. In the 1990s, the CSD was in collaboration with fewer than ten NGOs. This was extended to about 60 NGOs in 2006 (Pang, 2007) and over 80 in 2014 (Hong Kong Correctional Services 2014). The number of collaborations has increased eightfold over the last two decades. Since 2005, NGO forums have been organised every year to let stakeholders exchange views, expectations and experiences. A Rehabilitation Volunteer Group was formed in 2004 to provide training and services to prisoners in correctional institutions. The group comprises people from all walks of life, such as professionals, university students, housewives and retired persons. Most of them have attained post-secondary education. A variety of community education and publicity actions, such as a drama series and concerts, have been organised to appeal for community acceptance of, and support for, rehabilitated offenders.

A common phenomenon is that prisoners released from CSD institutions are still at risk of reoffending if they do not have sufficient support in the community, as many ex-prisoners may maintain contact with deviant friends, indulge in pleasure-seeking activities, run an imbalanced lifestyle between work and leisure, and encounter difficulties in adjustment after institutionalisation. In 1998, an NGO launched Project Dawn to help discharged inmates of the detention centre through intensive group activities, training and supportive programmes in the community. In the first few years, the response of participants was relatively passive, as reflected in the small number of referrals to the project. With increasing attention to community support and partnership in recent years, the

CSD has, under the auspices of the Continuing Care Project, extended its scope to include seven NGOs to provide community support, guidance and counselling services to discharged inmates (Kwok, 2007; APCCA, 2014: 73).

Since 2008, the CSD has organised the Rehabilitation Pioneer Project in which educational talks and prison visits are organised for students. Under the auspices of this project, the Encounter with Prisoners Scheme is organised for school youths to visit designated correctional institutions. Through the visits and meetings with inmates who have reformed themselves, they witness the hardships of correctional life and the pain that inmates suffer from the loss of liberty. The purpose is to enable these youths to understand the serious consequences of crime, and to deter them from committing crimes. Similarly, in the Green Haven Scheme, young people visit drug addiction treatment centres to learn about the harmful effects of drug abuse from inmates' personal experiences and feelings about being placed in custody. They also go through a closing ritual declaring their determination to remain drug-free. Both schemes have drawn very good responses. The CSD has also organised Student Forums and other educational activities for students (Hong Kong Correctional Services, 2014), such as the Reflective Path, with applied theatre format and strengthened interactive effect to help young people understand the dire consequences of committing crimes.

Conclusion

To conclude the development of correctional services in Hong Kong, in the 1970s the CSD tended to emphasise coercive custody and undermine the importance of rehabilitation and treatment of offenders. In the 1990s, increasing attention was paid to the rehabilitation and reintegration of offenders. In the 2000s, the appeal for community support and the formation of community partnerships became the CSD's focal concern. Although the Chinese criminal justice system emphasises punitiveness (Bakken, 2008), the rehabilitative nature of the correctional services in Hong Kong remained intact even after China resumed sovereignty of Hong Kong in 1997. The main reason is that the Hong Kong people regard the rule of law as sacrosanct and thus resist the 'mainlandisation' of Hong Kong's criminal justice system (Lo, 2012).

The Hong Kong prison model is similar to the one promoted by Mathiesen (1990) but modified to suit the local cultural context, with five main strategies: strict discipline training, timely and appropriate rehabilitation services, comprehensive aftercare services, public support and acceptance of rehabilitated offenders, and strengthening cooperation with NGOs (Kwok, 2007). Such a model has evolved through a few decades of trial and error, with a previous staff force with low academic qualifications, insufficient resources and poor community support. To date, the CSD has more staff with bachelor's and master's degrees than ever before. We have witnessed the professionalisation of correctional services through the use of X-ray body scanners to maintain centre discipline and the development of various assessment and rehabilitative programmes to reintegrate offenders into the community. Despite the fact that difficulties still arise in providing quality education, vocational training and treatment programmes to all inmates, the CSD has found its vision, mission and core values of corrections as well as different intervention and community approaches. Such sound philosophical and practice frameworks of corrections begin to be shared by members of the 6,500-strong staff from top management to frontline operation staff.

Review questions

1 What is the prevailing trend of penal population and how does it affect the overcrowding situation of prisons in Hong Kong?
2 Are custodial sentences expensive means in the rehabilitation of offenders? If they are, what are the major justifications?
3 What are the daily programmes offered to prisoners in correctional institutions? Do you think they can achieve the goal of rehabilitating offenders and prepare them to be reintegrated into the community after release?
4 In recent years, the CSD has been active in promoting community participation in helping released prisoners. What other community programmes should the CSD organise to further engage community and business organisations to help the released?
5 How would you measure the success rates of correctional services? How would you compare Hong Kong's success rate with those of overseas jurisdictions?

References

Asia and Pacific Conference of Correctional Administrators (APCCA) (2005) *25th APCCA Conference Report*, Seoul: APCCA.

Asia and Pacific Conference of Correctional Administrators (APCCA) (2011) *31st APCCA Conference Report*, Tokyo: APCCA.

Asia and Pacific Conference of Correctional Administrators (APCCA) (2014) *34th APCCA Conference Report*, Victoria, Canada: APCCA.

Bakken, B. (2008) 'The culture of revenge and the power of politics: A comparative attempt to explain the punitive', *Journal of Power*, 1(2): 169–187.

Britt, C.L. (1995) 'Reconsidering the unemployment and crime relationship: Variation by age group and historical period', *Journal of Quantitative Criminology*, 13(4): 405–428.

Caulkins, J.P. and Reuter, P. (1998) 'What price data tell us about drug markets', *Journal of Drug Issues*, 28(3): 593–612.

Chan, H.C., Lo, T.W. and Zhong, L. (forthcoming) 'Identifying the self-anticipated reoffending risk factors of incarcerated male repeat offenders in Hong Kong', *The Prison Journal*.

Chan, H.C., Lo, T.W., Zhong, L. and Chui, W.H. (2015) 'Criminal recidivism of incarcerated male nonviolent offenders in Hong Kong', *International Journal of Offender Therapy and Comparative Criminology*, 59(2): 121–142.

Chui, W.H. (1999) 'Residential treatment programs for young offenders in Hong Kong: A report', *International Journal of Offender Therapy and Comparative Criminology*, 43(3): 308–321.

Chui, W.H. (2001) 'Detention center in Hong Kong: A young offender's narrative', *Journal of Offender Rehabilitation*, 41(1): 67–84.

Chui, W.H. and Cheng, K.K.Y. (2013) 'Self-perceived role and function of Christian prison chaplains and Buddhist volunteers in Hong Kong prisons', *International Journal of Offender Therapy and Comparative Criminology*, 57(2): 154–168.

Collins, M.F. and Weatherburn, D. (1995) 'Unemployment and the dynamics of offender populations', *Journal of Quantitative Criminology*, 11(3): 231–245.

Harris, G.T., Rice, M.E. and Quinsey, V.L. (1993) 'Violent recidivism of mentally disordered offenders: The development of a statistical prediction instrument', *Criminal Justice and Behavior*, 20(4): 315–335.

Home Office (2001) *Making Punishments Work: Report of a Review of the Sentencing Framework for England and Wales*, London: Home Office.

Hong Kong Correctional Services (2002) *Annual Review 2002*, Hong Kong: Correctional Services Department.

Hong Kong Correctional Services (2003) *Annual Review 2003*, Hong Kong: Correctional Services Department.

Hong Kong Correctional Services (2004) *Annual Review 2004*, Hong Kong: Correctional Services Department.

Hong Kong Correctional Services (2005) *Annual Review 2005*, Hong Kong: Correctional Services Department.

Hong Kong Correctional Services (2014) *Annual Review 2014*, Hong Kong: Correctional Services Department.

Kwok, L.M. (2007) *Services for Rehabilitated Offenders Provided by the Correctional Services Department of Hong Kong SAR*, Hong Kong: Correctional Services Department (in Chinese).

Laidler, K.J. (2009) 'Correctional Services Department', in M.S. Gaylord, D. Gittings and H. Traver (eds) *Introduction to Crime, Law and Justice in Hong Kong* (pp. 185–203), Hong Kong: Hong Kong University Press.

Laidler, K.J., Peterson, C. and Emerton, R. (2007) 'Bureaucratic justice: The incarceration of mainland Chinese women working in Hong Kong's sex industry', *International Journal of Offender Therapy and Comparative Criminology*, 51(1): 63–83.

Langan, P.A. and Levin, D.J. (2002) *Bureau of Justice Statistics Special Report: Recidivism of Prisoners Released in 1994. U.S.*, Washington, DC: US Department of Justice, Office of Justice Programs.

Lee, M. (2001) 'Diversion', in E. McLaughlin and J. Munice (eds) *The Sage Dictionary of Criminology* (pp. 102–103), London: Sage.

Lo, T.W. (2008) 'Custodial sentences and correctional services', in W.H. Chui and T.W. Lo (eds) *Understanding Criminal Justice in Hong Kong* (pp. 224–247), Cullompton: Willan.

Lo, T.W. (2012) 'Resistance to the mainlandization of criminal justice practices: A barrier to the development of restorative justice in Hong Kong', *International Journal of Offender Therapy and Comparative Criminology*, 56(4): 627–645.

Lo, T.W., Wong, S.W., Chan, W.T., Leung, S.K., Yu, C.S. and Chan, C.K. (1997) *Research on the Effectiveness of Rehabilitation Programmes for Young Offenders: Full Report*, Hong Kong: Government Printer.

Lo, T.W., Wong, S.W., Chui, W.H., Zhong, L. and Senior, P. (2010) *Report on Comprehensive Review of the Rehabilitation Centre Programme for Correctional Services Department*, Hong Kong: City University of Hong Kong.

Lo, T.W., Zhong, L., Rochelle, T. and Chui, W.H. (2008) *Report on Performance Measurements of the Reintegration Programmes and Services of the Correctional Services Department*, Hong Kong: City University of Hong Kong.

Mathiesen, T. (1990) *Prison on Trial: A Critical Assessment*, London: Sage.

Morgan, R. (2002) 'Imprisonment: A brief history, the contemporary scene, and likely prospects', in M. Maguire, R. Morgan and R. Reiner (eds) *The Oxford Handbook of Criminology* (3rd edn) (pp. 1113–1167), Oxford: Oxford University Press.

Mulder, E., Brand, E., Bullens, R. and van Marle, H. (2011) 'Risk factors of overall recidivism and severity of recidivism in serious juvenile offenders', *International Journal of Offender Therapy and Comparative Criminology*, 55(1): 118–135.

Pang, S.Y. (2007) *Public Lecture on Correctional Services in Hong Kong: 1971 to 2006*, delivered by the former Commissioner of Correctional Services at City University of Hong Kong on 6 March 2007 (unpublished).

Post-Release Supervision Board (2003) *Post-Release Supervision Board 2001–2003: Fifth Report*, Hong Kong: Post-Release Supervision Board.

Post-Release Supervision Board (2005) *Post-Release Supervision Board 2003–2005: Sixth Report*, Hong Kong: Post-Release Supervision Board.

Radzinowicz, L. and Hood, R. (1990) *The Emergence of Penal Policy in Victorian and Edwardian England*, Oxford: Clarendon Press.

Raphael, S. and Winter-Ebmer, R. (2001) 'Identifying the effect of unemployment on crime', *Journal of Law and Economics*, 44(1): 259–283.

Ruck, S.K. (ed.) (1951) *Paterson on Prisons: Prisoners and Patients*, London: Hodder and Stoughton.

Vagg, J. (1991) 'Corrections', in H. Traver and J. Vagg (eds) *Crime and Justice in Hong Kong* (pp. 139–152), Hong Kong: Oxford University Press.

Vagg, J. (1994) 'The Correctional Services Department', in M.S. Gaylord and H. Traver (eds) *Introduction to the Hong Kong Criminal Justice System* (pp. 145–160), Hong Kong: Hong Kong University Press.

Walmsley, R. (2006) *World Female Imprisonment*, London: International Centre for Prison Studies, School of Law, King's College London.

Whitfield, D. (1997) *Tackling the Tag – The Electronic Monitoring of Offenders*, Winchester: Waterside Press.

Zamble, E. and Quinsey, V.L. (1997) *The Criminal Recidivism Process*, Cambridge: Cambridge University Press.

Zimring, F.E. and Hawkins, G. (1991) *The Scale of Imprisonment*, Chicago, IL: Chicago University Press.

Newspaper article cited

South China Morning Post (2014) 'Number of prisoners hits record low', 7 September.

Legislation cited

Criminal Procedure Ordinance (Cap. 221)
Detention Centres Ordinance (Cap. 239)

Drug Addiction Treatment Centres Ordinance (Cap. 244)
Hong Kong Bill of Rights Ordinance (Cap. 383)
Immigration Ordinance (Cap. 115)
International Covenant on Civil and Political Rights
Long-Term Prison Sentences Review Ordinance (Cap. 524)
Post-Release Supervision of Prisoners Ordinance (Cap. 475)
Prisoners (Release Under Supervision) Ordinance (Cap. 325)
Prison Rules (Cap. 234A)
Prisons Ordinance (Cap. 234)
Rehabilitation Centres Ordinance (Cap. 567)
Training Centres Ordinance (Cap. 280)

Cases cited

Chan Chung Kan v The Post-Release Supervision Board (2000) HCAL 1149/2000
Lui Tat Hang Louis v The Post-Release Supervision Board & Another (1999) HCAL 154/1999

Useful websites

Hong Kong Correctional Services www.csd.gov.hk
Long-term Prison Sentences Review Board www.sb.gov.hk/eng/links/ltpsrb/index.htm
Post-Release Supervision Board www.sb.gov.hk/eng/links/prsb/index.htm
Release Under Supervision Board www.sb.gov.hk/eng/links/rusb/index.htm

18

CRIME PREVENTION

Lena Y. Zhong

Introduction

As the proverb goes, prevention is better than cure. It is much better to stop crime before it occurs by taking preventive measures, for example residents installing anti-burglary doors to prevent burglary. Crime prevention is an important component in criminal justice. First, the benefits of crime prevention are in parallel to those of disease prevention. A sound public health system should provide education and guidance to the public on how to prevent cancer rather than just treat cancer after patients are diagnosed with the disease. In terms of crime, however, many popular media accounts of crime, both real-life and fictional, tend to convey the message that the most effective way to control crime is to arrest offenders. This reactive approach to crime is no more than closing the stable door after the horse has bolted. Second, it has been demonstrated in the extant literature that a small number of people commit a disproportionate amount of crime, and that a criminal history is a significant factor of future re-offending (see, for example, Zamble and Quinsey, 1997). It follows logically then that to 'prevent' people from having a criminal record in the first place has substantial effects on recidivism, and therefore overall crime in society. Third, crime prevention has economic benefits. Simply put, crime prevention could save money and therefore put to greatest use the resources allocated to the criminal justice system (Swaray, 2006). Last but not least, a particular crime involves a network including the offender, the victim, their family members and the whole community. To prevent it from ever occurring spares the whole network from the impact and damage of crime.

Hong Kong is among the safest cities around the world, both in terms of official crime statistics and crime victim surveys (see Chapters 4 and 5 of this edited volume). While this high level of safety could be attributed to a wide range of factors, the crime prevention efforts made by the law enforcement agencies (particularly the police) and the community at large should not be discounted. This chapter aims to highlight the various crime prevention programmes and initiatives in Hong Kong against the backdrop of international efforts in crime prevention. It is organised into three sections: definitions of crime prevention, classifications of crime prevention, and selected local crime prevention programmes and initiatives.

Definition of crime prevention

According to Lab (1988, 2004), crime prevention entails any action designed to reduce the actual level of crime and/or the perceived fear of crime. Van Dijk (1990: 205) referred to crime prevention as 'the total of all policies, measures, and techniques, outside the boundaries of the criminal justice system, aiming at the reduction of the various kinds of damages caused by acts defined as criminal by the state'. The targets of most crime prevention programmes include not just crime per se, but also behaviours associated with incivility and disorder, an essence of the 'broken windows' theory (Wilson and Kelling, 1982; Kelling and Coles, 1996).

The 'broken windows theory', as developed by Wilson and Kelling (1982), suggests that physical disorder (e.g. broken windows and accumulated trash) and social disorder (e.g. vandalism and rowdy youth) in a neighbourhood could lead to crime in the neighbourhood, because 'one unrepaired broken window is a signal that no one cares, and so breaking more windows costs nothing' (ibid.: 3).

Crime prevention also entails the reduction of any harm or suffering which may result from crime, including fear of crime. Some crime prevention programmes such as Neighbourhood Watch also strive to strengthen community cohesion and informal social control in the hope of defending against crime (Rosenbaum, 1988). An even broader definition of crime prevention includes reduction of risk factors for crime (such as gang membership) and increases in protective factors (such as completing high school) (see Sherman et al., 1997).

Crime prevention is not the sole responsibility of the criminal justice system. The role of other government agencies (such as labour and welfare) and the general public is crucial (see Garland, 1996). In contrast to the traditional compartmentalised response to crime (especially the police solution to crime), a holistic approach to fostering partnership is adopted to prevent crime (see Zhong and Broadhurst, 2007). In Hong Kong crime prevention is regarded as a multi-agency business. The Hong Kong Police Force (HKPF) has a Crime Prevention Bureau (CPB) at the Police Headquarters and Regional Crime Prevention Units at each of the six regions. The Police Public Relations Branch (PPRB) also engages in publicity of crime prevention. The community is organised to prevent and fight crime, as evidenced by the establishment of the Fight Crime Committee (FCC) and the Mutual Aid Committees (MACs), and by the active involvement of various faith organisations and non-governmental organisations (NGOs) such as the Chinese Young Men's Christian Association of Hong Kong, the Evangelical Lutheran Church of Hong Kong, and the Society of Rehabilitation and Crime Prevention, Hong Kong.

Sometimes crime prevention and crime control are used interchangeably. Strictly speaking, the two concepts should be distinguished from each other.

Lab (1988) differentiated them by arguing that 'crime prevention' is an attempt to eliminate crime either prior to the initial occurrence or before further activity, while crime control is the maintenance of a given or existing level and the management of certain behaviour by authorised regulating and coercive institutions.

Classifications of crime prevention

Many theoretical models have been offered to classify crime prevention interventions and programmes. This section introduces the three models of crime prevention that are prevalent in the literature and relevant to the Hong Kong context.

Public health model

This model draws on the approaches utilised in disease prevention. Based on the principal population target, crime prevention is distinguished between primary, secondary and tertiary prevention. According to Brantingham and Faust (1976), primary prevention targets the general population and intends to prevent crime from ever occurring, secondary prevention aims to prevent crime among the at-risk population based on the prediction of their predispositional or probabilistic risk factors, and tertiary prevention aims to prevent known offenders from committing further offences.

The public health model does not draw the boundaries of 'outside' or 'inside' the criminal justice system. In spite of its heuristic value, this model lacks sufficient explanation of the different philosophical, ideological and political assumptions underlying different crime prevention initiatives (Crawford, 1998). It fails to take into account who does the preventive action, and ignores the fact that a particular party such as the police can engage in all three levels of prevention activities (Graham and Bennett, 1995). Furthermore it seems primarily to address crime or criminality of offenders, potential or known. As demonstrated, crime can be prevented through changing the behaviour of potential victims or the characteristics of the community where both the offenders and the victims usually reside.

Social/situational approach

This approach addresses the nature of the intervention. Social crime prevention is concerned with measures aimed at tackling the root causes of crime and the dispositions of individuals to offend (Crawford, 1998; Rosenbaum et al., 1998). Currie (1996) advocated the strategies of social crime prevention at both the macro and micro levels of the social structure. At the macro level, he proposed three policies: a supportive labour market; a concerted, unapologetic strategy to reduce extremes of social and economic inequality; and an active supportive child and family policy. At the micro level, he pointed out the three most urgent interventions of social crime prevention in American society: 1) comprehensive child and family support programmes; 2) a youth intervention strategy that focuses on the expansion of tangible opportunities; and 3) a 'user-friendly' approach to drug abuse prevention and treatment.

Whereas social crime prevention addresses the root causes or *ultimate/push* factors of crime, situational crime prevention involves the management, design or manipulation of the immediate physical environment so as to tackle the *proximate/pull* factors of crime with the aim of reducing the opportunities for specific crimes (see, for example, Clarke, 1995, 1997; Crawford, 1998). Thus the underlying rationale for social crime prevention is that crime is the product of complex social, economic and cultural processes, while for situational crime prevention crime is opportunistic and can be controlled through the manipulation of the physical environment.

Tonry and Farrington's four-level model

In Tonry and Farrington's (1995) typology, crime prevention is classified into four categories: law enforcement, developmental, community, and situational prevention. Crime prevention by law enforcement emphasises the general prevention in enacting and implementing the criminal law. It achieves the goal indirectly through effects on socialisation and directly through deterrence, incapacitation and rehabilitation. On the basis of a series of research studies in the USA, Tonry and Farrington (1995) argued that even pre-adjudication criminal processes, such as mandatory arrest policies for domestic violence, could produce preventive effects.

Situational crime prevention, as referred to earlier, is based on the premise that a large proportion of crime is contextual and opportunistic. Therefore crime can be blocked by adopting target-hardening measures such as locking the door, shuttering the windows, purchasing dogs, and installing alarm systems. However, of concern are the consequences of the 'fortress society' (Blakely and Snyder, 1997). In terms of its effectiveness, 'displacement' is the Achilles heel (Crawford, 1998), while 'diffusion of benefits' shows the hidden benefits in that efforts to prevent one crime cause the unintended prevention of another, and crime control efforts in one locale reduce crime in other, untargeted areas (Clarke and Weisburd, 1994).

Community crime prevention refers to actions intended to change the social conditions that are believed to sustain crime in residential communities. It is premised on the insight that individuals' criminality is related to the community where they live and therefore changing the community may change the behaviour of its residents. This initiative can be dated back to the pioneering work of Shaw and McKay's Chicago School of Criminology, which focused on ecological and community explanations for crime and promoted the crime prevention role played by community organisations. This ecological approach has gained a revival in recent years and is further developed by scholars along its tradition (e.g. Bursik and Grasmick, 1993; Sampson et al., 1997; Sampson, 2002). Prevention efforts under the community approach have focused on altering the physical and social organisation of communities such as community organising, tenant involvement, resource mobilisation and community defence (Hope, 1995). Apparently there are overlaps between community crime prevention and situational crime prevention.

The last category in Tonry and Farrington's typology is developmental prevention. Through locating the risk factors and protective factors in childhood, the links between developmental processes and later delinquency are clarified. Thus interventions in children's development process, by decreasing risk factors and increasing protective factors, can have either delinquency-reducing effects or beneficial effects on other indicators such as school performance, hyperactivity and impulsivity which are associated with reduced probabilities of offending.

Selected local crime prevention programmes and initiatives

The selected programmes and initiatives are grouped into three areas: youth crime prevention, situational crime prevention and community crime prevention. Youth crime is always a concern in the local community and indeed a lot of resources are devoted to its prevention (Wong, 2000). Thus various efforts to prevent youth crime in Hong Kong are introduced. Given the wide use of situational crime prevention worldwide, several local initiatives along that line are introduced. Initiatives of community crime prevention are described to illustrate the partnership between the government and the public in crime prevention.

Youth crime prevention

Crime by young people is always high on the agenda of the local community (Choi and Lo, 2004). The official crime statistics showed that shop theft and serious assaults were the most common crimes committed by young people under the age of 21 in Hong Kong in recent years. For example, in 2014 1,510 juveniles (aged under 16) were arrested for crime, a drop of 27.5% compared with 2,083 in 2013. Most of them were arrested for shop theft (324 persons or 21.5%), miscellaneous theft (241 persons or 16.0%), and wounding and serious assault (231 persons or 15.3%). In 2014 2,814 young persons (aged between 16 and 20) were arrested for crime in 2014, a drop of 15.1% compared with 3,314 in 2013. Most of them were arrested for wounding and serious assault (451 persons or 16.0%), serious drug offences (367 persons or 13.0%) and miscellaneous theft (306 persons or 10.9%) (Hong Kong Police Force, 2014, 2015). According to Ambrose Lee, then secretary of security, the government adopts a strategy of tackling youth crime through deterring first-time offenders and reducing recidivism (Press Release, 2006). This strategy is implemented through a multi-agency holistic approach. This section reviews the following schemes:

the Police Superintendent's Discretion Scheme, Junior Police Call, Police School Liaison Programme, Working with Gangs, anti-school bullying, the Personal Encounter with Prisoners Scheme, and the Youth Ambassador Against Internet Piracy Scheme.

Police Superintendent's Discretion Scheme (PSDS)

PSDS is designed to divert young offenders from the criminal justice system with the aim of preventing their future criminal activity (Laidler, 2005). As an initiative of diversion, it is classified as secondary crime prevention in the public health model. Under PSDS, a police officer of the rank of superintendent or above may, at his or her discretion, caution a young offender instead of initiating a criminal prosecution against the offender. The following guidelines are used to assess the eligibility of juvenile offenders for PSDS:

- at the time the caution is administered, the offender is under the age of 18;
- the offender has no previous criminal record;
- the evidence available is sufficient to support a prosecution;
- the offender voluntarily and unequivocally admits the offence; and
- the offender and his or her parents or guardians agree to the caution.

Starting in 2007, the criterion of no previous criminal record has been removed. Instead, it stipulates that an offender with a previous criminal conviction would not normally be considered for a caution, but each case rests on its own merits. PSDS is only applied to a juvenile offender involved in a less serious offence (such as shop theft). Other factors for consideration include the prevalence of the offence, the degree of harm and damage to property suffered by the victim, and the attitude of the victim and the offender's parents or guardian(s). The most common reasons for not giving cautions include the serious nature of the offence and the previous caution record of the offender (Fight Crime Committee, 1997–2013).

If the police superintendent holds the view that aftercare is necessary in addition to caution, the offender will be referred to one or more of the following organisations for follow-up: Juvenile Protection Section (JPS), Community Support Service Scheme (CSSS), Social Welfare Department (SWD), or Education and Manpower Bureau (EMB). With effect from 1 November 2008, all cautioned juveniles under the PSDS are referred to the police's JPS for regular supervisory visits. If 'aftercare' is required in addition to the post-caution visits by the JPS, the offender will be referred to one or more of the agencies/schemes of CSSS, SWD and EMB. Table 18.1 shows the number of juveniles arrested and cautioned from 1997 to 2013, and Table 18.2 shows the distribution of the referrals among the four agencies/schemes from 1997 to 2013. The recidivism rate for those undergoing PSDS from 1997 to 2011 stays around 16%, fluctuating between 12.6% in 2011 and 19.6% in 2003. Here recidivism is defined as a

Table 18.1 Juveniles* arrested and cautioned under PSDS

Year	*No. of arrested*	*% eligible for PSDS*	*No. of cautioned*	*% of arrested/cautioned*
1997	8,810	54.5	3,256	37.1
1998	8,708	52.0	3,190	36.6
1999	8,646	54.7	3,216	37.2
2000	9,173	54.5	3,760	41.1
2001	8,732	53.5	3,585	41.0
2002	8,156	54.7	3,345	41.0
2003	7,918	50.4	3,012	38.0
2004	7,566	51.9	2,929	38.7
2005	6,821	55.6	3,026	44.4
2006	6,891	– **	2,774	40.3
2007	6,875	–	2,736	39.8
2008	6,303	–	2,358	37.4
2009	6,049	–	2,220	36.7
2010	5,454	–	2,076	38.1
2011	5,355	–	1,987	37.1
2012	4,198	–	1,453	34.6
2013	3,413	–	1,059	31.0

Source: Fight Crime Committee (1997–2013, various issues.

Notes: * Since 1 July 2003, the minimum age of criminal liability has been raised from seven to ten. ** The Fight Crime Committee stopped reporting the percentage of juveniles eligible for PSDS in its annual reports in 2006.

re-arrest for a crime within two years from the date of the caution, or before he or she reaches 18 years of age, whichever occurs first.

Junior Police Call (JPC) scheme

The JPC scheme was launched in 1974. Its objectives are: 1) to encourage and improve communication and mutual understanding between the police and the youth of Hong Kong; 2) to foster police–youth partnership in the fight against crime; 3) to develop young people's sense of responsibility towards society and to instil positive values in them; and 4) to provide a wide range of activities and training for young people in order to equip them as future leaders and develop their potential leadership.

JPC headquarters is established in the Police Public Relations Branch (PPRB) and its branches are distributed in 20 police districts in Hong Kong. The JPC and Youth Liaison Section of the PPRB are responsible for organising JPC activities in Hong Kong and for formulating work plans and policies, and the police

Table 18.2 Referrals for juveniles cautioned under PSDS*

Year	*Juvenile Protection Section (JPS)***	*Community Support Service Scheme****	*Social Welfare Department*	*Education Department*	*Total number*****
1997	85.8%	11.3%	2.7%	0.2%	2,258
1998	74.6%	24.1%	1.0%	0.3%	2,761
1999	77.0%	20.6%	2.2%	0.2%	2,724
2000	73.9%	22.5%	3.2%	0.4%	3,702
2001	73.2%	21.6%	5.1%	0.1%	3,500
2002	54.6%	43.2%	1.5%	0.7%	3,952
2003	48.9%	48.2%	1.5%	1.4%	3,576
2004	42.1%	55.9%	1.5%	0.5%	3,730
2005	46.1%	53.3%	0.5%	0.1%	4,056
2006	37.5%	61.6%	0.7%	0.2%	3,950
2007	40.3%	54.9%	2.9%	1.8%	5,082
2008	43.0%	52.0%	2.6%	2.4%	4,499
2009	45.4%	51.0%	1.9%	1.7%	4,888
2010	49.6%	49.4%	0.7%	0.4%	4,189
2011	47.2%	52.0%	0.5%	0.4%	4,213
2012	46.2%	53.1%	0.6%	0.2%	3,148
2013	46.4%	52.1%	1.2%	0.3%	2,282

Source: Fight Crime Committee (1997–2013, various issues.

Notes: * A cautioned juvenile offender may be referred to one or more agencies/schemes. ** With effect from 1 November 2008, all cautioned juveniles under the PSDS are referred to the JPS for regular supervisory visits. *** The referrals to CSSS have seen rapid growth since 2002. It may be due to the fact that in 2001 three more units of CSSS run by three NGOs were set up in Hong Kong (see Lee, 2005). **** The statistics are based on the actual take-up date of the referrals by the respective agencies/schemes.

community relations officer of individual police districts is responsible for all affairs of its JPC branch. With its membership expanding rapidly over the years, JPC has become one of the largest youth organisations in the world with strong police ties. Since 1974, over 1,000,000 young people have joined JPC as members. As at 31 May 2015, it had 121 JPC advanced leaders, 377 JPC leaders, and 203,457 JPC members. Since 1975, JPC has striven to develop School Clubs in primary and secondary schools in order to recruit JPC members, disseminate the anti-crime message within the school, promote JPC activities within the school, train students to perform crowd control duties in school, and provide suitable students for the school prefect system. Presently the number of School Clubs is 758, including 382 in primary schools and 376 in secondary schools (see JPC website and Lo and Cheuk, 2004).

Police School Liaison Programme (PSLP)

The PSLP was first introduced in 1974 by HKPF as part of the strategy on community policing (Press Release, 2001a, 2001b). In the first ten years the function was performed by police officers appointed as School Liaison Officers (SLOs). In 1984, SLOs' function was integrated into the duties of Neighbourhood Police Coordinators who also had the overall responsibility for community relations. However, given the rising juvenile crime, 25 SLO posts were re-established in September 1995 in all police districts except those lacking student populations (e.g. the airport and rail districts), in order to focus efforts on police–school liaison. As part of a comprehensive programme of support services for youth at risk, 33 Secondary School Liaison Officer (SSLO) posts at the rank of sergeant were created in August 2001 to strengthen police commitment in juvenile crime prevention work with secondary school children. In 2015 104 SLO/SSLO posts had been established (Hong Kong Police Force, 2016a). One of the primary objectives is to give school children an understanding of the role of the police and a respect for law.

Working with gangs

Based on the information provided by 153 frontline social workers (Lee, 2005), in Hong Kong the average number of youth gang members ranged from five to eight. The members are predominantly male, and even in gangs of mixed genders males outnumber females, with females assuming an inferior and subordinate status. Triad affiliations are quite common among youth gangs. As early as 1979, outreach social work services were provided to street gangs and deviant youth as a government policy on social welfare. Three approaches were used by many outreach teams to work with street gangs: gang work, group work and casework. If the gang is a delinquency-oriented one, social workers would reduce the gang's cohesiveness, thus controlling the delinquent behaviour of its members; otherwise, the aim was to transform it into a formal youth club. Social workers also handle gang members' personal problems through casework (Lo, 1986).

A juvenile gang murder case in 1997 in Sau Mau Ping prompted a round of soul searching in the community on how to address juvenile gangs in Hong Kong. A study was carried out to understand gang dynamics, with a psycho-social approach. Data were collected through relevant court papers and school records, interviews with the young offenders (nine of the 14 offenders), their parents (from five families), police officers investigating the case, youth workers who had provided services to the youth, and the principal and teachers of one school where six of the 14 juveniles attended. The study identified a series of factors leading to the tragic event: 1) insufficient family support or supervision and unsuccessful school life; 2) affiliation with undesirable peers to form a juvenile gang; 3) insufficient early intervention to control budding behavioural problems;

and 4) synergetic effect of gang dynamics and the influence of the dominant members as the precipitating factor of the tragic murder event. The study recommended a series of strategies to tackle juvenile gangs: 1) primary preventive work – public education; 2) secondary preventive programmes – early identification and early intervention; 3) tertiary preventive and intervention programmes – training for youth workers and teachers; and 4) measures and mechanisms for promoting district collaboration for tackling the problems of juvenile gangs (for details see Chapter 7 of the *Fight Crime Committee Report 2000*).

Anti-school bullying

School bullying gained broad attention in the local community with the wide media coverage of two high-profile school bullying cases in December 2003 and February 2004 (South China Morning Post, 2004). Surveys conducted by Wong et al. (2002) and Wong (2004a) showed that school bullying is common among students in both primary and secondary (or high) school in Hong Kong. For instance, Wong et al. (2002) found that about 31.7% of 7,025 primary school students reported being bullied physically. Wong's (2004a) survey found that 18.3% of 3,297 secondary school students were victims of physical school bullying. With the rapid development of information and communication technology, cyber-bullying has aroused public concern in Hong Kong. Wong et al. (2014) found that cyber-bullying is positively correlated with traditional bullying in a sample of 1,917 secondary adolescents from seven schools in Hong Kong. However, Wong and Lo (2002) were dismayed by the fact that so little was done in local schools after a survey of 905 teachers.

Wong (2004b) argued strongly that unresolved school bullying problems are often a precursor of school violence and delinquency, and hence called for the deployment of a comprehensive anti-bullying strategy instead of suppressive tactics such as reprimanding bullies and suspension. For example, Wong and Lee (2005) advocated the use of a whole-school approach to tackle school bullying in Hong Kong. The theoretical underpinning of the whole-school approach is team building and communication theories, which involve all parties, including parents, teachers, social workers and students. Applying this approach, Wong and Lee (2005) introduced a pilot anti-bullying programme in a secondary school, the first of its kind in Hong Kong. The objective of this pioneering programme was to create a peaceful and happy learning culture among students, to enhance students' interpersonal skills and to decrease the number of bullying incidents. The students, teaching staff and school principals viewed this programme very positively, and positive changes were observed among the students, such as improved self-discipline, greater concern for others' feelings among some troubled students, better sense of belonging and a decreased number of bullying cases. This whole-school approach involves all the 'stakeholders' to implement a multiple-element strategy. Research has shown that such complex prevention programmes have a greater chance of being effective in reducing offending than programmes based on only one type of prevention technique (see Tonry and Farrington, 1995).

Personal Encounter with Prisoners Scheme (PEPS)

PEPS, one of the major activities of the Rehabilitation Pioneer Project initiated by the Hong Kong Correctional Services Department, has been launched to target at-risk students or school drop-outs at the age of 13 to 18 in response to rising youth crime since 1993. Through an 'encounter' with inmates, the students experience the atmosphere of custodial life, feel the pains of the inmates who have lost freedom because of committing crime, correct their misconception of triad members as heroes, and reflect on their own lifestyles. The scheme aims to strengthen participants' determination in leading a crime-free life and is promoted as 'an integrated effort in crime prevention'. It consists of a site visit to prison facilities and discussions with selected prisoners in a group meeting in the company of school teachers, disciplinary school officers or social workers.

Sy (1996) evaluated the scheme. Some 50 students in three groups were administered pre- and post-visit questionnaires on their attitudes and self-reported delinquency. There are changes in attitudes among the students: after the visit the students showed less approval for delinquent behaviour but tended to be less afraid of prisons. Sy (1996: 83) observed that 'without adequate follow-up, changes in behavior will not be realized and "at-risk" students may be less fearful of the consequences'. This finding is not surprising. Schemes under the roof of 'Scared Straight' demonstrated similar results. Petrosino et al. (2006) undertook an extensive review of 'Scared Straight' and other juvenile awareness programmes conducted over a quarter-century in eight different jurisdictions and involving nearly 1,000 participants. They found that those programmes are not effective as a stand-alone crime prevention strategy. On the contrary, the empirical evidence showed that the programmes result in an increase in criminality in the experimental group when compared to a no-treatment control group. Notwithstanding the harmful effects, as Petrosino et al. (2006) pointed out, 'Scared Straight' and its derivatives continue in use. The 'Personal Encounter with Prisoners' Scheme in Hong Kong shows no signs of abating.

Youth Ambassador Against Internet Piracy Scheme (Youth Ambassador Scheme)

The Youth Ambassador Scheme aims to enlist youth in protection of intellectual property rights (IPRs). IPRs are vigorously protected in Hong Kong. This is reflected in the conviction, after appeal to the Court of Final Appeal, of a man nicknamed 'Big Crook' for attempting to distribute movies using Bit Torrent peer-to-peer file-sharing technology, a case hailed as unprecedented worldwide (South China Morning Post, 2007b). The scheme encourages young people aged nine to 25 from 11 local youth uniform organisations (increased to 13 since April 2013) to report online copyright infringements to the authorities via a website (www.iprpa.org/eng/anti_campaign.php). Initiated by the Hong Kong Customs and Excise Department in cooperation with the Intellectual Property Department, it was one of the main campaigns in a series of publicity and educational programmes for IPRs protection launched by the Commerce, Industry and Technology Bureau on 29 May 2006. The scheme has three main objectives: promoting the importance of IPRs, expanding the avenues for monitoring illegal Internet activities by involving young people, and reducing the flow of infringing Bit Torrent seeds on the Internet.

A Secretariat Office has been set up in the Customs and Excise Department with designated personnel to manage the day-to-day operation of the notification mechanism, facilitate communication with the youth uniformed groups, and sustain the momentum of participation of the Youth Ambassadors. The Secretariat Office also organises a variety of social activities and training for participating members, such as seminars, leadership training, photography competitions, gala competitions, and visits to production venues of copyright works, in addition to the publication of the *Youth Ambassador Newsletter*. In 2013 the scheme was supported by a membership of 200,000 youngsters from 13 youth uniform organisations, as well as representatives from six copyright owners, which represent most of the copyright works ranging from foreign and local movies, TV series, MTV and local comics. However, the scheme has raised eyebrows in the local community concerning privacy and the role of children in law enforcement. Suggestions were made that the government was recruiting young people to spy on others.

As the above youth crime prevention programmes show, a multi-agency approach has been adopted to prevent youth crime. In particular the police work closely with the community and schools. In fact, in the police there is a section dedicated to juveniles – the Juvenile Protection Section (JPS), as referred to earlier in PSDS. Since late 2004, the services of the JPS have been extended to children below the age of ten. At the district level, innovative initiatives were made to reach out to school children. For example, Wan Chai District and the University of Hong Kong jointly rolled out a police–school website in 2006. Such initiatives, together with the Youth Ambassador Scheme, also show the deployment of high technology in youth crime prevention. Moreover, in the Youth Ambassador Scheme, compared with traditional crime prevention programmes, the young people play a different role: they are not just the recipients of crime prevention service; they help to prevent crime.

Situational crime prevention

The next section reviews three situational crime prevention programmes, namely the police publicity and education campaign in opportunity reduction, crime prevention in the Hong Kong subway system (Mass Transit Railway – MTR), and the use of surveillance cameras, or closed circuit television (CCTV).

Police publicity and education campaign in opportunity reduction

The police, through the Crime Prevention Bureau (CPB) and Regional Crime Prevention Offices, adopt a wide range of measures to educate the public that taking sensible, common-sense and usually simple measures could prevent crime. For example, announcements in the public interest (APIs) are periodically made by the police through television and radio broadcasts for crime prevention tips. The police have produced a number of television programmes jointly with Radio Television Hong Kong, for example *Police Magazine* (30 minutes), *Police Report* (5 minutes), and *Police Bulletin* (10 minutes), broadcast on local TV channels to appeal to the general public on recent crime trends and to give crime prevention advice. The CPB officers educate the public, especially the elderly, on how not to fall prey to street scams, such as spiritual blessing scams (South China Morning Post, 2007a). They organise displays, exhibitions, seminars and lectures. They visit business and residential premises to give advice to occupants. Robotcop, equipped with an LCD monitor and an advanced digital and electronic audio-visual system, visits schools, family days and festivals to teach school children civic responsibility and personal safety, and is a very popular medium for crime prevention publicity (Hong Kong Police Force, 2016b).

In 2015 there was widespread panic over telephone deception in the local community. Between January and July 2015, the police received 2,371 reports of telephone deception and in 378 cases the fraudsters succeeded in defrauding victims of money. Various modus operandi were used by the fraudsters, including impersonating couriers (54.5%), pretending to be the Mainland Chinese Law Enforcement Agents (21%), officials of the Liaison Office of the Central People's Government in the Hong Kong Special Administrative Region (14.5%), as well as other public officials (10%) such as the staff of China Post, China Banking Regulatory Commission or the telecommunication companies (Hong Kong Police Force, 2016c). A highly publicised case involved an elderly couple who lost HK$22 million in August 2015 (*South China Morning Post*, 2015). The ten biggest telephone deception cases in July and August 2015 incurred a monetary loss of nearly HK$100 million on the part of the victims (*The Hong Kong Economic Times*, 15 August 2015). The police made every effort to alert the public to telephone deception, to the point of even sending text messages to local mobile phone users registered with some local telephone companies. By the end of 2015, the number of victims had subsided, but not disappeared.

In the past sometimes it was frustratingly difficult for CPB officers to persuade the public, especially merchants, to use common sense and install opportunity reduction devices. For example, the refusal of goldsmith shops to install unbreakable glass, steel grilles and to examine customers before staff open doors to let them into shops frequently led to robberies. Apart from the loss of millions of dollars, violent gangsters sometimes shot policemen and killed innocent bystanders while escaping from the scene of robberies. So CPB officers persuaded the owners of jewellery outlets to heed the advice, coupled with action from the insurance industry. The recent decade has seen a change in awareness of crime prevention on the part of the public and the commercial industry. Access control systems in the form of biometrics, cards, door phones, keypads and hybrid devices to limit entrance and exit to authorised persons are commonly installed in commercial and residential buildings. There is a full standard security system for domestic blocks of the Housing Department, consisting of security gates at block entrances and staircase exits; a door phone system; CCTV cameras inside lifts and at main entrances, and a security counter in the ground-floor lobby. The CPB Security Advisory Section offers advice on crime prevention through environmental design to encourage architects and planners to incorporate security concepts into the design of new premises prior to their construction. The CPB also has a display room featuring a wide range of security-related products and equipment.

It is common in Hong Kong for housing estates, whether private or public, to employ security guards to watch the entrance. This provides capable guardians according to the routine activity theory advanced by Cohen and Felson (1979). The Security and Guarding Services Industry Authority was established on 1 June 1995 under the *Security and Guarding Services Ordinance* (Cap. 460) to administer a licensing scheme to regulate the security industry. The CPB Security Companies Inspection Unit is responsible for the examination of applications by security companies for security company licences in accordance with the ordinance. Since 2012, the police have established Best Security Services Awards schemes through the CPB and the Regional Crime Prevention Offices to commend security companies and personnel in the security industry on an annual basis for their outstanding performance in helping the police combat crime.

Crime prevention in the MTR

The MTR provides a vivid illustration of how to 'design out' crime. A senior police officer was involved in the whole planning process of the subway system. From the construction planning stage, concepts were introduced to 'design out' anything that would facilitate crime. Stations were designed to minimise dark corners, dangerous niches and blind spots, thus denying potential criminals hiding places and points of ambush. Where such places could not be eliminated, as in multi-level station access tunnels and bends in corridors, mirrors and CCTV were installed. There are no public toilets in the MTR, no fast-food facilities, and no left luggage lockers where bombs or drugs could be planted.

Gaylord and Galliher (1991) attributed the design to the suggestions made by the Hong Kong police: 1) a key ingredient of the effective policing in the MTR is the communications system; 2) stations have been designed to promote easy observation; 3) stations offer a limited number of entrances and can therefore be sealed off quickly should a crime or other incident occur; 4) 'exact fare' systems obviate cash transactions; and 5 building on the above-mentioned principles, the MTR has been designed to act as a 'physical policeman'. Good planning pays: the safety standard on the system is the best in the world. Gaylord and Galliher (1991: 21) spoke highly of the use of the 'magnetized single- or return-journey ticket about the size of a credit card', at their time of writing. They would be amazed at the widespread use of the Octopus cards nowadays in Hong Kong.

The use of closed circuit television (CCTV)

CCTV cameras are very popular in some countries as a situational crime prevention measure. For example, in England and Wales, it is the single most heavily funded non-criminal justice crime prevention measure. A meta-analysis of the 19 CCTV evaluations with solid research designs shows that crime decreased by 21% in experimental areas (installation of CCTV) compared to control areas (Welsh and Farrington, 2006).

CCTV is also widely used in Hong Kong by public and private sectors such as the MTR, as referred to earlier. The CCTV systems in the public sectors are under the purview of the Transport Department (TD), Housing Department (HD) and the Leisure and Cultural Services Department (LCSD), and HKPF. The CCTV systems of the TD are for traffic surveillance, control and management purposes, and the cameras are generally installed at strategic locations to provide real-time traffic conditions to TD's Area Traffic Control (ATC) centres. For the HD, two types of CCTV systems are installed in public housing estates and shopping centres: a security system inside lifts and a falling object monitoring system at the façade of domestic buildings. The LCSD operates CCTV systems at the airport, stadiums and its other facilities. However, the HKPF has not installed CCTV systems at fixed locations in public places. Separately, CCTV systems have been installed in the land boundary of Hong Kong for security purposes, particularly for the detection of illegal immigrants.

It is not known how many CCTV systems are currently used in Hong Kong, either in the public or private sector (Press Release, 2001c). While CCTV surveillance cameras are widely used in the private sector, their limited use by the HKPF in public places on a temporary basis for law and order purposes is very different from other jurisdictions such as England and Wales. HKPF has only used temporary CCTV systems in crowd management operations during major festivals and events such as the millennium celebrations, at Christmas Eve and Lunar New Year firework displays, and large-scale international conferences. In 2002, the then deputy police commissioner announced a pilot scheme to permanently install CCTV cameras in Lan Kwai Fong for crime prevention and crowd control purposes. The proposal attracted widespread media coverage and a public debate on the possibility of infringing personal data privacy and 'Big Brother'-style surveillance. It roused strong objections in the Legislative Council, and the proposed scheme was withdrawn at a late stage (Legislative

Council, 2002; Office of the Privacy Commissioner for Personal Data, 2003). It is unknown to what extent those temporary cameras used by the police are effective in preventing crime. As for the cameras used in private and public housing estates in Hong Kong, CCTV seems to help prevent crime such as through quick identification of a suspect or with a deterrence effect. For example, in 1999 CCTV cameras were installed by the Housing Department in each of its 25 management districts to tackle the malpractice of throwing objects from a height on public housing estates (see *Fight Crime Committee Report 1999* for the details).

Community crime prevention

The Fight Violent Crime Committee was established in March 1973 to tackle rising crime since the early 1970s. Its terms of reference were to plan, organise and coordinate government and public efforts to assist the police in combatting violent crime. In 1975, the Fight Violent Crime Committee was renamed the Fight Crime Committee (FCC), with its membership expanded to include non-official members. In May 1983, the FCC was tasked to draw up plans to reduce crime, to coordinate efforts in fighting crime, to monitor the results and to report progress to the then governor.

The FCC consists of 16 members, eight of whom are members of the public appointed by the Chief Secretary for Administration, and eight are heads of relevant government policy bureaux and departments. There are two sub-committees under the FCC: the Standing Committee on Young Offenders and the Publicity Sub-committee. The FCC holds an average of five meetings every year, in order to examine the crime situation, monitor progress of the PSDS, implement the fight crime publicity work, and oversee the work of District Fight Crime Committees (DFCCs). Apart from that, at the meetings the FCC also addresses issues of major concern to the community. For example, in 2005, the committee revisited the strategies on the war against drugs and money laundering, and discussed the strategies and measures to prevent and tackle crime related to domestic violence.

DFCCs are established in the 18 districts of the territory in Hong Kong and comprise official and non-official members. They play an important part in promoting the fight against crime and in encouraging public participation at the district level. They have cross-membership with district councils and are the only committees that are directly concerned with law and order issues in each of the districts. The DFCCs meet every two to three months to monitor the state of crime and significant trends in district crime statistics, and address law and order issues specific to the individual districts. The FCC and DFCCs are supposed to serve as an important bridge between the community and the government, but it is unknown to what extent they have fulfilled such a role, apart from the studies conducted in the 1990s (see, for example, Chau (1992) and Wai (1995)) to assess the effectiveness of FCC and DFCCs in crime prevention.

Mutual Aid Committees (MACs) are another form of community crime prevention, and they are voluntary self-help organisations formed by residents of individual buildings. They are under the purview of the Home Affairs Department (HAD) through the HAD District Offices and liaison officers. MACs were initially promoted in private multi-storey buildings, and then quickly extended to public housing estates, industrial buildings, temporary housing and squatter areas. Two sets of Model Rules have been prepared by the HAD: Model Rules for a MAC in a Public Housing Estate and Model Rules for a MAC in a Private Building. By 30 April 2016, there were 1,762 MACs in Hong Kong (Home Affairs Department, 2016). The primary aims of MACs are to promote a sense of neighbourliness, mutual help and responsibility among residents, and to promote better security, a better environment and generally more effective management within the building. They serve as an important channel of communication between the government and the residents on matters affecting the well-being of the individual and the community, and also provide opportunities for residents to participate in community activities (Press Release, 2007).

The government departments, such as the HAD and Food and Environmental Department, actively engage the MACs on issues of concern to the residents. For example, the HAD addresses notices to the MACs to advise and guide the property owners on building management such as purchasing third-party liability insurance to minimise losses to property owners. The Food and Environmental Department has sent notices to the MACs on how to deal with rodents and how to maintain a clean and hygienic environment. As the 'Broken Windows' thesis demonstrates, the focus on physical environment could have enormous implications for crime and fear of crime at the neighbourhood level (Kelling and Coles, 1996). Moreover, opportunities are provided to MAC members to better deal with conflicts and disputes at the neighbourhood level, such as through training on 'professional mediation service'.

With the pace of urbanisation and industrialisation accelerating, there has been an outcry that the old community spirit is being lost: people living in high-rise buildings seldom get to know their neighbours next door and the old proverb 'it takes a village to raise a child' simply no longer applies. However, research along the lines of neighbourhood and informal social control demonstrates that the community, i.e. where you live, still matters a lot. For example, a large-scale study entitled Human Development in Chicago Neighborhoods, demonstrated that 'collective efficacy', defined as social cohesion among neighbours combined with their willingness to intervene on behalf of the common good, is linked to reduced violence at the neighbourhood level. The effects that remain after individual-level characteristics, neighbourhood characteristics and prior violence at the neighbourhood level are taken into account (Sampson et al., 1997). It attests to the importance of grassroots organisations such as the MACs as they are important media for promoting 'collective efficacy' and ultimately law and order at the community level.

Conclusion

While a wide range of policies and initiatives are adopted in Hong Kong to prevent crime, they are seldom evaluated, with a few exceptions. Indeed, not all crime prevention programmes are proven to be effective. Some crime prevention initiatives continue to receive widespread social and political support despite their limited usefulness, such as DARE (Drug Abuse Resistance Education), a school-based anti-drug programme in the USA and other countries (see Lab, 2004). Hence, ideally crime prevention should be based on the best possible evidence. The most appealing approach to evaluating crime prevention programmes is an experimental or quasi-experimental design (Sherman et al., 1997). Evaluations of crime prevention increasingly stress the employment of both process and output (outcome) evaluations (Ekblom and Pease, 1995). The mechanisms presumed to underpin the causal relationships of crime reduction should be established and tested (Pawson and Tilly, 1994). Effectiveness of crime prevention goes beyond the question of 'does it work?' to questions of 'what works?' and 'at what price?', as reflected in costs measurement and cost-benefit analysis (see Welsh and Farrington, 2000; Swaray, 2006).

Crime prevention in Hong Kong involves a multi-agency approach, and all facets of the society are organised to pursue the common goal of preventing crime and maintaining law and order. Some prevention measures are common sense, such as locking up and watching out, but whether they will be adopted entails consciousness, sensibility and sensitivity on the part of the individuals and merchants. Other measures are not so straightforward, and involve resolve, dedication and perseverance on the part of the multiple agencies involved in the process. Some strategies are demonstrated to work effectively. For some strategies, their effectiveness is still unknown. Some are demonstrated to be harmful elsewhere, but are still in use locally. Some strategies invoke concerns in the local community, although their effectiveness is demonstrated elsewhere.

Review questions

1. What aspects should a sound definition of crime prevention include?
2. How should crime prevention be classified?
3. Try to use the three typologies of crime prevention to classify every local initiative of crime prevention.

References

Blakely, E.J. and Snyder, M.G. (1997) *Fortress America: Gated Communities in the United States*, Washington, DC: The Brookings Institution & Lincoln Institute of Land Policy.

Brantingham, P.L. and Faust, F.L. (1976) 'A conceptual model of crime prevention', *Crime and Delinquency*, 22(3): 284–296.

Bursik, R.J. and Grasmick, H.G. (1993) *Neighborhood and Crime*, New York: Lexington Books.

Chau, A.K.Y. (1992) *An Assessment of the Work of the Fight Crime Committee*, unpublished Master of Public Administration thesis, Hong Kong: The University of Hong Kong.

Choi, A. and Lo, T.W. (2004) *Fighting Youth Crime: A Comparative Study of Two Little Dragons in Asia* (2nd edn), Singapore: Eastern University Press.

Clarke, R.V. (1995) 'Situational crime prevention', in M. Tonry and D.P. Farrington (eds) *Building a Safer Society: Strategic Approaches to Crime Prevention* (pp. 91–150), Chicago, IL: University of Chicago Press.

Clarke, R.V. (ed.) (1997) *Situational Crime Prevention: Successful Case Studies* (2nd edn), Guilderland, NY: Harrow and Heston Publishers.

Clarke, R. and Weisburd, D. (1994) 'Diffusion of crime control benefits: Observations of the reverse of displacement', in R. Clarke (ed.) *Crime Prevention Studies, Vol. 2* (pp. 165–183), New York: Criminal Justice Press.

Cohen, L.E. and Felson, M. (1979) 'Social change and crime rate trends: A routine activity approach', *American Sociological Review*, 44(4): 588–608.

Crawford, A. (1998) *Crime Prevention and Community Safety: Politics, Policies and Practices*, London: Longman.

Currie, E. (1988) 'Two visions of community crime prevention', in T. Hope and M. Shaw (eds) *Communities and Crime Reduction* (pp. 280–292), London: Home Office Research and Planning Unit.

Currie, E. (1996) 'Social crime prevention strategies in a market society', in J. Muncie, E. McLaughlin and M. Langan (eds) *Criminological Perspectives: A Reader* (pp. 343–354), London: Sage.

Ekblom, P. and Pease, K. (1995) 'Evaluating crime prevention', in M. Tonry and D.P. Farrington (eds) *Building a Safer Society: Strategic Approaches to Crime Prevention* (pp. 585–662), Chicago, IL: University of Chicago Press.

Fight Crime Committee (1997–2013, various issues) *Fight Crime Committee Report*, Hong Kong: Government Logistics Department.

Garland, D. (1996) 'The limits of the sovereign state: Strategies of crime control in contemporary society', *British Journal of Criminology*, 36(4): 445–471.

Gaylord, M.S. and Galliher, J.F. (1991) 'Riding the underground dragon: Crime control and public order on Hong Kong Mass Transit Railway', *British Journal of Criminology*, 31(1): 15–26.

Graham, J. and Bennett, T. (1995) *Crime Prevention Strategies in Europe and North America*, Helsinki: European Institute for Crime Prevention and Control Affiliated with the United Nations.

Home Affairs Department (2016) *Mutual Aid Committees*, www.had.gov.hk/en/public_services/district_administration/mutual.htm (accessed 15 June 2016).

Hong Kong Police Force (2014) *Hong Kong Police Review 2013*, Hong Kong: Hong Kong Police Force.

Hong Kong Police Force (2015) *Hong Kong Police Review 2014*, Hong Kong: Hong Kong Police Force.

Hong Kong Police Force (2016a) *Development of PSLP*, www.police.gov.hk/ppp_en/11_useful_info/youth/pslp_develop.html (accessed 15 February 2016).

Hong Kong Police Force (2016b) *Crime Prevention*, www.police.gov.hk/ppp_en/04_crime_matters/cpa/ (accessed 15 February 2016).

Hong Kong Police Force (2016c) *Telephone Deception*, www.police.gov.hk/ppp_en/04_crime_matters/ccb/cct_09.html (accessed 15 February 2016).

Hope, T. (1995) 'Community crime prevention', in M. Tonry and D.P. Farrington (eds) *Building a Safer Society: Strategic Approaches to Crime Prevention* (pp. 21–90), Chicago, IL: University of Chicago Press.

Kelling, G.L. and Coles, C.M. (1996) *Fixing Broken Windows: Restoring Order and Reducing Crime in Our Communities*, New York: Touchstone.

Lab, S.P. (1988) *Crime Prevention: Approaches, Practices and Evaluations*, Cincinnati, OH: Anderson.

Lab, S.P. (2004) 'Presidential address: Crime prevention, politics, and the art of going to nowhere fast', *Justice Quarterly*, 21(4): 681–692.

Laidler, K.A.J. (2005) 'Police diversion measures for juveniles at risk', in F.W.-L. Lee (ed.) *Working with Youth-at-Risk in Hong Kong* (pp. 53–74), Hong Kong: Hong Kong University Press.

Lee, F.W.-L. (2005) 'Service programmes for "youth-at-risk" in Hong Kong', F.W.-L. Lee (ed.) *Working with Youth-at-Risk in Hong Kong* (pp. 7–14), Hong Kong: Hong Kong University Press.

Legislative Council (2002) *Legislative Council – Official Record of Proceedings*, 3 July, www.legco.gov.hk/yr01-02/chinese/counmtg/floor/cm0703ti-confirm-c.pdf (accessed 15 February 2016).

Lo, C.W.-H. and Cheuk, A.C.-Y. (2004) 'Community policing in Hong Kong: Development, performance and constraints', *Policing: An International Journal of Police Strategies and Management*, 27(1): 97–127.

Lo, T.W. (1986) *Outreaching Social Work in Focus: Report of an Outreaching Social Work Project for Street Gangsters in Tung Tau*, Hong Kong: Outreaching Service, Caritas.

Office of the Privacy Commissioner for Personal Data (2003) *Community Perceptions towards Surveillance Cameras in Public Places*, Hong Kong: Office of the Privacy Commissioner for Personal Data.

Pauson, R. and Tilly, N. (1994) 'What works in evaluation research?', *British Journal of Criminology*, 34(3): 291–306.

Petrosino, A., Petrosino, C.-T. and Buehler, J. (2006) 'Scared Straight and other juvenile awareness programmes, in B.C. Welsh and D.P. Farrington (eds) *Preventing Crime: What Works for Children, Offenders, Victims, and Places* (pp. 87–102), Dordrecht: Springer.

Press Release (2001a) 'LCQ10: Secondary School Liaison Officers Programme' (17 October), www.info.gov.hk/gia/general/200110/17/1017180.htm (accessed 15 February 2016).

Press Release (2001b) 'Secondary School Liaison Officers help curb juvenile crime' (19 September), www.info.gov.hk/gia/general/200109/19/0919238.htm (accessed 15 February 2016).

Press Release (2001c) 'LCQ12: Closed circuit television cameras in public places' (7 November), www.info.gov.hk/gia/general/200111/07/1107179.htm (accessed 15 February 2016).

Press Release (2006) 'LCQ8: Effective strategies formulated to handle juvenile crime' (8 February), www.info.gov.hk/gia/general/200602/08/P200602080211_print.htm (accessed 15 February 2016).

Press Release (2007) 'LCQ14: Operation of Mutual Aid Committees' (5 December), www.info.gov.hk/gia/general/200712/05/P200712050109.htm (accessed 15 February 2016).

Rosenbaum, D.P. (1988) 'Community crime prevention: A review and synthesis of the literature', *Justice Quarterly*, 5(3): 323–395.

Rosenbaum, D.P., Lurigio, A.J. and Davis, R.C. (1998) *The Prevention of Crime: Social and Situational Strategies*, Belmont, CA: West/Wadsworth.

Sampson, R.J. (2002) 'Transcending tradition: New directions in community research, Chicago style', *Criminology*, 40(2): 213–230.

Sampson, R.J., Raudenbush, S.W. and Earls, F. (1997) 'Neighborhoods and violent crime: A multilevel study of collective efficacy', *Science*, 277(5328): 918–924.

Sherman, L.W., Gottfredson, D., MacKenzie, D., Eck, J., Reuter, P., Bushway, S. in collaboration with members of the Graduate Program (1997) *Preventing Crime: What Works, What Doesn't, What's Promising (A Report to the United States Congress)*, Maryland: Department of Criminology and Criminal Justice, University of Maryland.

Swaray, R. (2006) 'Economic methodology and evaluations: The costs and benefits of criminal justice interventions', in A.E. Perry, C. McDougall and D.P. Farrington (eds) *Reducing Crime: The Effectiveness of Criminal Justice Interventions* (pp. 143–162), West Sussex: John Wiley & Sons.

Sy, M.L.J. (1996) *An Assessment of the 'Personal Encounter with Prisoners Programme' of CSD*, unpublished MSocSc thesis, Hong Kong: University of Hong Kong.

Tonry, M. and Farrington, D.P. (1995) 'Strategic approaches to crime prevention', in M. Tonry and D.P. Farrington (eds) *Building a Safer Society: Strategic Approaches to Crime Prevention* (pp. 1–21), Chicago, IL: University of Chicago Press.

Van Dijk, J. (1990) 'Crime prevention policy: Current state and prospects', in G. Daiser and H.-J. Albrecht (eds) *Crime and Criminal Policy in Europe: Criminological Research Report (Vol. 43)* (pp. 205–220), Freiburg: Max Planck Institute.

Wai, W.H.-C. (1995) *Crime Prevention: The Role of the District Fight Crime Committees*, unpublished MSocSc thesis, Hong Kong: University of Hong Kong.

Welsh, B.C. and Farrington, D.P. (2000) 'Monetary costs and benefits of crime prevention programs', in M. Tonry (ed.) *Crime and Justice: A Review of Research (Vol. 27)* (pp. 305–362), Chicago, IL: University of Chicago Press.

Welsh, B.C. and Farrington, D.P. (2006) 'CCTV and street lighting: Comparative effects on crime', in A.E. Perry, C. McDougall and D.P. Farrington (eds) *Reducing Crime: The Effectiveness of Criminal Justice Interventions* (pp. 95–104), West Sussex: John Wiley & Sons.

Wilson, J.Q. and Kelling, G.L. (1982) 'The police and neighborhood safety: Broken windows', *Atlantic Monthly*, 127 (March), 29–38.

Wong, S.W. (2000) 'Juvenile crime and responses to delinquency in Hong Kong', *International Journal of Offender Therapy and Comparative Criminology*, 44(3): 279–292.

Wong, S.W. (2004a) 'School bullying and tackling strategies in Hong Kong', *International Journal of Offender Therapy and Comparative Criminology*, 48(5): 537–553.

Wong, S.W. (2004b) *School Bullying and Responding Tactics: A Life Education Approach* (2nd edn), Hong Kong: Arcadia Press (in Chinese).

Wong, S.W., Chan, O.H.C. and Cheng, C.H.K. (2014) 'Cyberbullying perpetration and victimization among adolescents in Hong Kong', *Children and Youth Services Review*, 36(1): 133–140.

Wong, S.W. and Lee, S.S.-T. (2005) 'Strategies for tackling school bullying: A whole-school approach', in F.W.-L. Lee (ed.) *Working with Youth-at-Risk in Hong Kong* (pp. 39–52), Hong Kong: Hong Kong University Press.

Wong, S.W. and Lo, T.W. (2002) 'School bullying in secondary schools: Teachers' perceptions and tackling strategies', *Educational Research Journal*, 17(2): 253–272.

Wong, S.W., Lok, D.P., Lo, T.W. and Ma, S. (2002) *A Study of School Bullying in Primary Schools in Hong Kong*, Hong Kong: Department of Applied Social Studies, City University of Hong Kong (in Chinese).

Zamble, E. and Quinsey, V.L. (1997) *The Criminal Recidivism Process*, Cambridge: Cambridge University Press.

Zhong, L.Y. and Broadhurst, R.G. (2007) 'Building little safe and civilized communities: Community crime prevention with Chinese characteristics?', *International Journal of Offender Therapy and Comparative Criminology*, 51(1): 52–67.

Legislation cited

Security and Guarding Services Ordinance (Cap. 460)

Newspaper articles cited

Hong Kong Economic Times (2015) 'In the ten biggest telephone deception cases victims were deceived 100 million dollars', 15 August (in Chinese).

South China Morning Post (2004) 'Schools must face up to bullying problem', 17 February.

South China Morning Post (2007a) 'Is Hong Kong wising up to the con men?', 22 April.

South China Morning Post (2007b) 'Internet film pirate sent to jail after appeals fails', 19 May.

South China Morning Post (2015) 'From street con-artists to phone fraud: A history of Hong Kong scams ... and how to avoid becoming another victim', 11 August.

Useful websites

Customs and Excise Department www.customs.gov.hk/eng/content_e.html
Fight Crime Committee Report (various issues) www.sb.gov.hk/eng/pub/index.htm
Hong Kong Police Force www.police.gov.hk
Intellectual Property Department www.ipd.gov.hk/eng/home.htm
Junior Police Call Scheme www.hkpjpc.org.hk
Mutual Aid Committees, Home Affairs Department www.had.gov.hk/en/public_services/district_administration/mutual.htm
National Crime Prevention Council (USA) www.ncpc.org
National Criminal Justice Reference Service – Crime Prevention (USA) www.ncjrs.gov/App/Topics/Topic.aspx?TopicID=49
Security and Guarding Services Industry Authority www.sb.gov.hk/eng/links/sgsia/index.htm
Security Bureau www.sb.gov.hk/eng/about/welcome.htm

19

THE FUTURE OF HONG KONG'S CRIMINAL JUSTICE[1]

T. Wing Lo

Introduction

Britain handed Hong Kong back to China as a special administrative region (SAR) on 1 July 1997. The *Sino-British Joint Declaration* guaranteed Hong Kong would maintain high-level autonomy and retain its capitalist system for 50 years under the model of 'One Country, Two Systems'. Under the *Basic Law of the Hong Kong Special Administrative Region of the People's Republic of China* (hereafter referred to as the *Basic Law*), the mini-constitution of Hong Kong, the governor was replaced by a locally elected but Beijing-appointed chief executive, and the criminal justice system was to continue, together with the political, legal, economic and social systems.

In fact, China has opposed any radical reforms that would establish a fully democratic government in Hong Kong, even though China has promised a high degree of autonomy. To China, the problem of Hong Kong is mainly one of sovereignty and not human rights (Lee, 1987), and thus its old colonial political system is ideal because of the great concentration of power in the hands of the chief executive and SAR government. It is not surprising to see that since the transfer of sovereignty, Hong Kong's political development has not been progressive. The calls for universal suffrage by the pro-democracy camp have not been thoroughly addressed (Ma, 2007). They are worried that Beijing will interfere with the internal affairs of Hong Kong and tighten its control over political activities.

The year 2014, characterised by the Umbrella Movement, represented a watershed in the political history of Hong Kong. The SAR government was confronted by young people who did not share their appreciation of Mainland China, and coercion was used to suppress their demonstrations. The police became the SAR government's reserve army (Hall et al., 1978: 202) and were brought in to maintain legal order, force the youths back into conformity and preserve the status quo. However, in a politically divided society, rule by coercion functions less effectively. Although the government was successful in suppressing the demonstrations, it failed to convince the people of the pro-democracy camp of its legitimacy. Political events had already sensitised them to such problems as corruption, injustice and social inequality and so, when they became conscious of this suppression, they questioned the validity of 'One Country, Two Systems', giving rise to localism power.

Against this backdrop, this concluding chapter examines the future challenges faced by certain major sectors of the criminal justice system of Hong Kong. In view of the quickening pace of political change and the rapid progress of 'mainlandisation' (Mainland China) within Hong Kong's political, economic and legal systems, this chapter argues that Hong Kong's legal system is losing its autonomy; the Independent Commission Against Corruption (ICAC) is challenged by increasing conflicts of interest among senior officials; the police are overwhelmed by political policing; and the court has become a site of struggle and contestation between opposing political forces.

Mainlandisation of criminal justice practices

Lo (2007: 186) refers to mainlandisation as the 'policy of making Hong Kong politically more dependent on Beijing, economically more reliant on the Mainland's support, socially more patriotic toward the motherland, and legally more reliant on the interpretation of the *Basic Law* by the PRC [People's Republic of China] National People's Congress'. Since 1997, Hong Kong has attempted to retain and develop a legal system based on principles that are consistent both with its past as a British colony and with its ongoing position as part of the international community. The best shield against the arbitrary use of power so often witnessed in Asian nations (Ghai, 1993) is the upholding of the rule of law that the Hong Kong people cherish so much.

In Mainland China, patriotism is highly appreciated. China's criminal law stipulates clearly the kinds of crime that endanger national security, known as counter-revolutionary crimes in the old version of the law. All Chinese people, especially members of the Chinese Communist Party (CCP) and government cadres, are required to stand in line with the CCP and fight against any counter-revolutionary crimes to safeguard territorial integrity, national union and independence under a one-party socialist state controlled by the CCP. Thus, 'toeing the Party line' in response to crimes against the state or counter-revolutionary crimes is one of the working principles in China's criminal justice system (Davidson and Wang, 2000). Hong Kong people have been concerned with how national security will be interpreted and applied in the SAR. They are worried that some of the Chinese criminal justice concepts will seep into their legal system through the process of mainlandisation, such as 'rule by the people', 'toeing the Party line', 'leniency for self-confession, severity for resistance', and 'the absence of the presumption of innocence' (Davidson and Wang, 2000).

Conflict between offenders' rights and collective interests

Criminal justice in China to date has departed from mass-line justice of the past (Lo, 1993) and is run through a well-defined bureaucratic process, including investigation by the public security authorities, prosecution by the procurator, and the trial and sentencing of cases by the court. Mass education and mass mobilisation are still in place, but it is now the criminal justice officials 'who finally define what the masses want in the field of public security' (Wang, 2000: 179). In addition, communities in China have changed from traditional informal social control to semi-formal social control. The two types of control are intertwined together and are hard to distinguish (Klein and Gatz, 1989; Zhong and Grabosky, 2009).

In China, mediation has always been the main method to resolve disputes in the neighbourhood. The tradition of maintaining a network of social control comprising various kinds of neighbourhood committees and mediation committees still exists. As social control agents, these committees are often involved in making decisions about offending. Mediation or reconciliation conducted by them has been used to settle disputes and conflicts (Lo et al., 2006; Di, 2009). This is regarded as a control-restorative model because the Chinese practice does not include fully restorative elements and the restorative outcomes are always shaped by the authority (Lo et al., 2005). The committees are not mandated under legislation or potentially accountable to the court for their decisions. Thus, under the dual influences of 'rule by the people' and 'toeing the Party line', impartiality is difficult to maintain and the restorative ways to handle offending could breach the important principles of proportionality, consistency and due process.

Due to the dominance of the people's or the Party's interest, the protection of the public interest, rather than the defendant's interest, is paramount (Davidson and Wang, 2000). Di (2009: 2) argued that 'based on collective interests, the mediators would consider all kinds of factors, such as law, power, social relationships, and reputation to convince the parties concerned, regardless of the conversation and negotiation between the parties themselves, and sometimes the mediators even overbear the parties to accept the result'. Thus, mediation in Mainland China may be biased because of the overemphasis on collective interest and social control.

Di (2009: 1) further contends that 'the characteristics of power are becoming more and more obvious during the continuing systematization of Chinese mediation'. The personal social network (*guanxi*) is so rampant in China that penal decisions are often affected by personal relations rather than the nature of the offence (Jiang et al., 2012). For instance, Zhang and Liu (2004) found that the official status of individual offenders had a negative effect on the swiftness of arrest. Di (2009: 2) argued that 'the self-governing mediation organizations are powerless in face of the disputes involving government'. Criminal justice in China is always related to power, ideology and conflict within society (Lo,

1993). Criminal justice practices are particularly susceptible to the influence of personal power and persuasion, and outcomes may favour those who have close affiliations with those in power.

Insufficient protection of offenders' rights to due process

China's criminal law emphasises punishment with leniency in the light of special circumstances. 'Leniency for self-confession and severity for resistance' is a very popular slogan in public security departments, detention centres and prisons. The main purpose is to terrify suspects into confessing and thus bring about prompt termination of a criminal case. This reflects the emphasis of Chinese criminal justice on expediency and the swift capture and punishment of offenders as a means of crime control (Davidson and Wang, 2000; Trevaskes, 2010). There are provisions in the criminal law that allow for less severe charges or sentences in return for 'contributions', including initial confession, reporting other people's crimes, and serving as a tainted witness (Felkenes, 1989). Therefore, 'leniency for self-confession and severity for resistance' works as both propaganda and a real criminal justice practice, but a practice that is likely to endanger the fairness of a trial.

Although it could be argued that plea bargaining is also encouraged in Western jurisdictions in order to save time and cost in criminal justice, the problem in the Chinese criminal justice system is its emphasis on confession as superior to any other kind of evidence. Confession extorted by means of torture or other illegal and immoral means frequently occurs because of the lack of powerful court supervision, limited independence of the judiciary, shortage of law enforcement resources, ineffective police training and the slow development of due process (Bakken, 2008).

Furthermore, it is observed that the presumption of innocence is a hidden concept in the criminal justice system of China because it 'has been regarded as a manifestation of idealism and metaphysics and has been rejected in favor of a more practical or pragmatic approach, for two reasons. First, China does not wish criminals to escape penalty under a presumption of innocence. Second, China has its own guideline, the principle of 'seeking truth from facts' (Davidson and Wang, 2000: 213). The prevailing principle in China is: 'When there is a borderline case with a choice to arrest an individual or not, always choose to arrest and if there is a choice to prosecute or not, always choose to prosecute' (Trevaskes, 2010: 349). Thus, although China's criminal law presumes the innocence of suspects, in actual practice, judicial personnel are inclined to presume them guilty. Suspects have to prove that they are not guilty with strong evidence. As the presumption of innocence is not fully recognised, suspects' legal rights are often ignored and the powerless may be urged to confess in order to resolve the incident quickly. In this respect, the Chinese model of criminal justice would carry the danger of offering insufficient protection to individuals against the most powerful and the organs of government.

The mirror effect

Taking into account the inherited weaknesses of these Chinese justice practices, the issue is actually not just about the problems of criminal justice, but about the existence of a *mirror effect* in Hong Kong. The mirror effect involves people living under 'One Country, Two Systems', indicating that the Hong Kong people have perceived through a mirror some Chinese criminal justice concepts or approaches that have been conveyed to them through the process of mainlandisation. In the absence of a well-established legal or administrative code to guide them, criminal justice decisions in China can be made and 'ruled' by the people, and practices would appear to vary enormously from place to place and case to case. Trevaskes (2009) has voiced the criticism that in the recent penal reform of China the practice of paying compensation to victims in return for a reduced sentence is a form of 'McDonaldisation' of criminal justice (Bohm, 2006; Ritzer, 2013) with Chinese characteristics, rather than a step towards achieving justice. In toeing the Party line, the Chinese criminal justice system leaves considerable room for abuse of human rights. Some of those in power can be above the law, or 'more equal' before the law than others. It is difficult for the ordinary people to resist the arbitrary interference by the powerful in judicial decisions, and the rights of the innocent are not always protected. The existential function of the mirror enables Hong Kong people to see the management of criminal justice relations in the shadow of Mainland China, thus provoking them into defending their last asset, the rule of law, which they have possessed for decades under the British administration.

Former Chief Secretary of Hong Kong Sir David Akers-Jones (2004: 268) contended that 'One Country, Two Systems' is interpreted as the 'superiority of our system and its proud possession of the rule of law, our freedom, our administration, our simple tax structure and our economic well-being'. However, in recent years, the economic bargaining power of Hong Kong vis-à-vis Mainland China has been rapidly losing ground, and this special administrative region of China is now 'simply a Mainland Chinese city with the exception of possessing the rule of law' (Lo, 2007: 221–222). Although China has been quite successful in speeding up the processes of political and economic convergence between Hong Kong and the mainland, there is strong resistance to any attempt of mainlandisation of Hong Kong's criminal justice system. In the continued contestation by liberal groups and human rights advocates, the rule of law is amplified as a shield against any attempt to mainlandise its legal system.

Colonising Hong Kong for 155 years, the British government at first lacked the will and later lacked the power to make Hong Kong's democracy genuine. Despite the lack of democracy, the rule of law has been regarded as a cornerstone of Hong Kong's success as a leading international financial centre in Asia and a gateway to China. The rights and freedoms of the citizens have been protected, the independence of the judiciary has been upheld, and the capitalist way of life in Hong Kong has been maintained. All these indicate that the rule of law worked very well before the transfer of sovereignty. Jones and Vagg (2007) explained why the rule of law was essential for the British colonial administration: 'The introduction of the rule of law probably owed as much to the *realpolitik* of the colonial rule as the "civilizing mission" – experience elsewhere had taught the Colonial Office that the best means of establishing the *pax Britannica* was by attaching the native population to colonial rule through rule of law and associated institutions' (Jones and Vagg, 2007: 3). It is quite true that democracy and the rule of law are twins in some developed countries, but in Hong Kong, where the people know they have no democracy, the rule of law becomes most valuable.

The challenges to Hong Kong's criminal justice system

The law: diminishing autonomy

The Hong Kong legal system is closely modelled on the English common law system, modified slightly by traditional Chinese laws and customs. One important feature of the common law system is its stress upon the rule of law and the existence of a judiciary free from executive influences and other political and personal pressures. Although both the *Sino-British Joint Declaration* and the *Basic Law* assure that there shall be an independent judiciary in Hong Kong after 1997, Article 160 of the *Basic Law* confers upon the Standing Committee of China's National People's Congress (NPC) the power to decide whether any existing law in Hong Kong contravenes the *Basic Law*. This was criticised as compromising the authority and independence of the Hong Kong judiciary after the transfer of sovereignty (Lo, 2012).

Since the power of interpretation of the *Basic Law* rests with the NPC, members of the pro-democracy camps and legal community believe that the independence of Hong Kong's judiciary and common law system has been under threat. Examples of the NPC's interpretation of the *Basic Law* include the right of abode for mainland-born children with Hong Kong parents who arrived in Hong Kong without proper documentation (Lo, 2007), and the direct elections of the chief executive and the Legislative Council in 2004. The legal profession, in particular, reacted strongly to all moves by the SAR government and Beijing administration to dilute the judicial autonomy of Hong Kong (Lo, 2007: 207). In the mid-2000s, around 900 members of the legal profession protested against the NPC's move to interpret the *Basic Law*. They reiterated that the Court of Final Appeal in Hong Kong should not be deprived of the right to interpret the *Basic Law* (Lo, 2007), indicating their efforts to minimise Hong Kong's legal convergence with Mainland China. However, Beijing's White Paper on Hong Kong published in June 2014 reconfirmed that 'as a unitary state, China's central government has comprehensive jurisdiction over all local administrative regions, including the HKSAR' (BBC News, 2014).

Incidentally, there was a need to enact a national security law in Hong Kong, laid down in Article 23 of the *Basic Law*, to outlaw treason, secession, sedition and subversion (Lo, 2007). Members of the public expressed grave concerns that their civil liberties would continue to be mainlandised, and this aroused public distrust both of Beijing's increasing influence on Hong Kong's legal system and the expansion of police power associated with the new law. Many people felt they had been confronted by tightening political and legal forces since 1997. Coupled with other social issues and problems, the proposed enactment of Article 23 of the *Basic Law* triggered public outcry and resulted in a demonstration by half a million people, who marched in the streets on 1 July 2003 (Cheng, 2005).

Eventually, the SAR government acquiesced and withdrew the draft law. Following the Umbrella Movement in 2014, there were calls for the reconsideration of the enactment of Article 23 in Hong Kong. In July 2015, China passed a national security law to counter emerging threats, ranging from cybercrime to terrorism. It was also regarded as a measure designed to purge political dissent (Wong, 2015). Although this law is not applied in the territories of Hong Kong, Hong Kong citizens may be arrested and prosecuted in Mainland China if their behaviour in Hong Kong is regarded as treasonous and subversive.

The ICAC: weakened shield

In the 1960s and 1970s, Hong Kong faced the problem of corruption and gangs, where the police and triad societies worked together to rule Hong Kong's underworld. Many people suffered during that period. Modern-day Hong Kong is no longer the corrupt and criminal city of the past, and is rather a city that enjoys a very low crime rate. A whole host of factors have contributed to Hong Kong's success.

First, the government has developed the strong political will necessary to fight corruption, including an amnesty for past corrupt officials. Hong Kong has very powerful laws governing the behaviour of civil servants; for example, civil servants' assets cannot exceed their total earnings during their civil service (Lo, 2003). Most importantly, the ICAC was formed, with 1,200 anti-graft fighters, for a city with a population of 7.2 million. The ICAC has adopted an innovative three-pronged attack approach of corruption prevention, community education against corruption, and investigation and prosecution. These anti-corruption measures are supported by various civil service reforms that have been implemented throughout the years, including a generous salary package, continuous training, enhanced transparency, integrity checks, and the declaration and disclosure of investments of senior officials.

Over the years, Hong Kong has developed into a very strong civil society that does not tolerate corruption; indeed, it boasts a mass media that serves as a watchdog of the government and politicians (Lo, 2003). Furthermore, judicial independence and the British rule of law are maintained. This whole anti-corruption package has cut the undesirable link between law enforcement and organised crime, and thus has substantially reduced the crime rate of Hong Kong.

It was expected that the curbing of the draconian powers of the ICAC brought about by the ICAC Review in 1994 would undermine the effectiveness of this graft fighter. However, the elimination of its powers had no negative impact on its effectiveness and public perceptions of its credibility and legitimacy remained high (Lo and Yu, 2000). In addition, in the view of the international community, Hong Kong is still a clean city. In recent years, however, the ICAC has been confronted by increasing conflicts of interest among senior government officials. For instance, former Chief Executive Donald Tsang was accused of accepting travel hospitality and a post-retirement luxury apartment from business tycoons (Li, 2014). Although there are established guidelines on gifts and hospitality for civil servants, no such guidelines are available for the chief executive. In another case, former ICAC Commissioner Timothy Tong Hin-ming was accused of lavish spending on official entertainment and gifts for *guanxi* building with Mainland Chinese officials (*South China Morning Post* (SCMP), 2013). These two high-profile cases have fuelled public concern and undermined confidence in the ICAC. In the third case, former Chief Secretary for Administration Rafael Si-Yan Hui was found guilty of corruption-related charges. The conviction of Hui helped to improve the image of the ICAC, but simultaneously confirmed the general public's perception that collusion still existed between senior officials and property tycoons; in particular, there was concern that additional conflicts of interest could have been covered up (SCMP, 2014).

The police: reserve army of domination

During the Umbrella Movement, there were two opposing views concerning the use of statutory powers by the police. Members of the pro-democratic camp were of the opinion that there was no real justification for the police to use extraordinary powers. They had to remain neutral in response to the public demand for universal suffrage and human rights. On the other hand, supporters of the pro-government camp argued that the police should be vested with stronger powers to ensure social stability.

The SAR government decided to rule by coercion, not by consent. There was an intensification of mass demand from the pro-government camp for coercive solutions to the crisis of occupation. Thus, the police became a political weapon in the pursuit of government interests, with the capacity to colonise political enemies (political policing is used by those in power against political opponents). This form of policing was highly targeted and served as a legitimate means to denounce and colonise the occupiers in their struggle for wider democratic participation, resulting in oppression and injustice. This coincides with the idea of Mao (1961: 417) that the state apparatus was an instrument for the oppression of antagonistic classes; it was violent and not benevolent.

The arrest of occupiers should not necessarily be regarded as retribution for the harm they caused society. Rather, it can also be viewed as a kind of coercion imposed by the rulers on the law-breakers, with the standards being set by the rulers. The arrest of occupiers is a flagrant punishment for their political association and ideology, rather than a punishment for the actual 'crime' itself. In this context, criminality can only be regarded as a political status rather than as a kind of law-breaking behaviour.

However, there was strong resistance from the opposition to redefine this censure. The police were accused as public security, a negative label classifying them in terms of their role in serving the interests of the CCP. Eventually, political policing resulted in disgracing, demoralising and isolating the police from a critical mass of the community. The Umbrella Movement signified a real political struggle between opposing political forces. Occupiers were able to resist and negotiate its content, but its capacity remained very weak. The SAR government was able to control and eliminate political opposition from occupied sites through the police and court orders.

The court: arena for contestation

In fact, political policing failed to perform hegemonic functions for the SAR government. Rather, the coercion created a new crisis of legitimation for the government. The coercive responses created new political tensions and a hegemonic crisis that everyone wanted to avoid. The court thus became a battlefield in the political arena, where it was open to negotiation and contest by political rivals. It is reasonable to suggest that the successful clearance of the occupied sites resulted from the effectiveness of the police, backed by court orders and bailiffs. The main characteristic of the intervention was to transfer a number of vital powers from the hands of the police to those of the court. Under the court orders, the abusive powers of the police had become more judicially confined and the likelihood of them being abused was drastically minimised.

Moreover, during the political struggle, the court had been used as an arena in which the two opposing camps could contend and be adjudicated under the rule of law. The symbolic function that has been achieved outshines the actual value of securing a judicial ruling on the legal status of the respective legislation. It reiterates and reinforces the fact that Hong Kong courts represent the interests of both the pro-democracy and pro-government camps. While the former cast doubt on the neutrality of the police, the latter asserted that, whilst the Umbrella Movement was a serious problem, the court released the demonstrators too easily.

Li (2014) contends that the root cause of Hong Kong's current problem originates in the *class conflicts* characterised by the land and property hegemony and the sharp disparity between the rich and the poor. However, this root cause has been overshadowed by *ideological conflicts* focused on Mainland China–Hong Kong inharmonious convergence. To date, the civil society of Hong Kong remains seriously divided as a result of these ideological conflicts. However, the court is not the SAR government's repressive apparatus against the pro-democracy camp; it also protects the interests of political rivals. Laws have not yet served as political weapons. The court remains relatively autonomous and this provides a degree of judicial space which members of the two political camps appropriate for their own defence and protection; it also gives the court a measure of freedom to police and regulate the real deviants. Thus, the court represents the interests of both the dominated and the dominant, albeit unequally. It is a site of struggle among a plurality of unequal social forces. The contestation provides constructive channels through which the people can express discontent and contain their demise. In this way, the court mutes class conflicts and preserves the interests of the land and property hegemonic group.

The legal censure of those who offended during the Umbrella Movement expounds a juridico-political ideology. The exemplary sentences imposed on members of both camps appear to support the claim that the court is a neutral entity: everyone is subject to legal constraints. As a setting for forceful symbolic rituals of sentencing deviants of both camps, the court has become an effective ideological apparatus that secures and constructs hegemony for Hong Kong. The positive elements of judicial functions serve the ideology of upholding the basic principles of accountability and fairness under the rule of law, resulting in the production of the people's consent in maintaining Hong Kong's stability.

Conclusion

The quickening pace of political change in Hong Kong will undoubtedly affect the criminal justice system. Required to answer to a Communist Chinese outlook, Hong Kong may be forced to re-examine its commitment to the rule of law. The rule of law is the principle that governmental authority is legitimately exercised only in accordance with written, publicly disclosed legal codes that are adopted and enforced in accordance with established procedures. The principle is intended to be a safeguard against arbitrary governance and to protect the interests and rights of all individuals so that no individual is above the law (Neumann, 2002). To put the rule of law into practice in criminal justice, the legal system of a society should ensure the following for every individual, irrespective of political affiliation, gender and race within the jurisdiction: recognition and equality before the law, not to be tried or punished twice, rights in criminal proceedings, humane treatment when deprived of liberty, no retrospective criminal laws, the right to liberty and security, the right to privacy and reputation, freedom of movement, fair hearings, and protection from torture and inhuman or degrading treatment (Ward and Langlands, 2008).

Yet, many Asian governments state that universal suffrage and human rights should fall within the sovereignty of their own countries, which differ from Western nations in history, culture, political structure, religion, social and economic development. Western individual rights sometimes do not suit Asian values, which stress greatly national interests and consensus (Ghai, 1993). They argue that human rights are not absolute but relative. They should be subject to a certain degree of limitations and restrictions so as to achieve communal good and social harmony, and to protect the rights of other people. As such, the Western perspective of human rights should be carefully appraised, and should not be universalised. On the other hand, human rights activists contend that:

> cultural relativism ... does not lead to the conclusion that civil and political rights have to be restricted and suppressed. It can hardly justify detention without trial, arbitrary killing, suppression of critics and dissidents, or denial of fair trial ... The collective good and consensus become the justifications for authoritarian government, paternalism, suppression of minorities and dissidents, or even financial corruption and the naked abuse of power.
>
> (Chan, 1997: 139)

With the threat of diminishing civil liberties and judicial independence, the rule of law has been treasured in Hong Kong. Its people want democracy and other basic human rights to be respected and safeguarded so as to ward off dictatorial control and interference from the communist regime. Reliance on the good will of the rulers always falls far short of a legally entrenched political system, the realisation of human rights and the rule of law. Without universal suffrage, the rule of law would therefore provide a better bulwark against communist oppression than other alternatives. Without the rule of law, it will be impossible to sustain for long the freedoms and human rights that are now enjoyed by the people and maintained by the existing status quo.

The above discussion presents a conflict between the ideals of an interesting trinity of influences, all ostensibly seeking justice: Western due process, Chinese criminal justice practices, and Asian culture. Mainlandisation is shaking up Hong Kong's criminal justice system. The protection of offenders' rights to due process and the balance between individual rights and collective interests may well be jeopardised in any society where the rule of law is at risk.

Review Questions

1 "Mainlandisation is shaking up Hong Kong's criminal justice system." In what aspects do you agree or disagree with this statement?

2 In your opinion, what are the key challenges facing the criminal justice system in Hong Kong? Give illustrative examples to support your answer.

Note

1 This chapter is a modified version of the paper 'Resistance to the mainlandisation of criminal justice practices: A barrier to the development of restorative justice in Hong Kong', published in 2012 in the *International Journal of Offender Therapy and Comparative Criminology*, 56(4): 627–645.

References

Akers-Jones, D. (2004) *Feeling the Stones: Reminiscences by David Akers-Jones*, Hong Kong: Hong Kong University Press.

Bakken, B. (2008) 'The culture of revenge and the power of politics: A comparative attempt to explain the punitive', *Journal of Power*, 1(2): 169–187.

Bohm, R.M. (2006) 'McJustice: On the McDonaldization of criminal justice', *Justice Quarterly*, 23(1): 127–146.

Chan, J. (1997) 'Human rights: From one era to another', in Joseph Y.S. Cheng (ed.) *The Other Hong Kong Report 1997* (pp. 137–167), Hong Kong: Chinese University Press.

Cheng, J.Y.S. (ed.) (2005) *The July 1 Protest Rally: Interpreting a Historic Event*, Hong Kong: City University of Hong Kong Press.

Davidson, R. and Wang, Z. (2000) 'The court system in the People's Republic of China with a case study of a criminal trial', in O.N.I. Ebbe (ed.) *Comparative and International Criminal Justice Systems: Policing, Judiciary, and Corrections* (pp. 205–218), Boston, MA: Butterworth-Heinemann.

Di, X.H. (2009, April) *Report on the Victim-offender Reconciliation of Minor Criminal Case in People's Procuratorate of Xinbei District*. Paper presented at the International Symposium on Preventing Offending and Reducing Re-offending, Hong Kong.

Felkenes, G.T. (1989) 'Courts, sentencing, and the death penalty in the PRC', in R. Troyer, J. Clark and D. Rojek (eds) *Social Control in the People's Republic of China* (pp. 141–158), New York: Praeger Publishers.

Ghai, Y. (1993) 'Asian perspectives on human rights', *Hong Kong Law Journal*, 23: 342–357.

Hall, S., Critcher, C., Jefferson, T., Clarke, J. and Roberts, B. (1978) *Policing the Crisis*, London: Macmillan.

Jiang, G., Lo, T.W. and Garris, C.P. (2012) 'Formation and trend of guanxi practice and guanxi phenomenon', *International Journal of Criminology and Sociology*, 1, 207–220.

Jones, C. and Vagg, J. (2007) *Criminal Justice in Hong Kong*, London: Routledge-Cavendish.

Klein, M.W. and Gatz, M. (1989) 'Professing the uncertain: Problems of lecturing on Chinese social control', in R.J. Troyer, J.P. Clark and D.G. Rojek (eds) *Social Control in the People's Republic of China* (pp. 169–187), New York: Praeger.

Lee, T.L. (1987) 'Hong Kong: The human rights dimension', in H. Chiu, Y.C. Jao and Y.L. Wu (eds) *The Future of Hong Kong: Towards 1997 & Beyond* (pp. 115–138), New York: Quorum Books.

Li, L. (2014) *Senior Officials' Corruption-Related Malpractice in Hong Kong after 1997*, unpublished doctoral dissertation, Hong Kong: The City University of Hong Kong.

Lo, S. (2007) 'The mainlandization and recolonization of Hong Kong: A triumph of convergence over divergence with Mainland China', in J.Y.S. Cheng (ed.) *The Hong Kong Special Administrative Region in its First Decade* (pp. 179–232), Hong Kong: City University of Hong Kong Press.

Lo, T.W. (1993) *Corruption and Politics in Hong Kong and China*, Buckingham: Open University Press.

Lo, T.W. (2003) 'Minimizing crime and corruption in Hong Kong', in R. Godson (ed.) *Menace to Society: Political-criminal Collaboration around the World* (pp. 231–256), London: Transaction Publishers.

Lo, T.W. (2012) 'Resistance to the mainlandization of criminal justice practices: A barrier to the development of restorative justice in Hong Kong', *International Journal of Offender Therapy and Comparative Criminology*, 56(4): 627–645.

Lo, T.W., Maxwell, G. and Wong, S.W. (2006) 'Diversion from youth courts in five Asia Pacific jurisdictions: Welfare or restorative solutions', *International Journal of Offender Therapy and Comparative Criminology*, 50(1): 5–20.

Lo, T.W., Wong, S.W. and Maxwell, G. (eds) (2005) *Alternatives to Prosecution: Rehabilitative and Restorative Models of Youth Justice*, Singapore: Marshall Cavendish Academic.

Lo, T.W. and Yu, R.C.C. (2000) 'Curbing draconian powers: The effects of Hong Kong's graft-fighter', *The International Journal of Human Rights*, 4(1): 54–73.

Ma, N. (2007) 'Democratic development in Hong Kong: A decade of lost opportunities', in J.Y.S. Cheng (ed.) *The Hong Kong Special Administrative Region in its First Decade* (pp. 49–74), Hong Kong: City University of Hong Kong Press.

Mao, T.T. (1961) *Selected Works of Mao Tse-Tung IV*, Beijing: Foreign Languages Press.

Neumann, M. (2002) *The Rule of Law*, Burlington, VT: Ashgate.

Ritzer, G.F. (2013) *The McDonaldization of Society*, Thousand Oaks, CA: Sage.

Sumner, C.S. (1990) *Censure, Politics and Criminal Justice*, Milton Keynes: Open University Press.

Trevaskes, S. (2009) 'Restorative justice or McJustice with Chinese characteristics?', in M. Farquhar (ed.) *21st Century China: Views from Australia* (pp. 77–96), Newcastle: Cambridge Scholars Publishing.

Trevaskes, S. (2010) 'The shifting sands of punishment in China in the era of "harmonious society"', *Law & Policy*, 32(3): 332–361.

Wang, Z. (2000) 'The police system in the People's Republic of China', in O.N.I. Ebbe (ed.) *Comparative and International Criminal Justice Systems: Policing, Judiciary, and Corrections* (pp. 171–182), Boston, MA: Butterworth-Heinemann.

Ward, T. and Langlands, R.L. (2008) 'Restorative justice and the human rights of offenders: convergences and divergences', *Aggression and Violent Behavior*, 13(5): 355–372.

Zhang, L. and Liu, J. (2004) 'Official status and the swiftness of criminal arrest: A Chinese case of the impact of social position on criminal justice', *Policing: An International Journal of Police Strategies and Management*, 27(1): 82–96.

Zhong, L.Y. and Grabosky, P.N. (2009) 'The pluralization of policing and the rise of private policing in China', *Crime, Law and Social Change*, 52(5): 433–455.

Newspaper articles cited

BBC News (2014) 'China media: White Paper on Hong Kong', 11 June, www.bbc.com/news/world-asia-china-27790302 (accessed 15 February 2016).

South China Morning Post (SCMP) (2013) 'Former ICAC chief Timothy Tong grilled on spending by lawmakers', 25 September, www.scmp.com/news/hong-kong/article/1317566/former-icac-chief-timothy-tong-grilled-spending-lawmakers (accessed 15 February 2016).

South China Morning Post (SCMP) (2014) 'Rafael Hui trial leaves nagging questions', 28 December, www.scmp.com/news/article/1668430/rafael-hui-trial-leaves-nagging-questions (accessed 15 February 2016).

South China Morning Post (SCMP) (2015) 'China adopts sweeping national-security law', 1 July, www.wsj.com/articles/china-adopts-sweeping-national-security-law-1435757589 (accessed 15 February 2016).

Legislation cited

Basic Law of the Hong Kong Special Administrative Region of the People's Republic of China

Sino-British Joint Declaration

INDEX